A Creative Approach to the Classical Progymnasmata

Writing & Rhetoric

Thesis Part 1

Teacher's Edition

Paul Kortepeter

Writing & Rhetoric Book 10: Thesis Part 1 Teacher's Edition
© Classical Academic Press®, 2019
Version 1.0

ISBN: 978-1-60051-378-7

All rights reserved. This publication may not be reproduced,
stored in a retrieval system, or transmitted, in any form or by any means,
without the prior written permission of Classical Academic Press.

All scripture is taken from THE HOLY BIBLE: NEW INTERNATIONAL VERSION®. NIV®.
Copyright © 1973, 1978, 1984 by Biblica. All rights reserved worldwide. Scripture quoted by permission.

Classical Academic Press
515 S. 32nd Street
Camp Hill, PA 17011
www.ClassicalAcademicPress.com

Series content editor: Christine Perrin
Series editor: Gretchen Nesbit
Illustrations: Katharina Drees
Book design: Lenora Riley

PGP.01.24

Thesis Part I

TABLE OF CONTENTS

Foreword

One of the most promising aspects of classical education is that it can help revive civil public discourse. It can ignite thoughtful, courteous conversations between people about what we value most.

Unfortunately, many of us nowadays are strutting our disputes like roosters fanning our feathers. In the words of philosopher Charles Taylor, we have become a culture of "mutual display." Showing off our opinions and shutting down those with whom we disagree has become more important than respectfully trying to win their hearts and minds. And this lack of civil discourse surely damages our society. Without kindness and respect, communication deteriorates into altercation. Without honoring our common cultural bonds, our nation disintegrates into cliques that focus on their own self-interest.

I have strong opinions. You have strong opinions. How do we come to a place where we can communicate respectfully? I would argue that to do this, civil conversation must be part of a child's comprehensive education. It must be taught at dinner tables and at bedsides before parents turn out the lights. It must be taught in schools of every kind—public, private, and religious—and it must be consistently modeled by teachers in their classrooms. It will take intentionality to counter the loud and crass voices that flood pop culture, the media, and the halls of government.

One way that ancient teachers prepared to entrust civil society to the next generation, and to help young people enter the public discourse, was to teach rhetoric. Rhetoric is imperfect, and it can be misused. Certainly the adage is true: "Whoever does not study rhetoric will be a victim of it." On the other hand, because it requires evidence, clarity, and ethical behavior as the support structure of an argument, rhetoric can help to create the kind of sustained and careful thinking that is needed for properly understanding the problems of our day.

Here, in the thesis exercise, all the best of rhetoric finds its full expression. The thesis essay and the thesis speech are, with little competition, two of the best ways to train our young people in civil communication and principled critical thinking. To those ends this book is dedicated.

A Typical Teaching Week

These guidelines are intended to help bring some predictability to lesson planning.

Although the elements of grammar are important aspects of this course, its primary focus is writing and rhetoric. We recommend that you teach a simple, but rich, grammar curriculum in parallel with the lessons in *Writing & Rhetoric: Thesis Part 1*. By simple, we mean to suggest that you avoid a grammar program with a writing component. Two different writing methods would most likely work against each other and cause an imbalance in the school day. Instead, look for a grammar program that focuses on grammatical concepts, provides plenty of practice sentences, and encourages diagramming.

You may want to provide same-day grammar instruction several days a week, preferably separating Writing & Rhetoric from grammar study by an hour or two. Or, you may want to alternate weeks between a grammar program and Writing & Rhetoric. This requires some negotiation in your language arts program for the year. If you aim to do two Writing & Rhetoric books per school year, that would equal approximately twenty lessons. The introductory lessons (1–6) each can be completed in a week. The essay-writing lessons (7–10) each may take two or three weeks to complete. You will have to choose a grammar program with this consideration in mind.

Please note that multiple opportunities for practice are built into the Writing & Rhetoric series. If you find that your students have mastered a particular form of writing, you should feel free to skip some lessons. In this case, some teachers choose to present the literature from skipped lessons as part of their history or English lessons. Some teachers may also provide their students with practice in summarizing, critical thinking, and sentence manipulation by doing only the Tell It Back, Talk About It, and Copiousness sections from skipped lessons.

The following table illustrates some possible options for scheduling lessons. As always with Writing & Rhetoric, teachers have the freedom to pick and choose the lesson elements, schedule, and pace that suits the needs of their classrooms. You can even schedule each lesson over two weeks if your students need the extra time.

Lessons 1–6, Option 1

Day 1 ● Read **lesson introduction** ● Tell back (narrate or summarize) text (**Tell It Back**) ● Engage in **Talk About It** discussions	**Day 2** ● Work on **Write & Discuss** exercise ● Begin **Go Deeper** if time allows
Day 3 ● Continue to work on **Go Deeper**	**Day 4 (if needed)** ● Finish **Go Deeper**

Lessons 1–6, Option 2

Day 1	Day 2
• Read part of **lesson introduction**, assign remainder for homework	• Tell back (narrate or summarize) text (**Tell It Back**) • Engage in **Talk About It** discussions • Work on **Write & Discuss** exercise

Day 3	Day 4	Day 5 (if needed)
• Begin **Go Deeper**	• Continue to work on **Go Deeper**	• Finish **Go Deeper**

Lessons 7–10, Option 1[A]

Day 1	Day 2
• Read **lesson introduction** • Tell back (narrate or summarize) text (**Tell It Back**) • Annotate text if time allows, or assign for homework (**Tell It Back**) • Engage in **Talk About It** discussions	• Work on readings and follow-up exercises (lesson 9) or **Writing Time** exercises (lessons 7–8, 10)

Day 3	Day 4	Day 5
• Continue to work on readings and exercises or **Writing Time** exercises	• Engage in **Speak It** exercises • Continue to work on readings and exercises or **Writing Time** exercises	• Work through **Revise It** section

Lessons 7–10, Option 2

Day 1	Day 2
• Read part of **lesson introduction**, assign remainder for homework • Assign annotations for homework (**Tell It Back**)	• Tell back (narrate or summarize) text (**Tell It Back**) • Engage in **Talk About It** discussions • Work on readings and follow-up exercises (lesson 9) or **Writing Time** exercises (lessons 7–8, 10)

Day 3	Day 4	Day 5
• Continue to work on readings and exercises or **Writing Time** exercises	• Engage in **Speak It** exercises • Continue to work on readings and exercises or **Writing Time** exercises	• Work through **Revise It** section

[A]There will be some exceptions to these schedules in lessons 9 and 10 based on variations in their format. Teachers will need to adjust the schedule accordingly for those lessons.

Day One

1. The teacher models fluency by reading the introductory text aloud while students follow along silently. If the lesson introduction contains a longer reading, such as a short story or a biography, teachers may read part of the selection in class as a "teaser" and assign the remainder for homework, or simply assign the entire reading for homework.

2. Tell It Back and Talk About It should immediately follow the reading of the text, while the text is still fresh in the students' minds. (In lesson 9 there are multiple Tell It Back and Talk About It sections that follow each reading. They should be completed at whatever pace the class goes through the readings. There is no Tell It Back or Talk About It work for lesson 10.) Annotation can be an important aid to memory for longer readings, and it is included under Tell It Back in certain lessons in this book as part of the reading process. If time allows, students can complete their annotations in class, or annotation can be assigned for homework. If the lesson reading is assigned as homework (see previous step), annotation also can be assigned for homework and teachers can engage students with Tell It Back and Talk About It the following day.

   Narration, the process of "telling back," can be done in a variety of ways. Pairs of students can retell the text to each other, or selected individuals can narrate orally to the entire class. Solo students can tell back the text into a recording device or to an instructor. Students in middle or high school are capable of written summary narrations, which is the focus in this book. Summary writing should be completed individually and then can be shared with the class as desired. At this age, narrative summaries, outlines, and dramatic reenactments can be done with skill.

   The process of narration is intended to improve comprehension and long-term memory. Please note that oral narration, often emphasized for younger students, can still be useful for older students, particularly those who struggle with writing. If you prefer longer, in-depth oral narration to the written summary narrations in this book, please consider these tips:

- Avoid rereading a passage to students. Let them rely on the strength of their memories. Students will pay more attention if they know they will hear a passage only once and be expected to tell it back.
- Remember that oral narrations are typically detailed retellings in chronological order, complete with names, events, and rich vocabulary words.
- Ask other students to assist if the narrator falters in his or her retelling. Be sure, however, to give enough quiet space for the narrator to think clearly about what he or she has just heard. Don't be hasty to jump in and "rescue" a narrator.

Annotation can help a student easily locate vocabulary words, proper nouns, and important concepts for drafting essays.

Talk About It is designed to help students analyze the meaning of their reading and to see analogous situations, both in the world and in their own lives. This book also includes several opportunities for picture analysis.

Days Two and Three

1. If some or all of the lesson reading was assigned for homework on day 1, Tell It Back and Talk About It can be completed on day 2. If only annotations were completed as homework, the teacher might engage students in conversations about the important ideas they underlined or the questions they jotted down in the margins.
2. In lessons 1–6, students will encounter the Write & Discuss exercise in which short writing assignments precede class discussions. Writing is always an excellent way to improve the quality of participation in any academic conversation. By giving students time to consider their answers on paper, teachers will find that even quiet and reticent students are more likely to engage in the discussion. Following Write & Discuss, students work with the text through the Go Deeper exercises. Go Deeper is all about practicing important skills essential to each lesson.

   In lessons 7, 8, and 10, students will work through the Writing Time section, which includes copiousness and the thesis exercises themselves. You will probably want to take multiple days for this step.

   Lesson 9 contains readings and comprehension exercises that will help students complete the thesis essay in lesson 10.

Day Four

1. Students may need the fourth day (or more) to complete the Go Deeper and Writing Time exercises (or the readings and exercises in lesson 9).

   In lessons 7, 8, and 10, if students complete the first draft of their thesis essays by day 3, we recommend that they take a breather from writing while they work on their speaking skills. Keeping a day between essay completion and revision helps students to look at their work with fresh eyes. However, teachers may find it valuable to pair students together to read their essays out loud and give each other ideas for revision. A rubric is included at the back of the book as an aid to partner feedback or grading by teachers.
2. The Speak It section creates opportunities for students to memorize, recite, discuss and debate, and read dramatically. Please consider using a recording device whenever it suits the situation. When using electronics, students should listen to their recordings to get an idea of what sounds right and what needs to be improved. Have students read the elocution instructions at the back of the book to help them work on skill in delivery. Speak It does not appear in lessons 1–6 and 9, and no work is required on day 4 for those lessons.

Day Five

At this level, students will continue to work toward a foundation in revision. The Revise It section provides basic exercises that develop students' skills in revision and proofreading. Revise It also provides a list that covers some of the most important steps toward improving an essay. Most students can do moderate self-editing at this age and provide thoughtful feedback to each other. However, teachers are still the best source for giving editorial feedback and requesting rewrites. Revise It does not appear in lessons 1–6 and 9, and no work is required on day 5 for those lessons.

Introduction to Students

You may not realize it, but you've just walked into a gym. No, no—of course not the kind of gym where you pump iron. You won't be doing biceps curls, leg presses, and barbell lifts here! What I mean is that you've entered a writing gym. This is the place for you to do your sentence curls, your critical-thinking presses, and your composition lifts. It goes without saying that the more you lift weights, the stronger your muscles become. Similarly, the more you work out with pencil, pen, and keyboard, the stronger your writing muscles become.

▲ This is me, the author. Actually, this is Charles Atlas, the famous twentieth-century strongman. However, you can bet my writing muscles are every bit as developed.

"The World's Most Perfectly Developed Man" circa 1935. Image courtesy of Wellcome Images, https://commons.wikimedia.org/wiki/File:%22The_World%27s_Most_Perfectly_Developed_Man%22_Wellcome_L0027452.jpg.

If you've been with us for a while, you know that these writing exercises are called the *progymnasmata*. They've been around for over 2,000 years, but nobody knows how ancient they really are.[1] They were created in the Greek-speaking part of the Roman Empire and they were used by schools to train the best writers and teachers in all of Rome. You can see most of the word "gymnasium" in *progymnasmata*, which means "preliminary exercises."

Milo of Kroton knew the value of weight training some 2,500 years ago. He was a famous athlete who grew up in the Greek colony of Kroton, which was located in southern Italy. When he was just a kid, Milo decided that he could build his muscles by pumping beef . . . literally! He would walk around with a baby calf in his arms and lift that calf above his head. As the calf grew heavier, Milo kept lifting it. And as that calf grew into a full-sized bull, he still lifted it daily and his muscles grew stronger. No wonder Milo won six Olympic titles for wrestling! It was relatively easy to throw a man down when he could lug a bull around. That's what the legends tell us, anyway.

Instead of lugging around a growing bull, you have been writing compositions that grow in difficulty. Writing exercises such as these *progymnasmata* build from simple forms to more complex, and from concrete ideas to more abstract. In this series, you've written fables, narratives, chreias, refutations, confirmations, commonplaces, encomia, vituperations, comparisons, descriptions, impersonations, and now—ta dah!—at long last you've reached thesis. Thesis is the last stage of rippin' those writing muscles before you get to formal rhetoric! You could say that it's the supreme workout.

If this is your first time to join us in the gym, there's no better exercise to get started with than thesis. It brings together the four modes of writing and discourse—narration, description, exposition, and persuasion—and it strengthens your ability to make an argument, organize your thoughts, and supply evidence. Thesis works every one of your writing muscles! You've got two books ahead to learn all about thesis writing and why this essay form is so important to your life and your ability to communicate personally and professionally. Consider these books to be your personal trainers.

OK, so come on now, let's get those muscles working! Let's break a sweat. Let's make 'em burn!

---

1. The oldest surviving text of the *progymnasmata* dates back to the first century and was written by a teacher of rhetoric named Aelius Theon of Alexandria.

Introduction

Two thousand-plus years ago, the Greeks developed a system of persuasive speaking known as rhetoric. The Romans fell in love with rhetoric because it both was practical for the real world and served the need of training orators in their growing republic. In order to prepare their students for oration, the Romans invented a complementary system of persuasive writing known as the *progymnasmata*: *pro-* meaning "preliminary" and *gymnas* meaning "exercises." The *progymnasmata* were the primary method used in Graeco-Roman schools to teach young people the elements of rhetoric. This happened in a grammar school (called a *grammaticus*) sometime around the age of ten for upper-class students.

There are several ancient "*progyms*" still in existence. The most influential *progyms* were by Hermogenes of Tarsus, who lived in the second century, and by Aphthonius of Antioch, who lived during the fourth century just as the western Roman Empire was collapsing. Even after the great cities of Rome lay in ruins, the *progym* continued as the primary method for teaching writing during the Middle Ages and even into early modern times.

The Writing & Rhetoric series is based on the *progymnasmata* of ancient Rome. This method assumes that students learn best by reading excellent examples of literature and by growing their writing skills through imitation. It is incremental, meaning that it goes from simpler exercises to more complex exercises, and it moves from the concrete to the abstract. One of the beauties of the *progym* is that it grows with the student through the stages of childhood development that are dubbed by modern classical educators as the "trivium," a term borrowed from medieval education.[1] These exercises effectively take a young writer from the grammar phase through the logic phase and finally to the rhetoric phase.

In a democracy such as Athens or a republic such as Rome, rhetoric was a powerful way to enter into public conversations. In the words of Yale rhetorician Charles Sears Baldwin, "Rhetoric is conceived by Aristotle as the art of giving effectiveness to the truth." He adds that "the true theory of rhetoric is the energizing of knowledge, the bringing of truth to bear upon men. . . ." Rhetoric thus had an intentional public purpose, that is, to persuade people to embrace truth and its corollaries: goodness and beauty. It was designed to enjoin right behavior by holding up to public scrutiny examples of virtue and wickedness. Of course, the person using rhetoric was also supposed to be virtuous—above all honest and just.

There is an urgency and a real purpose to rhetoric. It was never meant to be empty forms of speaking and composition. It was never meant to be only eloquence and skill of delivery. It was certainly never meant to be manipulative sound bites and commercials made to benefit an unscrupulous political or economic class. Rather, it was intended for every citizen as a means to engage articulately with the urgent ideas of the day. As the old saying goes, "Whoever does not learn rhetoric will be a victim of it."

1. In medieval times, the trivium was originally the lower division of the seven liberal arts. For the modern idea that these studies correspond to childhood development, please refer to Dorothy Sayers, *The Lost Tools of Learning*.

The best preparation for rhetoric is still the *progymnasmata*, the preliminary exercises. In this book you will find these exercises creatively updated to meet the needs of modern children. We have embraced the method both as it was used for Roman youth and as it develops the skills demanded by contemporary education.

- It teaches the four modes of discourse—narration, exposition, description, and argumentation—while at the same time blending them for maximum persuasive impact.
- It is incremental, moving from easier forms to harder forms. The level of challenge is appropriate for students as they mature with the program.
- It uses "living" stories, from ancient to modern, and is not stuck in any particular time period. Rather, it follows a timeline of history so that the stories can be integrated with history lessons.
- Its stories engage the imagination and also spark a desire in young people to imitate them. In this way, Writing & Rhetoric avoids the "blank-page syndrome" that can paralyze many nascent writers by giving students a model from which to write.
- It promotes virtue by lifting up clear-cut examples of good and bad character.
- It fosters the joy of learning by providing opportunities for creative self-expression as well as classroom fun.
- It uses speaking to enhance the development of persuasive writing.
- It teaches students to recognize and use the three persuasive appeals to an audience: pathos, ethos, and logos.
- It provides opportunities for students to learn from other students' work as well as to present their own work.

As educators, I think we need to admit that teaching writing is difficult. This is because writing makes big demands on cognitive function and, for many young writers, can easily become overwhelming. Our brains need to simultaneously

- utilize motor skills
- process vocabulary
- sequence and organize ideas
- employ grammatical concepts
- and draw upon a reservoir of good writing—hopefully the reservoir exists—as a template for new writing

That's a tall order. Also, writing contains a subjective element. It's not as clear-cut as math. And when you add argumentation to the mix, you have a very complex process indeed. To be properly educated, every person needs to be able to make and understand arguments.

It is from this list of complexities that a desire for a relatively easy-to-implement curriculum was born. While the task of teaching writing is difficult, it is my sincere belief that reconnecting the tree of modern composition to its classical roots in rhetoric will refresh the entire process. Regardless of your personal writing history, I trust that these books will provide a happy and rewarding experience for your students.

Best Foot Forward

The *Progym* and the Practice of Modern Writing

Although the *progym* are an ancient method of approaching writing, they are extraordinarily relevant today. This is because modern composition developed from the *progym*. Modern writing borrows heavily from many of the *progym's* various exercises. For example, modern stories are essentially unchanged from the ancient fable and narrative forms. Modern expository essays contain elements from the ancient commonplace, encomium/vituperation, and other *progym* exercises. Persuasive essays of today are basically the same as the ancient thesis exercises, although often (unfortunately) missing the robust challenge of antithesis. In this series, you can expect your students to grow in all forms of modern composition—narrative, expository, descriptive, and persuasive—while at the same time developing unique rhetorical muscle.

The *progym* cover many elements of a standard English and Language Arts curriculum. In *Thesis Part 1* these include:[2]

- experiencing both the reading of a story (sight) and listening to it (hearing)
- identifying a variety of genres, including description, history, short story, biography, and autobiography
- determining the meaning of words and phrases, including figures of speech, as they are used in a text
- increasing knowledge of vocabulary by considering word meaning, word order, and transitions
- analyzing text that is organized in sequential or chronological order
- demonstrating an understanding of texts by annotating, summarizing, and paraphrasing in ways that maintain meaning and logical order within a text
- gathering relevant information from multiple sources, and annotating sources
- drawing evidence from literary or informational texts to support analysis, reflection, and research
- articulating an understanding of ideas or images communicated by the literary work
- establishing a central idea or topic
- composing a topic sentence and creating an organizational structure in which ideas are logically grouped into coherent paragraphs to support the writer's purpose
- supporting claim(s) with clear reasons and relevant evidence, using credible sources, facts, and details
- writing informative (explanatory) and descriptive texts to examine a topic and convey ideas and information clearly

---

2. This list was derived from the Texas Administrative Code (TAC), Title 19, Part II, Chapter 110: Texas Essential Knowledge and Skills for English Language Arts and Reading (http://ritter.tea.state.tx.us/rules/tac/chapter110/index.html), the Core Knowledge Foundation's Core Knowledge Sequence: Content and Skill Guidelines for Grades K-8 (http://www.coreknowledge.org/mimik/mimik_uploads/documents/480/CKFSequence_Rev.pdf), the English-Language Arts Content Standards for California Public Schools: Kindergarten Through Grade Twelve (http://www.cde.ca.gov/be/st/ss/documents/elacontentstnds.pdf), the English Language Arts Standards of the Common Core State Standards Initiative (http://www.corestandards.org/ELA-Literacy), the English/Language Arts Standards Grade 6, Indiana Department of Education (http://www.doe.in.gov/standards/englishlanguage-arts), and the English Standards of Learning for Virginia Public Schools, Grade 7 (http://www.doe.virginia.gov/testing/sol/standards_docs/english/2010/stds_all_english.pdf).

- developing the topic with relevant facts, definitions, concrete details, quotations, or other information and examples
- providing a concluding statement or section that follows from the topic presented
- using precise language and domain-specific vocabulary
- using appropriate transitions to clarify the relationships among ideas and concepts
- producing clear and coherent writing in which the development, organization, and style are appropriate to task, purpose, and audience
- avoiding plagiarism through summary
- with some guidance and support from peers and adults, developing and strengthening writing as needed by planning, revising, editing, rewriting, or trying a new approach
- using technology as an aid to revision and oration
- using pictures and photos to analyze and interpret the past
- participating civilly and productively in group discussions

While these standards are certainly worthwhile and are addressed in this curriculum, the *progym* derive their real strength from the incremental and thorough development of each form of writing. The Writing & Rhetoric series does not skip from form to form and leave the others behind. Rather, it builds a solid foundation of mastery by blending the forms. For example, no expository essay can truly be effective without description. No persuasive essay can be convincing without narrative. All good narrative writing requires description, and all good persuasive writing requires expository elements. Not only do the *progym* demand strong organization and implement many of the elements of modern language arts, but they also retain all of the power of classical rhetoric.

Here is how the *progym* develop each stage of modern composition:

1. Fable—Narrative
2. Narrative—Narrative with descriptive elements
3. Chreia & Proverb—Expository essay with narrative, descriptive, and persuasive elements
4. Refutation & Confirmation—Persuasive essay with narrative, descriptive, and expository elements
5. Commonplace—Persuasive essay with narrative, descriptive, and expository elements
6. Encomium & Vituperation—Persuasive essay with narrative, descriptive, and expository elements
7. Comparison—Comparative essay with narrative, descriptive, and expository elements
8. Description & Impersonation—Descriptive essay with narrative, expository, persuasive, and comparative elements
9. Thesis Part 1—Persuasive essay with narrative, descriptive, expository, and comparative elements
10. Thesis Part 2—Persuasive speech with narrative, descriptive, expository, and comparative elements, as well as the three rhetorical appeals
11. Declamation—Persuasive essay or speech that marshals all the elements of the *progym* and brings them to bear upon judicial matters

As you can see, the *progym* move quickly to establish the importance of one form to another.

Objectives for *Thesis Part 1*

The following are some of the major objectives for the exercises found in each section of this book:

Reading

1. Expose students to narrative, autobiographical, and philosophical writing.
2. Model fluent reading for students and give them practice reading diverse texts.
3. Aid student reading and recall by teaching techniques for annotation.
4. Facilitate student interaction with well-written texts through discussions and exercises in evaluation and critical thinking.

Writing

1. Enhance research skills by giving students multiple texts to read and having them summarize and create a topic from the material.
2. Support the development of invention (inventing topics and ideas to write about).
3. Grow awareness of different types of audiences along with the purpose of the author.
4. Introduce a wide variety of essay "hooks" to help capture audience attention.
5. Encourage students to map (prewrite) their information before they write a paragraph.
6. Strengthen descriptive capabilities with an emphasis on specific, vivid words and sensorial language.
7. Support students in writing thesis essays focused on literary and thematic analysis, as well as on answering the speculative question, "What is beauty?" These essays include the development of an awareness of transitions, tone, and writing style.
8. Practice writing theses, topic sentences, and antitheses.
9. Improve conclusions so that they extend and enhance the original thesis.
10. Strengthen the skill of deriving information from texts and organizing and summarizing it in expository paragraphs.
11. Continue the development of revision, proofreading, and joint critiquing.
12. Grow awareness of the stylistic vices of redundancy, padding, mixing formal and informal language, dangling modifiers, and faulty predication.
13. Increase understanding of formal and informal language.
14. Reinforce grammatical concepts.

Related Concepts

1. Aid in the development of vocabulary and analysis of language.
2. Strengthen students' power of observation.
3. Reinforce the ability to summarize and paraphrase, as well as to amplify through description, for greater rhetorical flexibility.
4. Strengthen working memory through recitation (memoria), thus improving storage of information and rhetorical power.
5. Increase understanding of the flexibility and copiousness of language by practicing sentence variety.

Speaking

1. Strengthen students' oratory skills by providing opportunities for public speaking and for working on delivery—volume, pacing, and inflection.
2. Practice tone and inflection by means of dramatic reading.
3. Encourage students to see the relationship between writing and speaking as they consider their ideas orally and to use oration as an aid to the process of revision.

Teaching Thesis Part I

In this tenth book of the Writing & Rhetoric series, your students will be crafting persuasive essays with expository, descriptive, and narrative elements. In other words, these thesis essays integrate the four traditional modes of discourse. A persuasive essay cannot stand by itself. To persuade, it needs compelling information (exposition), vivid word pictures (description), and engaging stories (often in summary form). The persuasive writer marshals all these elements together in one seamless and extended argument.

The thesis essay is the most important form of academic writing. Any student who hopes to succeed in college must learn to write it well. In a respected publication by Harvard University, the author lists the fundamentals for academic writing, and many of these fundamentals are found in the thesis essay: the thesis itself, evidence, analysis, structure (or arrangement), counterargument, sources, and reflection.[1] Thus, even schools and students who have not yet worked with the *progymnasmata* will still greatly benefit from doing the exercises in this book.

In addition to academic writing, the thesis essay will help students to examine and sustain ideas, skills much needed to raise the level of discourse in today's public conversations. We live in a time of poisonous sound bites, memes, and partisan news, but what is necessary for the flourishing of a republic is an informed citizenry capable of engaging in rational and civil discussions. The principles of rhetoric that helped build the Roman republic for over four hundred years are still valuable—no, vital—for citizens of the American republic today.

The ancient authors of the *progymnasmata* (Graeco-Roman manuals of composition) certainly saw the value of thesis writing and made it one of the culminating exercises of the program. Nicolaus the Sophist[2] tells us that thesis provides practice for two species of rhetoric (judicial and epideictic) and includes all the parts of a classic oration: the introduction, the confirmations, the antitheses, the refutations (solutions), and the conclusion (epilogue).[3] We would add that writing persuasively has myriad uses, from requesting a raise at work to pleading for the release of a prisoner of conscience.[4]

Modern persuasive essays are inspired by the thesis exercise found in the ancient *progymnasmata*. The rhetorician Aphthonius tells us that "thesis is a logical examination of any matter under inspection."[5] These investigations would involve general topics in answer to speculative questions such as: Should people marry? Should people sail? Should a city be surrounded by walls? In this book, students will answer speculative questions as they analyze a short story (fiction) and a chapter from an autobiography (nonfiction) as well as seek to define the abstract idea of beauty.

In a thesis essay, the writer argues for a logical position and, at the same time, includes counterarguments so that the opposition has a chance to be heard. The writer essentially articulates the opposition's rebuttals and then disproves them with fresh arguments. These tertiary arguments are known as refutations. While the writer must certainly defend her position, the fact that she must consider other positions makes the thesis essay a genuine exploration and thought experiment.

---

1. Gordon Harvey, "A Brief Guide to the Elements of the Academic Essay," Harvard Writing Project Brief Guide Series (Harvard College Writing Program, 2009), https://writingproject.fas.harvard.edu/files/hwp/files/hwp_brief_guides_elements.pdf.
2. Nicolaus the Sophist lived in the fifth century AD and was the last of the writers of the existing *progymnasmata*. Although sophists have a bad reputation today as artful deceivers, they were the philosophers who developed rhetoric and were often very sincere teachers, not practicing deception at all. The word "sophist" (wise one) is related to the word "philosopher" (lover of wisdom).
3. George A. Kennedy, trans., Progymnasmata: *Greek Textbooks of Prose Composition and Rhetoric* (Atlanta: Society of Biblical Literature, 2003), 170.
4. prisoner of conscience: someone imprisoned for his religious or political views
5. George A. Kennedy, trans., Progymnasmata: *Greek Textbooks of Prose Composition and Rhetoric* (Atlanta: Society of Biblical Literature, 2003), 120.

This exploration is of great and lasting value for students. It forces them to consider: "Do I really believe what I'm saying? Have I provided enough evidence to convince myself and others? Am I expressing myself in a credible manner?"

In writing thesis essays, students take another step forward toward the goal of mastering rhetoric. The readings will continue to be a foundation of pleasure and instruction, but students will use the content of the readings to develop arguments. They will continue working with topic sentences and they will expand the meaning of those sentences through evidence, quotations, and explanation. In other words, all the basics are in place for creating an ethos, pathos, and logos based on careful reasoning, compelling illustrations, and reliable sources. By looking more deeply into texts, students will extend their dialogic (conversational) relationship with reading. The kinds of questions asked in the exercises in this book will lead students to consider the readings in the context of their lives and the world about them.

Unpacking *Thesis Part 1*

You will find nearly every lesson organized around the chapter readings. Narration, questions for discussion, and exercises in composition all emerge within the context of the readings. We find that contextualization helps to reinforce memory and the laddering of skills.

This book is divided into two portions:

Lessons 1 to 6—The first portion develops the vital aspects of writing a thesis essay from the opening hook to the concluding paragraph.

Lessons 7 to 10—The second portion guides students step by step through three thesis essays.

To stretch and strengthen the process of writing and speaking, both portions of this book contain special features such as Write & Discuss, Go Deeper, Writing Time, Speak It, and Revise It. These sections are explained in the following paragraphs.

The Lesson Reading

Every lesson contains excerpts from various sources: articles, speeches, stories, and biographies. The Writing & Rhetoric series uses readings that are culturally significant and that contain lasting insights. In making our selections, we seek to apply the admonition of educator Charlotte Mason: "The intellectual life . . . has but one food whereby it lives and grows—the sustenance of living ideas."[6] We choose readings that contain "living ideas"—i.e., ideas that encourage the intellectual development of children by being challenging and important.

All of the readings in the book are recorded in a downloadable MP3 file so that your students can experience the pleasure of being read to.

Tell It Back—Narration

Every time students hear a substantial reading in this book, they will also practice narrating it back, either orally or in writing. Multiple intelligences—memory, sequence, main idea—are developed by this practice. In addition to exercising their executive functions, students will continue to internalize an outline of the material. Some educational models have based their entire strategy on the important skill of narration.

As part of narration, students are encouraged to annotate select texts for main idea, vocabulary words, questions, and points of interest. Annotation will help to make a text truly "sink into" a student's imagination and develop the habit of reading closely.

Talk About It and Speak It

These two sections promote our conviction that writing, speaking, and thinking are critical skills that work together. Some educators believe that difficulties with writing stem from a lack of deeper

6. Charlotte Mason, *School Education*, AmblesideOnline, accessed January 24, 2019, https://amblesideonline.org/CM/vol3complete.html#3_01.

thought. These books use comprehension, reading aloud, discussion, and even oral performance as ways to help students become critical thinkers according to the way their bodies (and brains) are made. These three abilities—thinking, speaking, and writing—enlarge one another when practiced together.

Write & Discuss

While students anticipate writing their thesis essays, Write & Discuss (lessons 1–6, 9) keeps their writing and persuasive skills active. This section invites students to respond to thought-provoking readings of various lengths—or paintings in lesson 3—by writing down their ideas prior to a class discussion. Writing sets up students for a more rigorous and engaged discussion. It gives them time to reflect on the reading and to know their thoughts better. As Flannery O'Connor said, "I write because I don't know what I think until I read what I say." The principle of writing in order to know what we think is the main purpose of Write & Discuss. When students have their ideas tangibly spelled out on a piece of paper, it is easier for them to courageously engage in a challenging conversation.

Go Deeper

This section, found in lessons 1–6, seeks to deepen comprehension of the skills taught in those particular lessons. Students will variously examine summary, main idea, amplification, speculative questions, thesis statements, audience, antitheses, hooks, rhetorical devices, supporting arguments, direct quotes and paraphrasing, appeals to authority, and citations.

Writing Time

This aspect of the book, found in lessons 7–8 and 10, is the most obvious. Each Writing Time section features an opportunity to write copiously or abundantly. Copiousness stretching exercises teach students to reach for new words to express variations of the same idea. That way they can experience the joy of the abundance of language as well as of finding precise words.

In this book students will also learn to write well-crafted persuasive essays, which include an introduction, body paragraphs, and a conclusion. Practice in this section includes instruction on transitions and style. Each essay follows clear prewriting prompts, and the principle of imitation is always at work.

The thesis essay follows a clear—and ancient—outline. It starts with an introduction that grabs audience attention with a hook and then states and explains the paper's main argument or thesis. The next two paragraphs confirm (support) the thesis with sound reasoning and backing from textual sources. The next two paragraphs consider counterarguments to the thesis (antitheses) and refute them, also with sound reasoning and textual support. Finally, a conclusion wraps up the essay by expanding on the original thesis.

Revise It

In this book, students will continue to critically analyze their own writing. The Revise It section (lessons 7–8, 10) offers students the opportunity to improve their writing, and the writing of others, by strengthening phrasing, finding grammar errors, and proofreading.

Historical Note

The material covered in much of the Writing & Rhetoric series is loosely tied to periods in history. *Fable* and *Narrative I* borrow their stories from Greek and early Roman times. *Narrative II* picks up with the late Roman Empire, while *Chreia & Proverb* continues into the Middle Ages. *Refutation & Confirmation* moves into the experience of colonial America. In *Commonplace*, students read selected writings from late colonial America, the American Revolution, and the Federalist period. *Encomium & Vituperation* covers many colorful personalities from the Civil War era to that of the Wild West. *Comparison* covers the part of American history from the Gilded Age to the Great Depression. *Description & Impersonation* focuses primarily on twentieth-century writers, including two figures from the world wars. The purpose of this progression is to provide rich content that helps timeline-based schools integrate history with the language arts. As one discipline reinforces the other, students will retain a powerful impression of the periods of history they study.

This volume, *Thesis Part 1*, begins a new effort to synthesize the ancient and the modern, using readings that span the course of history. Our next book, *Thesis Part 2*, will also be comprehensive in approach as students study great speeches and apply the principles of the thesis essay to speech writing.

Important Notes

Flexibility is built into the program.

We have crafted this book to be useful to students at different levels with different needs. For instance, teachers can ask their students to complete some exercises verbally instead of in writing. If, on the other hand, teachers desire more written work, they can ask students to respond to Talk About It questions in writing. Teachers can also have students work together to tackle parts of lessons that are difficult. Education is personal, and one size does not fit all. Please use your judgment to determine what is best for your student(s) in terms of discipline and delight.

Review summary instructions.
This icon directs students to a section of the book with some pointers on how to summarize. Here, students will learn how to shorten a lengthy paragraph into a much more succinct form. To be brief is to use words wisely. It is a way to communicate important information to the audience while showing concern for its needs (and its attention span).

Practice a rhetorical device.
Some new rhetorical devices are introduced in this book, and others are reviewed. The formal study of rhetoric collects and draws upon these devices throughout a student's life as a writer and a speaker. We wanted to make special note of these to help you track the growing number of "tools" in your students' rhetorical "toolbox."

Begin prewriting.
This icon indicates that students will be doing prewriting exercises, including creating hooks, theses, and supporting arguments.

Include elocution instruction.
This icon indicates that elocution instruction should be included with the exercise and guides you to a section of the book that provides full elocution instructions. We believe that speaking well makes students better writers and that writing well makes for better speakers. In this book, we focus on the various aspects of speaking well, which include recitations, speeches, dramatic presentation, and the sharing of student work. Your students should practice one aspect of elocution every time they do public speaking.

Use a recording device.
This icon indicates that, depending on the size of the class and the availability of technology, you may want to have your student(s) record their work from the Speak It and sometimes the Revise It sections and play it back. This is an excellent way for them to hear the words and the qualities of their performances. They will learn elocution faster if they hear themselves as well as each other.

Best wishes as you embark upon these new and fascinating exercises with your students!

The purpose of this lesson is to introduce the idea that those who use the power of rhetoric also should strive for goodness.
In this lesson, students will practice:

- narration in summary form
- critical thinking
- written reflection and follow-up discussion
- writing summaries and identifying main ideas
- amplification

Lesson 1

Quintilian and the Classical Ideal: First Strive for Goodness

Rhetoric is the art of writing and speaking persuasively. Having mastery of rhetoric is like having a superpower. It may not be as dramatic as bulletproof skin or a Jedi mind trick, but it will help you to influence how some people think and how other people act. Of course, that influence can be a good thing or a bad thing, depending on who's using it.

One of the earliest philosophers of rhetoric, Aristotle (384–322 BC), recognized that rhetorical powers could be useful for defending truth and justice in public discussions. He also believed that a master rhetorician could persuade difficult audiences to believe his arguments by appealing to his own good character and by stirring up emotions. Old Aristotle believed so strongly in the usefulness of rhetoric that he wrote an instruction manual about how to become a rhetorical master and dubbed it—you guessed it—*Rhetoric*.

At the same time, Aristotle acknowledged that some people might use rhetorical powers to harm and manipulate others. "One who uses such power of speech unjustly might do great harm . . . ," he declared.[1] However, he added that any good thing—strength or health, wealth or leadership—can also be used for evil purposes. Although these things can be abused, Aristotle

1. Aristotle, *Rhetoric*, trans. W. Rhys Roberts, The Internet Classics Archive, accessed January 19, 2018, http://classics.mit.edu/Aristotle/rhetoric.1.i.html.

asserts that individuals "can confer the greatest of benefits by a right use of these."[2] As the Romans used to say, "*Abusus non tollit usum*": The abuse of something is not an argument against its proper use. Indeed, Aristotle believed that, even though rhetoric could be abused and misused, mastering the art of rhetoric was very important. He said, "It is absurd to hold that a man ought to be ashamed of being unable to defend himself with his limbs, but not of being unable to defend himself with speech and reason."[3] In other words, people should value the ability to defend themselves with rhetoric just as much as they value the ability to use their arms and legs to fend off a physical attack.

▲ The dark side: Rhetoric can be misused.
Mansudae Grand Monument, April 29, 2010. Image courtesy of John Pavelka, https://commons.wikimedia.org/wiki/File:Mansudae_Grand_Monument_(4610364189).jpg.

Flash forward a few hundred years after Aristotle to the first-century Roman Empire. It was then that one of the greatest teachers of all time, Quintilian, trained his students to be top-notch persuaders. He believed that the best thing any school could do for a young person was to make him an amazing orator. Like Aristotle, Quintilian thought it was absurd for anyone to give up using rhetoric simply because it could be misused. He joked, "Let us give up eating, it often makes us ill; let us never go inside houses, for sometimes they collapse on their occupants; let never a sword be forged for a soldier, since it might be used by a robber."[4] Rather, Quintilian said it was a useful and worthwhile task

> for a good [person] to defend his friends, to guide the senate by his counsels, and to lead peoples or armies to follow his bidding. . . . Is it not a noble thing, by employing the understanding which is common to mankind and the words that are

Maya Angelou visits York College, Feb. 2013. Image courtesy of York College ISLGP, https://commons.wikimedia.org/wiki/File:Maya_Angelou_visits_YCP_Feb_2013.jpg.

2. Aristotle, *Rhetoric*.
3. Aristotle, *Rhetoric*.
4. Quintilian, *Institutes of Oratory*, trans. Harold Edgeworth Butler (Loeb Classical Library, 1920–1922), bk. 2, chap. 16, http://penelope.uchicago.edu/Thayer/E/Roman/Texts/Quintilian/Institutio_Oratoria/home.html.

used by all, to win such honor and glory that you seem not to speak or plead, but rather, as was said of Pericles,[5] to thunder and lighten?[6]

Note that different cultures and people groups have differing ideas about what it means to be good. The Roman idea of goodness, as explained by Quintilian, emphasizes some slightly different aspects of goodness than some of the world's great religions. For instance, Judaism and Christianity emphasize selflessness and charity in addition to the virtues that Quintilian thought of as goodness.

Wow. Quintilian implies that with rhetoric our words can be as powerful as thunder and lightning! But don't miss that he said that rhetoric was good when it was used by "a good person." Without mincing words, he says, "I hold that no one can be a true orator unless he is also a good [person]."[7]

What did Quintilian mean by "a good person"? More than likely he meant someone who worked to develop within herself the solid Roman virtues of courage, self-control, generosity, justice, piety, and wisdom. There are many different opinions about what makes a person good, but the bottom line is that Quintilian felt it was important to use rhetoric for the good of others.

When a person who strives for goodness writes or speaks, rhetoric can become a significant power to bring about good ends. What about you? Do you strive for goodness?

More than likely you'll say "yes," and you probably already have many qualities that are good. Yet developing goodness doesn't happen all at once. It is the study of a lifetime, and a young person such as yourself may have a lot of learning and growing left to do when it comes to goodness. In fact, too often people think that they are better than they really are, and that misbelief can get in the way of developing goodness. A professor at Princeton University asked his students what their position on slavery would have been if they had been white and living in the South before abolition. Guess what? According to this professor, the students all claimed they would have been abolitionists!

5. Pericles (c. 495–429): the renowned statesman and leader of Athens during its Golden Age
6. Quintilian, *Institutes of Oratory*, bk, 2, chap. 16.
7. Quintilian, *Institutes of Oratory*, bk. 1, chap. 2.

> They all would have bravely spoken out against slavery, and worked tirelessly in the cause of freeing those enslaved. . . .
>
> Of course, it is complete nonsense. Only the tiniest fraction of them, or of any of us, would have spoken up against slavery or lifted a finger to free the slaves. Most of them—and us—would simply have gone along. Many would have supported the slave system and, if it was in their interest, participated in it as buyers and owners or sellers of slaves.
>
> So I respond to the students' assurances that they would have been vocal opponents of slavery by saying that I will credit their claims if they can show me evidence of the following: that in leading their lives today they have embraced causes that are unpopular among their peers and stood up for the rights of victims of injustice whose very humanity is denied, and where they have done so knowing (1) that it would make THEM unpopular with their peers, (2) that they would be loathed and ridiculed by wealthy, powerful, and influential individuals and institutions in our society, (3) that it would cost them friendships and cause them to be abandoned and even denounced by many of their friends, (4) that they would be called nasty names, and (5) that they would possibly even be denied valuable educational and professional opportunities as a result of their moral witness.
>
> In short, my challenge to them is to show me where they have at significant risk to themselves and their futures stood up for a cause that is unpopular in elite sectors of our culture today.[8]

To put it bluntly, very few people would actually risk their popularity, their money, their friendships, their education, or their opportunities in order to take an unpopular stand. In other words, we often are not as good as we think we are, and recognizing this should motivate us to keep working at developing goodness. Taking an unpopular stand requires serious courage and other virtues as well: determination, for instance, and sound judgment and prudence. Just as mastering rhetoric takes time and practice, so does developing those virtues. It is more of a journey than an arrival.

No one ever becomes perfectly good and has nothing left to work on. You must constantly, deliberately own up to your weaknesses and actively support what is noble and right. In this way, your life will be held up to an honest mirror similar to the one in the story of Snow White. You may say, "Mirror, mirror on the wall, am I improving after all?" And the mirror may say back, "Oh, Man (or Oh, Woman), in this life you won't arrive; the vital thing is that you strive." Or it might dispense with the rhyme and tell you bluntly, "You were really kind to that elderly woman yesterday, but then afterward you bragged about it to your friends. Let's work on a little humility now." Throughout all your days, your mirror will keep saying, "You can still improve," but perhaps you

8. Robert P. George, Facebook, August 17, 2017, https://www.facebook.com/robert.p.george.39/posts/10212810047458661. Used by permission of the author.

can also say back to it, “You’re right. I’m not yet perfectly good. I still have room to grow, but I am living well along the way.”

One of the purposes of these books, these *progymnasmata*, is to give you the tools for influencing others—for example, to stand up for what you believe in. When the time comes for you to take a stand, you will need to be able to express yourself clearly in writing or speech. The thesis essay is really the highest height of the *progymnasmata* because it can marshal every skill that came before it to make the strongest case for your ideas. You’ve made the climb and you’ve reached the pinnacle! But please remember: While you are learning to master rhetoric, to influence others, you must also strive to develop goodness, so that your influence is used for the good of others.

Narcissism

Nowadays it seems as though there are a lot of young people who are obsessed with their images—posting a bazillion selfies online; fixating on diet, clothes, celebrities; snapping photos back and forth. While it’s not necessarily bad to take selfies or think about how you look, being obsessed with doing those things can lead to excessive self-love, which is also known as narcissism. Narcissism can lead people to believe that they are better than they really are, that they don’t need to strive to improve. A professor of psychology in California recently surveyed thousands of students and found that 30 percent were narcissistic, a 15 percent leap from 1982![9] This rapid growth in narcissism among young people is a cause for concern for the health of our American culture.

Most people like to see themselves in the best possible light, and that’s perfectly natural. However, we must be on guard against thinking we are good (and special and remarkable) without questioning whether or not this assessment is based on reality. We must be on guard against the kind of thinking that leads us to use powerful tools such as rhetoric for our own selfish purposes, such as winning admiration or building power, rather than for the good of others. By working to develop the qualities of goodness, we can help ourselves to avoid the pitfalls of narcissistic thinking.

9. Jean M. Twenge and Joshua D. Foster, “Birth Cohort Increases in Narcissistic Personality Traits Among American College Students, 1982–2009,” *Psychology Today*, accessed June 8, 2018, https://www.psychologytoday.com/files/attachments/4330/npitimeupdatespps.pdf.

Tell It Back—Summary

This icon points to more tips on summarizing at the back of the book.

TE

Summarize aloud three or four important ideas in this lesson. Then, in the space provided, write one well-crafted sentence that tells the main idea of the lesson as best as you understand it. To arrive at the main idea, ask yourself, "What is the chief purpose of the lesson?"

Main idea:

Sample main idea: A person who uses the power of rhetoric should strive to be good in ways that can include courage, self-control, generosity, justice, piety, and wisdom.

Talk About It—

TE

1. Anne Shirley of *Anne of Green Gables* by Lucy Maud Montgomery asks the question, "Which would you rather be if you had the choice—divinely beautiful or dazzlingly clever or angelically good?" If you had to choose one of those qualities, which would it be and why? Why do teachers of rhetoric care about whether or not a person wants to be good?

TE

2. The word "narcissism" means "excessive self-love." The word is derived from a Greek myth about a handsome young man named Narcissus who rudely rejected all of his suitors, including the mountain nymph Echo. As punishment for his conceit, he was fated to fall in love with his own reflection on the surface of a pond. There he lay on the grassy bank, staring into his own two eyes, pining to embrace himself, until he withered away and died. Rhetoricians say that people must desire goodness and be concerned for the good of others. How does narcissism undermine the goodness demanded by the practice of rhetoric? What do you think happens to friendships and other important relationships in the life of a person who is a narcissist?

▲ *Echo and Narcissus* by John William Waterhouse

TE

3. Can you think of a situation or issue today in which it would be very costly to an individual if he or she were to take an unpopular stand?

Write & Discuss—

We find the following reflection in the Jewish book of moral teachings entitled *Chapters of the Fathers*, or *Pirkei Avot*:

Who is wise?
He who learns from everyone.
Who is strong?
He who conquers himself.
Who is rich?
He who is content with his lot.
Who is honorable?
He who treats all men honorably.[10]

Throughout the ages, rhetoric has demanded that its practitioners be people who strive after goodness. The *Pirkei Avot* contains some universal ideas defining goodness in human beings: wisdom, self-control, contentment, and honor.

What would you say are the qualities of a good person? Think carefully about an individual from history or from your own experience whom you respect and admire. Then take fifteen minutes to write down your thoughts about the qualities of goodness and how those qualities are expressed in that particular person. After that, share your thoughts with your teacher or with a partner, and try to arrive at a description of a person who strives for goodness—the kind of person who would use the skills of rhetoric for good purposes. Write your description in the space provided.

Observations of the individual:

Sample answer: Although he was imperfect—like all human beings—I really respect George Washington as a man of great goodness. He sacrificed his comfort and happiness to lead the ragged Continental Army to victory, and then, through wisdom and prudence, he led the struggling United States to stability. He showed courage in the face of danger, both on and off the battlefield. He willingly gave up power instead of grasping it like a dictator. He was hospitable to hundreds of visitors to Mount Vernon every year, and he loved his wife, Martha, faithfully for forty years.

10. The words of Simon Ben Zoma from *Pirkei Avot*, chapter 4. The full text of this book can be found at https://www.chabad.org/library/article_cdo/aid/680274/jewish/Pirkei-Avot-Ethics-of-the-Fathers.htm.

Description of a person who strives for goodness:

Sample answer: A person who strives for goodness is self-sacrificing, wise, prudent, courageous, kind, and loyal.

Go Deeper—

1. **SUMMARY, MAIN IDEA, AND DEFINITION**—One of the fascinating things about folk-tales and fairy tales is that they entertain us at the same time that they teach us lessons about life. We learn to avoid talking to strangers from "Little Red Riding Hood." We learn not to make rash promises from "Rumpelstiltskin." We learn that looks can be deceiving from "Beauty and the Beast." We learn that it's important to use our wits from "Hansel and Gretel."

Perhaps even more important than these moral lessons, which are similar to the lessons taught by fables, is the clear picture of good and evil that we get from many folk- and fairy tales. We know pretty quickly which characters are decent and kind, and we know which characters are harmful. This clear picture of good and evil—along with the way good characters are rewarded—helps children tilt toward wanting to live a good life.

Look at the following short tales. For each one, summarize the tale, as instructed, in the space provided. Then identify and write down the tale's main idea and describe how each tale defines goodness or wickedness. (Keep in mind that most narratives are subject to interpretation and there may be more than one suitable main idea or definition of goodness or wickedness. If you compare your answer with the answers of your classmates, you may be surprised by the variety of perspectives.)

Summary vs. Main Idea—What's the Difference?

A summary is a shortened, condensed version of a piece of writing. The main idea is the most important thought that comes out of the writing. For example, look at the following summary and main idea for "The Tortoise and the Hare":

Summary: In a race between a slow-moving tortoise and a fast-running hare, the tortoise crosses the finish line first by persevering toward the goal.

Main idea: Success depends on persistence.

Example:

"Odds and Ends," a German Tale

There was once upon a time a maiden who was pretty, but idle and negligent. When she had to spin she was so out of temper that if there was a little knot in the flax, she at once pulled out a whole heap of it, and strewed it about on the ground beside her. Now she had a servant who was industrious, and gathered together the bits of flax which were thrown away, cleaned them, [spun] them fine, and had a beautiful gown made out of them for herself. A young man had wooed the lazy girl, and the wedding was to take place. On the eve of the wedding, the industrious one was dancing merrily about in her pretty dress, and the bride said,—"Ah, how that girl does jump about, dressed in my odds and ends." The bridegroom heard that, and asked the bride what she meant by it. Then she told him that the girl was wearing a dress [made] of the flax which she had thrown away. When the bridegroom heard that, and saw how idle she was, and how industrious the poor girl was, he gave her up and went to the other, and chose her as his wife.[11]

Tip: Use quotation marks to punctuate the title of a short story, short poem, TV episode, or essay. Italicize or underline the title of a longer work, such as a book, movie, play, TV show, or collection of poems, stories, or essays.

a. Summarize the tale "Odds and Ends" in one sentence.

In "Odds and Ends," a bridegroom nearly marries a spoiled, lazy maiden, but marries her servant instead when he discovers that the hardworking servant made a dress out of discarded flax.

b. State the main idea of the tale in one sentence.

Hard work and thrift, rather than beauty and idleness, receive a reward.

c. How does the tale define goodness?

"Odds and Ends" defines goodness as working hard and making the best of your situation in life.

A. **"The Star-Money," a German Tale**

There was once on a time a little girl whose father and mother were dead, and she was so poor that she no longer had any little room to live in, or bed to sleep in, and at last she had nothing else but the clothes she was wearing and a little bit of bread in her hand which some charitable soul had given her. She was, however, good and pious.

And as she was thus forsaken by all the world, she went forth into the open country, trusting in the good God. Then a poor man met her, who said, "Ah, give me something to eat, I am so hungry!" She reached him the whole of her piece of bread, and

11. The Brothers Grimm, "Odds and Ends," in *Household Tales*, trans. Margaret Hunt (London: George Bell and Sons, 1884; Project Gutenberg, 2004), https://www.gutenberg.org/files/5314/5314-8.txt.

said, "May God bless it to thy use," and went onwards. Then came a child who moaned and said, "My head is so cold, give me something to cover it with." So she took off her hood and gave it to him; and when she had walked a little farther, she met another child who had no jacket and was frozen with cold. Then she gave it her own; and a little farther on one begged for a frock, and she gave away that also. At length she got into a forest and it had already become dark, and there came yet another child, and asked for a little shirt, and the good little girl thought to herself, "It is a dark night and no one sees thee, thou canst very well give thy little shirt away," and took it off, and gave away that also.

And as she so stood, and had not one single thing left, suddenly some stars from heaven fell down, and they were nothing else but hard smooth pieces of money, and although she had just given her little shirt away, she had a new one which was of the very finest linen. Then she gathered together the money into this, and was rich all the days of her life.[12]

a. Summarize the tale "The Star-Money" in one sentence.

Sample answer: In "The Star-Money," a poor orphan girl wanders through the world giving away what little she possesses until she is rewarded by money from heaven.

b. State the main idea of the tale in one sentence.

Sample answers: Even when a person feels poor, she can still be generous.
Goodness and piety will be rewarded in the end.

c. How does the tale define goodness?

Sample answer: "The Star-Money" defines goodness as giving generously, even if it hurts.

B. **"How the Wicked Sons Were Duped," an Indian Tale**

A very wealthy old man, imagining that he was on the point of death, sent for his sons and divided his property among them. However, he did not die for several years afterwards; and miserable years many of them were. Besides the weariness of old age, the old fellow had to bear with much abuse and cruelty from his sons. Wretched, selfish ingrates! Previously they vied with one another in trying to please their father, hoping thus to receive more money, but now they had received their patrimony,[13] they cared

12. The Brothers Grimm, "The Star-Money," in *Household Tales*, trans. Margaret Hunt (London: George Bell and Sons, 1884; Project Gutenburg, 2004), https://www.gutenberg.org/files/5314/5314-8.txt.
13. patrimony: inheritance from one's father

not how soon he left them—nay, the sooner the better, because he was only a needless trouble and expense. And they let the poor old man know what they felt.

One day he met a friend and related to him all his troubles. The friend sympathized very much with him, and promised to think over the matter, and call in a little while and tell him what to do. He did so; in a few days he visited the old man and put down four bags full of stones and gravel before him.

"Look here, friend," said he. "Your sons will get to know of my coming here to-day, and will inquire about it. You must pretend that I came to discharge a long-standing debt with you, and that you are several thousands of rupees[14] richer than you thought you were. Keep these bags in your own hands, and on no account let your sons get to them as long as you are alive. You will soon find them change their conduct towards you. Salaam.[15] I will come again soon to see how you are getting on."

When the young men got to hear of this further increase of wealth they began to be more attentive and pleasing to their father than ever before. And thus they continued to the day of the old man's demise, when the bags were greedily opened, and found to contain only stones and gravel![16]

a. Summarize the tale "How the Wicked Sons Were Duped" in three sentences.

Sample answer: In "How the Wicked Sons Were Duped," several wicked sons treat their father abusively after he gives them their inheritance. Seeing the old man in despair, a friend gives him four bags of stones and recommends that he pretend they are a repayment of a debt. By pretending to be rich again, the old man again receives the kind attention of his sons.

b. State the main idea of the tale in one sentence.

Sample answers: It is unwise to give away one's wealth before one is dead.
A parent may not even trust his own children to care for him when he is poor.

c. How does the tale define wickedness?

Sample answer: "How the Wicked Sons Were Duped" defines wickedness as mistreating elders or one's own parents.

14. rupee: the basic money unit of India, Pakistan, and Nepal
15. Salaam: a greeting and farewell that means "peace"
16. "How the Wicked Sons Were Duped," in *Indian Fairy Tales*, ed. Joseph Jacobs (London: David Nutt, 1892; Project Gutenburg, 2003), https://www.gutenberg.org/files/7128/7128-h/7128-h.htm.

C. **"The Old Man and His Grandson," a German Tale**

There was once a very old man, whose eyes had become dim, his ears dull of hearing, his knees trembled, and when he sat at table he could hardly hold the spoon, and spilt the broth upon the table-cloth or let it run out of his mouth. His son and his son's wife were disgusted at this, so the old grandfather at last had to sit in the corner behind the stove, and they gave him his food in an earthenware bowl, and not even enough of it. And he used to look towards the table with his eyes full of tears. Once, too, his trembling hands could not hold the bowl, and it fell to the ground and broke. The young wife scolded him, but he said nothing and only sighed. Then they bought him a wooden bowl for a few pennies, out of which he had to eat.

They were once sitting thus when the little grandson of four years old began to gather together some bits of wood upon the ground. "What are you doing there?" asked the father. "I am making a little trough," answered the child, "for father and mother to eat out of when I am big."

The man and his wife looked at each other for a while, and presently began to cry. Then they took the old grandfather to the table, and henceforth always let him eat with them, and likewise said nothing if he did spill a little of anything.[17]

a. Summarize the tale "The Old Man and His Grandson" in three sentences.

Sample answer: In "The Old Man and His Grandson," an old man lives with his son and daughter-in-law. Disgusted by the old man's inability to hold his bowl steady and by daily spills on the table, the younger couple seat him out of the way behind the stove. It's only when the grandson, while playing, mimics the selfishness of the younger couple that the couple realize that they must treat the old man with kindness.

b. State the main idea of the tale in one sentence.

Sample answers: Treat others as you want yourself to be treated.
We can learn wisdom from people of all ages.

c. How does the tale define goodness?

Sample answer: "The Old Man and His Grandson" defines goodness as patience with weakness, and kindness toward others.

17. The Brothers Grimm, "The Old Man and His Grandson," in *Household Tales*, trans. Margaret Hunt (London: George Bell and Sons, 1884; Project Gutenburg, 2004), https://www.gutenberg.org/files/5314/5314-8.txt.

D. **"The Miraculous Cow," a Filipino Tale**

There was once a farmer driving home from his farm in his cart. He had tied his cow to the back, as he was accustomed to do every evening on his way home. While he was going along the road, two boys saw him. They were Felipe and Ambrosio. Felipe whispered to Ambrosio, "Do you see the cow tied to the back of that cart? Well, if you will untie it, I will take it to our house."

Ambrosio approached the cart slowly, and untied the cow. He handed the rope to Felipe, and then tied himself in the place of the animal.

"Come on, Ambrosio! Don't be foolish! Come on with me!" whispered Felipe impatiently.

"No, leave me alone! Go home, and I will soon be there!" answered the cunning Ambrosio.

After a while the farmer happened to look back. What a surprise for him! He was frightened to find a boy instead of his cow tied to the cart. "Why are you there? Where is my cow?" he shouted furiously. "Rascal, give me my cow!"

"Oh, don't be angry with me!" said Ambrosio. "Wait a minute, and I will tell you my story. Once, when I was a small boy, my mother became very angry with me. She cursed me, and suddenly I was transformed into a cow; and now I am changed back into my own shape. It is not my fault that you bought me: I could not tell you not to do so, for I could not speak at the time. Now, generous farmer, please give me my freedom! for I am very anxious to see my old home again."

The farmer did not know what to do, for he was very sorry to lose his cow. When he reached home, he told his wife the story. Now, his wife was a kind-hearted woman; so, after thinking a few minutes, she said, "Husband, what can we do? We ought to set him free. It is by the great mercy of God that he has been restored to his former self."

So the wily boy got off. He rejoined his friend, and they had a good laugh over the two simple folks.

The next day the farmer went to the market to buy a new cow and found his own cow for sale. He grieved at his own foolishness and vowed to thrash the boys if he ever saw them again.[18]

a. Summarize the tale "The Miraculous Cow" in two sentences.

Sample answer: In "The Miraculous Cow," two boys steal a farmer's cow from the back of his cart, and one of the boys tethers himself to the cart using the cow's rope. The boy pretends that he is the cow, now turned back to his original form, and the farmer foolishly believes him, but after he lets the boy go, he finds his own cow for sale at the market.

18. Adapted from "The Miraculous Cow," in *Filipino Popular Tales*, ed. Dean S. Fansler (Lancaster, PA: American Folklore Society, 1921; Project Gutenburg, 2008), https://www.gutenberg.org/files/8299/8299-h/8299-h.htm.

b. State the main idea of the tale in one sentence.

Sample answers: A preposterous story should never be believed.
With cleverness it is easy to trick the simple-minded.

c. How does the tale define wickedness?

Sample answers: "The Miraculous Cow" defines wickedness as using one's wits to fool kindhearted, simple folk.
"The Miraculous Cow" defines wickedness as foolishly believing impossible stories.

2. **AMPLIFICATION**—When we give readers a chance to enter more fully into an experience, they often become more open to our ideas. Amplification can do exactly that—help readers enter into an experience—by making a story richer with detail. Good rhetoric requires good storytelling.

The story in this exercise is a tale from China that warns the reader to treat people kindly, to protect them, and to avoid assuming the worst about them. You will see that this story, like some of the tales in the previous exercise, teaches about goodness by showing what goodness is not—by describing wickedness in action. After you read it over, rewrite the story in the space provided, adding dialogue and description that would enhance your audience's enjoyment of the story and help them to better understand what you think the story is saying about goodness.

- You can use vivid, descriptive words to:
  - more fully describe the farmers
  - more fully describe the settings of the field and the temple
  - more fully describe the storm
- You can go into more detail about the wicked background of the farmers or help your audience better understand the "mind" of the lightning.
- You can use dialogue to:
  - give more details about the actions and motives of the farmers
  - enhance the personality and character of several of the farmers

"Who Was the Wicked Man?", a Chinese Tale

Once upon a time there were ten farmers, who were crossing a field together. They were surprised by a heavy thunder-storm, and took refuge in a half-ruined temple. But the thunder drew ever nearer, and so great was the tumult that the air trembled about them, while the lightning flew around the temple in a continuous circle. The farmers were greatly frightened, and thought that there must be a wicked man among them, whom the lightning would strike. In order to find out who it might be, they agreed to hang their straw hats up before the door, and he whose hat was blown away was to yield himself up to his fate.

No sooner were the hats outside, than one of them was blown away, and the rest thrust its unfortunate owner out of doors without pity. But as soon as he had left the temple, the lightning ceased circling around and struck the temple with a crash, killing the remaining nine farmers.

The one whom the rest had thrust out had been the only good man among them, and for his sake the lightning had spared the temple. So the other nine had to pay for their hard-heartedness with their lives.[19]

Amplification:

Sample amplification:

Once upon a time there were ten farmers. As they sloshed across the rice fields together, they were suddenly caught in a storm with heavy rain and fearsome flashes of lightning. They ran for their lives and took refuge in the ruins of an old temple. As the thunder boomed louder and louder, nearer and nearer, they pressed their backs against the brick walls in an effort to stay dry under the half-collapsed roof. And then came a crash so loud, so earsplitting, that they felt the air shudder and the ground tremble beneath their feet.

"We will all surely die!" cried one of the farmers.

"What have we done to deserve this fate?" shrieked another.

Now, one of the farmers, a tall, bearded fellow with burly muscles, took leadership of the group. He shouted, "How foolish we are! We must sacrifice one of us to save the others. Surely the lightning god is angry with us for good reason. Perhaps we are sheltering an evildoer among us!" The tall man then urged the other farmers to hang their straw hats on a rafter in front of the broken-down door. "Whichever man has his hat blown away first, that is the man we shall send into the storm!"

19. *The Chinese Fairy Book*, ed. Dr. R. Wilhelm, trans. Frederick H. Martens (New York: Frederick A. Stokes Company, 1921; Project Gutenberg, 2009), http://www.gutenberg.org/files/29939/29939-h/29939-h.htm.

Only one farmer, a thin old man with gray hair, argued against the idea. "It would be cruel to send any man back into the storm," he said. "We must wait for the storm to pass."

The burly farmer made a fist and said, "You silly old coot! I'll knock your block off if you resist!"

Not all the farmers wanted to hang their hats on the rafter. It seemed like a desperate idea, but they were afraid of the burly farmer with the beard. They were afraid that if they appeared reluctant, they would be identified as the evildoer. It took another loud crash of thunder to send them all scurrying toward the door, and there they hung up their hats. The old man reluctantly waded across the muddy floor to the rafter and hung up his hat as well.

In less than a minute, a powerful gust of wind burst through the door. And whose hat did it lift off the hook? The old, gray-headed man's. It flew like a dart across the room.

"Aha!" gloated the burly farmer. "We might have known it was you, you old scoundrel. You wicked, selfish man! How dare you hide among us and try to get us killed? Get out in the storm. Now!"

The old man looked to his comrades for help, but they all cowered against the dripping brick wall. A flash of lightning showed them all to be trembling and unwilling to say a word.

"Get out!" one of them said.

"Get out!" they all shouted in unison.

And so the old man picked up his hat and plodded out the door. The wind was fierce and threatened to knock him down. The rain struck hard and stung him all over. But when he was only thirty paces from the temple, a giant shaft of lightning hit its roof. The roof and all the walls caved in on top of the other farmers, killing them instantly, leaving only a smoking ruin.

In a short while, the sun came up on the rice fields and the birds began chirping once more. The old man kept walking, walking, walking. The lightning god had spared the only good man in the bunch. It was for the old farmer's sake that he had avoided the temple, but once the old man had departed, the lightning god had struck the temple with all of his might.

Lesson 1: Quintilian and the Classical Ideal: First Strive for Goodness

Tell It Back—Summary

Sample important ideas:

- Both Aristotle and Quintilian saw rhetoric as a good and useful skill for public discussions, although they acknowledged that it could be misused.
- Most people are not as good as they think they are, and recognizing this should motivate us to keep working at developing goodness.
- Becoming a good person is the study and challenge of a lifetime.

Talk About It—

1. I would want to be good even though it would be tempting to choose beauty or cleverness. Beauty doesn't last forever, and some beauties are really rotten to other people. Clever people are intelligent and can be wise, but cleverness without goodness can also be used hurtfully. If someone is truly good, he or she is always helpful and kind to other people.

   Teachers of rhetoric care about a person's desire to be good because they believe that anyone who practices rhetoric must have this aspiration. If a person isn't working on self-improvement, he might do more harm than good in the use of rhetoric.

   Teachers: You may find it useful to share the following sample answer with your students as well, to give them an idea of how the question might be answered by someone in a different stage of life. This is how the author of this series would answer the question:

   When I was a young man, I wanted to be divinely beautiful so that I could find love. When I found love, I wanted to be dazzlingly clever so that I could win fame and fortune. Now that I'm older, I don't value fame or fortune all that much. Instead, I would like to be good so that young people, including my children, can see me as a role model and emulate my care and concern for others. The world needs people who are striving to be good more than it needs beautiful, famous, or wealthy people.

2. Narcissism undermines goodness by making selfishness a person's priority. A narcissist may use rhetoric to build power, wealth, or prestige, but not to help others or his society.

   Because narcissists love to be the center of attention, they probably don't have much time to pay attention to the needs of others. All relationships require mutual care and attention to be healthy, and a narcissist who can't give to others will fast suck the life out of a relationship. Eventually the narcissist's friends will tire of always putting the narcissist at the center. And what happens when the friends of a narcissist stop giving him so much admiration? I'll bet the narcissist will dump those friends and move on to others who will admire him more,

TE

and the cycle will start all over again. Every one of a narcissist's friendships are likely to be shallow because they don't last long.

3. Answers will vary. Topics might include abortion, sexual orientation, combat enlistment of women, doctor-assisted suicide, sex selection of children, religious freedom, human cloning, animal rights, and rights for robots with artificial intelligence. In many countries today, freedom of worship and freedom of political activism are forbidden. Many millions are forced to take unpopular stands for the sake of their consciences and they pay the price in persecution.

Notes

The purpose of this lesson is to introduce thesis statements and thesis essays as useful tools for effective argument.
In this lesson, students will practice:
- narration in summary form
- critical thinking
- written analysis of a literary topic and follow-up discussion
- identifying and writing speculative questions
- identifying and writing persuasive thesis statements

Lesson 2

Of Thesis Statements, Disagreements, and Speculative Questions

You'll come across the word "thesis" in this book about as often as you'll come across the word "burger" at a fast food joint. When we use the word "thesis," it will mean one of two things:

1. a thesis statement—the main idea or argument of an essay, oration, or discussion
2. a **thesis essay**—a persuasive paper that defends a thesis statement

Now, don't let your eyes glaze over! To be honest, your pulse should be quickening, your knees should be getting wobbly, and you should have butterflies in your tummy. No, you're not about to fall in love. Rather, you're about to learn about two of the most important ways to communicate in your life as a student. The thesis statement and the thesis essay—these are the fireworks of rhetoric!

The Thesis Statement—

One way that you can argue more effectively, or go deeper in your thinking, is to advance a thesis statement. Depending on the type of paper you are writing, some thesis statements merely explain a subject, such as jazz or photosynthesis or appendicitis. Other thesis statements analyze topics, such as hunting or plastic surgery or lottery games, in an essay that breaks down the topic and weighs its pluses and minuses. The thesis statement in a persuasive paper is a little different. It is still the main idea of the essay, but it makes a claim that can be argued and tries to persuade the audience that the claim is right. This is how old Aristotle or Cicero or Aphthonius would have used a thesis statement. In other words, using a thesis as the main argument of a paper is a classic idea. Here's an example of a persuasive thesis:

> Due to high expenses and frequent injuries, football should be dropped as a high school sport.

Now, a fair number of people might agree with this statement, but quite a few football fans would disagree. The beauty of a thesis is that you can make a case for it—argue for it—to help you win your audience to your side. It is not a simple factual statement such as "Water is wet" or "Purple is a color." A thesis statement requires support to back it up.

Unless I'm mistaken, you already have some practice at making a case. Most people have considerable experience arguing for the things they want. When you urge your dad or mom to go out to eat or watch a particular movie, you are most likely making some sort of attempt at an argument. (Keep in mind that an argument is different than a quarrel. An argument is a clear line of thinking aimed at proving a point. A quarrel is any sharp or angry disagreement.) So let's say that you want to make the case for eating out tonight, but you haven't really thought about it too carefully. You put forth your thesis:

"I'm hungry."

No, that's not a thesis—or at least it's not a *persuasive* thesis. It's a statement of fact; it really can't be argued. Also, it's not clear about what you really want: to eat out. You try again.

"Can we go out to eat tonight?"

Again, not a thesis. A question is not a statement. You try again.

"I've been dreaming of sushi."

Nice try. Although this attempt is another statement, it's a fuzzy statement that can't be argued. You haven't even mentioned your purpose yet, which is to go out to eat.

"We should go out for sushi."

Now that's a clear and debatable statement! If you want to make it even more persuasive, you could include supporting details and reasons for the statement: "We should go out for sushi because it offers health benefits and a taste experience that can't be matched by the food in our refrigerator."

Word Roots!

Our English word "thesis" comes from the Greek *thesis*, which means a "setting down" or "something set down." This comes from the verb *tithenai*, which means "to put, set down." It is very similar to the Latinate word "proposition" from the Latin *proponere*, which means "to put before." When we present a thesis, we put or set forth a claim.

OK, now that's a solid thesis statement! Although it is expressed with all the force of a statement of fact, the sentence really needs some support to carry the day. In other words, it is a statement that could be argued. Your parents could agree *or* disagree with you. To make your case, you will need to be able to explain how sushi offers taste and health benefits when compared to the grub that's currently in the fridge. You will need to support your statement in such a way that your parents will take your idea seriously.

> **Word Roots!**
>
> The word "statement" is derived from the Latin *sto, stare* (I stand, to stand). A statement is a declaration of the status of something, declaring "how things stand."

Of course, parents have every right to override suggestions from their children with counterarguments, or to provide no explanation at all. Please don't get the impression that I'm saying it's OK to nag your mom and dad. But knowing how to express your desires or opinions by using and supporting a thesis can help you to clarify your thinking and improve your discussions with your parents—and anyone else as well.

The Nature of Disagreement—

Think about all the disagreements you can have—such as whether or not to go out to dinner—in a small family or circle of friends and then extend those disagreements to the big family we call humanity. We are surrounded by disagreement!

There's an old Jewish proverb that goes, "Whenever there are two people in a room, there are three opinions." And then there's this Yiddish[1] joke:

> Two men come to their rabbi[2] to settle a dispute. One man holds one opinion while the other man holds exactly the opposite opinion. So the rabbi listens patiently to the first man. After he finishes, the rabbi exclaims, "You're right!" But the second man jumps in and tells his side of the story. When he's done, the rabbi cries, "And you're right, too!" A bystander who has listened to the whole dispute breaks in and says, "What's wrong with you, rabbi? They're arguing two totally different sides! They can't both be right!" To which the rabbi replies, "You're right!"

Both proverb and joke illustrate the fact that people don't agree perfectly on anything. Not a single belief held by one person hasn't been disputed by another person. Does this prove there aren't any right or wrong answers? No. It only proves that the thoughts of people are all over the map.

The reasons for our disagreements are many. We live in diverse cultures. We have conflicting sources of information. Some people think more logically while others think more emotionally. We take selfish positions; we take selfless positions. Some speak from deep knowledge; others speak from ignorance. Finally, for some inexplicable reason, human beings like to disagree. We love to dispute, to debate, to bump heads.

1. Yiddish: a language fusion of German, Hebrew, and Slavic; originally spoken by the Jews of Central and Eastern Europe
2. rabbi: a teacher of Jewish law and religion

Word Roots!

Although the words "quarrel" and "argue" are often used interchangeably today, they have two decidedly different original meanings. "Quarrel" is from the Latin *queri* (to complain) and *querela* (a complaint). "Argument" is from *arguer* (to prove on the basis of evidence, assert, make known, show, make clear).

Oftentimes disagreements arise that are not terribly serious, but simply matters of taste. Is pepperoni pizza better than mushroom? Are rainy days more pleasant than sunny? Are brown eyes more beautiful than blue? There is no universal answer to any of these questions because there's no accounting for taste. I like chocolate mint chip ice cream; you like butter pecan. We can try to persuade each other to appreciate a different kind of ice cream, but in the end it's neither good nor bad to like only one or the other—or to dislike ice cream altogether.

Disagreements of a more serious nature arise when there's a moral component to the question. That's because every moral question implies a right or a wrong answer. Not only that, but morality greatly impacts our happiness, as well as the health of our society. It's not simply a matter of taste when a mother rebukes her defiant daughter for cheating on a test. Or if a father has a problem with his son listening to music with dark or violent lyrics. The mother is concerned about a host of moral issues. How does her daughter's cheating hurt the honest students? How has the daughter cheated herself out of her own education, which includes working hard? Will the cheating cause her daughter to make a habit of dishonesty and laziness? This is not a debate about roses and peonies here. Likewise, the father has moral concerns that go beyond whether or not he likes the sound of violent music. If he was raised on surf pop or blues music, the dad may wince at the different sound. But the dad also worries that violent music will deaden his son's conscience. Will the explicit lyrics coarsen his behavior toward girls? Will the obscenities make him more inclined to taint thoughtful conversations with a sewer stream of four-letter words? Morality is so much more important than taste. It's all about right or wrong attitudes and behavior. It's all about reaching for what's good or sliding in the opposite direction. Because of this, moral matters almost always lead us to sharper disagreements.

You've heard it said, "There are two sides to every question," but for moral issues that is an understatement! Two sides are much too few. It would be better to describe each moral debate as having two opposing extremes with a spectrum of opinions in between. Here's a short list of some of the topics of hot moral debates that are happening today:

- gun rights
- recreational drugs
- social media
- abortion
- sexual behaviors
- pornography

- human rights
- immigration
- "designer" babies (embryos genetically modified for some desirable trait, such as curly hair or high intelligence)
- climate change
- robots and artificial intelligence

In each of these debates, there are many, many different opinions. Some of the opinions strongly and directly oppose each other, and there are many others that fall someplace in between.

Take a look at one moral issue that at first you might think would be cut and dried: homicide. Most people would agree that killing a human being is a terrible crime. However, it's not quite that simple. Many people believe that homicide is permitted in self-defense or in certain instances of warfare. On the other hand, a few people believe that the killing of any person is wrong, even if it's done in self-defense.

Some people even take it farther than that. Not too long ago, I saw graffiti spray-painted on the side of a steak house that said, "Meat is murder!" Some people believe that butchering and eating animals is homicide as well. Now, it's understandable if someone's conscience will not allow the eating of meat. But this steak-house vandal wanted to create equivalence between people and animals, as if cows are as valuable as people. If meat is murder, then pity the lion or tiger that must "murder" fellow animals in order to eat. Should big cats become vegans, too?

Some cultures of the world permit and even celebrate murder. The ancient Canaanites sacrificed infants to their deity Moloch and then burned the infants' remains. In fact, human sacrifice happened with deplorable regularity among almost all the early civilizations of the earth. Throughout history, we see terrorists and criminal rulers praising murder as if it were a virtue. Consider this twisted thinking by Maximilien Robespierre, one of the leaders during the Reign of Terror in France: "Terror is nothing other than justice, prompt, severe, inflexible; it is therefore an emanation of virtue." Thousands of people lost their heads to the guillotine thanks to this rubbish about virtue. Robespierre's thoughts were mirrored by the terrorist Osama bin Laden when he said, "We say that our terror against America is a blessed terror." On another occasion he said, "The pieces of the bodies of infidels were flying like dust particles. If you would have seen it with your own eyes, you would have been very pleased, and your heart would have been filled with joy."

As you can see, there is a spectrum of opinion on the topic of homicide, and you'll find that's the case with any moral issue. With so many divergent ideas in the world, and also many extreme, debased ideas, disagreements about moral issues can have great consequences. There's often a serious reason for our disagreements, and we need to learn to defend the good, the true, and the beautiful.

When moral issues are up for debate, it's important that wise people take part in the conversation so that we are arguing constructively rather than quarreling destructively. By your "clear line of thinking aimed at proving a point," you may be able to prevent or subdue some quarrels and promote helpful discussion instead—that is, of course, if people are actually willing to listen. Hopefully we want more from our conversations than to hear ourselves blow hot air. Hopefully we want to arrive at a deeper understanding of each other and of the truth. Dr. Ruth Simmons, former president of Brown University, once said, "It is easy enough to exist in a realm where everyone is like-minded and speaks only of unimportant matters. That's easy. While comfort may be found in silence, truth cannot dwell there."[3] In other words, it is vital that people can freely discuss their differences. That is the only way to arrive at truthful understandings. Your ability to argue well will enable you to consider and understand other viewpoints. It will also help you, when necessary, to dispel bad or unhelpful ideas.

Word Roots!

The word "essay" comes from the Latin *exagium* (a weighing) and is related to the verb *exagere* (to examine, test; literally, to drive out). An essay is an effort or an attempt to weigh, evaluate, examine, and test an idea. It is related to the idea of melting gold until the dross (impurities) floats to the top, so that it can be skimmed off and removed, thus purifying the gold. An essay "purifies" or distills an idea.

The Thesis Essay—

The thesis essay is intended to do just that—defend your ideas against uninformed, foolish, and dangerous ideas—as well as to help you to take a stand on many everyday issues as well. Every thesis essay begins by answering a speculative question.

- Is it better to live in the city or the country?
- What is the future of atomic energy?
- Which is the most important amendment in the Bill of Rights?
- Is it ethical to eat meat?
- How young is too young for owning a cell phone or smartphone?
- Has peer pressure forced students to all think alike on important issues?
- What can be done to stop binge drinking in college?

A speculative question doesn't have a definite answer; rather, it can have more than one answer, and these answers are open to opinion, counterarguments, and debate. Keep in mind, however, that some answers will be better than others. Some answers will be thoughtful and well supported; others will be careless and weak. For example, if someone were to ask "What is a helpful way to motivate students to study hard?" one person could answer, "Have high expectations for the student," which is a thoughtful answer, while another person could say, "Give the student a swift kick in the pants," which isn't particularly thoughtful or helpful.

3. Ruth J. Simmons, "Text of the President's Opening Convocation Address" (speech), Brown University, September 4, 2001, Providence, Rhode Island, transcript, http://www.brown.edu/Administration/News_Bureau/2001-02/01-014t.html.

Recognizing Dichotomies

Notice how the question "Is it better to live in the city or the country?" implies that there are only two possible answers. This implication creates a divide (or dichotomy) between country lovers and city lovers. There are other possible answers: Neither is better, a hybrid lifestyle is better, the suburbs are better, both are equally good. Dichotomies aren't necessarily bad, but it is important to recognize that some speculative questions—the way they are phrased—can limit the possible answers.

In addition, some speculative questions are not as open-ended as they may seem even if they do not create dichotomies. The question "What can be done to stop binge drinking in college?" assumes that binge drinking is universally injurious. While that is undoubtedly true, the question limits our possible opinions because it assumes from the start that we agree that binge drinking is a problem. Even if they are wrong, some people may say, "Binge drinking should be allowed in college as long as students are monitored by chaperones." The limitations of the question do not allow for that kind of answer.

It's sometimes tricky to see that even open-ended questions may restrict how we think about a problem. In some situations, questions that limit possible answers are meant to make our responses focused and well defined. On the other hand, in some situations it may be good to notice that a question is too limiting or creates a dichotomy so that you can rephrase it in your mind in order to consider a wider array of answers.

As you write a thesis essay, your thesis statement will be your thoughtful answer to a speculative question. The question will have many possible answers. For example, here's a typical open-ended, speculative question: "What is the best form of government?"

Here's a possible thesis that answers the question: "A republic is the best form of government because it limits the power of both the government and the majority, and keeps them both in balance."

And here's a different possibility: "A constitutional monarchy is the best form of government because kings and queens provide unmatched stability and are a force for national unity."

The thesis essay is a logical investigation of a speculative question. It works to defend the thesis statement. Before you think in detailed terms of the essay's defensive system, however, take some time to get some more practice with thesis statements and speculative questions.

As you discuss thesis essays with your students, you may want to point out that the process of considering a debatable topic and forming and defending a persuasive thesis statement helps us to learn more about the debate and about our own ideas and beliefs.

Tell It Back—Summary

TE Summarize aloud three or four important ideas in this lesson. Then, in the space provided, write one well-crafted sentence that tells the main idea of the lesson as best as you understand it. To arrive at the main idea, ask yourself, "What is the chief purpose of the lesson?"

Main idea:

Sample main idea: Thesis statements and essays can help people to argue effectively, especially when it comes to serious disagreements about moral issues.

Talk About It—

TE 1. Do you enjoy debates and arguments, or are you a person who generally likes to avoid them? Explain your answer.

TE 2. In his play *Magic*, G.K. Chesterton says, "I object to a quarrel because it always interrupts an argument." How might a quarrel end an argument, and an argument end a quarrel?

TE 3. Is it important to look at questions from different sides? If so, why? And is it possible to be too open-minded? Why would that be a concern?

Write & Discuss—

Too often what begins as a reasonable discussion ends up as a quarrel. At age sixteen, George Washington copied down some ideas for keeping conversations reasonable and polite in his commonplace book. Today, these ideas can be found in a collection called *110 Rules of Civility & Decent Behavior in Company and Conversation.* Read over the following partial list of Washington's rules and then identify one or two that strike you as the most important. Consider why you think they are important. Would you subtract any rules from this list as not helpful or add any of your own rules? Take fifteen minutes to write down your thoughts in the space provided. After that, share your thoughts with your teacher or with your class.

Rule 1: Every Action done in Company ought to be with Some Sign of Respect to those that are Present.

Rule 40: Strive not with your Superiors in argument, but always Submit your Judgment to others with Modesty.

Rule 47: Mock not nor Jest at any thing of Importance; break no Jest that are Sharp Biting[4]. . .

Rule 49: Use no Reproachful Language against anyone, neither Curse nor Revile.

Rule 58: Let your Conversation be without Malice or Envy, for 'tis a Sign of a Tractable and Commendable Nature: And in all Causes of Passion admit Reason to Govern.[5]

Rule 61: Utter not base and frivolous things amongst grave and Learned Men nor very Difficult Questions or Subjects among the Ignorant or things hard to be believed, and Stuff not your Discourse with Sentences amongst your Betters nor Equals.[6]

Rule 65: Speak not injurious Words; neither in Jest nor Earnest. Scoff at none although they give Occasion.

Rule 73: Think before you Speak. Pronounce not imperfectly nor bring out your Words too hastily but orderly & distinctly.

Rule 74: When Another Speaks be attentive your Self and disturb not the Audience. If any hesitate in his Words help him not nor Prompt him without desired, Interrupt him not, nor Answer him till his Speech be ended.

Rule 76: While you are talking, Point not with your Finger at him of Whom you Discourse nor Approach too near him to whom you talk especially to his face.[7]

Thoughts and observations:

Sample answer: Rule 65, "Speak not injurious Words; neither in Jest nor Earnest. Scoff at none although they give Occasion," strikes me as the most important of Washington's rules because it gets at the heart of respecting people. Even though disagreements will crop up, I think it's vital not to mock someone or scoff arrogantly at the person you disagree with, because ridicule will not change her mind. What is important is the respectful, free exchange of ideas. The first part of Rule 73 also strikes me as essential: "When Another Speaks be attentive your Self and disturb not the Audience." I always like the saying that we have two ears and one mouth for a reason. We need to listen twice as much as we speak. Following this rule is vital to a good conversation because listening carefully is the only way to truly understand what a person is saying.

I wouldn't add any rules or subtract anything from this list; it covers a host of helpful ground rules for all sorts of discussion.

4. "break no Jest that are Sharp Biting": In other words, don't use sarcasm or harsh humor in conversation.
5. In modern English this rule would read "By avoiding cruelty or jealousy in your conversations, you will show yourself to be an amenable and praiseworthy person. Make sure that your enthusiasms are guided by reason."
6. Washington is suggesting that it's rude for a person to say crass or silly things among serious and intelligent people and to utter "lofty ideas" among people who have little understanding. He also urges a person to avoid speaking excessively when in the company of peers.
7. Adapted from "The Rules of Civility," George Washington's Mount Vernon, Mount Vernon Ladies' Association, accessed June 28, 2018, http://www.mountvernon.org/george-washington/rules-of-civility.

Go Deeper—

1. A speculative question doesn't have a definite answer; rather, it can have more than one answer, and these answers are open to opinion, counterarguments, and debate. "Is the moon made of Swiss cheese?" This is not a speculative question. The answer is definitively "No!" "What is the taste of serenity?" This is also not a speculative question. There is no answer to such a question. On the other hand, this is a speculative question: "Will people one day colonize Mars?" The answer is still up in the air and can be debated.

   Speculative questions can help a writer or speaker form a thesis because the question causes the speaker to think about a topic and develop an opinion. A thesis statement directly answers a speculative question.

   A. Read the following questions and circle those that are speculative and would be helpful in forming a thesis.

      Example:

      Is it good to be single?
      Are hurricanes destructive when they strike land?
      What is the meaning of life?
      When is a rainbow not a rainbow?

      a. Can monkeys create art?
      b. What was the color of George Washington's white horse?
      c. Does the earth revolve around the sun?
      d. What is the main cause of poverty?
      e. Are you sleeping?
      f. What is the formula for the surface area of a pyramid?
      g. Were history's queens better rulers than history's kings?
      h. What is love?
      i. What is the color of the wind?
      j. Is there life after death?
      k. How can human trafficking be stopped?
      l. How many angles are part of a circle?
      m. To what extent should robots replace human labor?
      n. Should voters be required to pass a civics test?
      o. When should students have access to a smartphone?

   B. Now write three speculative questions of your own that could prompt a thesis essay.

      Question 1:

      Sample answer: Who is the most important person in history?

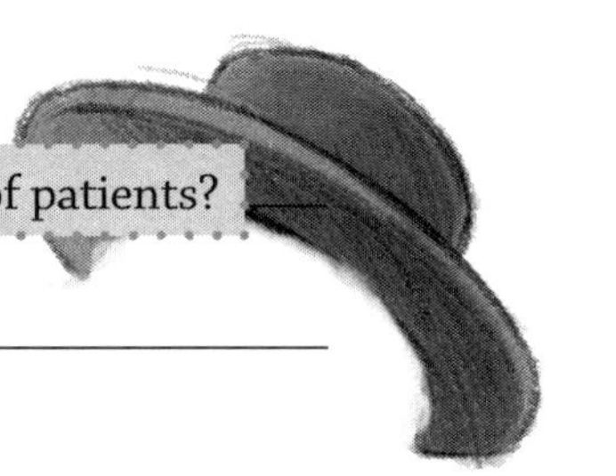

Question 2:

Sample answer: Should physicians be allowed by law to assist in the suicide of patients?

Question 3:

Sample answer: Are today's video games too violent and sexual?

2. A thesis statement is the main idea or argument of an essay, oration, or discussion. In an expository essay, its purpose is to explain. In an analytical essay, its purpose is to analyze and weigh strengths and weaknesses. In a persuasive essay, such as the thesis essays in this book, its purpose is to persuade an audience and provide structure for the rest of the essay. A good persuasive thesis takes a position or expresses an opinion and is open to debate.

   Read the following essay excerpts and underline the thesis statement for each one.[A] Then in the space provided write a speculative question that might have prompted the author to write about that topic.

[A]When you search for a thesis, keep in mind that thesis statements are as varied as writers themselves. This is the style of simple thesis statements you will be asked to write in this book:

- Those who would give up essential Liberty, to purchase a little temporary Safety, deserve neither Liberty nor Safety. —Ben Franklin

However, when you are asked to identify thesis statements in some of the exercises, you will see that not every statement is found in a single, discreet sentence. Sometimes the thesis can be made in two or three sentences. For example:

- Man is born broken. He lives by mending. —Eugene O'Neill[8]
- Progress, far from consisting in change, depends on preserving some of the past. When change is absolute there is nothing left to improve. . . . Those who cannot remember the past are condemned to repeat it. —adapted from George Santayana[9]

Or sometimes the thesis statement can be found within a longer sentence, as in the following example:

- Life, liberty, and the pursuit of property were just what Aristotle did not talk about; they are the conditions of happiness, but the essence of happiness, according to Aristotle, is virtue. —Allan Bloom[10]

It is good to keep this in mind if you are having difficulty identifying a thesis.

8. Eugene O'Neill, *The Great God Brown*, act 4, scene 1; quoted in Anne Lamott, *Traveling Mercies* (New York: Pantheon Books, 1999), 112.
9. Adapted from George Santayana, *The Life of Reason; or the Phases of Human Progress* (New York: Charles Scribner's Sons, 1905), 172.
10. Allan Bloom, "Commerce and 'Culture,'" in *Giants and Dwarfs* (New York: Simon & Schuster, 1990), 263.

Example:

Sports are replacing religion for masses of Americans today. If you doubt this is true, consider that the fastest growing religious category in America is "not religious." While attendance is shrinking at churches and synagogues, more and more time is devoted by families and student athletes to travel leagues and to semiprofessional teams at schools and colleges. Consider that sports fans have their saints—the top athletes of the day—and their holy places—million-dollar stadiums and any room dedicated to game-watching on TV. Sports fans wear their holy garb, their team colors, and they paint their faces and wave their flags like the true believers of any faith. At sports games there are chants and songs and anthem singing that resemble the singing of hymns.

Speculative question:

What is replacing religion for masses of Americans today?

Regarding Writing Tips

A. Vigorous writing is concise. A sentence should contain no unnecessary words, a paragraph no unnecessary sentences, for the same reason that a drawing should have no unnecessary lines and a machine no unnecessary parts. This requires not that the writer make all his sentences short, or that he avoid all detail and treat his subjects only in outline, but that every word "tell." —from *The Elements of Style* by William Strunk Jr.[11]

Speculative question:

Sample answer: How can writing be made more vigorous?

B. When a tiny word gives you a big headache, it's probably a pronoun. Pronouns are usually small (I, me, he, she, it), but they're among the biggest troublemakers in the language. If you've ever been picked on by the pronoun police, don't despair. You're in good company. Hundreds of years after the first Ophelia cried, "Woe is me," only a pedant would argue that Shakespeare should have written "Woe is I" or "Woe is unto me." . . . The point is that no one is exempt from having his pronouns second-guessed. Put simply, a pronoun is an understudy for a noun. *He* may stand in for "Ralph," *she* for "Alice," *they* for "the Kramdens" and *it* for "the stuffed piranha." —from *Woe Is I* by Patricia T. O'Conner[12]

Speculative question:

Sample answer: What part of speech causes the biggest grammar headaches?

11. William Strunk Jr., *The Elements of Style* (New York: Harcourt, Brace and Company, 1919), xiv.
12. Patricia T. O'Conner, *Woe Is I: The Grammarphobe's Guide to Better English in Plain English*, 4th ed. (New York: Riverhead Books, 2019), 1. Used by permission of the author.

Regarding Cooking

C. To me the word "curry" is as degrading to India's great cuisine as the term "chop suey" was to China's. But just as Americans have learned, in the last few years, to distinguish between the different styles of Chinese cooking and between the different dishes, I fervently hope that they will do the same with Indian food instead of lumping it all under the dubious catch-all title of curry. "Curry" is just a vague, inaccurate word which the world has picked up from the British who in turn got it mistakenly from us. —from *An Invitation to Indian Cooking* by Madhur Jaffrey[13]

Speculative question:

Sample answer: What should Americans learn about Indian cuisine?

D. Louisiana is a terrific setting for a cook because of its bountiful natural resources, including a variety of wildlife and a wealth of fresh seafood that is extraordinary because of the state's diverse water resources: the brackish waters in the coastal wetlands and in many of the southernmost lakes, the saltwater of the Gulf, and the freshwater lakes and streams throughout the state. Also, our subtropical climate produces a taste in fruits and vegetable that is unmatched—when the taste is there, it's just really staggering. —from *Chef Paul Prudhomme's Louisiana Kitchen* by Paul Prudhomme[14]

Speculative question:

Sample answer: Which state provides the best setting for a cook?

Regarding the Chinese Revolution and Mao Tse-Tung

E. A revolution is not a dinner party, or writing an essay, or painting a picture, or doing embroidery; it cannot be so refined, so leisurely and gentle, so temperate, kind, courteous, restrained and magnanimous. A revolution is an insurrection, an act of violence by which one class overthrows another. —from *Report on an Investigation of the Peasant Movement in Hunan* by Mao Tse-Tung[15]

Speculative question:

Sample answer: What is a revolution?

13. Madhur Jaffrey, *An Invitation to Indian Cooking* (New York: Alfred A. Knopf, 1973), 5. Copyright © 1973 by Madhur Jaffrey. Used by permission of Alfred A. Knopf, an imprint of the Knopf Doubleday Publishing Group, a division of Penguin Random House LLC (US), and by permission of Harold Ober Associate Incorporated (UK). Any third party use of this material, outside of this publication, is prohibited. Interested parties must apply directly to Penguin Random House LLC for permission.
14. Paul Prudhomme, *Chef Paul Prudhomme's Louisiana Kitchen* (New York: William Morrow & Company, 1984), 14.
15. Mao Tse-Tung, *Report on an Investigation of the Peasant Movement in Hunan*, March 1927, Marxists.org, https://www.marxists.org/reference/archive/mao/selected-works/volume-1/mswv1_2.htm.

F. The Chinese dictator Mao was one of the worst dictators in human history. In terms of numbers murdered, he was worse than Hitler and Stalin combined. Between mass executions of his political enemies, death and labor camps, and terror sprees, Mao inspired the murder of some 60 to 70 million people. Of that incomprehensible number, about 45 million died in the famine caused by the Great Leap Forward. In those dark times, between 1958 and 1962, starving farmers were forced to eat rats and mud to fill their bellies.[16] Mao famously said, "It is better to let half of the people die so that the other half can eat their fill."[17]

Speculative question:

Sample question: Was Mao Tse-Tung a good leader?

Regarding Totalitarianism

Totalitarianism is a form of government headed by a dictator who uses terror and secret police to exert control over his people. Totalitarian governments such as those of Nazi Germany and the Soviet Union caused many of the great calamities of the twentieth century and represented a substantial challenge to human rights and freedom.

G. The totalitarian brand of tyranny has perfected an awesome technique for stripping the individual of all material and spiritual resources which might bolster his independence and self-respect. It deprives him of every alternative and refuge—even that of silence or retreat into solitariness. Not only is he cut off from the outside world, but his fellow men around him—including relatives, friends, and neighbors—are a threat rather than a support. He stands alone and naked, deprived even of the magic of words to sustain him in his total aloneness. For Stalin[18] has murdered all potent words, and drained the lifeblood out of "honor," "truth," "justice," "liberty," "equality," "brotherhood," "humanity."[19] —from *The Ordeal of Change* by Eric Hoffer[20]

Speculative question:

Sample answer: What does a totalitarian government do to destroy the individual?

16. Jung Chang and Jon Halliday, *Mao: The Unknown Story* (New York: Anchor Books, 2006), n.p.
17. As quoted in Frank Dikötter, "Mao's Great Leap to Famine," *New York Times,* December 15, 2010, http://www.nytimes.com/2010/12/16/opinion/16iht-eddikotter16.html.
18. Stalin: dictator of the Soviet Union from the late 1920s until his death in 1953
19. This passage is saying that a totalitarian government strips away all of our freedom as individuals, and it even takes away the words and ideas that would give us hope. The dictator Stalin was particularly skillful at killing the historical meaning of words and twisting them to mean something entirely different. For example, he might say that "honor" was spying on a neighbor and reporting him to the police. He might say that "justice" was murdering his enemies because they disagreed with him. By changing the meanings of words in this way, he took away the power and the hope that might be found in those words.
20. Eric Hoffer, *The Ordeal of Change* (Titusville, NJ: Hopewell Publications, 2006), n.p. Reprinted with permission from Hopewell Publications, LLC.

President Ronald Reagan was a foe of totalitarian dictatorships. In 1982, he addressed the British government, known as Parliament, with the goal of reawakening its confidence in "individual liberty, representative government, and the rule of law under God." He wanted Britain to work with the United States in stopping the spread of totalitarianism in the world. (Please note that although this passage contains several paragraphs, it answers a single speculative question and contains one overall thesis.)

H. We're approaching the end of a bloody century plagued by a terrible political invention—totalitarianism. Optimism comes less easily today, not because democracy is less vigorous, but because democracy's enemies have refined their instruments of repression. Yet optimism is in order, because day by day democracy is proving itself to be a not-at-all-fragile flower. . . .

[In El Salvador the] silent, suffering people were offered a chance to vote, to choose the kind of government they wanted. Suddenly the freedom-fighters in the hills were exposed for what they really are—Cuban-backed guerrillas[21] who want power for themselves, and their backers, not democracy for the people. They threatened death to any who voted, and destroyed hundreds of buses and trucks to keep the people from getting to the polling places. But on election day, the people of El Salvador, an unprecedented 1.4 million of them, braved ambush and gunfire, and trudged for miles to vote for freedom.

They stood for hours in the hot sun waiting for their turn to vote. Members of our Congress who went there as observers told me of a woman who was wounded by rifle fire on the way to the polls, who refused to leave the line to have her wound treated until after she had voted. A grandmother, who had been told by the guerrillas she would be killed when she returned from the polls, and she told the guerrillas, "You can kill me, you can kill my family, kill my neighbors, but you can't kill us all." The real freedom-fighters of El Salvador turned out to be the people of that country—the young, the old, the in-between. . . .

No, democracy is not a fragile flower. Still it needs cultivating. If the rest of this century is to witness the gradual growth of freedom and democratic ideals, we must take actions to assist the campaign for democracy. —from "Address to Members of the British Parliament" by Ronald Reagan, delivered June 8, 1982[22]

Speculative question:

Sample answer: Do we have reason for optimism in an era of totalitarianism?

21. During the Salvadoran Civil War (1979–1992), guerillas who were supported by communist Cuba and who claimed to be "freedom fighters" opposed the military-run Salvadoran government. When the government gave civilians the chance to vote, the guerillas threatened the civilians with murder if they participated in the voting. In the end, both the government and the guerillas proved guilty of many atrocities.

22. Ronald Reagan, "Address to Members of the British Parliament" (speech), Palace of Westminster, June 8, 1982, London, England, Ronald Reagan Presidential Library & Museum, transcript, https://www.reaganlibrary.gov/research/speeches/60882a.

Regarding Technology Compulsion

Technology compulsion is the inability of a person to resist using a digital device, such as a cell phone or video game console, or a social media platform or other app. Compulsive behaviors take a negative toll on the health and happiness of many people. Other compulsions include gambling and shopping, and are often termed addictions. "Compulsion" is the more accurate psychological term.

I. It should come as no surprise that we are all hopelessly addicted to our devices, particularly our smartphones. Why shouldn't we be? We are now able to carry a powerful computer around 24/7 in our pocket or purse. The new "WWW" really means "Whatever, Wherever, Whenever." And we are all succumbing to its draw. Just look at any restaurant table and you will see phones sitting next to forks and knives. It is normal to see someone pick up a smartphone, tap tap tap and put it back down while in the middle of talking. Is this healthy or are we all headed down a slippery slope toward what I call an "iDisorder"? An iDisorder is where you exhibit signs and symptoms of a psychiatric disorder such as OCD, narcissism, addiction or even ADHD, which are manifested through your use—or overuse—of technology. Whether our use of technology makes us exhibit these signs or simply exacerbates our natural tendencies is an open question. —from an article by Larry D. Rosen, author of *IDisorder*[23]

Speculative question:

Sample answer: Do people have unhealthy relationships with their digital devices?

J. One of the ironies of iGen life is that despite spending far more time under the same roof as their parents, today's teens can hardly be said to be closer to their mothers and fathers than their predecessors were. "I've seen my friends with their families—they don't talk to them," Athena told me. "They just say 'Okay, okay, whatever' while they're on their phones. They don't pay attention to their family." Like her peers, Athena is an expert at tuning out her parents so she can focus on her phone. She spent much of her summer keeping up with friends, but nearly all of it was over text or Snapchat. "I've been on my phone more than I've been with actual people," she said. "My bed has, like, an imprint of my body."

In this, too, she is typical. The number of teens who get together with their friends nearly every day dropped by more than 40 percent from 2000 to 2015; the decline has been especially steep recently. It's not only a matter of fewer kids partying; fewer kids are spending time simply hanging out. That's something most teens used to do:

23. Larry D. Rosen, "Face the Facts: We Are All Headed for an iDisorder," *Lifehack*, accessed January 30, 2018, http://www.lifehack.org/articles/lifehack/face-the-facts-we-are-all-headed-for-an-idisorder.html. Used by permission of the author.

nerds and jocks, poor kids and rich kids, C students and A students. The roller rink, the basketball court, the town pool, the local necking spot—they've all been replaced by virtual spaces accessed through apps and the web.

You might expect that teens spend so much time in these new spaces because it makes them happy, but most data suggest that it does not. . . . The results could not be clearer: Teens who spend more time than average on screen activities are more likely to be unhappy, and those who spend more time than average on nonscreen activities are more likely to be happy. —from "Have Smartphones Destroyed a Generation?" by Jean M. Twenge[24] **A**

TE

Speculative question:

Sample answer: What is a negative side effect of excessive cell phone usage?

3. **WRITING THESIS STATEMENTS**—Guns. Should Americans be permitted to own and carry guns? If so, what kind of guns and how much ammunition? Does the US Constitution protect the right of private citizens to own guns, or does it restrict gun ownership to policemen, the military, and trained militias? There are many, many sides to this complex moral issue.

   In this exercise you will read two excerpts with two different perspectives on the topic. At the end of each excerpt, follow the instructions to get some practice with thesis statements. Please note that you do not have to agree with the statements you create in completing this exercise. This is a contentious issue, and you are not expected to agree with one side or the other.

   Remember that a persuasive thesis statement **B**

TE

   - is clear and specific and avoids being too broad. For example, "Crime does not pay" is too broad a thesis statement. It does not specify what type of crime (among a myriad of crimes) or what it means by "pay." A more specific thesis statement would be "All medically able prison inmates should be required to pay restitution to society by working jobs during their imprisonment."
   - takes a position and expresses an opinion that others can argue or dispute. It is not an obvious fact or observation. For example, "Butterflies belong to the insect order of Lepidoptera" is both an obvious fact and observation. No one can

24. Jean M. Twenge, "Have Smartphones Destroyed a Generation?", *The Atlantic*, September 2017, https://www.theatlantic.com/magazine/archive/2017/09/has-the-smartphone-destroyed-a-generation/534198/; from *iGen* by Jean M. Twenge, PhD. Copyright © 2017 by Jean M. Twenge, PhD. Reprinted with the permission of Atria Books, a division of Simon & Schuster, Inc. All rights reserved.

argue that butterflies are not Lepidoptera. A better, more debatable thesis would be: "Butterflies are the main reason to visit the cloud forests of Costa Rica."

- is not a question, but is written in response to a speculative question. For example, this is not a thesis statement: "Should walnut growers be permitted to label their products as a medicine for the heart?" When turned into a statement, however, this question becomes a proper thesis: "Walnut growers should be permitted to label their products as a medicine for the heart."
- can be supported with evidence. The thesis about walnuts in the previous point can be supported, as there are many studies that show that walnuts provide nutrients for proper heart function and can lower "bad cholesterol" in the blood. On the other hand, the statement "Pie makers should be permitted to label sugar cream pies as a medicine for the heart" is insupportable, as there is no evidence to back up this claim.

A. **"Gun-Control Ignorance" by Thomas Sowell**

How many times do the same arguments need to be refuted?

Must every tragic mass shooting bring out the shrill ignorance of "gun control" advocates? The key fallacy of so-called gun-control laws is that such laws do not in fact control guns. They simply disarm law-abiding citizens, while people bent on violence find firearms readily available. If gun-control zealots[25] had any respect for facts, they would have discovered this long ago, because there have been too many factual studies over the years to leave any serious doubt about gun-control laws being not merely futile but counterproductive.

▲ Thomas Sowell

Places and times with the strongest gun-control laws have often been places and times with high murder rates. Washington, D.C., is a classic example, but just one among many. The rate of gun ownership is higher in rural areas than in urban areas, but the murder rate is higher in urban areas. . . . For the country as a whole, hand-gun ownership doubled in the late 20th century, while the murder rate went down.

The few counter-examples offered by gun-control zealots do not stand up under scrutiny. Perhaps their strongest talking point is that Britain has stronger gun-control laws than the United States and lower murder rates. But, if you look back through history, you will find that Britain has had a lower murder rate than the United States for more than two centuries—and, for most of that time, the British had no more stringent gun-control laws than the United States. Indeed, neither country had stringent gun control for most of that time. . . .

25. zealots: people who show passion or fanaticism for a cause

*	Neither guns nor gun control were the reason for the difference in murder rates. People were the difference. Yet many of the most zealous advocates of gun-control laws on both sides of the Atlantic have also been advocates of leniency toward criminals. In Britain, such people have been so successful that legal gun ownership has been reduced almost to the vanishing point, while even most convicted felons are not put behind bars. The crime rate, including the rate of crimes committed with guns, is far higher in Britain now than it was back in the days when there were few restrictions on Britons buying firearms. In 1954, there were only a dozen armed robberies in London but, by the 1990s—after decades of ever tightening gun-ownership restrictions—there were more than a hundred times as many armed robberies.

Gun-control zealots' choice of Britain for comparison with the United States has been wholly tendentious,[26] not only because it ignored the history of the two countries, but also because it ignored other countries with stronger gun-control laws than the United States, such as Russia, Brazil, and Mexico. All of these countries have higher murder rates than the United States. You could compare other sets of countries and get similar results. Gun ownership has been three times as high in Switzerland as in Germany, but the Swiss have had lower murder rates. Other countries with high rates of gun ownership and low murder rates include Israel, New Zealand, and Finland.

Guns are not the problem. People are the problem—including people who are determined to push gun-control laws, either in ignorance of the facts or in defiance of the facts. There is innocent ignorance and there is invincible, dogmatic,[27] and self-righteous ignorance. Every tragic mass shooting seems to bring out examples of both among gun-control advocates.[28]

a. Identify and underline the thesis statement for the entire excerpt. The thesis may be one or two sentences long. **C**

TE

26. tendentious: tainted by bias and prejudice
27. dogmatic: stubborn [in asserting an opinion]
28. Adapted from Thomas Sowell, "Gun-Control Ignorance," *National Review*, December 18, 2012, http://www.nationalreview.com/article/335848/gun-control-ignorance-thomas-sowell. Used by permission of Thomas Sowell and Creators Syndicate, Inc.

b. Next, paraphrase the thesis statement you underlined—in other words, put the author's main idea into different words—or create a new statement based on your understanding of the excerpt. Write your "new" thesis statement in the space provided. New thesis statement:

Sample answer: Laws that seek to control gun ownership don't actually keep guns from violent criminals, but only succeed in disarming citizens who respect the law.

c. One paragraph in the excerpt is marked with an asterisk in the margin. In this paragraph the author implies that there is a cause of gun violence and crime that has nothing to do with gun ownership. If this paragraph were expanded to make an entire speech, what would the thesis statement of the speech be? In other words, what is the paragraph's main idea, and how would you phrase that main idea as a thesis statement for an entire speech? Write your thesis in the space provided. Thesis statement for a speech based on the marked paragraph:

Sample answer: The same people who push for gun control also allow criminals to go unpunished; consequently, crime is bound to go up.

B. **"Remarks by the President on Common-Sense Gun Safety Reform" by Barack Obama**

▲ Official photographic portrait of US President Barack Obama, January 13, 2009. Image courtesy of The Obama-Biden Transition Project, https://commons.wikimedia.org/wiki/File:Official_portrait_of_Barack_Obama.jpg.

Every single year, more than 30,000 Americans have their lives cut short by guns—30,000.[29] Suicides. Domestic violence. Gang shootouts. Accidents. Hundreds of thousands of Americans have lost brothers and sisters, or buried their own children. Many have had to learn to live with a disability, or learned to live without the love of their life. . . .

The United States of America is not the only country on Earth with violent or dangerous people. We are not inherently more prone to violence. But we are the only advanced country on Earth that sees this kind of mass violence erupt with this kind of frequency. It doesn't happen in other advanced countries. It's not even close. And as I've said before, somehow we've become numb to it and we start thinking that this is normal.

And instead of thinking about how to solve the problem, this has become one of our most polarized, partisan[30] debates—despite the fact that there's a general consensus[31] in America about what needs to be done. . . .

I'm not on the ballot again. I'm not looking to score some points. I think we can disagree without impugning[32] other people's motives or without being disagreeable. We don't need to be talking past one another. But we do have to feel a sense of urgency about it. In Dr. King's words, we need to feel the "fierce urgency of now." Because people are dying. And the constant excuses for inaction no longer do, no longer suffice.

That's why we're here today. Not to debate the last mass shooting, but to do something to try to prevent the next one. To prove that the vast majority of Americans, even if our voices aren't always the loudest or most extreme, care enough about a little boy like Daniel[33] to come together and take common-sense steps to save lives and protect more of our children.

29. The author of *Thesis Part 1* notes that two-thirds of the deaths in this statistic are suicides. (Drew Desilver, "Suicides Account for Most Gun Deaths," May 24, 2013, Pew Research Center, http://www.pewresearch.org/fact-tank/2013/05/24/suicides-account-for-most-gun-deaths/.)
30. partisan: one-sided; adhering to the position of one political party
31. consensus: agreement
32. impugning: opposing or attacking
33. This is a reference to Daniel Barden, a seven-year-old victim of the Sandy Hook school shooting on December 14, 2012.

Now, I want to be absolutely clear at the start—and I've said this over and over again . . . I believe in the Second Amendment.[34] It's there written on the paper. It guarantees a right to bear arms. No matter how many times people try to twist my words around—I taught constitutional law, I know a little about this—I get it. But I also believe that we can find ways to reduce gun violence consistent with the Second Amendment.

I mean, think about it. We all believe in the First Amendment, the guarantee of free speech, but we accept that you can't yell "fire" in a theater. We understand there are some constraints on our freedom in order to protect innocent people. We cherish our right to privacy, but we accept that you have to go through metal detectors before being allowed to board a plane. It's not because people like doing that, but we understand that that's part of the price of living in a civilized society.

And what's often ignored in this debate is that a majority of gun owners actually agree. A majority of gun owners agree that we can respect the Second Amendment while keeping an irresponsible, law-breaking feud from inflicting harm on a massive scale.

* Today, background checks are required at gun stores. If a father wants to teach his daughter how to hunt, he can walk into a gun store, get a background check, purchase his weapon safely and responsibly. This is not seen as an infringement on the Second Amendment. Contrary to the claims of what some gun rights proponents have suggested, this hasn't been the first step in some slippery slope to mass confiscation. Contrary to claims of some presidential candidates, apparently, before this meeting, this is not a plot to take away everybody's guns. You pass a background check; you purchase a firearm. The problem is some gun sellers have been operating under a different set of rules. A violent felon[35] can buy the exact same weapon over the Internet with no background check, no questions asked. A recent study found that about one in 30 people looking to buy guns on one website had criminal records—one out of 30 had a criminal record. We're talking about individuals convicted of serious crimes—aggravated assault, domestic violence, robbery, illegal gun possession. People with lengthy criminal histories buying deadly weapons all too easily. And this was just one website within the span of a few months.

34. The Second Amendment is often known as "the right to bear arms." It states, "A well-regulated Militia, being necessary to the security of a free State, the right of the people to keep and bear Arms, shall not be infringed."
35. felon: a criminal who commits a major crime

So we've created a system in which dangerous people are allowed to play by a different set of rules than a responsible gun owner who buys his or her gun the right way and subjects themselves to a background check. That doesn't make sense. Everybody should have to abide by the same rules. Most Americans and gun owners agree. And that's what we tried to change three years ago, after 26 Americans—including 20 children—were murdered at Sandy Hook Elementary. . . .

How did we get here? How did we get to the place where people think requiring a comprehensive background check means taking away people's guns?

Each time this comes up, we are fed the excuse that common-sense reforms like background checks might not have stopped the last massacre, or the one before that, or the one before that, so why bother trying. I reject that thinking. We know we can't stop every act of violence, every act of evil in the world. But maybe we could try to stop one act of evil, one act of violence.

All of us should be able to work together to find a balance that declares the rest of our rights are also important—Second Amendment rights are important, but there are other rights that we care about as well. And we have to be able to balance them. Because our right to worship freely and safely—that right was denied to Christians in Charleston, South Carolina. And that was denied Jews in Kansas City. And that was denied Muslims in Chapel Hill, and Sikhs in Oak Creek. They had rights, too.

Our right to peaceful assembly—that right was robbed from moviegoers in Aurora and Lafayette. Our unalienable right to life, and liberty, and the pursuit of happiness—those rights were stripped from college students in Blacksburg and Santa Barbara, and from high schoolers at Columbine, and from first-graders in Newtown. First-graders. And from every family who never imagined that their loved one would be taken from our lives by a bullet from a gun.

Every time I think about those kids it gets me mad. And by the way, it happens on the streets of Chicago every day.

So all of us need to demand a Congress brave enough to stand up to the gun lobby's lies. All of us need to stand up and protect its citizens. All of us need to demand governors and legislatures and businesses do their part to make our communities safer. We need the wide majority of responsible gun owners who grieve with us every time this happens and feel like your views are not being properly represented to join with us to demand something better.[36]

36. Barack Obama, "Remarks by the President on Common-Sense Gun Safety Reform" (speech), The White House, January 5, 2016, Washington, DC, transcript, https://obamawhitehouse.archives.gov/the-press-office/2016/01/05/remarks-president-common-sense-gun-safety-reform.

a. Identify and underline the thesis statement for the entire excerpt. Please note that the thesis may not appear in the first paragraph of the excerpt.

b. Next, paraphrase the thesis statement you underlined—in other words, put the author's main idea into different words—or create a new statement based on your understanding of the speech. Write your "new" thesis statement in the space provided. New thesis statement:

Sample answer: Sensible gun laws can help prevent some gun violence in America without harming the Second Amendment.

c. One paragraph in the excerpt is marked with an asterisk in the margin. In this paragraph the former president implies that supporters of gun rights have a mistaken idea. If this paragraph were expanded to make an entire speech, what would the thesis statement of the speech be? In other words, what is the paragraph's main idea, and how would you phrase that main idea as a thesis statement for an entire speech? Write your thesis statement in the space provided.
Thesis statement for a speech based on the marked paragraph:

Sample answer: Background checks effectively monitor legal gun ownership without infringing on the rights of gun owners, but violent felons can too easily bypass the checks and obtain weapons over the Internet.

Lesson 2: Of Thesis Statements, Disagreements, and Speculative Questions

Tell It Back—Summary

Sample important ideas:

- A persuasive thesis statement makes a claim that can be argued.
- When moral issues are up for debate, it's important that wise people take part in the conversation so that we are arguing constructively rather than quarreling destructively.
- A thesis essay is useful for defending one's ideas against uninformed, foolish, and dangerous ideas.
- The thesis essay is a logical investigation of a speculative question and defends a thesis statement.

Talk About It—

1. Answers will vary. Sample answer: As long as I know the conversation is welcomed by the other people involved, I generally enjoy debates and arguments. I like listening to other points of view and exchanging ideas. It's a valuable way to build understanding between people. However, I don't enjoy debating anyone whose mind is so closed that he doesn't want to hear what I have to say or who feels it necessary to jump on or interrupt everything I have to say.
2. If an argument, which is a clear line of thinking aimed at proving a point, breaks down into a quarrel, it can disrupt the original argument. The thinking and courtesy of the argument go out the window. A quarrel always involves anger and possibly name-calling and really diminishes the possibility of continuing to share perspectives and evidence. However, good, clear thinking—the kind demanded by an argument—may stop a quarrel from continuing if the people involved are willing to listen to one another.
3. Yes, I think it's important to look at questions from different sides, because it helps people to avoid the pitfalls of arrogance and simplemindedness. Arrogant individuals blindly ignore the insights of others and often assert their ideas as right even when they're wrong. Looking at a question from only one side can lead to simpleminded thinking, which can be easily defeated or twisted by someone who is better informed, but perhaps less scrupulous. Even when a person's ideas are right, he can still be led away from the truth by faulty reasoning. People gain wisdom by seeing the complexity of issues. By anticipating different sides, a well-trained thinker can argue decisively for the truth and defeat falsehood.

   I do think that it is possible to be too open-minded. While it's healthy to avoid being narrow-minded, it's also important that we're not so open-minded that we forget to use

TE

caution. If people are crazy enough to surf ninety-foot waves, as tall as a large apartment building, it should come as no surprise that people the world over are also surfing reckless, dangerous ideas. The world is a stormy sea of competing opinions, some of them bizarre and openly harmful. If we agree with everything and stand on nothing, we may accept ideas that are unhelpful and even dangerous.

Go Deeper—

[A]Please note that students may find it challenging to identify the overall thesis statement for this excerpt. Feel free to offer assistance as needed.

[B]For more information on the writing of thesis statements, please consult *Writing & Rhetoric: Commonplace* and *Writing & Rhetoric: Encomium & Vituperation.*

[C]Please allow for some latitude in the sentences students choose for thesis statements. They should be able to provide sound reasons for the choices they make.

Notes

The purpose of this lesson is to introduce the important considerations of audience and purpose in writing, as well as the concept of antithesis.
In this lesson, students will practice:

- narration in summary form
- critical thinking
- picture narration and analysis using comparison
- identifying audience and purpose
- identifying and writing thesis statements
- writing antitheses

Lesson 3

Audience and Antithesis

On the jet, flying home to California from Indiana, I wrote in my journal, "I've just met the girl I'm going to marry." After spending only two days in her company, I was determined to keep in touch with this dazzling young woman. And sure enough, three years later, after hundreds of letters and phone calls, we tied the knot!

I'm one of the few guys who keeps a journal, and it is intended for an **audience** of one—me! I would be terribly embarrassed if all the inner workings of my mind were suddenly released to the public, at least in my lifetime. My correspondence with my future bride was meant for an audience of two—me and her—and I would be equally embarrassed if those letters fell into the hands of anybody but the two of us. (You can't believe all the wonderful mush that was part of letter writing and courtship in the days before texting.) On the other hand, when a writer pens a speech, a lecture, an essay, or a sermon, he's writing for a wider audience, and that will have an effect on how and what he writes. He's not likely to confess his deepest, darkest secrets to the audience like someone who's writing a journal or gush about his one true love like someone writing a love letter. Can you picture a dentist addressing a gathering of dentists and saying, "I hate staring into mouths! Teeth give me the heebie jeebies and gum disease makes me want to throw up! The only lips I love belong to my sweet Mabelline!" No, any good writer will consider who his audience is, and he will write differently depending on who he's writing for.

Know your audience. That's a key principle of any type of effective writing, whether an essay, speech, social media post, or the next great American novel. Know your audience and think about it while you're writing. Only by considering your audience can you sort out what information matters to it and what will best hold its attention. An essay with the title "Transgressing the Boundaries: Towards a Transformative Hermeneutics of Quantum Gravity"[1] will not be a hit with five-year-old kids, even if it's made into a pop-up book. On the other hand, an audience of kids *will* be grabbed by a classic picture book such as *The Snowy Day* by Ezra Jack Keats or *Blueberries for Sal* by Robert McCloskey—stories written on their level.

When you consider your audience, you'll want to think about who they are: Are they adults or children, or a mix of both? Men or women or both? Is your audience made up of people who do a certain job—doctors, mechanics, teachers? Or have certain interests—sports, painting, music? Or is there a mix of professions or interests? You'll also want to think about the audience's disposition: Is it a friendly audience, eager to hear what you have to say? Or is it a hostile audience that will need some serious persuasion to be convinced of your message?

You should also consider the purpose of your writing. Say you're writing for a friendly audience about something they already know and fancy. In that case, your purpose might be to entertain or to give additional information or to encourage some new action. On the other hand, you may be writing for a friendly audience but want to challenge their thinking. In that case, your work will affirm your mutual interests but then lean in on the point of concern, sometimes with gentleness and sometimes with "tough love." If you're writing for a neutral or indifferent audience, then your purpose may be to persuade them to care about your topic or even to wake them up with a sense of urgency. The hardest audience to persuade is a hostile audience. In many cases your purpose with a hostile audience will be to get it to consider a different perspective. To do that, you are going to need to find some common ground with its members and appeal to their emotions, their reason, and your own credibility.

In the real world, of course, there are a multitude of different types of audiences and purposes for writing—not just these four situations. Even an audience that seems to be all one type—all doctors, all children, all athletes—is made up of a hodgepodge of individuals, and no two people are alike, so you will always have to figure out how best to write for each specific audience. Still, it can help you to consider your audience and your purpose by looking more closely at some of the more basic situations you might encounter.

1. This is the actual title of an article that appeared in *Social Text*, an academic journal of culture. After publication, the author acknowledged that the article was pure nonsense and that he had written it to reveal the bias of the editors.

Type of Audience	Possible Purpose of Author	Famous Example
friendly	to encourage, support, inform, celebrate	Martin Luther King Jr., "I've Been to the Mountaintop"
friendly	to challenge, instruct, persuade, advise	Elie Wiesel, "The Perils of Indifference"
neutral or indifferent	to alert, awaken, justify, motivate	Winston Churchill, "Iron Curtain Speech"
hostile	to defend, argue, illustrate, influence	Clarence Thomas, "Statement Before the Senate Judiciary Committee"

Take a quick look at excerpts from each of the examples given in the chart. **A**

TE

Friendly Audience:

Martin Luther King Jr., "I've Been to the Mountaintop"

Martin Luther King Jr. delivered his last speech, "I've Been to the Mountaintop," to friends and supporters at Mason Temple in Memphis, Tennessee, on April 3, 1968. The next day he was assassinated on the balcony of his hotel.

▲ Martin Luther King Jr.

In this speech, King continues his call for boycotts and other nonviolent action to move forward the civil rights of African Americans. However, the speech is mainly a retrospective and celebration of the achievements of the Civil Rights Movement to that date.[2] He ends the speech with the following:

> Well, I don't know what will happen now. We've got some difficult days ahead. But it really doesn't matter with me now, because I've been to the mountaintop. And I don't mind.
>
> Like anybody, I would like to live a long life. Longevity has its place. But I'm not concerned about that now. I just want to do God's will. And He's allowed me to go up to the mountain. And I've looked over. And I've seen the Promised Land. I may not get there with you. But I want you to know tonight, that we, as a people, will get to the Promised Land!
>
> And so I'm happy, tonight. I'm not worried about anything. I'm not fearing any man! Mine eyes have seen the glory of the coming of the Lord![3]

2. Civil Rights Movement: a widespread protest movement that was begun in the 1950s by African Americans to end segregation and discrimination
3. Martin Luther King Jr., "I've Been to the Mountaintop" (speech), Mason Temple, April 3, 1968, Memphis, TN, The King Institute, Stanford University, transcript, http://kingencyclopedia.stanford.edu/encyclopedia/documentsentry/ive_been_to_the_mountaintop/.

King knows his audience—it's filled with friends and admirers. His purpose is to celebrate with them, and also to encourage them. He knows that his fellow travelers in the Civil Rights Movement need to hear that they can go on and achieve victory with or without him. Notice how King achieves his purpose in the way he writes for his audience. The warm and happy tone of the speech, and the sense of triumph tinged with a winsome humility, communicate a feeling of celebration. In addition, by using the pronoun "we," King includes everyone in his audience in the celebration and in a shared sense of purpose for the future.

Friendly Audience: Elie Wiesel, "The Perils of Indifference"

▲ Elie Wiesel
Elie Wiesel, Professor of the Humanities, Boston University, USA, speaks during the session "269 A New Agenda: Combining Efficiency and Human Dignity" at the "Annual Meeting 2003" of the World Economic Forum in Davos, Switzerland, January 28, 2003. Copyright by World Economic Forum swiss-image.ch/photo by Sebastian Derungs, https://upload.wikimedia.org/wikipedia/commons/4/42/Elie_Wiesel.jpg.

While Elie Wiesel—a survivor of Nazi concentration camps—is actually talking to a friendly audience in this speech, his purpose is to challenge his listeners and make them uncomfortable. He wants them to remember how indifference to the plight of the Jews during World War II, when they were seeking to immigrate to safer shores, enabled the Nazis to capture and murder millions. Wiesel believes that remembering the horrors of the Holocaust may prevent genocides in the future.[4]

> Indifference is always the friend of the enemy, for it benefits the aggressor—never his victim, whose pain is magnified when he or she feels forgotten. The political prisoner in his cell, the hungry children, the homeless refugees—not to respond to their plight, not to relieve their solitude by offering them a spark of hope is to exile them from human memory. And in denying their humanity, we betray our own. Indifference, then, is not only a sin, it is a punishment. . . .
>
> The depressing tale of the *St. Louis*[5] is a case in point. Sixty years ago, its human cargo—nearly 1,000 Jews—was turned back to Nazi Germany. And that happened after the Kristallnacht, after the first state sponsored pogrom, with hundreds of Jewish shops destroyed, synagogues burned, thousands of people put in concentration camps. And that ship, which was already in the shores of the United States, was sent back. I don't understand. Roosevelt was a good man, with a heart. He understood those who needed help. Why didn't he allow these refugees to disembark? A thousand people—in America, the great country, the greatest democracy, the most generous of all new nations in modern history. What

4. Sadly, genocides continue to this day. Some examples include the Cambodian genocide from 1975–1979, the Rwandan genocide of the Tutsi in 1994, the Darfur genocide in 2003 by the Sudanese government, and the genocide of Yazidis and Christians in Iraq by Islamic State militants in 2014.
5. The *St. Louis* was a transatlantic German ocean liner that in 1939 was filled with Jews who were fleeing persecution. The ship first landed in Cuba on May 27, but its passengers were not allowed to disembark. It traveled next to the United States, but there the *St. Louis* met the same fate. Eventually the passengers were sent back to Europe. Some of the passengers went on to find refuge in Great Britain and France, but in the end, 254 of them were murdered in concentration camps.

> happened? I don't understand. Why the indifference, on the highest level, to the suffering of the victims?[6]

Like King, Wiesel knows his audience and writes his speech with that audience in mind. He uses a kindly tone in his speech, because the audience is friendly, but he leaves his questions unanswered because he wants the individuals in his audience to consider what sort of stand they would take under similar circumstances. Also like King, he uses the pronoun "we" to show that all people, without exception, are accountable to take care of fellow human beings. In addition, he appeals to the audience's desire to be remembered well by future generations. In other words, he knows that his listeners are concerned about their legacy, and he uses this knowledge to nudge them to embrace activism instead of indifference.

▲ Winston Churchill

Neutral Audience: Winston Churchill, "Iron Curtain Speech"[7]

Winston Churchill visited the United States after World War II to deliver a serious message: The Soviet Union (communist Russia) was trying to dominate the surrounding countries of Europe and Asia with its totalitarian government. At that time, few Americans wanted to hear that these distant lands needed protection from communist expansion. World War II had been so costly in human life and in resources that the United States just wanted to remain neutral and not take sides. In this speech, Churchill tries to wake up the US to the new threat of the Soviet superpower.

> The United States stands at this time at the pinnacle of world power. It is a solemn moment for the American democracy. For with this primacy in power is also joined an awe-inspiring accountability to the future. As you look around you, you must feel not only the sense of duty done, but also you must feel anxiety lest you fall below the level of achievement. Opportunity is here now, clear and shining, for both our countries. . . .
>
> It is my duty, however, to place before you certain facts about the present position in Europe. From Stettin in the Baltic to Trieste in the Adriatic an iron curtain has descended across the Continent. Behind that line lie all the capitals of the ancient states of Central and Eastern Europe. Warsaw, Berlin, Prague, Vienna, Budapest, Belgrade, Bucharest and Sofia; all these famous cities and the populations around them lie in what I must call the Soviet sphere, and all are subject, in one form or another, not only to Soviet influence but to a very high and in some cases increasing measure of control from Moscow.[8]

---

6. Elie Wiesel, "The Perils of Indifference" (speech), April 12, 1999, Washington, DC, American Rhetoric, transcript and audio mp3, http://www.americanrhetoric.com/speeches/ewieselperilsofindifference.html.
7. This speech is also known as "Sinews of Peace."
8. Winston Churchill, "Sinews of Peace" (speech), Westminster College, March 5, 1946, Fulton, MO, National Churchill Museum,

Notice that in this speech Churchill first compliments the United States for its strength and power, which would please his audience. Churchill knows his audience. It represents a country that has just fought an exhausting war, a country that would like to lick its wounds and not get involved, and so it's only after he makes a neutral audience smile that he tells it of a new burden they must bear—the need to turn back Soviet aggression.

Hostile Audience: Clarence Thomas, "Statement Before the Senate Judiciary Committee"

▲ Clarence Thomas

Before any judge is elevated to the Supreme Court, the Senate must give its approval. In 1991, Clarence Thomas faced a number of hostile senators on the Senate Judiciary Committee who were determined to keep him off the Supreme Court. His detractors claimed that he had committed personal misconduct, but those who supported him believed that those accusations were false and were politically or even racially motivated. In this fiery speech, Thomas dispenses with polite answers and compares his treatment to the worst of racist violence.

> I think that this today is a travesty. I think that it is disgusting. I think that this hearing should never occur in America. This is a case in which this sleaze, this dirt, was searched for by staffers of members of this committee, was then leaked to the media, and this committee and this body validated it and displayed it at prime time over our entire nation. How would any member on this committee, any person in this room, or any person in this country, like sleaze said about him or her in this fashion? Or this dirt dredged up and this gossip and these lies displayed in this manner? How would any person like it?
>
> The Supreme Court is not worth it. No job is worth it. I am not here for that. I am here for my name, my family, my life, and my integrity. . . .
>
> This is a circus. It's a national disgrace. And from my standpoint as a black American, as far as I'm concerned, it is a high-tech lynching for uppity blacks who in any way deign to think for themselves, to do for themselves, to have different ideas, and it is a message that unless you kowtow[9] to an old order, this is what will happen to you. You will be lynched, destroyed, caricatured by a committee of the U.S.—U.S. Senate, rather than hung from a tree.[10]

---

transcript, https://www.nationalchurchillmuseum.org/sinews-of-peace-iron-curtain-speech.html. Reproduced with permission of Curtis Brown, London, on behalf of The Estate of Winston S. Churchill. Copyright The Estate of Winston S. Churchill.

9. kowtow: to bow low and touch one's forehead to the ground in servile submission
10. Clarence Thomas, "Statement Before the Senate Judiciary Committee," October 11, 1991, Washington, DC, American Rhetoric, transcript and audio mp3, http://www.americanrhetoric.com/speeches/clarencethomashightechlynching.htm.

The tone of Thomas's speech is very different from King's, isn't it? Thomas knows he is facing a hostile audience and that to achieve his purpose—which is to win their vote—he must speak with that audience in mind. He knows that to win them over, he must find common ground and appeal to the audience's emotions and reason. Thomas appeals to powerful images of injustice and asks the senators to consider how they would like to be treated if they were standing in his shoes. He brings their attention to their personal responsibility by mentioning "any person in the room" as opposed to a collective group. He suggests that they will be remembered well or poorly for how they handle his case, just as we remember those who made decisions surrounding slavery, Jim Crow, and its aftermath. His skillful use of rhetoric carried the day despite lingering questions about his candidacy and he was confirmed as a justice of the Supreme Court in 1991.

Whatever you write will need to be relevant to your audience or it will lose interest and remain unmoved. When you know the makeup and disposition of your audience, you can better determine your purpose—to inform, to persuade, to encourage, to entertain, and so on. Only then can you shape your essays and speeches so that they will be effective with your audience.

Questions to Ask about Audience—

When considering your audience, ask yourself these important questions:

1. Who is my audience? How much do they know about my topic? What do they currently think or believe about the topic? Will they be friendly, neutral, or hostile toward my message? Is my message something they care about deeply or only superficially?
2. What is my purpose in trying to reach this audience? In other words, what effect do I want my essay or speech to have on the audience? Do I want to delight them, inform them, challenge them, or persuade them? Do I want their understanding of the topic to change after they finish reading my work or listening to me speak?
3. What is my relationship with the audience? Do I want to be prominent in the essay or speech, or do I want to minimize my presence? What do I want the audience to think of me? Am I the bringer of good news, or am I the bearer of bad news? What point of view will I take to best appeal to the audience: first, second, or third person? In other words, what pronouns will I use to make my case: I, you, and we, or will I remain objective in the third person ("he," "she," "it," "one")?
4. What rhetorical devices will best create interest for my topic and grab the audience's attention? How do I organize my work to best accomplish my purpose for the audience?

Antithesis (Testing Your Thesis)—

Analyzing your audience before you start your work will help you to reach it better, and when you are writing a persuasive essay, it will also help you to make your thesis stronger.

Picture yourself as a lawyer in the middle of a courtroom drama in which a person (or two) stands up in the middle of the proceedings and shouts, "I object!" That person then gives reasons for his objection. How are you going to deal with this disagreement? You can always say, "Shut up!" but that won't refute the objection. You can personally attack the objector by calling him names—"Sit down, you stupid idiot!"—but again, you've done nothing to refute the objection. In fact, the rest of the audience may suspect that your argument is pretty weak if you can't handle disagreement.

Unfortunately, we see examples of ineffective disagreement all the time in real life. The 2016 presidential election was particularly irksome when it came to personal attacks.[11] Along the way, candidate Hillary Clinton was called "Crooked Hillary," "Wicked Witch of the West Wing," and "Hilla the Hun." Candidate Donald Trump, known for the orange cast of his skin, was called "Tangerine Tornado," "Decomposing Jack-O-Lantern," and the "Burning of Rome in Man Form." While personal attacks can be clever and temporarily effective, they are ultimately destructive to necessary conversations and to the mocker's own character. In the long run, they change no one's minds.

In addition to helping you prepare counterarguments, considering objections to your thesis also can help you determine how strong your thesis is in the first place. Although you believe in your thesis, your big idea, you must soberly consider objections to it so that you will know whether it stands up to those arguments. In some cases, you may even abandon your position if you realize that your thesis is too weak or ill-considered.

If you want to continue your argument and maintain your credibility, you must respond intelligently to objections. Recognize in advance that an audience—especially a hostile audience—may want to argue with your message, and prepare for those arguments. Knowing your audience will help you to anticipate its objections to your thesis and be prepared to handle them. By reflecting on objections, you will be able to think through possible responses and have counterarguments ready. Approaching persuasive thesis writing in this way, from a position of strength, means that you don't need to stoop to personal attacks.

An argument against a thesis is aptly called an **antithesis**.[12] These counterarguments can take the opposite position from that of the entire thesis, or they can challenge a certain aspect of a thesis's position. Let's say this is the thesis of Edward Abbey, an environmental activist and writer:

> Wilderness is not a luxury but a necessity of the human spirit, and as vital to our lives as water and good bread.[13]

---

11. Personal attacks are also known as ***ad hominem* attacks**.
12. "Antithesis" also refers to a rhetorical device that makes use of antonyms to consider opposing ideas. This device is used mostly to capture interest rather than to make an argument (e.g., "The world will not long remember what we say here, but it can never forget what they did here." —Abraham Lincoln).
13. Edward Abbey, *Down the River* (New York: Plume, 1991), n.p.

If you're like me, you probably agree with this thesis. Wilderness is essential to life on earth as well as to the thriving of human beings. However, objections to the thesis need to be considered so that the strongest possible argument for the thesis can be presented. Here is an antithesis that takes the opposite position:

> Wilderness is a luxury, and it can only be enjoyed by hikers and other wealthy elites.

This antithesis confronts the most important assertion of Abbey's thesis. Abbey takes the position that wilderness is not a luxury, whereas the objector says the exact opposite: Wilderness is a luxury enjoyed only by a few.

Now here are two antitheses that challenge only an aspect of the thesis:

> Wilderness is not as necessary to the human spirit as beautiful parks.

> Humans can survive without wilderness, but not without water or food.

The first antithesis takes issue with the idea that wilderness is more necessary than other types of natural settings, such as parks. It doesn't say that wilderness is not important, but it does assert that other natural settings (such as parks) are more important. To refute this antithesis, Abbey would need to weigh the idea of wilderness—a wild, out-of-reach natural setting—against the idea of parks, which are natural settings more accessible to people. Abbey makes a claim that there is something special about wilderness that is worth defending, and it's up to him to articulate that specialness in the comparison between wilderness and parks.

The second antithesis does not argue with wilderness being necessary to the spirit, but it quibbles with the second part of the thesis by stating that wilderness is not literally as important to life as water or food. To refute this antithesis, Abbey would need to recognize that it insincerely attempts to undermine the thesis by misinterpreting the author. Abbey is not being literal, but rather figurative, when he says that wilderness is "as vital to our lives as water and good bread." The antithesis, however, takes the phrase literally in order to claim that it is wrong. You can see why it's important to stay on your toes when arguing for your point of view.

When you write your thesis essay or speech, you will be asked to consider the strongest objections to your argument and seek to refute them in your writing. Using antitheses in this way will make your essays more rich, engaging, and productive, because your ideas will be fully considered and strong. Knowing your audience will help you to use antitheses effectively.

Hopefully you see that if your purpose is to persuade an audience, you must first know your audience. In the next lesson you will learn about writing the actual thesis essay, but for the rest of this lesson you will be working on some exercises to help you better analyze audience and anticipate counterarguments.

Tell It Back—Summary

TE Summarize aloud three or four important ideas in this lesson. Then, in the space provided, write a well-crafted sentence that tells one of the main ideas of the lesson as best as you understand it. (There are two main ideas.) To arrive at one of the main ideas, ask yourself, "What is the chief purpose of the lesson?"

Main idea:

Sample main idea 1: It is important to know your audience before writing or speaking.

Sample main idea 2: It is important for an author or speaker to anticipate objections to his thesis so that he can prepare to respond to those objections.

Talk About It—

TE 1. The novelist John Steinbeck gives this advice about audience: "In writing, your audience is one single reader. I have found that sometimes it helps to pick out one person—a real person you know, or an imagined person and write to that one."[14] Do you think Steinbeck's advice is good? Why or why not?

TE 2. Personal (*ad hominem*) attacks can target a person's appearance, intelligence, character, age, race, sex, and so forth. Why do you suppose that personal attacks have been called "the last refuge of the thoughtless"? Although they might be momentarily effective, why aren't they convincing to audiences in the long run?

TE 3. In recent times, at college campuses around the country, students have taken to protesting guest speakers by trying to stop them from speaking. They may shout at the speaker to drown him out or chant so loudly that he can no longer be heard or even block the entrance to a building so that people who want to hear the speech can't enter. This is a change from the days when I was a college student. In the past, the student audience would sit politely through a speech, weigh the arguments for themselves, and then challenge the speaker during the question-and-answer time if they disagreed or wanted to clarify an idea. College was once known as a place where young people could be exposed to many different ideas and where they could decide what to think for themselves. Nowadays, even professors and teachers often are joining in the protests, as if they don't want the students to hear a point of view different from the one that they are pushing.**B** TE

14. John Steinbeck, "The Art of Fiction No. 45," interview by George Plimpton and Frank Crowther, *The Paris Review*, no. 63 (Fall 1975), https://www.theparisreview.org/interviews/4156/john-steinbeck-the-art-of-fiction-no-45-continued-john-steinbeck.

- Is there any problem with students protesting by blocking buildings and drowning out speakers?
- What are some things that a speaker could do when confronted with a hostile audience?
- What should a speaker do when an audience refuses to listen?

Write & Discuss—

Take a look at the images of the two paintings. The first is *Girl Reading a Letter by an Open Window* by Johannes Vermeer, and the second is *Two Girls Reading* by Pierre-Auguste Renoir. With a partner, compare the paintings to each other. Then take ten or fifteen minutes individually to jot down your answers to the following questions in the space provided. After that, discuss your thoughts with your class.

▲ *Girl Reading a Letter by an Open Window* by Johannes Vermeer

▲ *Two Girls Reading* by Pierre-Auguste Renoir

1. How are the paintings similar and how are they different? What is happening in the two paintings? What sort of texts are the Vermeer woman and the Renoir girls reading?

Sample answer: Both paintings capture a scene in which the subjects are reading and engrossed by the text. In the Vermeer painting, a young woman appears to be reading a letter by the light of an open window. In the Renoir painting, two girls are reading a book together while dressed in frilly outfits, and it's possible they are seated outdoors.

2. Every audience has different expectations. Some want to be informed, some to be entertained, some to be motivated, encouraged, challenged, and so on. The people in these paintings are the audience for the texts they are reading. What do you suppose are the expectations of the woman in the Vermeer painting and the girls in the Renoir painting?

Sample answer: The woman in the Vermeer painting most likely expects the letter to contain news and words of affection from someone who is close to her. The two Renoir girls likely are hoping to be entertained by a clever story and illustrations, or perhaps it's a book about nature and they are eagerly seeking information.

3. Who might the author of the letter be as compared to who might be the author of the book? How might the purpose of the two authors be different?

Sample answer: A letter is usually a very personal text, and the Vermeer woman may be hearing from a close friend or even from a lover. On the other hand, the girls reading the book are children, and the author of the book is most likely someone who writes stories for children. The author of the letter may want to convey that he is thinking about and cares about the Vermeer woman. If the writer is a young man, perhaps he is sharing his love for her for the first time. On the other hand, a children's book author would want to entertain her readers with a vivid and exciting story.

Go Deeper—

1. **IDENTIFYING AUDIENCE**—Read the following passages carefully. When you are done reading, underline the one sentence or part of a sentence in each passage that you think is most likely to be the thesis statement of the passage. Then, for each excerpt, briefly answer the following questions as best as you can in the space provided.
   - What is the most likely original audience for this passage? For example, is the audience more likely to be:
     - adults or children?
     - women, men, or both?
     - people with a particular interest, such as dog lovers, movie lovers, cooks, soldiers?
     - friendly, neutral, or hostile?
   - In your opinion, what is the purpose of the author? For example, does the author want to:
     - delight?
     - inform?
     - persuade?
     - awaken?
     - defend?
     - threaten?
     - encourage?

   Explain your answer.

   Example:

   "Grain-Free or Not Grain-Free? That Is the Question" by Jerry L. Risser, DVM, MA

   In this blog post on his professional website, Dr. Risser addresses a popular question about what to feed dogs. Dr. Risser recently served as the president of the Indiana Veterinary Medical Association and is a member of the Society of Veterinary Medical Ethics.

   > One of the routine questions asked during each dog physical is usually, "What are you feeding currently?" Seems innocent enough. Some clients are sheepish (not great food, they fear), and some are quite proud of their choice. "Grain-free" is one about which people are proud, because there's so much out there advocating it. But is it a good idea for dogs?
   >
   > Let me start by qualifying a few things. First, there are a lot of good choices for pet food out there. Much of what we see in animal nutrition spills over from human medicine. We do see a reasonable number of people with diseases like celiac disease, which can arise from an adverse reaction to gluten, a protein originating from grains.
   >
   > But we don't really see an identical disease in dogs and cats. It is true that any protein can cause an adverse or allergic reaction in a sensitive pet. . . . But grains in general (and

gluten specifically) are quite rare allergens. I contend that for the majority of dogs, grain-free diets are unnecessary. The wild dogs from whom our current pups descended are "omnivores," eating meat, grains, vegetables, even grass (which is part of why that fresh green spring grass can be such a delicacy). We have many years of excellent research from several companies that have created diets that have genuinely extended the lives of pets. My desire isn't to insult any well-meaning person who is seeking to take excellent care of their dog, but I'm convinced that the "grain-free" trend is a fad.[15]

a. Underline the likely thesis statement or main idea.

b. Briefly answer the following questions as best as you can.

- What is the most likely original audience for this passage?

  The original audience consists of dog owners who, judging from the pleasant, conversational tone of the writing, are inclined to be friendly toward the author.

- In your opinion, what is the purpose of the author?

  The author seeks to gently persuade his clients that grain-free diets for dogs are typically unnecessary.

Explain your answer.

The author states that grains are rarely an allergen for dogs and points to the fact that the ancestors of dogs ate a lot of wild foods, including grains.

TE

A. **Resolution of Protest by the Hiroshima City Council**[C]

In 1958, former US president Harry Truman made remarks on television that he felt "no compunction" or guilt for having ordered the atomic bomb dropped on the Japanese cities of Hiroshima and Nagasaki toward the end of World War II. He went so far as to say that he might consider using the bomb again in an emergency. The following resolution is the official reaction from the city of Hiroshima, published in American newspapers as an open letter.

> The citizens of Hiroshima who have led their life in tribulation of more than two hundred thousand lives taken in sacrifice consider it their sublime duty to be a cornerstone of world peace and hold that no nation of the world should ever be permitted to repeat the

15. Jerry L. Risser, "Grain-Free or Not Grain-Free? That Is the Question," *Fall Creek Veterinary Medical Center Blog*, August 10, 2018, https://www.fallcreekvet.com/Fall-Creek-Veterinary.html. Used by permission of the author.

error of using nuclear weapons on any people anywhere on the globe, whatever be the reason.

If, however, the statement made by Mr. Truman, former President of the United States, that he felt no compunction whatever after directing the atomic bombing of Hiroshima and Nagasaki, and that the hydrogen bombs would be put to use in future in case of emergency be true, it is a gross defilement committed on the people of Hiroshima and their fallen victims.

▲ Hiroshima, August 5, 1946

We, the City Council, do hereby protest against it in deep indignation shared by our citizens and declare that in the name of humanity and peace we appeal to the wisdom of the United States and her citizens and to their inner voice for peace that said statement be retracted and that they fulfil their obligations for the cause of world peace.[16]

a. Underline the likely thesis statement or main idea.

b. Briefly answer the following questions as best as you can.

- What is the most likely original audience for this passage?

Sample answer: The original audience is former president of the United States Harry Truman, as well as any American who happens to read the open letter in newspapers.

- In your opinion, what is the purpose of the authors?

Sample answer: The purpose of the authors is to persuade Truman to retract his statement that he felt no compunction about having used atomic bombs to end the war with Japan.

Explain your answer.

Sample answer: The resolution states plainly that Harry Truman's statement is a "gross defilement" and that, for the sake of peace in the world, "said statement [should] be retracted."

16. "Resolution to Declare Protest Against Broadcast Remarks of Mr. Truman, Former United States President," Hiroshima City Council, February 13, 1958, Harry S. Truman Presidential Library & Museum, https://www.trumanlibrary.org/whistlestop/study_collections/bomb/large/documents/index.php?documentid=73&pagenumber=4.

B. **Letter to Honorable Tsukasa Nitoguri, chairman of the Hiroshima City Council, by Harry S. Truman, thirty-third president of the United States**

Truman sent a letter to the chairman of the Hiroshima City Council in response to the council's resolution. (See previous exercise.) The following excerpt is a portion of that letter.

> On July 16, 1945, before the demand for Japan's surrender was made, a successful demonstration of the greatest explosive force in the history of the world had been accomplished.
>
> After a long conference with the Cabinet, the military commanders and Prime Minister Churchill, it was decided to drop the atomic bomb on two Japanese cities devoted to war and work for Japan. The two cities selected were Hiroshima and Nagasaki.
>
> When Japan surrendered a few days after the bomb was ordered dropped, on August 6, 1945, the military estimated that at least a quarter of a million of the invasion forces against Japan and a quarter of a million Japanese had been spared complete destruction and that twice that many on each side would, otherwise, have been maimed for life.[17]
>
> As the executive who ordered the dropping of the bomb, I think the sacrifice of Hiroshima and Nagasaki was urgent and necessary for the prospective welfare of both Japan and the Allies.
>
> The need for such a fateful decision, of course, never would have arisen, had we not been shot in the back by Japan at Pearl Harbor in December, 1941.
>
> And in spite of that shot in the back, this country of ours, the United States of America, has been willing to help in every way the restoration of Japan as a great and prosperous nation.[18]

17. Truman is saying that an invasion of Japan by land and sea would have been far more costly to life and limb for both Americans and Japanese than dropping the atom bomb was.
18. Harry S. Truman to Honorable Tsukasa Nitoguri, March 12, 1958, Harry S. Truman Presidential Library & Museum, https://www.trumanlibrary.org/whistlestop/study_collections/bomb/large/documents/index.php?documentid=73&pagenumber=1.

a. Underline the likely thesis statement or main idea.

b. Briefly answer the following questions as best as you can.

- What is the most likely original audience for this passage?

Sample answer: The original audience is the Hiroshima City Council, and specifically Tsukasa Nitoguri, chairman of the council.

- In your opinion, what is the purpose of the author?

Sample answer: Truman seeks to justify his decision to drop the atom bomb and to spread the responsibility of the decision to other people, including "the Cabinet, the military commanders and Prime Minister Churchill."

Explain your answer.

Sample answer: The former president places the blame squarely on Japan for causing the war in the first place, calling Pearl Harbor a "shot in the back," but he also shares that an invasion of Japan would have been more costly in life and limb than dropping the bomb was.

C. **"Silent Spring" by Rachel Carson, biologist and environmental activist**

Carson's series of articles on pollution first appeared in *The New Yorker* magazine and then were expanded into a best-selling book by the same title.

> In the mornings, which had once throbbed with the dawn chorus of robins, catbirds, doves, jays, and wrens, and scores of other bird voices, there was now no sound; only silence lay over the fields and woods and marshes. . . . What is silencing the voices of spring in countless towns in America? I shall make an attempt to explain. . . . The most alarming of all man's assaults upon the environment is the contamination of the air, earth, rivers, and seas with dangerous, and even lethal, materials. This pollution has rapidly become almost universal, and it is for the most part irrecoverable; the chain of evil it initiates, not only in the world that must support life but in living tissues, is for the most part irreversible. It is widely known that radiation has done much to change the very nature of the world, the very nature of its life; strontium 90, released into the air through nuclear explosions, comes to earth in rain or drifts down as fallout, lodges in

soil, enters into the grass or corn or wheat grown there, and, in time, takes up its abode in the bones of a human being, there to remain until his death. It is less well known that many man-made chemicals act in much the same way as radiation; they lie long in the soil, and enter into living organisms, passing from one to another. Or they may travel mysteriously by underground streams, emerging to combine, through the alchemy of air and sunlight, into new forms, which kill vegetation, sicken cattle, and work unknown harm on those who drink from once pure wells. As Albert Schweitzer has said, "Man can hardly even recognize the devils of his own creation."[19]

a. Underline the likely thesis statement or main idea.

b. Briefly answer the following questions as best as you can.

- What is the most likely original audience for this passage?

  Sample answer: The original audience was probably adult men and women who may have been neutral about environmental matters and who the author felt needed to be aroused from indifference.

- In your opinion, what is the purpose of the author?

  Sample answer: The purpose of the author is to inform the audience that pollution is devastating to nature.

Explain your answer.

Sample answer: Carson likens the assault of chemical pollution in the environment to nuclear radiation. She paints a vivid image of how it works through nature to create a "silent spring."

19. Rachel Carson, "Silent Spring—I," *The New Yorker*, June 16, 1962, https://www.newyorker.com/magazine/1962/06/16/silent-spring-part-1. Copyright © Condé Nast. Reprinted with permission.

D. **Wellesley College Commencement[20] Address by Toni Morrison, novelist and winner of the Nobel Prize in literature**

A commencement address is an inspirational speech given to high school or college graduates. Toni Morrison is most famous for her novel *Beloved*, a story about the terrifying repercussions of slavery. In this speech she encourages students not to be stuck in immaturity, but to grow up willingly and embrace adulthood.

> I'm sure you have been told that this is the best time of your life. It may be. But if it's true that this is the best time of your life, if you have already lived or are now living at this age the best years, or if the next few turn out to be the best, then you have my condolences.[21] Because you'll want to remain here, stuck in these so-called best years, never maturing, wanting only to look, to feel and be the adolescent that whole industries are devoted to forcing you to remain.
>
> One more flawless article of clothing, one more elaborate toy, the truly perfect diet, the harmless but necessary drug, the almost final elective surgery, the ultimate cosmetic—all designed to maintain hunger for stasis.[22] While children are being eroticized[23] into adults, adults are being exoticized[24] into eternal juvenilia.[25] [26] I know that happiness has been the real, if covert, target of your labors here, your choices of companions, of the profession that you will enter. You deserve it and I want you to gain it, everybody should. But if that's all you have on your mind, then you do have my sympathy, and if these are indeed the best years of your life, you do have my condolences because there is nothing, believe me, more satisfying, more gratifying than true adulthood. The adulthood that is the span of life before you. The process of becoming one is not inevitable. Its achievement is a difficult beauty, an intensely hard won glory, which commercial forces and cultural vapidity[27] should not be permitted to deprive you of.[28]

20. commencement: graduation ceremony
21. condolences: sympathy
22. statis: motionlessness, stoppage
23. eroticized: made appealing sexually
24. exoticized: made strange and unnatural
25. juvenilia: youthful objects
26. In other words, Morrison is saying that our culture is pushing children and adults to behave inappropriately for their level of maturity. Children are being forced by our culture to pretend to be sexually mature adults, while adults are being forced to act like kids.
27. vapidity: lifelessness, tastelessness
28. Toni Morrison, "Commencement Address to the Wellesley College Class of 2004" (speech), Wellesley College, May 28, 2004, Wellesley, Massachusetts, transcript, http://www.wellesley.edu/PublicAffairs/Commencement/2004/morrison.html. Copyright 2004 by Toni Morrison. Reprinted by permission of ICM Partners.

a. Underline the likely thesis statement or main idea.

b. Briefly answer the following questions as best as you can.

- What is the most likely original audience for this passage?

Sample answer: This speech is written for a friendly audience consisting of college students at a graduation ceremony.

- In your opinion, what is the purpose of the author?

Sample answer: The author wants to call the young adults to embrace maturity and adulthood and to leave behind childish preoccupations.

Explain your answer.

Sample answer: Morrison shares her sympathy for any student who wants to stay stuck in the college years and shows her disdain for the lifestyle of an adult who acts like a teenager.

2. **WRITING ANTITHESES**—For each thesis statement in this exercise, write an antithesis, or counterargument, in the space provided. Please keep in mind that you don't have to personally agree or disagree with your antitheses. You are simply practicing how to frame a counterargument.

Just like a persuasive thesis, an antithesis must be clear, specific, and debatable. Your answer can be directly opposite the entire thesis, or it can counter or qualify some aspect of the thesis. For example, if someone asserts that "Athletes are the greatest heroes," you could:

- oppose the entire thesis. One way to do this is by mirroring the format of the thesis and asserting something completely different; e.g., "Parents are the greatest heroes."
- undermine the thesis by disagreeing with some aspect of it; e.g., "Many athletes are self-absorbed and self-serving, and therefore not heroic at all." While this antithesis allows that *some* athletes may be heroes, it undermines the thesis by stating that *not all* athletes are heroic.

Examples:

Thesis: No beverage is more beneficial than coffee.

Antithesis:

Milk is more beneficial than coffee.

Coffee contains too much caffeine to be entirely beneficial.

Thesis: The battle between the armies of good and evil is the main theme in Tolkien's *The Lord of the Rings*.

Antithesis:

The main theme of *The Lord of the Rings* is the conflict between good and evil, but it is not the physical battle between the armies; rather, the main theme is the conflict that takes place within the story's characters.

The importance of friendship is the main theme in Tolkien's *The Lord of the Rings*.

A. Thesis: The best friendships grow slowly.

Antithesis:

Sample answer: The best friendships spring up suddenly.

B. Thesis: What does not kill me makes me stronger. —Friedrich Nietzsche

Antithesis:

Sample answer: Some things that might not kill me, such as antibiotics, might not make me stronger either.

C. Thesis: Might makes right.

Antithesis:

Sample answer: Might does not make right.

D. Thesis: The best season is autumn, bringer of apples and frost.

Antithesis:

Sample answer: The best season is summer, bringer of pool parties and popsicles.

E. Thesis: History is nothing more than a record of crimes and misfortunes. —Voltaire

Antithesis:

Sample answer: History is more than a record of crimes and misfortunes; it is also the story of courage and triumph.

F. Thesis: Religion is the opium of the people. —Karl Marx (In other words, religion acts like a drug to keep people stupefied and inactive.)
Antithesis:

Sample answer: True religion calls people to rise up and fight injustice.

G. Thesis: The only way to get rid of a temptation is to yield to it. —Oscar Wilde
Antithesis:

Sample answer: The only way to get rid of a temptation is to run away from it.

H. Thesis: Time strengthens friendship, but weakens love. —Jean de la Bruyère
Antithesis:

Sample answer: Time strengthens true love just as it strengthens friendship.

I. Thesis: Behind every great fortune, there is a crime. —paraphrase of Honoré de Balzac (In other words, massive wealth is gained unlawfully.)
Antithesis:

Sample answer: Behind many great fortunes, there is some luck and honest hard work.

3. **IDENTIFYING AUDIENCES AND ANTITHESES—**Read the following passages, and for each one, identify a possible audience and the passage's likely thesis statement. Write your answers in the space provided. Then, whether or not you agree with the thesis statements, write two possible antitheses for each one.

A. American companies can play a vital role to help make eating fruits and veggies fun and, yes, even cool. Study after study proves this point. . . . Imagine walking into any grocery store in America and finding the healthiest options clearly marked and centrally placed so that you know within seconds what's good for your family when you walk in that store. Imagine opening up a menu in any restaurant and knowing exactly what items will give your family the most nutrition for your hard-earned dollar. Imagine our kids begging and pleading, throwing tantrums to get you to buy more fruits, vegetables and whole grains. Yes, this is possible. —from "Remarks by the First Lady to the Partnership for a Healthier America" by Michelle Obama, delivered March 8, 2013[29]

a. Possible audience:

Sample answer: The audience might be representatives from food companies who are neutral and getting an earful from the First Lady because she wants them to push for healthier eating for their customers.

b. Thesis:

Sample answer: American companies can play a vital role to help make eating fruits and veggies fun.

c. Antithesis 1:

Sample answer: Nothing can be done to make eating fruits and veggies fun.

d. Antithesis 2:

Sample answer: American companies can play a vital role to help make eating fruits more fun, but veggies are hopelessly disgusting.

B. A good burger is a thing of beauty, a satisfying, messy manifestation of all things umami:[30] fine beef, sticky cheese, tomatoes: both fresh and in ketchup, all ready to be loaded up with your heart's content of bacon, relish, salad, pickles, chili. . . . There are few things culinary that can be relied on to do their job as effectively. But hey, even a bad burger, a Maccy D's[31] or a Burger King, isn't going to disappoint its legion of fans. They know what they want and they can get it, cheap and filling and—crucially—consistent, time after time. —from "In Search of the Perfect Burger" by Marina O'Loughlin[32]

a. Possible audience:

Sample answer: More than likely the audience consists of friendly food lovers—people who enjoy reading about their favorite foods.

29. Michelle Obama, "Remarks by the First Lady to the Partnership for a Healthier America," George Washington University, March 8, 2013, Washington, DC, The White House, transcript, https://obamawhitehouse.archives.gov/the-press-office/2013/03/08/remarks-first-lady-partnership-healthier-america-summit.
30. umami: a meaty or savory taste
31. Maccy D's: refers to McDonald's, the fast food restaurant; equivalent to the American nickname "Mickie D's"
32. Marina O'Loughlin, "In Search of the Perfect Burger," *The Guardian*, July 9, 2013, https://www.theguardian.com/lifeandstyle/2013/jul/09/perfect-burger-review-nationwide.

b. Thesis:

Sample answer: A good burger is a thing of beauty, a satisfying, messy manifestation of all things umami.

c. Antithesis 1:

Sample answer: A good burger may be a satisfying, savory feast on a bun, but its unhealthy fat is hardly beautiful.

d. Antithesis 2:

Sample answer: A messy, greasy, cheese-laden, ketchup-y burger has no redeeming value, either as art or as food.

C. We, the human species, are confronting a planetary emergency [in global warming]—a threat to the survival of our civilization that is gathering ominous and destructive potential even as we gather here. . . . Today, we dumped another 70 million tons of global-warming pollution into the thin shell of atmosphere surrounding our planet, as if it were an open sewer. And tomorrow, we will dump a slightly larger amount, with the cumulative concentrations now trapping more and more heat from the sun. . . . As a result, the earth has a fever. And the fever is rising. The experts have told us it is not a passing affliction that will heal by itself. . . . Science is warning us that if we do not quickly reduce the global warming pollution that is trapping so much of the heat our planet normally radiates back out of the atmosphere, we are in danger of creating a permanent "carbon summer." —from the Nobel lecture by Al Gore, delivered December 10, 2007[33]

a. Possible audience:

Sample answer: This Nobel lecture was most likely delivered to a friendly audience of adults concerned about global warming.

b. Thesis:

Sample answer: We, the human species, are confronting a planetary emergency [in global warming].

33. Al Gore, Nobel lecture, Oslo City Hall, December 10, 2007, Oslo, Norway, Nobelprize.org, transcript, https://www.nobelprize.org/nobel_prizes/peace/laureates/2007/gore-lecture_en.html. Copyright © The Nobel Foundation (2007).

c. Antithesis 1:

Sample answer: The possibility of nuclear bombs in the hands of terrorists—not global warming—is a planetary emergency.

d. Antithesis 2:

Sample answer: While global warming is a serious matter, it is not an emergency.

D. There is plenty of other evidence that CO_2 is trivial to climate change. Water vapor is by far the most important greenhouse gas, providing 96 to 98% of any greenhouse effect. CO_2 is a weak greenhouse gas and comprises only 0.04% of the atmosphere—and 97% of CO_2 is produced by nature, not mankind. Volcanoes, swamps, rice paddies, fallen leaves, even insects and bacteria produce CO_2 as well as methane, another greenhouse gas. Termites alone emit far more CO_2 than all the factories and automobiles in the world. (See *Science*, Nov. 5, 1982.) Natural wetlands emit more greenhouse gases than all human activities combined. If we could eliminate not only all human use of fossil fuels but all natural sources of greenhouse gases as well, 96% of any greenhouse effect would still remain, because of water vapor.

Carbon dioxide produces only tiny changes in atmospheric temperature. . . . At the time of the dinosaurs, the carbon dioxide content of the atmosphere was 3 to 5 times what it is today, but there was no runaway global warming. During the Ordovician period, the level of CO_2 in the atmosphere was 12 times what it is today, but the earth was in an Ice Age. If a theory contradicts reality, the theory must be wrong. During the Permian and the first half of the Triassic period, 250–320 million years ago, carbon dioxide concentration was half what it is today but the temperature was 10°C higher. From the Cretaceous to the Eocene 35 to 100 million years ago, a high temperature went with declining carbon dioxide. The theory that atmospheric carbon dioxide concentration is determining the earth's temperature is therefore wrong.

The key to the earth's climate is the sun, not CO_2. Mars, Neptune, Jupiter, Saturn and even distant Pluto are all experiencing global warming. Is the sun warming them while our warming is due to CO_2? —from "The Agenda Behind Global Warming Alarmism" by Edmund Contoski[34]

34. Edmund Contoski, "The Agenda Behind Global Warming Alarmism," July 18, 2017, The Heartland Institute, https://www.heartland.org/news-opinion/news/the-agenda-behind-global-warming-alarmism. Used by permission of the author.

a. Possible audience:

Sample answer: This article was probably written to a neutral or skeptical audience who believes that climate change is the fault of human activity.

b. Thesis:

Sample answer: CO_2 is trivial to climate change.

c. Antithesis 1:

Sample answer: CO_2 is significant to climate change.

d. Antithesis 2:

Sample answer: CO_2 is trivial to a cooling climate, but not to a warming climate.

Lesson 3: Audience and Antithesis

[A]We recommend reading the first three speeches in their entirety if time allows. Each speech is considered a gem of rhetorical power and makes a great example for budding rhetoricians. They are available at the following addresses online:

- Martin Luther King Jr., "I've Been to the Mountaintop": https://kinginstitute.stanford.edu/king-papers/documents/ive-been-mountaintop-address-delivered-bishop-charles-mason-temple
- Elie Wiesel, "The Perils of Indifference": http://www.americanrhetoric.com/speeches/ewieselperilsofindifference.html
- Winston Churchill, "Iron Curtain Speech": https://www.nationalchurchillmuseum.org/sinews-of-peace-iron-curtain-speech.html

Tell It Back—Summary

Sample important ideas:

- There are different types of audiences, including friendly, hostile, and neutral.
- To know your audience better, ask yourself questions about it.
- The antithesis is an objection or counterargument to the thesis and should be anticipated by the author.
- Knowing his audience can help an author to anticipate and deal with objections to his thesis.
- When an author considers the possible objections to his thesis, he can refute those objections in his speech or writing.

Talk About It—

1. Answers will vary.

   Sample answer 1: I don't think Steinbeck's advice is all that good or helpful. Most audiences don't consist of a single person, real or imaginary. Authors have to consider a lot of things when thinking about an audience, and one person is probably too small a sample, too individual and too quirky, to be relevant to a larger audience. For example, the people who read or listen to any text could be friendly, indifferent, or hostile. They might be male, female, or a mix of both. It might be a child audience or an adult audience or a blend. The author can't write to so many varieties of people if he only has a single person in mind.

   Sample answer 2: Steinbeck's advice is definitely helpful to writers. When writers think of a real person or, at least, a fully imagined person, it ensures that they stay grounded in the needs and desires of a clear-cut audience. If an audience is too fuzzy or abstract, it will be hard for writers to adequately prepare for it. By considering the needs, the prejudices, and the hopes of a real person, writers can make their work more real and relevant.

TE

2. Personal attacks are called "the last refuge of the thoughtless" because they don't take any serious thought to create. Anyone can call another person names. A truly thoughtful person will respond to an argument with eloquent persuasion.

   Personal attacks are ultimately unconvincing because the attacker loses credibility with his audience. Verbal abuse doesn't respond to the issue at hand so much as reveal the pettiness of the attacker. Not only are personal attacks irrelevant and thoughtless, but they are also unpleasant to listen to.

[B]Free thinking and free discourse at a college level have recently received a boost from a website called Heterodox Academy (https://heterodoxacademy.org). The site is dedicated to increasing viewpoint diversity on campuses as a way to solve some of "the world's most complex problems." High school and middle school teachers may find this site a helpful aid to understanding the problem of the "closing of the American mind" on college campuses. The importance of viewpoint diversity and constructive disagreement is very much at the heart of learning to write thesis essays. Another excellent resource is the Foundation for Individual Rights in Education (FIRE) at https://www.thefire.org.

3. Answers will vary. Sample answer: There is definitely a problem with students protesting by blocking buildings and drowning out speakers. Students who protest in this way aren't honestly engaging other points of view, and they're cutting off other people from a valuable learning experience. It's not respectful or productive to shut down other people without hearing and considering their ideas. If students so adamantly disagree with a particular idea, they should engage the speaker and seek to change his or her mind.

   When confronted with a hostile audience, a speaker can use her knowledge of antithesis to anticipate objections and defend her thesis in a persuasive way. A speaker could also recognize the audience's hostility and leave room for a question-and-answer session after the speech so that the opposing sides can discuss together.

   When an audience refuses to listen, the speaker has no choice but to depart and leave the audience to its ignorance. There's no point to wasting one's breath. An audience that is too close-minded to listen, that refuses to consider a different perspective, can't be forced to open its mind.

Go Deeper—

[C]Please note that students may find it challenging to identify the overall thesis statement for this excerpt. Two different possible theses have been underlined as examples. Feel free to offer assistance as needed.

The purpose of this lesson is to walk students through the first paragraph of a thesis essay and introduce a variety of methods for hooking audience attention.

In this lesson, students will practice:

- narration in summary form
- critical thinking
- written analysis of a literary topic and follow-up discussion
- writing *erotema*, which are rhetorical questions needing no answer
- writing *hypophora*, which are questions immediately followed by answers
- writing summaries of narratives using sentence limitations

Lesson 4

The Thesis Essay, Part I: Hooking the Audience

Should One Marry?

To marry or not to marry . . . That is the question most of us will need to consider sooner or later. Martin Luther tells us, "There is no more lovely, friendly, and charming relationship, communion, or company than a good marriage." But the cynics have had their say as well. According to H.L. Mencken, "He marries best who puts it off until it is too late."

Our teacher of rhetoric from the late Roman Empire, Aphthonius, has plenty of positive things to say about marriage in his sample thesis essay for the original *progymnasmata*. He delivers his thesis in a well-crafted essay that anticipates the antitheses of cynics. The essay reads like a speech to a room full of quarrelsome naysayers.

You've learned about the importance of the thesis statement and how it asserts the main idea or argument of a composition. You've also learned that audience analysis is important so that a writer can adapt her work to engage an audience and anticipate any objections the audience might have to her thesis. These next two lessons will now walk you through Aphthonius's thesis essay on marriage as preparation for writing your own essays in coming lessons. In this lesson, you'll tackle the essay's introduction, and in the next lesson you'll cover the rest.

The Introductory Paragraph—

TE

As in the previous persuasive essays you've practiced—from refutations and confirmations to encomiums and vituperations—Aphthonius begins his thesis essay with an introduction.[1] The purpose of the introduction is to grab the reader's attention and to announce the subject of the essay. Take a look:

> What would the universe be without marriage? Empty! Marriage enabled the gods to produce offspring and fill the heavens. First came the marriage of Gaia, the earth, to Uranus, the sky. Because Uranus mistreated his children, Gaia plotted with her son, Saturn, to overthrow him. Saturn succeeded in taking his father's throne and married Ops to produce many gods—including Jupiter. Father Jove—for that is the meaning of the name "Jupiter"—became the grandfather of Romulus and Remus, the two princes who founded the city of Rome. From one marriage, then, came gods and goddesses and the Roman people. The gift of life isn't the only reason to praise marriage, either. Marriage is worthy of praise because it gives men and women great courage and self-control.

In this introductory paragraph, Aphthonius uses both a question and an illustration to grab the reader's attention. The illustration also adds weight to his argument by claiming the authority of well-known mythology. Aphthonius is essentially saying, "Don't take my word for it. Even the gods would agree with me!" At the end of his introduction, Aphthonius throws down the gauntlet—his thesis statement—which tells us, "This is the point I intend to argue."

TE

▶What is the thesis statement of the essay?

Aphthonius of Antioch was a famous rhetorician who lived in the Greek-speaking part of the Roman Empire in the mid to late 300s (AD). His *progymnasmata*, a textbook of rhetorical exercises, is one of only four *progyms* to survive from ancient times and forms the backbone of this series.

◀ © Livius.org courtesy of Jona Lendering

1. As a Greek speaker, Aphthonius would have used the word ***exordium*** for "introduction." Some modern courses in rhetoric still use the Greek term.

While a good thesis always states the main idea or argument of a paper, a good hook catches the attention of the audience. When the audience is alert, it is more open to listening to the persuasive words that follow. Any rhetorical device used to snare the interest of the audience or wake it up is called a hook. Hooks for essays and speeches come in all shapes and sizes: narratives such as fables, parables, anecdotes, jokes, news flashes, and summaries; questions; descriptions and illustrations; proverbs and sayings; quotations and provocative statements; statistics and fascinating facts. Every audience is different, and your analysis of the audience may help you to determine what hook works best for the people you are writing or speaking to.

Aphthonius hooks the attention of his audience with questions and illustrations. A question gets attention because it puts an audience on the spot. Even though listeners and readers are rarely expected to provide an answer, questions are like pop quizzes and can cause the heart to pump a little faster. Proverbs, word pictures (illustrations or descriptions), and narratives grab the attention of readers because they are concrete (as opposed to abstract) and easy to grasp. Just as children love pictures in their storybooks, so audiences love illustrations that bring brainy ideas down to earth.

Take a closer look at the following variety of useful hooks:

Narratives—

Everybody loves a story, and there's no more compelling way to hook an audience's attention than to tell a story. (I suppose you could sneeze on your essay or dance on the podium to get attention, but you'd risk nobody taking you seriously.) Besides being easy to grasp, stories make great hooks because they are interesting or exciting.

Let's say you're writing an essay about the significance of Daniel Webster in preserving the Union prior to the Civil War. Wouldn't this anecdote be a riveting way to introduce your topic?

> Yes, Dan'l Webster's dead—or, at least, they buried him. But every time there's a thunderstorm around Marshfield, they say you can hear his rolling voice in the hollows of the sky. And they say that if you go to his grave and speak loud and clear,

▲ Examples of fishing swim baits made by Kanan Lures, March 18, 2013. Image courtesy of Kananlures, https://commons.wikimedia.org/wiki/File:Kanan_fishing_lures,_swim_baits.jpg.

Hooks come in all shapes and sizes:

- narratives: fables, parables, anecdotes, jokes, news flashes, summaries
- questions
- descriptions and illustrations
- proverbs and sayings
- quotations and provocative statements
- statistics and facts

"Dan'l Webster—Dan'l Webster!" the ground'll begin to shiver and the trees begin to shake. And after a while you'll hear a deep voice saying, "Neighbor, how stands the Union?" Then you better answer the Union stands as she stood, rock-bottomed and copper-sheathed, one and indivisible, or he's liable to rear right out of the ground. At least, that's what I was told when I was a youngster.[2]

There's enough tall tale in this anecdote to really make an audience's ears prick up.

A great thing about narratives is that they can be any size to fill the space you need, and there's a story for every purpose, whether a fable, a parable, an anecdote, a joke, a news flash, or a summary of a longer story.

Fable—a short story that teaches a simple moral lesson, usually with talking animals
Parable—a short story that teaches a moral lesson, always true to life
Anecdote—a brief account of a humorous or interesting event, often used to make a larger point
Joke—typically a crisp little story told to evoke amusement or laughter
News flash—a brief piece of urgent and up-to-the-minute news
Summary—a shortened or concise version of a longer text such as a folk tale or a biography

Notice how each of these definitions emphasizes the shortness of the narrative. In general, when you use a story as a hook, you'll want to keep the story brief. Stories that go on for a long time tend to overshadow the persuasive aspects of an essay, and people might forget your thesis and wonder what your point is.

Every type of story exists for a reason. Narrative has proven itself over time to be a powerful way to communicate. We started this series with stories and, I hope you can see, we've never dropped them. They are mighty rhetorical and learning tools and they make for stupendous hooks.

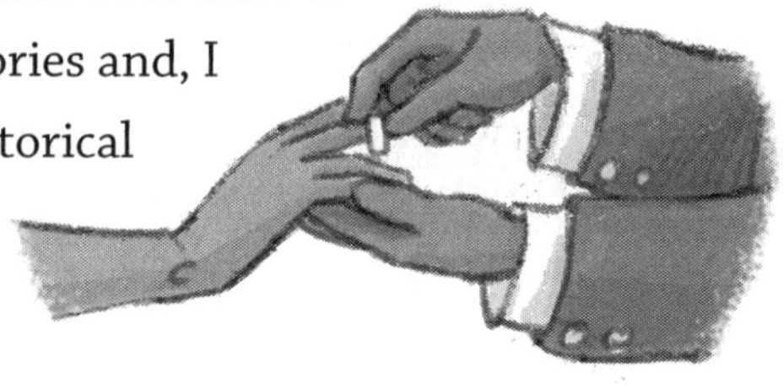

Questions—

Questions hook an audience because they make the audience think. Any sort of active brainwork means that the audience is awake, alert, and cogitating. ("Cogitating" is a show-off word for "thinking.")

Patrick Henry uses attention-grabbing questions throughout his "Give Me Liberty or Give Me Death" speech. He swiftly answers some of the questions, such as in the following excerpt:

> Has Great Britain any enemy, in this quarter of the world, to call for all this accumulation of navies and armies? No, sir, she has none. They are meant for us; they can be meant for no other.[3]

2. Stephen Vincent Benét, *The Devil and Daniel Webster* (New York: Penguin Books, 1999), n.p. Copyright © 1936 by Stephen Vincent Benét. Copyright renewed © 1964 by Thomas C. Benét, Stephanie B. Mahin, and Rachel Benét Lewis. Used by permission of Brandt & Hochman Literary Agents, Inc. Any copying or distribution of this text is expressly forbidden. All rights reserved.
3. Patrick Henry, "Give Me Liberty or Give Me Death" (speech), Henrico Parrish Church, March 23, 1775, Richmond, Virginia, American Rhetoric, transcript, http://www.americanrhetoric.com/speeches/patrickhenrygivemeliberty.html.

Some other questions Henry doesn't bother to answer because the answers are painfully obvious:

> Shall we gather strength by irresolution and inaction? Shall we acquire the means of effectual resistance by lying supinely on our backs, and hugging the delusive phantom of hope, until our enemies shall have bound us hand and foot?[4]

These two different types of questions have Greek names. A question that a writer or speaker poses and then immediately answers is called ***hypophora***. A question for which no reply is expected is called a rhetorical question or an ***erotema***. Examples of rhetorical questions include "Does a bear have hair?" and "Is rain wet?" In most cases you wouldn't expect an answer to these questions because the answers are so obvious.

One powerful rhetorical technique is to ask a series of *hypophoras* or *erotemata* all in a row. In his speech "Annihilation of Caste," B.R. Ambedkar uses this technique as he tries to awaken the consciences of his fellow Indians and show them the injustice of the caste system.[5]

> Are you fit for political power even though you do not allow a large class of your own countrymen like the untouchables[6] to attend public school? Are you fit for political power even though you do not allow them the use of public wells? Are you fit for political power even though you do not allow them the use of public streets? Are you fit for political power even though you do not allow them to wear what apparel or ornaments they like? Are you fit for political power even though you do not allow them to eat any food they like?[7]

These questions are all *erotemata* or, in other words, rhetorical questions. Ambedkar asks his questions one after the other because he doesn't think that they require answers. It's obvious to him that the politicians he's addressing are not fit for power because of the heartless way they treat the lowest class. Nobody should be treated so heartlessly. In addition, the use of multiple questions strung together adds emphasis to the point Ambedkar is making.

When used as hooks, questions like these can be an effective way to get an audience interested in hearing what you will say next.

4. Patrick Henry, "Give Me Liberty or Give Me Death."
5. caste system: a class structure in which every individual's status is determined by birth. In other words, if a person is born poor, the caste system determines that he will remain poor for his entire life. B.R. Ambedkar belonged to the Dalit caste in India, which meant that other classes considered him untouchable, or belonging to the lowest order.
6. untouchables: the lowest class of the Indian caste system
7. B.R. Ambedkar, *Annihilation of Caste* (self-pub., 1944; Ambedkar.org), http://www.ambedkar.org/ambcd/02.Annihilation%20of%20Caste.htm.

Descriptions and Illustrations—

Besides narratives and questions, writers and orators sometimes use vivid descriptions as hooks. For example, at the beginning of her book *Pilgrim at Tinker Creek*, Annie Dillard captures attention with a description of a dizzying, horrifying moment in nature. The full description is used here because the writing is so lovely, but you could pare it down for an essay by using your skills at summarizing. (For more information on how to properly summarize writing of any length, please refer to the section at the end of this book titled "Get to the Point: Tips for Summarizing.")

> At the end of the island I noticed a small green frog. He was exactly half in and half out of the water, looking like a schematic diagram of an amphibian, and he didn't jump. He didn't jump; I crept closer.
>
> At last I knelt on the island's winter killed grass, lost, dumbstruck, staring at the frog in the creek just four feet away. He was a very small frog with wide, dull eyes. And just as I looked at him, he slowly crumpled and began to sag. The spirit vanished from his eyes as if snuffed. His skin emptied and drooped; his very skull seemed to collapse and settle like a kicked tent. He was shrinking before my eyes like a deflating football. I watched the taut, glistening skin on his shoulders ruck, and rumple, and fall. Soon, part of his skin, formless as a pricked balloon, lay in floating folds like bright scum on top of the water; it was a monstrous and terrifying thing. I gaped bewildered, appalled. An oval shadow hung in the water behind the drained frog; then the shadow glided away. The frog skin bag started to sink.
>
> I had read about the giant water bug, but never seen one. "Giant water bug" is really the name of the creature, which is an enormous, heavy-bodied brown bug. It eats insects, tadpoles, fish, and frogs. Its grasping forelegs are mighty and hooked inward. It seizes a victim with these legs, hugs it tight, and paralyzes it with enzymes injected during a vicious bite. That one bite is the only bite it ever takes. Through the puncture shoot the poisons that dissolve the victim's muscles and bones and organs—all but the skin—and through it the giant water bug sucks out the victim's body, reduced to a juice. This event is quite common in warm fresh water. The frog I saw was being sucked by a giant water bug. I had been kneeling on the island grass; when the unrecognizable flap of frog skin settled on the creek bottom, swaying, I stood up and brushed the knees of my pants. I couldn't catch my breath.[8]

I think you'll agree that the vivid picture painted by Dillard's description is enough to get any audience to listen up!

Like descriptions, illustrations are another way to capture attention by appealing to the senses of readers: sight, hearing, taste, smell, and touch. They most often serve as a tangible example or

8. Annie Dillard, *Pilgrim at Tinker Creek* (New York: HarperCollins, 1974), 7–8, 9. Copyright © 1974 by Annie Dillard. Reprinted by permission of HarperCollins Publishers (US) and Russell & Volkening as agents for the author (UK).

picture of a difficult idea and help bring it down to earth. In this way, they serve the same function as pictures in a picture book.

Rather than luxuriating in lengthy description, illustrations are more likely to be brief flashes of vivid imagery, and their purpose is to help make a larger point. For example, Albert Einstein, the famous physicist, was the first person to identify the theory of special relativity. He demonstrated that space and time created a continuous fabric in the universe known as space-time and that mass and energy are equivalent. This theory also presupposes that the speed of light in a vacuum is the same no matter how fast an observer is traveling, even though speed creates the perception of time slowing down. The idea of relativity is a hard one to grasp, and a joke—possibly from Einstein himself—has circulated to help illustrate it: "Put your hand on a hot stove for a minute, and it seems like an hour. Sit with a pretty girl for an hour, and it seems like a minute. That's relativity." You can see how this vivid imagery not only grabs attention but also serves the larger purpose of helping a nonscientist better understand the perception of time differences as described by the theory of relativity.

Here's another example of illustrations in action. George Graham Vest, a nineteenth-century lawyer and US senator, delivered this next speech during a trial in which one man sued another for killing his dog. In the speech, Vest compares dogs to human friends.

> The one absolute, unselfish friend that man can have in this selfish world—the one that never deserts him, the one that never proves ungrateful or treacherous—is his dog.
>
> . . . [A] man's dog stands by him in prosperity and in poverty, in health and in sickness. He will sleep on the cold ground, where the wintry winds blow and the snow drives fiercely, if only he can be near his master's side. He will kiss the hand that ha[s] no food to offer, he will lick the wounds and sores that come in encounter with the roughness of the world. He guards the sleep of his pauper master as if he were a prince. When all other friends desert, he remains. When riches take wings and reputation falls to pieces he is as constant in his love as the sun in its journey through the heavens.[9]

Vest strings together a number of illustrations to create a sympathetic portrait of "dogginess." Each illustration—the cold of winter, the wet of a dog's tongue, the warm radiance of the sun—grabs attention by playing on the reader's senses. These sensory details cause the reader to have an emotional reaction in favor of Vest's client—to think what a tragedy it is that the client should lose such a good and faithful friend, a friend who would brave the wintry winds and driving snow! As you can see, using illustration to stir up the senses is a sure way to engage an audience.

9. George Graham Vest, "Eulogy on the Dog," 1870, in *Respectfully Quoted: A Dictionary of Quotations* (1989), excerpted by Bartleby.com, accessed May 1, 2018, http://www.bartleby.com/73/446.html.

Proverbs and Sayings—

Another attention grabber is the humble but mighty proverb.[10] Do you remember what a proverb is? A proverb is a short, pithy saying used to convey wisdom or some basic truth.

Here's a proverb that starts a speech about the horrors of war: "War is the sport of Death."

Here's a proverb to introduce an essay on the difficulty of writing a poem: "He who paints a flower cannot paint its fragrance."

In his speech on the death of Caesar, Shakespeare's Marc Antony creates his own proverb: "The evil that men do lives after them; The good is oft interred with their bones."[11]

A proverb helps you get off to a good start with your readers or listeners because they recognize in it some basic truth. When they hear a little pinch of common sense, they're more likely to agree with you, and as a result, more likely to want to hear more.

Common sayings can also be used to grab attention, but you have to be careful to avoid sayings that are tired and overused. The following is the start of a speech by Daniel Webster defending the Declaration of Independence: "Sink or swim, live or die, survive or perish, I give my hand and my heart to this vote."[12] [13] Notice how Adams strings common sayings together for a strong introduction that doesn't sound clichéd. If he had used each one separately, they may have sounded dull and uninspired.

Stringing sayings together is just one—not the only—way to give common sayings some zest. Common sayings that have fallen into disuse are often the most arresting. For example, sayings such as "That kid is knee high to a grasshopper," "The government is so broke it's deep in the ketchup," or "When that gangster is dead, he's going to be wearing a pine overcoat" sound pretty old-fashioned, and because of that they are interesting to hear.

Common sayings can have an especially strong effect when an author makes them more surprising by changing them slightly. Grammar writer Patricia T. O'Conner describes the effect of the transformation thus:

> Tallulah Bankhead once described herself as "pure as the driven slush." And bankruptcy has been called "a fate worse than debt."[14] We smile at expressions like these out of pure relief, because we're braced for the numbing cliché that doesn't arrive.

10. Some excellent sources of proverbs include the books of Proverbs and Ecclesiastes from the Hebrew scriptures, *Bartlett's Familiar Quotations* (especially the maxims of Publius Syrus and the proverbs of John Heywood), and *The Oxford Dictionary of Proverbs*.
11. William Shakespeare, *Julius Caesar*, ed. Barbara Mowat and Paul Werstine, 3.2.84–85, Folger Shakespeare Library, accessed May 1, 2018, http://www.folgerdigitaltexts.org.
12. Daniel Webster's speech is written in the voice of John Adams, as if Adams is the speaker.
13. Daniel Webster, "Imaginary Speech of John Adams," 1826, Bartleby.com, accessed May 2, 2018, http://www.bartleby.com/400/prose/786.html.
14. The clichés O'Conner refers to here are "pure as the driven snow" and "a fate worse than death."

> Nothing is wrong with using a figure of speech, an expression that employs words in imaginative (or "figurative") ways to throw in a little vividness or surprise. But it's an irony of human communication that the more beautiful or lively or effective the figure of speech, the more likely it will be loved, remembered, repeated, worn out, and finally worked to death.[15]

Like little firecrackers with gunpowder compacted inside, proverbs and common sayings pack a lot of meaning in a little space. When you set them off in your writing, they will be noticed—pow!—by your audience.

Quotations and Provocative Statements—

A quotation makes for a superb hook when you find one that is delightfully worded and made by an authority. In other words, the quote should ideally come from a trusted source who has a way with words. This gives the quote both weight and interest, which makes it rousing to an audience.

If I were writing a thesis essay on the purpose of science, I might quote John Polkinghorne, one-time professor of mathematical physics at Cambridge: "We know now that cosmic history is the astonishing tale of how initial simplicity has given rise to present multivarious complexity. What started as an expanding, almost uniform, ball of energy has become the home of life and self-conscious beings. It is the job of science to describe that marvelously fruitful process."[16] Or, along the same lines, I could quote physicist Stephen Hawking: "The eventual goal of science is to provide a single theory that describes the whole universe. . . . If we do discover a theory of everything . . . it would be the ultimate triumph of human reason—for then we would truly know the mind of God."[17] These quotes are hard to beat because the authors are respected scientists who know how to write with energy and also turn a beautiful phrase.

Some quotes take a provocative angle to hook the audience's interest. That means that they deliberately seek to surprise the audience. Tony Dungy, one of the most talented coaches to be inducted into the Football Hall of Fame, says this in the introduction to his autobiography *Quiet Strength*:

> The point of this book is not the Super Bowl. In fact, it's not football. Don't get me wrong—football is great. It's provided a living and a passion for me for decades. It was the first job I ever had that actually got me excited about heading to work. But football is just a game. It's not family. It's not a way of life. It doesn't provide any sort of intrinsic meaning. It's just football. It lasts for three hours, and when the game is over, it's over.[18]

Now that's a pretty provocative statement coming from a man whose career was dedicated to the game of football. Essentially he's saying, "Football is terrific, but it's not *that* terrific." Once

15. Patricia T. O'Conner, *Woe Is I: The Grammarphobe's Guide to Better English in Plain English*, 4th ed. (New York: Riverhead Books, 2019), 197. Used by permission of the author.
16. John Polkinghorne, "A Potent Universe," in *Evidence of Purpose*, ed. John Marks Templeton (New York: Continuum, 1994), 106.
17. Stephen Hawking, *A Brief History of Time* (New York: Bantam Books, 1996), 11.
18. Tony Dungy, *Quiet Strength* (Carol Stream, IL: Tyndale, 2007), xiv.

those words are out of a speaker's mouth, his audience is going to want to know what is even more important to Dungy than football.

Few hooks grab your audience like a provocative or razor-sharp direct quote. However, quotes are like pearls: The more you string together, the less an individual quote stands out. In order to be effective, you should use quotes sparingly, choosing only the best of the best. A few well-placed quotes are fantastic—just don't go overboard. And don't forget: You must be sure to credit the speaker of any quote you use. You'll take a closer look at direct quotations in lesson 6.

Of course, provocative statements are not limited to quotations. The author of a thesis essay can lob a bomb of his own invention into his introductory paragraph. He could start an essay on social media by saying, "The fakest of fake news is social media, where all users create phony lives for themselves online." Or he could say, "You've never really visited a beautiful place or had a great vacation until you post it on social media." Provocative statements are sharp hooks because provoking an audience is inherently an attention-getting activity.

Statistics and Facts—

In a hook, intriguing numbers and fascinating facts can play a similar role to that of quotes and provocative statements. They can often be surprising and also carry the weight of authority. Although some cynics disparage statistics as "numerical lies" because they are too often misused and manipulated, a well-documented statistic still has the power to arrest attention. Try these on for size:

- Today's children are spending an average of seven hours a day on entertainment media, including televisions, computers, phones, and other electronic devices.[19]
- What are your odds of winning the lottery? It depends how many tickets are sold, but generally speaking you are four times more likely to be struck by lightning than to win the lottery.[20]
- You are more likely to be killed by a toaster than by a shark. Toasters killed nearly 800 people in 2015, whereas sharks killed just 6.[21]

19. "Media and Children Communication Toolkit," American Academy of Pediatrics, accessed April 18, 2018, https://www.aap.org/en-us/advocacy-and-policy/aap-health-initiatives/Pages/Media-and-Children.aspx.
20. Courtney Taylor, "What Are the Odds of Winning the Lottery?", ThoughtCo, updated March 15, 2018, https://www.thoughtco.com/the-odds-of-winning-the-lottery-3126169.
21. Ingrid Sprake, "Why You Should Be Scared of Your Toaster, Not Sharks," CORE sea, June 29, 2016, http://coresea.com/4159-2/.

I'm guessing that each of these statistics had some surprise value for you, hence their effectiveness as hooks. Similarly, facts can have an edgy, attention-grabbing quality as well. Check these out:

- In a desperate situation, it's possible to amputate your own limb. For example, American outdoorsman Aron Ralston had his right hand and forearm trapped under a boulder while hiking alone in a canyon in the Utah wilderness. Without help and with no way to contact rangers, he amputated the arm with a blunt pocket knife and then exited the canyon by rappelling sixty-five feet down a sheer cliff.
- According to Suetonius, the emperor Caligula loved his horse Incitatus so much that he gave the animal a marble stall, an ivory manger, purple coverings, a jeweled frontlet,[22] and a retinue of slaves, and even sought to make it a consul over the Roman senate.[23]
- Some tarantulas have defensive hairs that they can flick off in a spray at predators. One tarantula owner had to go to the doctor because a number of these tiny hairs had lodged in his eye.[24]

These facts are all pretty shocking, but they are the kind of details that will certainly arrest the attention of your audience.

In addition to having a solid thesis statement, the introduction of a quality thesis essay will include a hook that makes its audience want to pay attention. Now that you've seen a good list of attention-grabbers for your introductions, take some time to experiment with some of them in the rest of this lesson.

22. frontlet: a band for a horse's forehead
23. Seutonius, *The Lives of the Twelve Caesars* (Project Gutenberg, 2004), http://www.gutenberg.org/cache/epub/6389/pg6389-images.html.
24. Lauren Cox, "Ouch! Tarantula Attacks Owner," ABC News, January 1, 2010, http://abcnews.go.com/Health/EyeHealthNews/tarantula-attack-pierces-owners-eyes/story?id=9458010.

Tell It Back—Summary

TE

Summarize aloud three or four important ideas in this lesson. Then, in the space provided, write one well-crafted sentence that tells the main idea of the lesson as best as you understand it. To arrive at the main idea, ask yourself, "What is the chief purpose of the lesson?"

Main idea:

Sample main idea: A good hook grabs an audience's attention, which makes the audience open to the persuasive words to follow.

Talk About It—

TE

1. What type of hook do you think might be most effective in grabbing the attention of an audience, and why? Pick from narratives, questions, descriptions, illustrations, proverbs, sayings, quotations, provocative statements, statistics, or facts, and explain your answer.

TE

2. The following excerpt is the beginning of Aleksandr Solzhenitsyn's *The Gulag Archipelago*, an investigation of the prison camps of the Soviet Union. These camps, known as gulags, were notorious for their brutal conditions and the high death rates of the prisoners. Most prisoners were taken there for "crimes against the state." They included peasants who were considered too rich, artists who created art that offended communists, starving people who stole a few potatoes, and teachers who joked about communism.

> How do people get to this clandestine[25] Archipelago?[26] Hour by hour planes fly there, ships steer their course there, and trains thunder off to it—but all with nary a mark on them to tell of their destination. . . .
>
> Those who go to the Archipelago to administer the camps get there via the training schools. . . . Those who go there to be guards are conscripted via the military conscription centers. And those who, like you and me, dear reader, go there to die, must get there solely and compulsorily[27] via arrest.
>
> Arrest! Need it be said that it is a breaking point in your life, a bolt of lightning which has scored a direct hit on you? That it is an unassimilable[28] spiritual earthquake not every person can cope with, as a result of which people often slip into insanity? The

25. clandestine: secret in a sinister way
26. Archipelago: a cluster of islands in an expanse of water
27. compulsorily: forcibly
28. unassimilable: not capable of being absorbed or understood

Universe has as many different centers as there are living beings in it. Each of us is a center of the Universe, and that Universe is shattered when they hiss at you: "You are under arrest."

If you are arrested, can anything else remain unshattered by this cataclysm? But the darkened mind is incapable of embracing these displacements in our universe, and both the most sophisticated and the veriest simpleton among us, drawing on all life's experience, can gasp out only: "Me? What for?" And this is a question which, though repeated millions and millions of times before, has yet to receive an answer. Arrest is an instantaneous, shattering thrust, expulsion, somersault from one state into another.[29]

What are some types of hooks Solzhenitsyn uses to draw his readers in? Why do you think he uses the second-person perspective with the pronoun "you""

Write & Discuss—

Here are the beginnings of three famous essays. Take fifteen minutes to write down, in the space provided, your thoughts about what makes each beginning interesting or effective in grabbing the reader's attention. Then discuss with your class which essay beginning you think is the most attention-grabbing and explain your answer.

"Notes of a Native Son" by James Baldwin

On the 29th of July, in 1943, my father died. On the same day, a few hours later, his last child was born. Over a month before this, while all our energies were concentrated in waiting for these events, there had been, in Detroit, one of the bloodiest race riots of the century. A few hours after my father's funeral, while he lay in state in the undertaker's chapel, a race riot broke out in Harlem. On the morning of the 3rd of August, we drove my father to the graveyard through a wilderness of smashed plate glass.[30]

"The Future Is Now" by Katherine Anne Porter

Not so long ago I was reading in a magazine with an enormous circulation some instructions as to how to behave if and when we see that flash brighter than the sun which means that the atom bomb has arrived. I read of course with the intense interest

29. Aleksandr I. Solzhenitsyn, *The Gulag Archipelago 1918–1956* (New York: HarperCollins, 2007), 1:3–4. Copyright © 1973 by Aleksandr I. Solzhenitsyn. English language translation copyright © 1973, 1974 by Harper & Row Publishers, Inc. Reprinted by permission of HarperCollins Publishers (US) and The Random House Group Ltd. © 1995 (UK).
30. James Baldwin, "Notes of a Native Son," in *Notes of a Native Son* (Boston: Beacon Press, 1984), 85. Copyright © 1955, renewed 1983, by James Baldwin. Reprinted with permission from Beacon Press, Boston.

of one who has everything to learn on this subject; but at the end, the advice dwindled to this: the only real safety seems to lie in simply being somewhere else at the time, the farther away the better; the next best, failing access to deep shelters, bombproof cellars and all, is to get under a stout table—that is, just what you might do if someone were throwing bricks through your window and you were too nervous to throw them back. This comic anticlimax to what I had been taking as a serious educational piece surprised me into real laughter, hearty and carefree. It is such a relief to be told the truth, or even just the facts, so pleasant not to be coddled with unreasonable hopes.[31]

"The Fallacy of Success" by G.K. Chesterton

There has appeared in our time a particular class of books and articles which I sincerely and solemnly think may be called the silliest ever known among men. They are much more wild than the wildest romances of chivalry and much more dull than the dullest religious tract. Moreover, the romances of chivalry were at least about chivalry; the religious tracts are about religion. But these things are about nothing; they are about what is called Success. On every bookstall, in every magazine, you may find works telling people how to succeed. They are books showing men how to succeed in everything; they are written by men who cannot even succeed in writing books. To begin with, of course, there is no such thing as Success. Or, if you like to put it so, there is nothing that is not successful. That a thing is successful merely means that it is; a millionaire is successful in being a millionaire and a donkey in being a donkey.[32]

Your thoughts:

Sample answer: The beginning of "Notes from a Native Son" is interesting because of the contrast between important life events (birth and death) and the background of extreme social events, such as race riots. The beginning of "The Future Is Now" is surprising because the author reacts with hilarity to the dire circumstances of an atom bomb explosion and the lack of any helpful action to take. The beginning of "The Fallacy of Success" is interesting because the author takes the provocative position that books on success are a waste of time. In my opinion, "Notes from a Native Son" has the most interesting beginning because it has more urgency and dramatic tension than the other essay beginnings. In Baldwin's piece, the father dies on the same day his son is born while, at the same time, the author's world is laid waste by a riot. It seems like a crazy set of circumstances into which a baby would make his grand entrance.

31. Katherine Anne Porter, "The Future Is Now," *Mademoiselle*, November 1950. Reprinted with the permission of The Katherine Anne Porter Literary Trust c/o The Permissions Company, Inc., www.permissionscompany.com.
32. G.K. Chesterton, "The Fallacy of Success," in *All Things Considered* (1915; Project Gutenberg, 2004), https://www.gutenberg.org/files/11505/11505-h/11505-h.htm.

Go Deeper—

1. A rhetorical question (*erotema*) requires no answer because the answer is obvious or unnecessary. Rhetorical questions often make a stronger impression and impact when they are asked in a series.

   A. For each of the following excerpts, add to the question or set of questions one more question that would make sense in the context of the quotation. Write your addition in the space provided.

   Examples:

   If everyone jumped off a cliff, would you?

   If everyone played with scorpions, would you?

   [*Mama to her daughter:*] Child, when do you think is the time to love somebody the most? When they done good and made things easy for everybody?

   When they are sunshine and smiles, and all comfortable to be with?

   Well then, you ain't through learning—because that ain't the time at all. . . . When you starts measuring somebody, measure him right, child, measure him right. Make sure you done taken into account what hills and valleys he come through before he got to wherever he is.[33]

   a. Is the sky blue?

   Sample answer: Is the grass green?

33. Lorraine Hansberry, *A Raisin in the Sun* (New York: Vintage Books, 1994), act 3.

b. If you prick us, do we not bleed? If you tickle us, do we not laugh? If you poison us, do we not die?[34]

Sample answer: If you hit us, do we not bruise?

c. Everyone [in my school] knew there would be no gum chewing, nail biting, unbuttoned shirts, loose shirt tails, jazzy walks, jive talk, or fingers snapping. I'd ask children, "How are you going to run a corporation if you can't run yourself? Are you going to sit around a conference table in an executive suit popping gum or sticking your fingers in your mouth? How are you going to keep your life in order if you can't keep your appearance or your desk or your notebook?"[35]

Sample answer: How are you going to take care of a family if you can't take care of tying your shoelaces?

d. We see totalitarian forces in the world who seek subversion and conflict around the globe to further their barbarous assault on the human spirit. What, then, is our course? Must civilization perish in a hail of fiery atoms? Must freedom wither in a quiet, deadening accommodation with totalitarian evil?[36]

Sample answer: Must we accept the iron boot of dictatorship like dumb driven cattle?

e. You can't own a human being.[37] You can't lose what you don't own. Suppose you did own him. Could you really love somebody who was absolutely nobody without you? You really want somebody like that? Somebody who falls apart when you walk out the door?

Sample answer: Somebody who can't wake up in the morning without you in the room?

You don't, do you? And neither does he.[38]

34. William Shakespeare, *The Merchant of Venice*, ed. Barbara A. Mowat and Paul Werstine, 3.1.63–65, Folger Shakespeare Library, accessed May 1, 2018, http://www.folgerdigitaltexts.org.
35. Marva Collins, *Marva Collins' Way* (New York: Tarcher/Putnam Books, 1990), n.p.
36. Ronald Reagan, "The Evil Empire" (speech), June 8, 1982, Washington, DC, Reagan 2020, transcript, https://patriotpost.us/pages/439-ronald-reagan-the-evil-empire-1.
37. In this passage, when Morrison refers to owning a human being, she means it in a sense of commanding the love of another person rather than literally owning a person in chattel slavery. However, the play on words is intentional.
38. Toni Morrison, *Song of Solomon* (New York: Vintage Books, 2004), n.p.

f. **ROSE:** I been standing with you! I been right here with you, Troy. I got a life, too. I gave eighteen years of my life to stand in the same spot with you. Don't you think I ever wanted other things? Don't you think I had dreams and hopes? What about my life? What about me?[39]

Sample answer: Don't I deserve to be treated with respect?

g. Now the trumpet summons us again—not as a call to bear arms, though arms we need—not as a call to battle, though embattled we are—but a call to bear the burden of a long twilight struggle, year in and year out, "rejoicing in hope, patient in tribulation"—a struggle against the common enemies of man: tyranny, poverty, disease and war itself. Can we forge against these enemies a grand and global alliance, North and South, East and West, that can assure a more fruitful life for all mankind? Will you join in that historic effort?[40]

Sample answer: Will you come together to make a brighter future?

B. In the space provided, write at least two of your own *erotemata* (rhetorical questions) in a row. Make sure that the questions all fit together naturally.

Sample answer: When a self-driving car runs someone over, does it go to jail? Can you sue a self-driving car for reckless driving? If its software acts loopy, does it take a Breathalyzer test?

39. August Wilson, *Fences* (New York: Plume, 1986), act 2, scene 1.
40. John F. Kennedy, "Inaugural Address" (speech), January 20, 1961, Washington, DC, The American Presidency Project, transcript, http://www.presidency.ucsb.edu/ws/index.php?pid=8032&.

2. *Hypophora* is a rhetorical device in which the author asks a question and then immediately answers it. After reading each of the following excerpts, turn the underlined statement into both a question and an answer to the question. Write them in the space provided.

Examples:
The purpose of art is washing the dust of daily life off our souls. —Pablo Picasso
Hypophora: What is the purpose of art? It is to wash the dust of daily life off our souls.

The library is inhabited by spirits that come out of the pages at night. —Isabel Allende
Hypophora: What inhabits a library? Spirits that come out of the pages at night.

A. A great people has been moved to defend a great nation. Terrorist attacks can shake the foundations of our biggest buildings, but they cannot touch the foundation of America. These acts shattered steel, but they cannot dent the steel of American resolve. America was targeted for attack because we're the brightest beacon for freedom and opportunity in the world. And no one will keep that light from shining.
—from "Address to the Nation" by George W. Bush, delivered on September 11, 2001[41]

Sample answer: Why was America targeted? It's because we're the brightest beacon for freedom and opportunity in the world.

B. On some positions, cowardice asks the question, is it expedient? And then expedience comes along and asks the question, is it politic? Vanity asks the question, is it popular? Conscience asks the question, is it right?

There comes a time when one must take the position that is neither safe nor politic nor popular, but he must do it because conscience tells him it is right.
—from "Remaining Awake Through a Great Revolution" by Martin Luther King Jr., delivered on March 31, 1968[42]

Sample answer: There comes a time when one must do what? One must take a position that is neither safe, nor politic, nor popular.

41. George W. Bush, "Address to the Nation" (speech), The White House, September 11, 2001, Washington, DC, transcript, https://georgewbush-whitehouse.archives.gov/news/releases/2001/09/20010911-16.html. This speech was delivered on the evening of September 11, 2001, as a way to encourage Americans.
42. Martin Luther King Jr., "Remaining Awake Through a Great Revolution" (speech), National Cathedral, March 31, 1968, Washington, DC, The Martin Luther King Jr. Research and Education Institute, transcript, https://kinginstitute.stanford.edu/king-papers/publications/knock-midnight-inspiration-great-sermons-reverend-martin-luther-king-jr-10.

C. The time is now near at hand which must probably determine whether Americans are to be freemen or slaves; whether they are to have any property they can call their own; whether their houses and farms are to be pillaged and destroyed, and themselves consigned to a state of wretchedness from which no human efforts will deliver them.

The fate of unborn millions will now depend, under God, on the courage and conduct of this army. Our cruel and unrelenting enemy leaves us only the choice of brave resistance, or the most abject submission. We have, therefore, to resolve to conquer or die. —from "Address to the Continental Army before the Battle of Long Island" by George Washington, delivered on August 27, 1776[43]

Sample answer: What time is now near at hand? The time which must probably determine whether Americans are to be freemen or slaves.

D. We must not be confused about what freedom is. Basic human rights are simple and easily understood: freedom of speech and a free press; freedom of religion and worship; freedom of assembly and the right of petition; the right of men to be secure in their homes and free from unreasonable search and seizure and from arbitrary arrest and punishment. —from a speech to the International Assembly for Human Rights by Eleanor Roosevelt, delivered on September 28, 1948[44]

Sample answer: What are some qualities of basic human rights? They are simple and easily understood.

43. George Washington, "Address to the Continental Army before the Battle of Long Island" (speech), August 27, 1776, New York, George Washington's Mount Vernon, Mount Vernon Ladies' Association, transcript, http://www.mountvernon.org/george-washington/quotes/article/the-time-is-now-near-at-hand-which-must-probably-determine-whether-americans-are-to-be-freemen-or-slaves-whether-they-are-to-have-any-property-they-can-call-their-own-whether-their-houses-and-farms-are-to-be-pillaged-and-destroyed-and-themselves-consigned/. The full text of this speech can be found at http://www.thirty-thousand.org/pages/Free_Men.htm.

44. Eleanor Roosevelt, "The Struggle for Human Rights" (speech), September 28, 1948, Paris, France, American Rhetoric, transcript, http://www.americanrhetoric.com/speeches/eleanorroosevelt.htm.

E. This Government, as promised, has maintained the closest surveillance of the Soviet Military buildup on the island of Cuba. Within the past week, unmistakable evidence has established the fact that a series of offensive missile sites is now in preparation on that imprisoned island. The purpose of these bases can be none other than to provide a nuclear strike capability against the Western Hemisphere.[45] —from the Cuban Missile Crisis speech by John F. Kennedy, delivered on October 22, 1962[46]

Sample answer: What is the purpose of these bases? It can be none other than to provide a nuclear strike capability against the Western Hemisphere.

3. **EFFICIENCY EXERCISE—SUMMARY**

An electric car that can drive 200 miles on a single battery charge is more efficient than a car that can go 100 miles on a charge. Whenever possible, your writing should be similarly efficient. You want it to travel as far as possible, in terms of its vigor and comprehensibility, with the fewest number of words. Efficiency of wording and arrangement is prized in today's fast-paced world.

Being efficient does not mean that you should always be cutting your words down to the bare bones of simple sentences. You should still craft beautiful sentences—including compound and complex sentences—but without rambling on and on. Precise words are key, as well as considering carefully what you want to say. This principle holds doubly true for essay hooks, when you are trying to grab and hold the attention of your audience.

One of the ways to train yourself to be more efficient, as well as more flexible, in your writing is to summarize a text using a limited number of sentences—and also to start the first sentence of your summary with a word or phrase that has already been selected for you. The chosen word or phrase forces you to invent a way to complete the summary, a way that you might not have considered had you been given nothing but blank lines. The following stories are all connected to the Civil Rights Movement, a twentieth-century movement that protested the unequal and oppressive treatment of African Americans from the earliest days of American history. After each excerpt you will be asked to summarize the narrative using a certain number of sentences. You also will be provided with a word or phrase with which to start your summary. Read each excerpt and then follow the instructions to complete the exercise.

45. In 1962, Soviet Russia began to build missile-launching sites on the island of Cuba, just south of Florida. President Kennedy immediately recognized the danger. From these sites, missiles carrying nuclear warheads could easily be launched into the United States.

46. John F. Kennedy, "Radio and Television Address to the American People on the Soviet Arms Build-Up in Cuba," October 22, 1962, John. F. Kennedy Presidential Library and Museum, transcript, https://www.jfklibrary.org/Asset-Viewer/sUVmCh-sB0moLfrBcaHaSg.aspx.

A. Nonfiction, Third-Person Narrative —from *Southern Horrors: Lynch Law in All Its Phases* by Ida B. Wells

▲ Ida B. Wells, c. 1893

In this passage, Ida B. Wells, an investigative journalist for antisegregationist newspapers, describes the incident that launched her crusade against lynching—the hanging or murder of a person by a mob. After the Civil War and during much of the early twentieth century, lynching was used as a weapon by white racists to terrorize African Americans. The men described in this passage were Wells's friends and workers in an African American–owned business, the People's Grocery.

On March 9, 1892, there were lynched in this same city (Memphis) three of the best specimens of young since-the-war Afro-American manhood. They were peaceful, law-abiding citizens and energetic businessmen. They believed the [racial] problem was to be solved by eschewing[47] politics and putting money in the purse.[48] They owned a flourishing grocery business in a thickly populated suburb of Memphis, and a white man named Barrett had one on the opposite corner.

After a personal difficulty which Barrett sought by going into the "People's Grocery" drawing a pistol and was thrashed by Calvin McDowell, he (Barrett) threatened to "clean them out." These men were a mile beyond the city limits and police protection; hearing that Barrett's crowd was coming to attack them Saturday night, they mustered forces, and prepared to defend themselves against the attack.

When Barrett came he led a *posse* of officers, twelve in number, who afterward claimed to be hunting a man for whom they had a warrant. That twelve men in citizen's clothes should think it necessary to go in the night to hunt one man who had never before been arrested, or made any record as a criminal has never been explained. When they entered the back door the young men thought the threatened attack was on, and fired into them. Three of the officers were wounded, and when the *defending* party found it was officers of the law upon whom they had fired, they ceased and got away.

Thirty-one men were arrested and thrown in jail as "conspirators," although they all declared more than once they did not know they were firing on officers. Excitement was at fever beat until

47. eschewing: avoiding
48. "putting money in the purse": The author means that economic prosperity in the black community would build acceptance for African Americans throughout the United States.

the morning papers, two days after, announced that the wounded deputy sheriffs were out of danger. This hindered rather than helped the plans of the whites. There was no law on the statute books which would execute an Afro-American for wounding a white man, but the "unwritten law" did. Three of these men, the president, the manager and clerk of the grocery—"the leaders of the conspiracy"—were secretly taken from jail and lynched in a shockingly brutal manner. "The Negroes are getting too independent," they say, "we must teach them a lesson."[49]

Summarize the story in three sentences in the space provided. Begin the first sentence with "although."

Although ____

Sample answer: Although the three African Americans who ran a successful grocery business in Memphis, Tennessee, were peaceful and law-abiding, they were targeted for "cleaning out" by the white grocery store owner across the street. This man, Barrett by name, led a posse of others against the African American–owned store at night, and the defending men fired guns at their attackers. As it turns out, the wounded attackers were police officers and, despite the fact that the black men had fired in legitimate self-defense, an angry mob pulled several of them out of jail and lynched them.

B. Nonfiction, First-Person Narrative —from a description of Bloody Sunday by John Lewis

In this excerpt, civil rights leader and congressman John Lewis recalls his experiences near the Edmund Pettus Bridge in Selma, Alabama, on March 7, 1965. Here peaceful marchers, protesting the murder of a black man by a state trooper and restrictions on their right to vote, encountered the forces of segregationist government. Lewis suffered not only a concussion but a fractured skull.

> We got to the top of the bridge. We saw a sea of blue—Alabama state troopers—and we continued to walk. We came within hearing distance of the state troopers. And a man identified himself and said, "I'm Major John Cloud of the Alabama state troopers. This is an unlawful march. It will not be allowed to continue. I give you three minutes to disperse and return to your church." And one of the

49. Ida B. Wells, *Southern Horrors: Lynch Law in All Its Phases* (1892; Project Gutenburg, 2005), http://www.gutenberg.org/ebooks/14975.

young people walking with me, leading the march, a man by the name of Hosea Williams, who was on the staff of Dr. Martin Luther King Jr., said, "Major, give us a moment to kneel and pray." And the major said, "Troopers, advance!" And you saw these guys putting on their gas masks. They came toward us, beating us with nightsticks and bullwhips, trampling us with horses. I was hit in the head by a state trooper with a nightstick. I had a concussion at the bridge. My legs went out from under me. I felt like I was going to die. I thought I saw Death. All these many years later, I don't recall how I made it back across that bridge to the church.[50]

▲ John Lewis, c. 1964

Summarize the story in two sentences. Begin the first sentence with "when."

When ______________________________

Sample answer: When the marchers reached the bridge, they were forced to halt by a crowd of Alabama state troopers. The marchers asked to pray, and that request unleashed a fierce response of violence, resulting in beatings and brutality, and John Lewis's head was battered by a nightstick.

C. Comedy Narratives —from comedy routines by Dick Gregory

Dick Gregory was a civil rights activist who used humor to shine a light on the evils of segregation and racism.

All the record stores are playing that subversive song again . . . *I'm Dreaming of a White Christmas* . . . It's kinda sad, but my little girl doesn't believe in Santa Claus. She sees that white cat[51] with the whiskers—and even at two years old, she knows damn well ain't no white man coming into our neighborhood at midnight . . . be honest now. How many of *you* have ever seen a black Santa

▲ Dick Gregory, c. 1964

50. John Lewis, "'I Thought I Saw Death': John Lewis Remembers Police Attack on Bloody Sunday in Selma 50 Years Ago," interview by Juan González and Amy Goodman, *Democracy Now!*, March 6, 2015, transcript and video, https://www.democracynow.org/2015/3/6/i_thought_i_saw_death_john. Used by permission.
51. "Cat" is a slang word for a cool person. It derives from "hepcat," also a slang word, which was a name for a person who performed or followed jazz and swing music.

Claus? He ain't even black after he comes down the chimney—and he *should* be![52]

Last time I was down South, I walked into this restaurant. This White waitress came up to me and said, "We don't serve colored people here." I said, "That's all right. I don't eat colored[53] people, no way! Bring me a whole fried chicken." About that time, these three cousins came in. You know the ones I mean—Ku, Klux, and Klan.[54] They said, "Boy,[55] we're givin' you fair warnin'. Anything you do to that chicken, we're gonna do to you." About then, the waitress brought me my whole chicken and the cousins said, "Remember, boy, anything you do to that chicken, we're gonna do to you." So I put down my knife and fork, picked up that chicken, and kissed it!"[56]

Summarize one of the jokes and its punch line in two sentences. A **punch line** is the last line of a joke that provides its humorous impact. Begin the first sentence with "Dick Gregory tells a story about."

Dick Gregory tells a story about ______________________________

Sample answer: Dick Gregory tells a story about how his daughter can't believe in Santa Claus because "ain't no white man coming into our neighborhood at midnight." He adds that it's strange that Santa isn't black "even after he comes down the chimney."

____

52. Dick Gregory, *From the Back of the Bus* (Dick Gregory Enterprises, Inc., 1962; Chicago Ex-Patriate blog, 2012), http://chicagoexpat.blogspot.com/2012/07/moving-forward-from-back-of-bus-by-dick.html.
53. Because the original author of this text chose to use the word "colored," we reprint it faithfully here. Language is always evolving, and this word as it refers to human beings has had a checkered career. According to the Oxford English Dictionary, emancipated slaves used the term "colored" as an expression of racial pride (https://en.oxforddictionaries.com/definition/coloured), and this usage survives in the National Association for the Advancement of Colored People (NAACP) as well as in today's preferred term "people of color." The word "colored" became increasingly offensive in the US, however, as it was associated with segregation.
54. The Ku Klux Klan is a racist, terrorist group dedicated to white supremacy. Though isolated today, it was a strong political force in the 1920s.
55. The term "boy" as used here is derogatory and offensive.
56. Dick Gregory, *Callus on My Soul* (New York: Kensington Publishing Corp., 2003), 47.

Lesson 4: The Thesis Essay, Part I: Hooking the Audience

The Introductory Paragraph—

Please note that Aphthonius's essay on marriage as it is found in lessons 4–5 of this book is a paraphrase and embellishment of the original. While the ancient thesis served as a springboard to practice orations, also known as declamations, they were not as comprehensive and evidence-based as current persuasive papers demand. Therefore, the structure of Aphthonius's work has been modified to conform to the format used in this book. Our changes to Aphthonius's example satisfy the requirements of modern persuasive writing while retaining the spirit of ancient thesis writing.

▶ What is the thesis statement of the essay?

The thesis statement is the last sentence of the introduction: "Marriage is worthy of praise because it gives men and women great courage and self-control."

Tell It Back—Summary

Sample important ideas:

- Rhetorical hooks are used in persuasive essays and speeches to grab the attention of the audience.
- Questions put the audience on the spot and cause it to think.
- Stories can be any size to fill the space needed, and there's a story for every purpose, whether a fable, a parable, an anecdote, a joke, a news flash, or a summary of a longer story.
- Descriptions and illustrations use the senses to grab attention and can serve the same purpose as pictures in a picture book.

Talk About It—

1. Answers will vary. Sample answer: Using illustrations might be the single best way to hook an audience because they are the most basic to human understanding. Illustrations make abstract ideas more concrete and bring hard-to-grasp ideas down to earth. While some people enjoy incessant deep thoughts, most audiences can't go for very long without some aid to understanding, such as a word picture. An audience that doesn't know what the writer or speaker means will nod off to sleep, but an audience that understands the author will be "hooked." In addition, creating understanding through vivid illustration also can stir up

an audience's senses and cause it to be emotionally engaged. For example, when a parent wants to awaken a child to the dangers of running across the street, an abstract concept, she might point out a dead animal on the road. Scientists use the vivid idea of a wormhole to illustrate the abstract idea of connections between points in space and time. In both of these examples, the illustrations help explain difficult ideas while also engaging the senses. It's also helpful that illustrations can use fewer words to get attention than many narratives and descriptions.

2. Solzhenitsyn begins his book by drawing readers in with a question, and a very intriguing question at that. He asks how people can get to the secret prison camps of the Soviet Union, the Gulag Archipelago. He also draws readers in with word pictures, or illustrations, about unmarked vehicles, which creates an air of mystery about the camps. Solzhenitsyn then switches to illustrations that tell readers about the type of people who go to the Gulag.

   I think he uses the second-person "you" to involve the reader in his word pictures. For example, by pointing out that arrest is the only way for people "like you and me" to get to the Gulag, he makes the reader feel as if she could be arrested too. This makes the experience of arrest feel so much more threatening and immediate.

Notes

The purpose of this lesson is to walk students through the body paragraphs and conclusion of a thesis essay.
In this lesson, students will practice:
- narration in summary form
- critical thinking
- picture analysis
- writing thesis statements from excerpts of literature
- using facts to support a position
- writing a paragraph confirming a thesis
- writing a paragraph refuting an antithesis

Lesson 5

The Thesis Essay, Part 2: Supporting the Thesis

Should One Marry?

Oddly enough, when I think about writing a thesis essay, the image of a concentric castle comes to mind. A concentric castle is a castle that has rings of walls, towers, and other defenses that surround the tallest tower, which is known as a keep. Castles built with these layers of protection could stand against a formidable attack of knights and foot soldiers and even missile-slinging catapults. The body paragraphs of a thesis essay are meant to support and defend the essay's thesis statement. So, if you think about the thesis statement of an essay as the keep, and the body paragraphs of the essay as rings of defense around the thesis, you'll see why the image of a concentric castle is so perfect.

Both castles and theses without a strong defense are vulnerable to attack. You don't want your thesis to share the fate of the castle in this twelfth-century poem:

> Great is my joy when I see knights and armored horses
> ranged on the battlefield.

. . . And it warms my heart to see strong castles besieged,
the palisades smashed and broken down,
and to see the army on the river-bank
protected on all sides by ditches,
and strong, tight-made palisades.

And I am well pleased by a lord
when he is the first to attack,
on horseback, armored, fearless:
thus does he inspire his men
with boldness, and worthy courage.

—by Bertran de Born, lord of Hautefort[1]

Just as a castle keep needs surrounding walls to stand against a siege, so a thesis needs supporting arguments to stand against opposition. The supporting arguments of a thesis essay are known as **confirmations**. They take a particular aspect of the thesis and show why this aspect is in some way true. By "true" we mean probable, logical, believable, clear, or proper.[A] These confirmations can form strong fortifications around the thesis, just like castle walls surround and fortify the castle.

To further defend the keep, many concentric castles also have outer defenses such as a second layer of walls, towers, a moat, or rock cliffs. In the same way, a writer or orator can further protect a thesis with another layer of protection known as **refutations**. Refutations rebut counterarguments—antitheses—by showing why the antithesis is somehow untrue. By "untrue" we mean improbable, illogical, unbelievable, unclear, or improper.

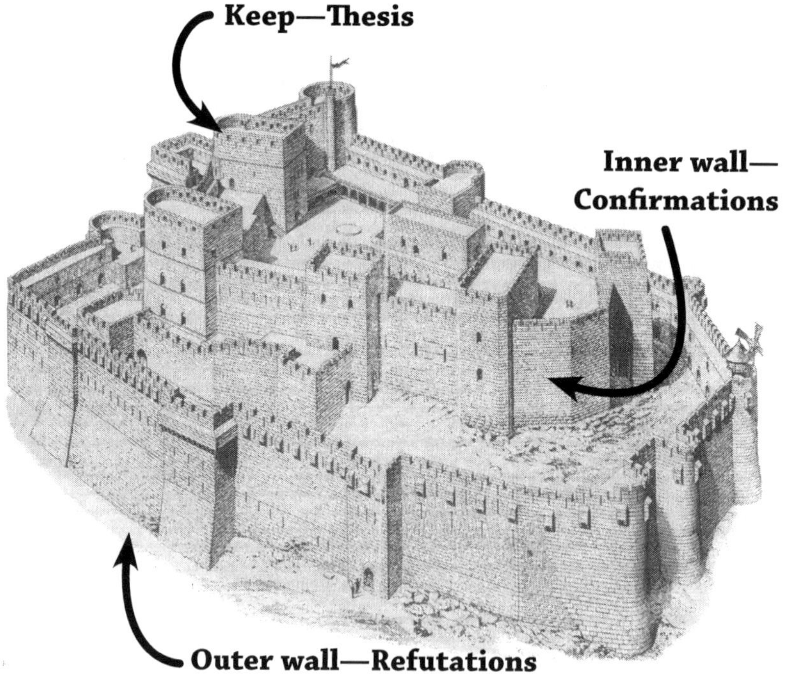

1. Bertran de Born (c. 1140–1215) was a French musician and poet who lived in medieval times. Bertran de Born, "Be'm plai lo gais temps de pascor," trans. Clifford J. Rogers, "Portions of Two Poems by the Twelfth-Century Knight-Troubadour Bertran de Born," De Re Militari, accessed July 1, 2018, http://www.deremilitari.org/RESOURCES/SOURCES/born.htm. Used by permission of the author.

In lesson 4 you saw how Aphthonius begins his sample thesis essay with an introduction paragraph. If you look at the rest of Aphthonius's essay on marriage, you can see how he protects his thesis with confirmations and refutations. In fact, you can see a summary of the two confirmations in his thesis statement. Here is the thesis again:

> Marriage is worthy of praise because it gives men and women great courage and self-control.

Why should a person marry? Aphthonius delivers two confirming arguments: Marriage helps spouses gain courage, and marriage gives people self-control. He explains his reasoning by following his introduction with two supporting paragraphs.

[A]These terms may remind you of *Writing & Rhetoric: Refutation & Confirmation*, in which you used confirmation to defend certain parts of a narrative as believable, probable, clear, or proper. (Note that by "clear" we mean "understandable," and by "proper" we mean "appropriate" or "morally sound.") Just as a confirmation essay defends parts of a narrative, so the paragraphs in a thesis essay defend aspects of the thesis. Although you won't be asked to use those specific terms in your writing for this book, they are aspects of a thesis that you can consider when defending it.

Body Paragraph 1: Confirmation—

In this paragraph, Aphthonius expands on the claim that marriage gives men and women great courage.

It takes courage to marry, doesn't it? To stand up in front of family and friends and pledge one's life to another person. To make huge promises "to love, to comfort, to honor and keep, in sickness and health" until death parts the couple. "To forsake all others." But Aphthonius means to say that marriage promotes courage in another way. Take a look at what he wrote:

Topic sentence——

> Because marriage unites a man and a woman, and often brings forth children, too, the man must learn to provide courageously for his family. He must make his way in the thorny world and fight for the sustenance of the ones he loves best. He is not likely to shirk his duty to take care of his family. A man will not let his loved ones starve. If war comes, his courage will rise up in the defense of them. What is true for a husband is true for a wife. She will defend her children to the death, if necessary, and work ceaselessly for their happiness.

Aphthonius shows how marriage leads to courage because it drives a person to care for his or her family at any cost. He uses this idea to show that his thesis is proper and logical: Marriage is worthy of praise because it has a positive consequence, the development of courage.

Keep in mind that Aphthonius was writing at a time when patriarchy was the norm. Patriarchy is a social system in which the husband is the head of the family and is most often the one to work at a job outside of the home. In fact, the word "husband" comes from the Old English word for "head of the house" and also meant "farmer" or "tiller of the soil." In a patriarchy, a wife's primary responsibilities would be the care of young children and the management of the house. Times have changed! Today wives often take careers outside of the home and also manage the affairs of the family. Sometimes husbands take on the primary care of young children and household management. Even today, however, Aphthonius's point stands true: Taking care of a family, no matter your role in a marriage, requires courage.

Body Paragraph 2: Confirmation—

In this paragraph, Aphthonius expands on the claim that marriage gives men and women self-control. Take a look:

Topic sentence— Just as marriage stirs up courage, it also helps men and women to have self-control. Pleasure is a part of marriage, but it is a tender pleasure, not the greedy pursuit of the flesh as so often happens outside of marriage. What can be destructive to a single person becomes admirable for a married person. Marriage provides a lawful pleasure that binds husbands and wives together in contentment and intimacy, which helps to remove the temptation of destructive actions. For single people, the satisfaction that comes from marriage gives them something to look forward to once they are married. When they trust their physical pleasure to marriage, single men and women can control their natural urges.

In this paragraph Aphthonius is referring specifically to sexual self-control. According to Aphthonius, the ability to look forward to pleasure in marriage helps men and women to exercise self-control when they are single. And later, during marriage, sex builds an intimacy that protects couples against destructive sexual behavior. He uses this idea to show that his thesis is proper and logical: Marriage is worthy of praise because it has another positive consequence, the development of self-control.

Do you see the pattern in both of these confirmation paragraphs? They each begin with a topic sentence, which states the main idea of the paragraph. The topic sentence is followed by explanations and illustrations that fill out the confirmation like mortar around the bricks of a wall. When you make a claim, your reader's first response is often "Why?" or "Prove it!" or "How do you know that?" Explanations and illustrations answer those concerns.

So now you've seen an example of the outer walls of the castle, the confirmation paragraphs. What about the next layer of defense? Without pausing for breath, Aphthonius turns to the cynics in his audience who might object to his claims. These might be people who feel they have been burned by a bad marriage or who are inclined to avoid a lifelong commitment. Aphthonius anticipates what his critics are thinking and he answers them squarely. He begins his two refutation paragraphs with two antitheses: Marriage causes strife and misfortune, and marriage is tiresome. These antitheses also function as topic sentences in the paragraphs, but rather than approving of them, Aphthonius explains why they are wrong ideas, and he uses illustrations to back up his perspective.

A Valiant Thesis Essay

Just as the knight guides the horse, so the thesis guides the essay.

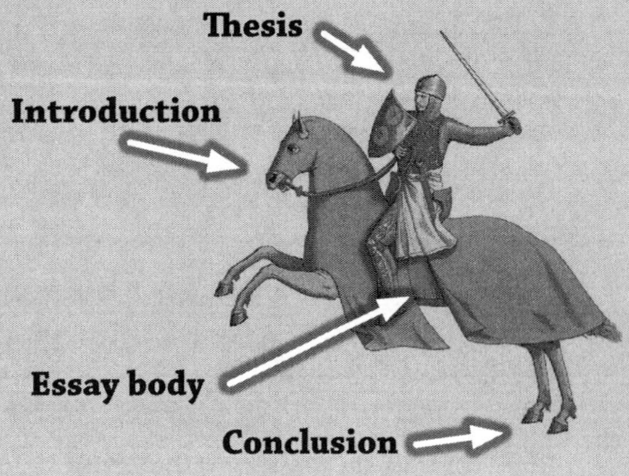

Body Paragraph 3: Refutation—

In the first refutation paragraph, Aphthonius tackles the idea that marriage causes strife and misfortune. This is what he says:

Antithesis

> Critics will say that <u>marriage causes strife and misfortune</u>. True, some marriages are filled with quarrels and beset by troubles. But is there any aspect of life that doesn't have strife or misfortune? Fans of team sports sometimes get into bloody fights and stampedes, even crushing other spectators underfoot. Does bad behavior argue against the proper use of stadiums? No! The worst aspects of human nature are always present to some degree in every earthly endeavor, and the presence of strife does not argue against the goodness of marriage in general. Likewise, lightning or hail can ruin a farmer's crops and sailors drown at sea, but it is silly to think that people should stop farming or seafaring. Marriage can likewise have its share of misfortune, but fortune[2] itself is to blame, not marriage.

In short, Aphthonius is saying that marriage does not cause strife and misfortune. Rather, strife and misfortune are present in many situations, including marriage, but they are not caused by the marriage and are not reasons to avoid marriage. By explaining why this antithesis is untrue, Aphthonius adds to the defense of his thesis.

2. The Roman concept of fortune included both good and bad luck. Devout Romans worshipped luck and chance in the form of the goddess Fortuna.

Body Paragraph 4: Refutation—

In his second refutation paragraph, Aphthonius takes on the criticism that marriage is tiresome:

> While misfortune sours some critics on marriage, others say that matrimony is just plain tiresome. Husbands and wives grow weary of each other, they say, and then life turns to unending drudgery. One of the flaws of human nature is that people are easily bored, but surprisingly unmarried couples are more dissatisfied than married couples. More often than not, married couples report that the boredom and burdens of life are relieved by marriage. When one spouse is fatigued, the other can help to enliven the hours. When one spouse is sick or injured, the other acts as a nurse. When one spouse is ridiculed at work, the other acts as a support and encourager. When children are needy, both husband and wife take turns helping them. Finally, when parents are truly tired out, made old and infirm by the years, their children, who are the result of the marriage, can show their full merit by energizing the parents and easing their burdens.

—Antithesis

In this paragraph, Aphthonius acknowledges that some critics feel that marriage is tiresome. Then he gives reasons why marriage is instead just the opposite, because it actually can help relieve burdens. Once again, he adds to the defense of his thesis by showing why this antithesis is untrue.

Notice that Aphthonius does not treat his critics with derision. He doesn't put them down or attack them with name-calling or bad language. Rather, he takes their criticisms seriously and answers them politely but firmly. He is trying to convince them with his arguments rather than cudgel them with his words and insults. In both of these refutation paragraphs he uses logic, comparisons, and illustrations to make his point.

After the walls and defenses—the confirmation and refutation paragraphs—are in place, Aphthonius ends his essay with a conclusion (or epilogue) in which he repeats his thesis and his main arguments for emphasis. He also widens his praise to include marriage's influence on society and adds a call to action. Notice that he avoids phrases that can be overused, such as "in conclusion" and "in closing." While these phrases are acceptable transitions in some cases, for the most part they aren't really necessary.

> Marriage is, in fact, a wonderful thing. It contains pleasure, and this pleasure brings forth new life and new generations. It teaches husbands and wives courage and self-control as well as relieves boredom and difficulties. Our society owes much of its health and happiness to marriage. It's time we gave it our highest esteem, and spread the word, so that more young people are encouraged to embrace a lifelong commitment.

That's a tidy ending for a pretty convincing composition. Your conclusion should always reaffirm the thesis and somehow answer the question, "Why is this topic important?" You can also encourage your reader to take some sort of action. Living in the classical age, Aphthonius could never have foreseen a time when singles might avoid getting married. In our modern times, however, it's appropriate to include the call for young people "to embrace a lifelong commitment."

Do you see the pattern established by this thesis essay? Here it is in a nutshell:

- Introduction—attention grabber and thesis, the main argument
- Two confirmation paragraphs—arguments supporting the thesis
- Two refutation paragraphs—arguments rebutting the antitheses
- Conclusion—reaffirmation of the thesis and answer to the question "Why is this topic important?"

With his confirmation and refutation paragraphs, Aphthonius has successfully defended his "castle," and you will follow the same pattern in your own writing. In lesson 7 you will put all the parts of the essay together when you write your first thesis. For now, take some time to get more practice with thesis statements and defending paragraphs.

The Entire Thesis Essay: Should One Marry?

hook using hypophora — hook using illustration — Introduction

What would the universe be without marriage? Empty! Marriage enabled the gods to produce offspring and fill the heavens. First came the marriage of Gaia, the earth, to Uranus, the sky. Because Uranus mistreated his children, Gaia plotted with her son, Saturn, to overthrow him. Saturn succeeded in taking his father's throne and married Ops to produce many gods—including Jupiter. Father Jove—for that is the meaning of the name "Jupiter"—became the grandfather of Romulus and Remus, the two princes who founded the city of Rome. From one marriage, then, came gods and goddesses and the Roman people. The gift of life isn't the only reason to praise marriage, either. Marriage is worthy of praise because it gives men and women great courage and self-control. — thesis statement

topic sentence — Confirmation paragraph 1—courage

Because marriage unites a man and a woman, and often brings forth children, too, the man must learn to provide courageously for his family. He must make his way in the thorny world and fight for the sustenance of the ones he loves best. He is not likely to shirk his duty to take care of his family. A man will not let his loved ones starve. If war comes, his courage will rise up in the defense of them. What is true for a husband is true for a wife. She will defend her children to the death, if necessary, and work ceaselessly for their happiness.

topic sentence—Just as marriage stirs up courage, it also helps men and women to have self-control. Pleasure is a part of marriage, but it is a tender pleasure, not the greedy pursuit of the flesh as so often happens outside of marriage. What can be destructive to a single person becomes admirable for a married person. Marriage provides a lawful pleasure that binds husbands and wives together in contentment and intimacy, which helps to remove the temptation of destructive actions. For single people, the satisfaction that comes from marriage gives them something to look forward to once they are married. When they trust their physical pleasure to marriage, single men and women can control their natural urges.

Confirmation paragraph 2—self-control

topic sentence/antithesis

Critics will say that marriage causes strife and misfortune. True, some marriages are filled with quarrels and beset by troubles. But is there any aspect of life that doesn't have strife or misfortune? Fans of team sports sometimes get into bloody fights and stampedes, even crushing other spectators underfoot. Does bad behavior argue against the proper use of stadiums? No! The worst aspects of human nature are always present to some degree in every earthly endeavor, and the presence of strife does not argue against the goodness of marriage in general. Likewise, lightning or hail can ruin a farmer's crops and sailors drown at sea, but it is silly to think that people should stop farming or seafaring. Marriage can likewise have its share of misfortune, but fortune itself is to blame, not marriage.

Refutation paragraph 1—strife and misfortune

While misfortune sours some critics on marriage, others say that matrimony is just plain tiresome. Husbands and wives grow weary of each other, they say, and then life turns to unending drudgery. One of the flaws of human nature is that people are easily bored, but surprisingly unmarried couples are more dissatisfied than married couples. More often than not, married couples report that the boredom and burdens of life are relieved by marriage. When one spouse is fatigued, the other can help to enliven the hours. When one spouse is sick or injured, the other acts as a nurse. When one spouse is ridiculed at work, the other acts as a support and encourager. When children are needy, both husband and wife take turns helping them. Finally, when parents are truly tired out, made old and infirm by the years, their children, who are the result of the marriage, can show their full merit by energizing the parents and easing their burdens.

topic sentence/antithesis

Refutation paragraph 2—tiresome

restatement of thesis and main arguments—Marriage is, in fact, a wonderful thing. It contains pleasure, and this pleasure brings forth new life and new generations. It teaches husbands and wives courage and self-control as well as relieves boredom and difficulties. Our society owes much of its health and happiness to marriage. It's time we gave it our highest esteem, and spread the word, so that more young people are encouraged to embrace a lifelong commitment.

Conclusion

widening of thesis

call to action

Tell It Back—Summary

TE 1. Summarize aloud three or four important ideas in this lesson. Then, in the space provided, write one well-crafted sentence that tells the main idea of the lesson as best as you understand it. To arrive at the main idea, ask yourself, "What is the chief purpose of the lesson?"

Main idea:

Sample main idea: In a thesis essay, confirmations and refutations are used to defend the thesis statement.

TE 2. In what way does a thesis essay resemble a concentric castle?

Talk About It—

TE 1. A persuasive thesis statement is easiest to defend when it is clear, specific, and supportable. If the thesis is unclear, you will never be sure precisely what position you are attempting to defend, and if it is too broad, it will require a great deal of research to cover every aspect of it. If adequate evidence to support a thesis is lacking, your defense will be weak.

The six statements in this exercise are about cities. If these sentences were used as persuasive thesis statements, which of them would be easier to defend with confirmations and refutations? Which statements would be more difficult to defend? Explain your answers.

- The modern city is ugly . . . because it is a jungle, because it is confused and anarchic, and surging with selfish and materialistic energies.[3]
- City life is millions of people being lonesome together.[4]
- The city is humanity's laboratory, where people flock to dream, create, build and rebuild.[5]
- In the country the darkness of night is friendly and familiar, but in a city, with its blaze of lights, it is unnatural, hostile and menacing.[6]
- American cities are like badger holes, ringed with trash—all of them—surrounded by piles of wrecked and rusting automobiles, and almost smothered in rubbish.[7]
- Every city contains some landmark of beauty and wonder.

3. G.K. Chesterton, "The Way to the Stars," in *Lunacy and Letters* (New York: Sheed & Ward, 1958), as quoted by The American Chesterton Society, https://www.chesterton.org/quotations-of-g-k-chesterton/.
4. Author unknown; often attributed to Henry David Thoreau.
5. Edward L. Glaeser, *Triumph of the City* (New York: Penguin, 2011), n.p.
6. Attributed to W. Somerset Maugham.
7. John Steinbeck, *Travels with Charley* (New York: Penguin, 1986), n.p.

TE

2. Look carefully at the painting *Honeymoon* by artist Marcus Stone (1840–1921) and then at the painting *The Waning Honeymoon* by George Henry Boughton (1833–1905). If the artists were using their paintings to represent thesis statements about marriage, what might those statements be? Explain your answer.

▲ *The Waning Honeymoon* by George Henry Boughton

▲ *Honeymoon* by Marcus Stone

Write & Discuss—

The following excerpts are passages from two twentieth-century novels set in Los Angeles. If these books were thesis essays and the paragraphs in this exercise were the essays' confirmations, what might the essays' thesis statements be? In other words, what main point does each excerpt seem to be supporting? Take fifteen minutes to read the paragraphs and consider what the authors are saying. Then, in the space provided, write a thesis statement for each "essay." When you've finished writing, compare thesis statements with a partner and try to judge which statement is more clear, specific, debatable, and supportable.

The Day of the Locust by Nathanael West

In this passage, West describes the houses that sit along a canyon road in Los Angeles.

> Not even the soft wash of dusk could help the houses. Only dynamite would be of any use against the Mexican ranch houses, Samoan huts, Mediterranean villas, Egyptian and Japanese temples, Swiss chalets, Tudor cottages, and every possible combination of these styles that lined the slopes of the canyon. . . .
>
> On the corner of La Huerta Road was a miniature Rhine castle with tarpaper turrets pierced for archers. Next to it was a little highly colored shack with domes and minarets out of the Arabian Nights. . . . Both houses were comic. . . . Their desire to startle was so eager and guileless.[8]

8. guileless: innocent

It is hard to laugh at the need for beauty and romance, no matter how tasteless, even horrible, the results of that need are. But it is easy to sigh. Few things are sadder than the truly monstrous.[9]

Thesis statement:

Sample answer: The mishmash of houses along the canyon road are monstrous and deserve to be destroyed.

The Little Sister by Raymond Chandler

In this passage, a private investigator reminisces about a more innocent time in Los Angeles.

"I used to like this town. . . . A long time ago. There were trees along Wilshire Boulevard.[10] . . . Los Angeles was just a big dry sunny place with ugly homes and no style, but goodhearted and peaceful. It had the climate they just yap about now. People used to sleep out on porches. Little groups who thought they were intellectual used to call it the Athens of America. It wasn't that, but it wasn't a neon-lighted slum either. . . .

"Now . . . We've got the big money, the sharp shooters, the percentage workers, the fast-dollar boys, the hoodlums[11] out of New York and Chicago and Detroit and Cleveland. We've got the flash restaurants and night clubs they run, and the hotels and apartment houses they own, and the grifters and con men and female bandits[12] that live in them. . . . The riffraff of a big hard-boiled city with no more personality than a paper cup. . . ."[13]

Thesis statement:

Sample answer: Los Angeles used to be a decent place to live, but it's been ruined by criminals and hoodlums.

9. Nathanael West, *Miss Lonelyhearts & The Day of the Locust* (New York: New Directions Publishing, 2009), 61. Copyright © 1939 by Estate of Nathanael West. Reprinted by permission of New Directions Publishing Corp.
10. Wilshire Boulevard: a very long and important street in Los Angeles
11. big money, sharp shooters, percentage workers, fast-dollar boys: shady characters involved in gambling or gang activities
12. grifters, con men, female bandits: criminals who steal money by deceiving their victims
13. Raymond Chandler, *The Little Sister* (New York: Vintage Books, 1988), n.p. Copyright © 1949 by Raymond Chandler. Used by permission of Vintage Crime/Black Lizard, an imprint of Penguin RandomHouse LLC (US), and the estate of the author c/o Rogers, Coleridge & White Ltd., 20 Powis Mews, London W11 1JN (UK). All rights reserved. Any third party use of this material, outside of this publication, is prohibited. Interested parties must apply directly to Penguin Random House LLC for permission.

Go Deeper—B

In this exercise you will practice confirmation and refutation by making some changes to Aphthonius's thesis essay on marriage. After reading the instructions, write your answers in the space provided.

1. **NEW SUPPORTING ARGUMENT: BETTER HEALTH**—Say that instead of "self-control" Aphthonius used "better health" as his reason that marriage is worthy of praise. His thesis would then read: "Marriage is worthy of praise because it gives men and women great courage <u>and better health</u>."

   Your task is to write a new confirmation paragraph supporting the argument that marriage should be praised because it gives better health. The following is some information you can use in shaping this new paragraph.[14]

   - Married people live longer than unmarried people, which is often a sign of good health.
     - Husbands live an average of ten years longer than unmarried men.
     - Wives live an average of four years longer than unmarried women.
   - Married people are generally happier than single people, and happiness means less susceptibility to physical and mental illness.
     - Sadness and loneliness depress the immune system and make people more susceptible to sickness.
     - Forty percent of spouses studied report being "very happy," whereas only twenty-five percent of singles report the same.
     - Married couples consistently report greater emotional well-being than single or divorced people.
     - Marriage is good for mental health. Married men and women are less likely to be anxious or depressed than unmarried men and women.
   - Married people are less likely to fall victim to violence and abuse.
     - In addition to causing physical injury, violence and abuse can cause long-term physical ailments including chronic pain, headaches, and heart problems.
     - Violence against women is more likely to be perpetrated by a boyfriend rather than a husband.
     - Cohabitating couples are more likely to be abusive than married couples.
     - Single women and bachelor men are four times more likely to experience violent crime.
   - Married people enjoy better heart health than unmarried people.
     - Married women between the ages of fifty-one to sixty-one have lower blood pressure than unmarried women.
     - Unmarried men are three times more likely to die of cardiovascular disease than married men.

14. These facts come from a variety of sources and studies, but especially *The Case for Marriage: Why Married People Are Happier, Healthier, and Better off Financially* by Linda J. Waite and Maggie Gallagher (New York: Broadway Books, 2002).

Which points stood out to you as the strongest reasons why marriage promotes good health? Choose two or three of the points and use them to construct a new confirmation paragraph. Start your paragraph with a topic sentence; then add your illustrations or supports in four or five more sentences.

Just as marriage stirs up courage, it also helps men and women to

Sample paragraph: Just as marriage stirs up courage, it also helps men and women to enjoy longer, healthier lives. Wives live an average of four years longer than unmarried women, and the benefit is even greater for married men—ten years! In addition to longevity, it's important to note that the incidence of domestic violence, which can affect a person's health, is much lower for married couples, and marriage even improves mental health. There is hardly an area of human happiness, which can have a significant influence on health, that marriage doesn't enhance. In fact, studies show that married couples are generally happier than any other demographic.[A]

[A]Whenever ideas or research are borrowed from another source, it's important to cite the source. However, in order to approach thesis writing incrementally, we do not require citations in this exercise or include them in our sample answer. We discuss citations more specifically in the next lesson.

[B]As you read and practice with Aphthonius's essay in this lesson, you may find that his glowing description of marriage in general differs from your own experience. For instance, maybe you come from a single-parent home, and you might be thinking, "My parents had good reasons to split up." Or, "Hey, my parents never got married and I turned out all right." Or you might be thinking the opposite: "I wish my parents hadn't split." Or "My parents' divorce really messed me up." Perhaps you come from an intact family in which parents fight frequently and you wish there could be more peace. These situations might make it seem that marriage isn't the good thing that Aphthonius says it is. I can understand why you might feel that way. However, it is rarely sound to argue from your personal experience alone. Your experiences are like tesserae, or small squares, in a larger mosaic. There may be dark pieces or light pieces, but you can't know how they fit into the big picture until you step back. Although there are always some exceptions, Aphthonius's views on marriage have been shown to be generally true nearly two thousand years later. Although it is not always perfect, marriage is worthwhile to defend and protect because it strengthens the fabric of our society. Studies show that when marriage is strong, violence and poverty decrease and public health increases. So even though your own experience may make marriage look less desirable than Aphthonius says it is, try to see the big picture, one that shows that despite the exceptions, marriage is generally a very good thing.

2. **NEW ANTITHESIS: GRIEF**—Next, replace the antithesis that claims that marriage is tiresome with another antithesis: that marriage causes deep pain and grief when a spouse dies. You will start your paragraph with this statement: "Because marriage creates such a deep, intimate bond, it causes husbands and wives to experience the deepest pain and grief possible when a spouse dies."**B**

How would you argue against such a claim? Your argument might be similar to Aphthonius's refutation of the claim that marriage causes misfortune. Is marriage to blame for the grief we feel when someone close to us dies? You might also question whether marriage is the only relationship in which a person would feel deep pain and grief at another person's death. What other relationships might be just as deep and intimate in their own special way?

Your task is to write a paragraph refuting the new antithesis. Start by stating the new antithesis and then be sure to explain what it means. You want to be fair to the antithesis by not immediately discarding it. After you explain the antithesis, follow with several sentences that refute it and discuss why it is wrong.

While misfortune sours some critics on marriage, others say that because marriage creates such a deep, intimate bond, it causes husbands and wives to experience the deepest pain and grief possible when a spouse dies.

Sample answer: While misfortune sours some critics on marriage, others say that because marriage creates such a deep, intimate bond, it causes husbands and wives to experience the deepest pain and grief possible when a spouse dies. Nothing seems more tragic than a husband or wife visited by the death of a spouse and the tears shed over a grave. Yet is marriage to blame for the grief we feel when someone close to us dies? No, death is the cause of our grief, not marriage. In addition, the deep pain of death is not unique to spouses. People involved in other types of deep, intimate relationships feel deep grief as well. Friends can love friends and parents can love children with similar emotional depth, and their grief can be equally intense. In the end, everyone feels grief over death, whether married or not. Therefore, the possibility of deep pain and grief is not a reason to criticize marriage. Since avoiding marriage does not mean the avoidance of death or grief, it's better to enjoy the benefits of marriage than to miss out on them.

B The new antithesis in this exercise is loosely based on an antithesis used by Aphthonius in his original *progymnasmata*.

Lesson 5: The Thesis Essay, Part 2: Supporting the Thesis

Tell It Back—Summary

1. Sample important ideas:
   - Just as a castle keep needs surrounding walls to stand against a siege, so a thesis needs supporting arguments to stand against opposition.
   - Supporting arguments are known as confirmations.
   - Rebuttals of counterarguments (otherwise known as antitheses) are called refutations.
   - Refutations rebut counterarguments by showing why the antithesis is somehow untrue.
2. Concentric castles were built with rings of protection around the central tower, the keep. In a similar way, confirmations and refutations provide rings of protection or defense around the thesis statement (the main argument) of a thesis essay.

Talk About It—

1. Answers may vary. Sample answer: Most likely the final two statements would be the easiest to defend because they are specific and clear, and there is abundant proof for each argument. Most American cities do have trashy areas and eyesores on their outskirts, including wrecked cars and rubbish. And it would not be hard to find some landmark of beauty or some architectural wonder in every major city.

   On the other hand, the first two arguments are very broad and would need a fair bit of research to prove, and would therefore be difficult to defend. At first glance, the third argument seems to be a factual statement that needs no defense, but it is rather unclear. What does the author mean by "laboratory," and what are the people actually creating, building, and rebuilding? We are left with fuzzy words and ideas that are not easy to define, which makes the thesis harder to defend. The fourth argument about darkness is a fascinating idea, but it would be difficult to prove with hard evidence because it depends on personal impressions. It may, however, be defensible in a philosophical way.
2. In Boughton's *The Waning Honeymoon*, the artist seems to be saying that not all marriages are warm and intimate, even in the beginning. The man is ignoring his bride for the sake of a book, and the bride's expression is none too pleased. Rather than getting comfortable with his wife, and holding her lovingly, the husband is carelessly petting the dog's head. In terms of added symbolism, the bench they are sitting on is situated in the middle of two diverging paths, and we might assume that the artist is saying the husband and wife will grow apart from each other as well.

TE

If Stone's *Honeymoon* were representing a thesis statement, the artist would seem to be saying that marriage makes for a comfortable and warm relationship. The man and woman lean upon one another in an intimate fashion. The man reads with his head resting comfortably on the woman, while the woman appears pleased to be reclining so closely to her husband.

Notes

The purpose of this lesson is to revisit the rhetorical concept of ethos and to show how quotes, paraphrases, and allusions can be used to improve ethos.

In this lesson, students will practice:

- narration in summary form
- critical thinking
- reading an essay, discussing it, and writing about its implications
- lifting quotes and putting them in context
- using in-text citations
- paraphrasing paragraphs
- creating allusions

Lesson 6

How to Be Appealing: Ethos, the Appeal to Authority

Wouldn't it be great to have an authority take your side every time you got into a disagreement? Say that you're arguing with a friend about the greatest quarterback in football history. You say it's Tom Brady. Your friend says it's Peyton Manning. So who is it, Tom Brady or Peyton Manning? All of a sudden, Don Shula, the winningest coach in football history, appears out of thin air and says to your friend, "Listen, kid, it's Tom Brady. He made 580 career touchdown passes, started as quarterback in 9 Super Bowls and won 6 of them, and won 237 career games.[1] Now run along and clean your messy room!"

▲ Don Shula knows how to settle a disagreement about football!

It would be pretty nice if that happened, wouldn't it? Your friend wouldn't be able to argue with an authority like Don Shula.

1. These statistics are as of March 2019. "Tom Brady," New England Patriots, accessed March 1, 2019, https://www.patriots.com/team/players-roster/tom-brady/.

What is an authority? An authority is a highly respected source of information. It is a person who has real expertise and influence. Lee Trevino is a true authority on golf. Indra Nooyi is a true authority on managing a big corporation. Duke Ellington is a true authority on music. Neil Armstrong is a true authority on flying to the moon. When you write a persuasive paper, any time you can show that an authority takes your side, you will enhance your persuasiveness. You are essentially borrowing the authority, the trustworthiness, of that individual to build your own trustworthiness.

In the previous book, *Description & Impersonation*, you encountered the concept of ethos. Ethos is one of three types of persuasive appeal along with pathos and logos. It attempts to persuade the audience that the writer or speaker is a trusted or credible authority on his subject. Keep in mind, however, that although today ethos is often seen simply as an appeal to the writer's or speaker's trustworthiness, it is more than that—it is an appeal to his entire character. If a person has good character, the audience will be more likely to believe him. Aristotle tells us, "We believe good men more fully and more readily than others; this is true generally whatever the question is, and absolutely true where exact certainty is impossible and opinions are divided. . . . [The speaker's] character may almost be called the most effective means of persuasion he possesses."[2] In other words, a person's good name is paramount to her ability to persuade others.

Think about it for a moment. A politician says, "Elect me and I'll keep the streets safe from drug dealers," and then he himself gets busted for taking illegal drugs. Or a politician expects the public to trust her with tax money, but cheats on her own taxes. How much credibility would these individuals have? Their ethos is shredded by their own behavior. They may be authorities on street crime and tax law respectively, but their audience may be unwilling to abide their hypocrisy. Our actions are important, as are the words we use and the motives we nurture. A student who cheats on tests and who lies about her friends may take a noble stand on some issue, but who will trust her? People are inclined to take the opposite action when they are urged to do something by someone they don't trust. Clearly authority works best with a strong dose of good character. Good character is authority in its own right—what we call moral authority.

When you combine good character with the support of an authority on your topic, you'll be building an ethos that is sure to persuade. In the thesis essays in this book, you will be required to quote respected authorities in order to strengthen your ethos. Just as Aphthonius uses the authority of mythology—which would have been authoritative in his day—you will call upon trustworthy texts and figures to back you up. As you write your confirmations and refutations, the appeal to authority provides another defensive layer to protect your thesis from attack.

2. Aristotle, *Rhetoric*, trans. W. Rhys Roberts, The Internet Classics Archive, accessed January 19, 2018, http://classics.mit.edu/Aristotle/rhetoric.1.i.html.

In-Text Citations

Whenever you use a direct quote or paraphrase in your writing, you'll want to not only give credit to its original author, but also help your reader find its source. It may be that readers will want to confirm your honesty or do more exploration on the subject themselves. Citations identify the source of a quotation or paraphrase and are like a trail of bread crumbs that you can leave behind for readers to follow if they want to check up on your research.

In-text citations are references found right at the end of a quote or paraphrase. Say you want to quote Shakespeare. At the end of the quote, you would cite the last name of the quote's author and the page number where you found the quote, in parentheses, like this:

> "To be or not to be, that is the question" (Shakespeare, 127).

If you introduce your quote by mentioning Shakespeare, then you would only have to put the page number in parentheses, like this:

> Shakespeare's character Hamlet says, "To be or not to be, that is the question" (127).

(Please note that if your source doesn't have page numbers, you might need to list a chapter number or paragraph number instead, or even forego the identifying numbers. Check with your teacher to see what she would prefer.)

Every in-text citation must have a corresponding full citation on the Works Cited page at the end of your essay. (An example of a Works Cited page can be found later in this lesson.)

How to write citations for both print and Internet sources will vary a bit based on the specific type of text you are quoting and your teacher's preferred style. For a complete list of variations in the Modern Language Association (MLA) style, please consult Purdue's Online Writing Lab: https://owl.english.purdue.edu/owl/resource/747/02/.[A]

[A]If you prefer that your students use a different style guide for citations, feel free to point them to a different source.

Direct Quotations—

There are a number of ways you can show that an authority supports your thesis. One way is to use a **direct quote**, which is the repetition of another person's exact words enclosed in quotation marks. Having the words of someone else support your argument is like having a strong sibling at the playground to back you up with the neighborhood bully. You can fend off the bully with a heavyweight backing you up; you can fend off counterarguments when you directly quote an authority. Your credibility—your ethos—will be bolstered by expert insight.

In 1935, disease specialist Hans Zinsser published a remarkably delightful history of horrible epidemics called *Rats, Lice, and History*. In the 1930s, there wasn't anyone on the planet who knew more about plagues than Zinsser, and he even came up with a vaccine for the dreaded disease typhus. Yet even though he was an authority in his own right, in his book, Zinsser quotes freely from other authorities—historians and doctors of the past. As a modern scientist, he needed to rely on the expert testimony of people who actually lived through plagues and who documented them. Here's an example in which Zinsser quotes Procopius, a historian of sixth-century Byzantium:

> His account reflects the terrified helplessness and panic which spread with this pestilence. Four months the plague remained in Byzantium. At first, few died—then there were 5,000, later 10,000 deaths a day. "Finally, when there was a scarcity of gravediggers, the roofs were taken off the towers of the forts, the interiors filled with the corpses, and the roofs replaced" (Procopius, bk. 2, XXIII, 10–15).[3]

Zinsser knows that he could not have done a better job of conveying the nightmare of the epidemic than by directly quoting the eyewitness account itself. In this example Zinsser holds off on quoting Procopius until he comes to the most shocking part of his ancient description, because he knows it will have the most impact on his readers. In the same way, you'll want to choose your quotations carefully to make the maximum impact.

Now here's another example. Liz Moyer, a reporter for the business news website CNBC.com, knows that the most successful investor of her day is Warren Buffett. Incredibly, Buffett is worth somewhere around $84 billion after starting out with only a few bucks in his piggy bank! Anyone that successful must be an authority on making money and have sage words of investing advice. In an article on bank stocks, Moyer quotes Buffett right off the bat:

> Warren Buffett has a saying about the stock market and investing in general: "Be fearful when others are greedy and greedy when others are fearful."[A] Time and again, the value investor has used this philosophy to pounce on opportunities.[4]

Moyer quotes Buffett to support her argument that it is wise to buy bank stocks when everybody else is selling them out of fear. Buffett's saying—"Be fearful when others are greedy and greedy when others are fearful"—has become something of a proverb among stock market investors. In fact, it is such a famous saying that it would be plagiarism to put it into other words and pass it off as your own.

Another example of a direct quote comes from columnist David Brooks. In his essay about Dorothy

[A]Note that this example demonstrates an exception to the rules: A citation is not included for the quote in this excerpt. Because Buffett's words are a known saying, rather than a quote that he put in print, there is no original source to cite. In cases such as this, you often will only be able to cite the name of the person who created the quote.

3. Adapted from Hans Zinsser, *Rats, Lice, and History* (New York: Routledge, 2017), 146.
4. Liz Moyer, "Warren Buffett's Big Bank Score Proves His Saying True Once Again: 'Be Greedy When Others Are Fearful,'" CNBC, June 30, 2017, https://www.cnbc.com/2017/06/30/buffetts-big-bank-score-proves-be-greedy-when-others-are-fearful.html.

Day, reporter and Catholic activist, Brooks relies heavily on direct quotes from Day herself. It makes sense for him to quote Day, as she is an authority on her own life. An autobiography is often an excellent source of authoritative material related directly to a particular person. Here is a passage describing the birth of Day's daughter, Tamar:

> When her daughter Tamar arrived, she [Dorothy Day] was overwhelmed by gratitude: "If I had written the greatest book, composed the greatest symphony, painted the most beautiful painting or carved the most exquisite figure, I could not have felt the more exalted creator than I did when they placed my child in my arms" (Day, ix).[5]

Notice that Brooks doesn't quote some ordinary lines from Day simply saying that she was happy to have a daughter. He quotes her rhapsody about giving birth—surely one of the most important moments of her life—and that quote convinces us of her authentic delight.

Similarly, any writer who is analyzing a work of literature or science will want to quote directly from the text itself. An analysis needs to be supported by what scholars call **textual evidence**—evidence taken straight from the source. If a writer is making a statement—an analysis—about a work, she should be able to show how the work demonstrates the idea she is putting forth. In other words, her quotation should strongly support the thesis statement, or main idea, of the analysis. Here is an example of using direct quotes as textual evidence that support a main idea:

> In the novel *Papillon* by Henri Charrière, the main character, a convict, finds deep satisfaction in the chance to remake his criminal past and become a respectable person. After his first escape from the penal colony, he is given shelter by an upright family. He tries to convey the "intense emotion" he feels over his "newfound self-respect" (88). He says, "This imaginary baptism, the immersion in purity, the elevation of my being above the filth in which I'd been mired and, overnight, this sense of responsibility, made me into a different man" (88). The question quickly becomes, can the convict keep his purity even when he is recaptured and sent back to the "hell" of prison?

The writer of this literary analysis wants to prove how deeply the convict feels about his newfound respectability. He picks quotes that show a vital moment when the convict feels made into a different man, a man who can be respected. The quotes perfectly support the writer's point of view.

5. Adapted from David Brooks, *The Road to Character* (New York: Random House, 2015), 84.

Here is some advice about including direct quotes in your thesis writing:

- Use quotes to support your thesis and appeal to authority.
- Keep quotes brief so they don't bore or confuse the audience.
- Use quotes that are so skillfully worded that they express an idea better than you can.
- Don't go overboard in using direct quotes. They tend to get lost, like a tree in a forest, if one quote follows another.
- Don't use a quote in a way that changes its meaning or is unfair to the author.
- For every quote, be sure to include a sentence or more to explain its purpose for the point you are making. This is called contextualizing your quote—giving it connection to your thesis and explaining its significance.
- Don't forget to introduce your quote and use quotation marks.

Actress Marlene Dietrich once summed up the significance of quotes. She said, "I love [quotations] because it is a joy to find thoughts one might have, beautifully expressed with much authority by someone recognizedly wiser than oneself."[6]

6. Marlene Dietrich, *Marlene Dietrich's ABC: Wit, Wisdom & Recipes* (New York: Open Road Media, 2012), n.p.

Paraphrase—

You can also appeal to authority with the use of paraphrase, or restating an original quote using different wording. Writers often paraphrase to make a quotation easier to understand or to summarize it.

The following is a direct quote from a letter written by physicist Albert Einstein to President Franklin Roosevelt. The scientist wanted to warn the president that Nazi Germany was probably attempting to build an atomic bomb. This famous letter is said to have launched the nuclear arms race during the Cold War.

> In the course of the last four months it has been made probable—through the work of Joliot in France as well as Fermi and Szilard in America—that it may become possible to set up a nuclear chain reaction in a large mass of uranium by which vast amounts of power and large quantities of new radium-like elements would be generated. Now it appears almost certain that this could be achieved in the immediate future.
>
> This [new] phenomenon would also lead to the construction of bombs, and it is conceivable—though much less certain—that extremely powerful bombs of a new type may thus be constructed. A single bomb of this type, carried by boat and exploded in a port, might very well destroy the whole port together with some of the surrounding territory.[7]

Now here is text from a booklet prepared by the Department of Defense that refers to the letter in the form of a paraphrase:

> The development of a nuclear weapon was a low priority for the United States before the outbreak of World War II. However, scientists exiled from Germany had expressed concern that the Germans were developing a nuclear weapon. . . . <u>In a letter sponsored by a group of concerned scientists, Albert Einstein informed President Roosevelt that German experiments had shown that an induced nuclear chain reaction was possible and could be used to construct extremely powerful bombs (Einstein).</u>[8]

Notice how the authors of the booklet paraphrased the original letter in order to summarize it. They captured some of the essential ideas from the letter: that induced nuclear chain reactions are possible and that these reactions can be used to build powerful bombs. At the same time, they left out many of the details of the letter, including the reference to uranium and the size of the bomb blast. Notice, too, that the authors made sure to use Albert Einstein's name. Einstein happened to be the leading scientist of his day, a true authority in the realm of nuclear physics, and his name helped to solidify the ethos of the authors.

---

7. Albert Einstein to F.D. Roosevelt, August 2, 1939, Atomic Heritage Foundation, accessed July 28, 2018, https://www.atomicheritage.org/key-documents/einstein-szilard-letter.
8. Adapted from Carl Maag and Steve Rohrer, *Project Trinity 1945–1946* (Arlington, VA: Department of Defense; Project Gutenberg, 2008), http://www.gutenberg.org/cache/epub/548/pg548-images.html.

Instead of using the exact words of an authority, a paraphrase borrows the authority's idea. Paraphrasing allows the writer to keep the flow of her own writing and adapt or abbreviate information and ideas according to her needs. Despite using new words, however, it's still important to use citations to give proper credit to the author of the original idea. Always keep in mind that "credit where credit's due" is a great way to build ethos—and it's the honest thing to do.

Allusion—

You can also appeal to authority using an **allusion**. An allusion makes reference to a well-known idea, often found in a story, speech, or poem, either by hinting at it indirectly or by borrowing its words directly.

Note that an allusion generally does not mention the name of the idea's original author, include a citation, or use quotation marks, even if exact words are quoted.[B] This is because an allusion is not directly presenting the idea, but rather making a reference to it, and because the borrowed idea is so well known that it has become a fixed part of our cultural heritage, an idea that many people will recognize. For example, if I were to say, "Your quarrel is much ado about nothing," you would likely recognize the reference to William Shakespeare and the title of his play *Much Ado About Nothing*. If you were to say, "You're stuck between Scylla and Charybdis!" I would know that you were alluding to the *Odyssey* and how Odysseus was trapped between two monsters—like being stuck between a rock and a hard place.

[B]Determining whether something is an allusion or a direct quotation can be somewhat subjective. If in doubt, use quotation marks and citations to be safe.

An allusion adds to a writer's credibility because it shows her to be well-read and well-educated. For example, Martin Luther King Jr. alludes to Abraham Lincoln's most famous speech, "The Gettysburg Address," when he begins his own famous speech, "I Have a Dream":

> Five score years ago, a great American, in whose symbolic shadow we stand today, signed the Emancipation Proclamation. This momentous decree came as a great beacon light of hope to millions of Negro slaves who had been seared in the flames of withering injustice.[9]

Here is Lincoln in his own words:

> Four score and seven years ago our fathers brought forth on this continent a new nation, conceived in Liberty, and dedicated to the proposition that all men are created equal.[10]

9. Martin Luther King Jr., "I Have a Dream" (speech), August 28, 1963, Washington, DC, The Martin Luther King Jr. Research and Education Institute, Stanford University, transcript, https://kinginstitute.stanford.edu/king-papers/documents/i-have-dream-address-delivered-march-washington-jobs-and-freedom.
10. Abraham Lincoln, "The Gettysburg Address," November 19, 1863, Gettysburg, PA, Our Documents, transcript, https://www.ourdocuments.gov/doc.php?flash=false&doc=36&page=transcript.

As you can see, King alludes to Lincoln's speech by mirroring the phrase "four score and seven years ago" with his own phrase, "five score years ago." The Gettysburg Address is one of the most respected speeches in the history of oratory, and King essentially borrows a little ethos from Lincoln before he launches into his own speech, which is now equally famous. Notice also that Lincoln himself makes an allusion in that first sentence of his speech. "All men are created equal" alludes to the following brilliant lines from the Declaration of Independence:

> We hold these truths to be self-evident, that all men are created equal, that they are endowed by their Creator with certain unalienable Rights, that among these are Life, Liberty and the pursuit of Happiness.[11]

In order to strengthen the cause of women's rights, Elizabeth Cady Stanton alludes to the same portion of the Declaration of Independence in her Declaration of Sentiments, with a slight twist:

> We hold these truths to be self-evident: that all men <u>and women</u> are created equal.[12]

Allusions are most useful when they are brief and make a quick point to demonstrate a writer's knowledge. With a wink and a nod, an allusion works swiftly to validate a claim. Be careful, though. Any idea longer than a word or a phrase, any idea not extremely well known, should be treated as a quotation or a paraphrase.

Introduce Your Quotes and Paraphrases and Give Them Context—

How often do you walk up to a total stranger and start talking to her without an introduction? Not often, I hope. Besides being unwise, it is a good way to be perceived as a little batty. Similarly, you should not just toss off a direct quote or a paraphrase without making introductions. Let your reader know whose words you are quoting or rewriting. Here are some ways to introduce a quote or paraphrase:

- <u>According to</u> Edmond Hoyle, the card game expert . . .
- <u>In the words of</u> Edmond Hoyle, the famed authority on card games . . .
- <u>To quote</u> Edmond Hoyle, rules maker for card games . . .
- Edmond Hoyle, renowned expert on card games, <u>says</u> . . .

In addition to "says," here are some other useful introductory verbs:

- argues (argued)
- asserts (asserted)—to affirm, to state positively
- believes (believed)
- claims (claimed)
- contends (contended)—to argue with force

11. Thomas Jefferson himself borrowed the phrase "the pursuit of happiness" from John Locke's *An Essay Concerning Human Understanding*. Locke states emphatically, "The necessity of pursuing happiness [is] the foundation of liberty."
12. Elizabeth Cady Stanton, Declaration of Sentiments, 1848, Seneca Falls, NY, The National Park Service, https://www.nps.gov/wori/learn/historyculture/declaration-of-sentiments.htm.

- describes (described)
- disputes (disputed)—to question, to argue against
- observes (observed)
- opines (opined)—to state an opinion
- states (stated)

Quotes and paraphrases need more than an introduction, however. They also need **context**. You could never keep a fish as a pet without water. An aquarium filled with water is the necessary context for having a pet fish; the fish would die without it. Similarly, context surrounds a quote or paraphrase and gives it life. When you give context, you are telling the reader how to better understand the quote and how it connects to your point. Here's an example:

> As with any human endeavor, science is not always harmonious. Scientists can have serious disagreements. Physicist Albert Einstein tells his fellow scientist Niels Bohr, "God does not play dice with the universe." Bohr shoots back, "Stop telling God what to do!"

Those are nice, attention-catching sayings, right? Except that they don't really make sense without more information. Why would one guy (Einstein) protest the randomness in the universe and the other guy (Bohr) tell him, essentially, to accept the universe as it exists? And what does their conversation have to do with the point that is being made? Here is a paragraph putting the sayings in context:

> As with any human endeavor, science is not always harmonious. Scientists can have serious disagreements. Albert Einstein and Niels Bohr were theoretical scientists who gave us new ways of thinking about physics. Even though they were good friends, they could never completely agree on how to explain the behavior of light, energy, and subatomic objects. The tools of measurement gave them different results even though the same object was being studied. For example, sometimes light acted like a stream of tiny bullets and sometimes it acted like a wave. Einstein believed that there had to be some explanation for such contradictory behavior, some way to predict how these objects would act. Legend tells us that he said, "God does not

play dice with the universe"[13] (Einstein, 88). He was determined to understand the ultimate reality behind the strange behavior of light and atoms and all matter. He wanted to find a master theory—a theory of everything—behind the many new scientific discoveries. Bohr, on the other hand, believed that objects behaved differently when they got very, very small and this behavior would never be fully predictable. Supposedly he said to Einstein, "Stop telling God what to do!" (Rae, 22). Bohr was comfortable with the idea that the universe was made to be ultimately unknowable. Though Einstein and Bohr were excellent physicists, their disagreement shows that some aspects of science are still open for debate.

Now that you know the context of the Einstein and Bohr sayings, you can see how they connect to each other. Even if you don't understand much about physics and subatomic particles, you can at least see that both men were seeking to understand the ultimate nature of reality. And you can see how the sayings connect to the paragraph's topic—that good scientists can sometimes disagree. Context helps us to understand the sayings and why they are important.

Citations—

A citation is used in writing to identify a source of information. By properly citing any works that you use to support your thesis, you can avoid plagiarism, which is passing off someone else's ideas or words as your own. Plagiarism is a serious form of cheating, and many young people have found themselves in academic jeopardy for pretending to write something that had already been written by someone else.[14]

There are a variety of ways to format citations, and your teacher will tell you which style she prefers. This book uses *The Chicago Manual of Style* (CMS) format for its citations, but the Modern Language Association (MLA) style is commonly used by students. We have demonstrated MLA style in the previous examples of direct quotes and paraphrases and in the following sections about the Works Cited page.

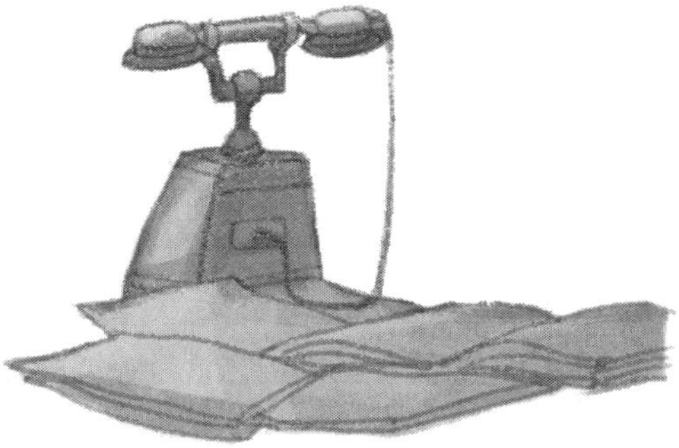

13. The actual quote, from a letter to Max Born, a German physicist, reads, "I am convinced that He [God] is not playing at dice."
14. For more on plagiarism, please see *Writing & Rhetoric: Encomium & Vituperation*.

Works Cited in This Lesson—

The following list is an example of a Works Cited page. It includes the full citations for the in-text citations in this lesson.

Works Cited

Charrière, Henri. *Papillon*. Pocket Books, 1970.

Day, Dorothy. *Thérèse*. Ave Maria Press, 2016.

Einstein, Albert. "Letter to Max Born 1926." *The Born-Einstein Letters 1916–1955*, edited by Max Born, Macmillan, 2005, p. 88.

Procopius. *History of the Wars, Books I–II*. Translated by H.B. Dewing, book 2, Harvard University Press, 1914. *Project Gutenberg*, 2005, https://www.gutenberg.org/files/16764/16764-h/16764-h.htm. Accessed July 21, 2018.

Rae, Alastair. *Quantum Physics: Illusion or Reality*. Cambridge University Press, 1994.

Shakespeare, William. *Hamlet*. Simon & Schuster, 2012.

MLA Format for a Works Cited List—

The following list demonstrates the format for full citations in the MLA style for some common types of sources.[15] Please note that even these examples may have variations that are specific to individual circumstances. Consult your teacher's preferred style guide to be sure your format is correct.

Note that it is sometimes difficult to find all of the information you need to make a proper citation, especially for a website. Style guides such as the MLA manual will typically give some direction for what to do if you are missing information. If you are still stumped, ask your teacher what he would like you to do.

Books and print media:

One author: Last Name, First Name. *Title of Book*. City of Publication (if required),[16] Publisher, Year.

Two authors: Last Name, First Name and First Name Last Name. *Title of Book*. City of Publication (if required), Publisher, Year.

A work within an anthology: Last Name, First Name. "Title of Work." *Title of Anthology*, edited by Editor's Name(s), City of Publication (if required), Publisher, Year, Page Range of Entry.[17]

---

15. Based on "MLA Formatting and Style Guide," Purdue Online Writing Lab, Purdue University, accessed July 21, 2018, https://owl.purdue.edu/owl/research_and_citation/mla_style/mla_formatting_and_style_guide/mla_formatting_and_style_guide.html.
16. According to the Purdue Online Writing Lab's guidelines for MLA style, the city of publication needs to be included only if the book's publication date is before 1900 or if the book's publisher is located in multiple countries or unknown outside of North America. "MLA Works Cited Page: Books," Purdue Online Writing Lab, Purdue University, accessed July 21, 2018, https://owl.english.purdue.edu/owl/resource/747/06/.
17. Some sources, such as electronic versions of books, may not include page numbers. In that case you might need to use a chapter number or paragraph number, or even forego the identifying number, in your citation. Consult your style guide for more specific information.

Magazine article: Last Name, First Name. "Title of Article." *Title of Magazine*, Day Month Year, Page Numbers.

Newspaper article: Last Name, First Name. "Title of Article." *Newspaper Name*, Day Month Year, Page Numbers.

Digital media:

Internet encyclopedia: Last Name, First Name (if available). "Title of Article." *Title of Encyclopedia*. Publication or Update Date (if available). *Name of Website*. URL. Access Date.

Internet website: Last Name, First Name (if available). "Title of Web Page." *Title of Website*. Name of Organization (that sponsors the site), Date of Creation or Update (if given), URL. Date Accessed.

You've come a long way in a short time in this lesson, but when all is said and done, what you've learned is this: It's important to build ethos by backing up your arguments with the support of trusted authorities. You can do this by using quotations, paraphrases, or allusions. And don't forget to cite your sources!

Tell It Back—Summary

TE

Summarize aloud three or four important ideas in this lesson. Then, in the space provided, write one well-crafted sentence that tells the main idea of the lesson as best as you understand it. To arrive at the main idea, ask yourself, "What is the chief purpose of the lesson?"

Main idea:

Sample answer: Several ways to build one's ethos include quoting directly, paraphrasing, and making allusions to an authority.

Talk About It—

TE

1. In his book *Rhetoric*, Aristotle writes, "There are three things which inspire confidence in the orator's own character. . . . Good sense, good moral character, and goodwill."[18] The first two seem obvious—a speaker needs to be sensible and honorable to be persuasive. But what about goodwill? Why does it matter that a speaker desires the best for her audience and for humanity in general?

TE

2. Recently a famous actor made a movie warning people about the dangers of global warming and carbon pollution. In a speech at the Oscar awards, he said, "It [climate change] is the most urgent threat facing our entire species, and we need to work collectively together and stop procrastinating."[19] Despite his beneficial message about pollution, this actor has been a huge polluter. He has used private jets and yachts to get to the playgrounds of the rich and famous, he has attended swanky parties with exotic imported foods, and he has, by his lifestyle, added tons of pollution a year to the air.[20] What are some of your thoughts about this actor's ethos—both his authority and his character?

18. Aristotle, *Rhetoric*, trans. W. Rhys Roberts, The Internet Classics Archive, accessed January 19, 2018, http://classics.mit.edu/Aristotle/rhetoric.2.ii.html.
19. Robert Rapier, "Leonardo DiCaprio's Carbon Footprint Is Much Higher Than He Thinks," *Forbes Magazine*, March 1, 2016, https://www.forbes.com/sites/rrapier/2016/03/01/leonardo-dicaprios-carbon-footprint-is-much-higher-than-he-thinks/#4500ca5e2bd5.
20. Rapier, "Leonardo DiCaprio."

Write & Discuss—

"Question Authority" has been a popular slogan found on bumper stickers and at college campuses. It is thought to have been coined by Timothy Leary, a psychologist who popularized doing psychedelic drugs during the 1960s. It means that people should often and even automatically ask questions about any widely held belief or any idea handed down by leaders, teachers, scientists, and other authorities. While it can be helpful to ask questions about the things we're taught by authority—indeed, that's one purpose of thesis essays—it can also be unhelpful to question all authority thoughtlessly and impulsively. Yes, sometimes authority is wrong or harmful, and we could all make a long list of rotten Pied Pipers and bad ideas that have led humanity astray. But no, not all traditional beliefs and long-standing moral truths are wrong or harmful—if heeded, they can make our world a better place.

The following opinion piece is by Christina Hoff Sommers, a professor at Clark University. In this article she laments the loss of respect that young people accord to the authority of tradition and moral truth. Read the article as a class or with a teacher and then follow the instructions at the end of the article. **B C** **TE**

Are We Living in a Moral Stone Age?

—by Christina Hoff Sommers

Christina Hoff Sommers is the W.H. Brady Fellow at the American Enterprise Institute in Washington, DC. She is also a professor of philosophy at Clark University, where she has served on the faculty since 1980. . . .

Sommers charges that today's young people are suffering from "cognitive moral confusion." They not only have trouble distinguishing right from wrong—they question whether such standards even exist. The threat this moral relativism poses to society is greater than any external danger. . . .

> We hear a lot today about how Johnny can't read, how he can't write, and the trouble he is having finding France on a map. It is also true that Johnny is having difficulty distinguishing right from wrong. Along with illiteracy and innumeracy, we must add deep moral confusion to the list of educational problems. Increasingly, today's young people know little or nothing about the Western moral tradition.
>
> This was recently demonstrated by *Tonight Show* host Jay Leno. Leno frequently does "man-on-the-street" interviews, and one night he collared some young people to ask them questions about the Bible. "Can you name one of the Ten Commandments?" he asked two college-age women. One replied, "Freedom of speech?" Mr. Leno said to

the other, "Complete this sentence: Let he who is without sin . . ." Her response was: "Have a good time?" Mr. Leno then turned to a young man and asked, "Who, according to the Bible, was eaten by a whale?" The confident answer was, "Pinocchio."

As with many humorous anecdotes, the underlying reality is not funny at all. These young people are morally confused. They are the students I and other teachers of ethics see every day. Like most professors, I am acutely aware of the "hole in the moral ozone."[21] One of the best things our schools can do for America is to set about repairing it—by confronting the moral nihilism that is now the norm for so many students.

I believe that schools at all levels can do a lot to improve the moral climate of our society. They can help restore civility and community if they commit themselves and if they have the courage to act.

Conceptual Moral Chaos

When you have as many conversations with young people as I do, you come away both exhilarated and depressed. Still, there is a great deal of simple good-heartedness, instinctive fair-mindedness, and spontaneous generosity of spirit in them. Most of the students I meet are basically decent individuals. They form wonderful friendships and seem to be considerate of and grateful to their parents—more so than the baby boomers[22] were.

In many ways they are more likable than the baby boomers—they are less fascinated with themselves and more able to laugh at their faults. An astonishing number are doing volunteer work (70 percent of college students, according to one annual survey of freshmen). They donate blood to the Red Cross in record numbers and deliver food to housebound elderly people. They spend summer vacations working with deaf children or doing volunteer work in Mexico. This is a generation of kids that, despite relatively little moral guidance or religious training, is putting compassion into practice.

Conceptually and culturally, however, today's young people live in a moral haze.[23] Ask one of them if there are such things as "right" and "wrong," and suddenly you are confronted with a confused, tongue-tied, nervous, and insecure individual. The same person who works weekends for Meals on Wheels, who volunteers for a suicide prevention hotline or a domestic violence shelter might tell you, "Well, there really is no such thing as right or wrong. It's kind of like whatever works best for the individual. Each person has to work it out for himself." The trouble is that this kind of answer, which is

21. The ozone layer in the upper atmosphere surrounding Earth filters out harmful radiation from the sun. During the 1970s, scientists recognized that certain man-made chemicals were depleting the ozone layer, creating a "hole" in the stratosphere. In this article, Sommers compares the lack of moral literacy to an ozone hole. She believes that the ability to think morally provides a layer of protection around culture and civilization.
22. baby boomers: the generation of Americans born roughly between the end of World War II (1945) and the beginning of the 1960s
23. Sommers means that young people are unable to form a clear understanding of morality, either in their heads or in the way they live.

so common as to be typical, is no better than the moral philosophy of a sociopath.[24]

I often meet students incapable of making even one single confident moral judgment. And it's getting worse. The things students now say are more and more unhinged. Recently, several of my students objected to philosopher Immanuel Kant's "principle of humanity"— the doctrine that asserts the unique dignity and worth of every human life. They told me that if they were faced with the choice between saving their pet or a human being, they would choose the former.

We have been thrown back into a moral Stone Age; many young people are totally unaffected by thousands of years of moral experience and moral progress. The notion of objective moral truths is in disrepute. And this mistrust of objectivity has begun to spill over into other areas of knowledge. Today, the concept of objective truth in science and history is also being impugned. An undergraduate at Williams College recently reported that her classmates, who had been taught that "all knowledge is a social construct,"[25] were doubtful that the Holocaust ever occurred. One of her classmates said, "Although the Holocaust may not have happened, it's a perfectly reasonable conceptual hallucination."[26]

A creative writing teacher at Pasadena City College wrote an article in the Chronicle of Higher Education about what it is like to teach Shirley Jackson's celebrated short story "The Lottery" to today's college students. It is a tale of a small farming community that seems normal in every way; its people are hardworking and friendly. As the plot progresses, however, the reader learns this village carries out an annual lottery in which the loser is stoned to death.

It is a shocking lesson about primitive rituals in a modern American setting. In the past, the students had always understood "The Lottery" as a warning about the dangers of mindless conformity, but now they merely think that it is "Neat!" or "Cool!" Today, not one of the teacher's current students will go out on a limb and take a stand against human sacrifice.

The Loss of Truth

It was not always thus. When Thomas Jefferson wrote that all men have the right to "life, liberty, and the pursuit of happiness," he did not say, "At least that is my opinion." He declared it as an objective truth. When Elizabeth Cady Stanton amended the Declaration of Independence by changing the phrase "all men" to "all men and women," she was not merely giving an opinion; she was insisting that females are endowed with the same rights and entitlements as males.

24. sociopath: someone who has a personality disorder that mutes his sense of right and wrong, and who has difficulty feeling concern for the suffering of others

25. social construct: a set of ideas accepted by a certain group of people, but not true for everybody

26. conceptual hallucination: a false, mistaken idea; a figment of the imagination

The assertions of both Jefferson and Stanton were made in the same spirit—as self-evident truths and not as personal judgments. Today's young people enjoy the fruits of the battles fought by these leaders, but they themselves are not being given the intellectual and moral training to argue for and to justify truth. In fact, the kind of education they are getting is systematically undermining their common sense about what is true and right.

Let me be concrete and specific: Men and women died courageously fighting the Nazis. They included American soldiers, Allied soldiers, and resistance fighters. Because brave people took risks to do what was right and necessary, Hitler was eventually defeated. Today, with the assault on objective truth, many college students find themselves unable to say why the United States was on the right side in that war. Some even doubt that America was in the right. To add insult to injury, they are not even sure that the salient events of the Second World War ever took place. They simply lack confidence in the objectivity of history.

Too many young people are morally confused, ill-informed, and adrift. This confusion gets worse rather than better once they go to college. If they are attending an elite school, they can actually lose their common sense and become clever and adroit intellectuals in the worst sense. George Orwell reputedly said, "Some ideas are so absurd that only an intellectual could believe them." Well, the students of such intellectuals are in the same boat. Orwell did not know about the tenured radicals of the 1990s, but he was presciently aware that they were on the way.

The Great Relearning

The problem is not that young people are ignorant, distrustful, cruel, or treacherous. And it is not that they are moral skeptics. They just talk that way. To put it bluntly, they are conceptually clueless.[27] The problem I am speaking about is *cognitive*.[28] Our students are suffering from "cognitive moral confusion."

What is to be done? How can we improve their knowledge and understanding of moral history? How can we restore their confidence in the great moral ideals? How can we help them become morally articulate, morally literate, and morally self-confident?

In the late 1960s, a group of hippies[29] living in the Haight-Ashbury District of San Francisco decided that hygiene was a middle class hang-up that they could best do without. So, they decided to live without it. For example, baths and showers, while not actually banned, were frowned upon. The essayist and novelist Tom Wolfe was intrigued by these hippies who, he said, "sought nothing less than to sweep aside all

27. conceptually clueless: unable to think clearly about ideas
28. cognitive: mental; intellectual
29. hippies: typically young people in the 1960s who rejected conventional lifestyles and created an alternative culture which often involved drugs, psychedelic rock music, antiwar protests, and promiscuity

codes and restraints of the past and start out from zero."

Before long, the hippies' aversion to modern hygiene had consequences that were as unpleasant as they were unforeseen. Wolfe describes them: "At the Haight-Ashbury Free Clinic there were doctors who were treating diseases no living doctor had ever encountered before, diseases that had disappeared so long ago they had never even picked up Latin names, such as the mange, the grunge, the itch, the twitch, the thrush, the scroff, the rot." The itching and the manginess eventually began to vex the hippies, leading them to seek help from the local free clinics. Step by step, they had to rediscover for themselves the rudiments of modern hygiene. Wolfe refers to this as the "Great Relearning."

▲ Jefferson Airplane was a popular band among hippies; they dressed in fairly typical hippie fashion.

The Great Relearning is what has to happen whenever earnest reformers extirpate[30] too much. When, "starting from zero," they jettison basic social practices and institutions, abandon common routines, defy common sense, reason, conventional wisdom—and, sometimes, sanity itself.

We saw this with the most politically extreme experiments of our century: Marxism, Maoism, and fascism.[31] Each movement had its share of zealots and social engineers who believed in "starting from zero." They had faith in a new order and ruthlessly cast aside traditional arrangements. Among the unforeseen consequences were mass suffering and genocide. Russians and Eastern Europeans are just beginning their own "Great Relearning." They now realize to their dismay, that starting from zero is a calamity and that the structural damage wrought by the political zealots has handicapped their societies for decades to come. They are also learning that it is far easier to tear apart a social fabric than it is to piece it together again.

America, too, has had its share of revolutionary developments—not so much political as moral. We are living through a great experiment in "moral deregulation," an experiment whose first principle seems to be: "Conventional morality is oppressive." What is right is what works for us. We question everything. We casually, even gleefully, throw out old-fashioned customs and practices. Oscar Wilde once said, "I can resist

30. extirpate: uproot or erase
31. Marxism, named after the political philosopher Karl Marx, is another name for communism. Maoism is a variation of communism named after Mao Zedong, the twentieth-century dictator of China. Fascism is a political system under the control of a nationalistic dictator such as Hitler or Mussolini. All three systems of government are totalitarian, as they seek total control of people through the use of terror and secret police.

everything except temptation." Many in the Sixties generation made succumbing to temptation and license their philosophy of life.

We now jokingly call looters "non-traditional shoppers." Killers are described as "morally challenged"—again jokingly, but the truth behind the jokes is that moral deregulation is the order of the day. We poke fun at our own society for its lack of moral clarity. In our own way, we are as down and out as those poor hippies knocking at the door of the free clinic.

We need our own Great Relearning. Here, I am going to propose a few ideas on how we might carry out this relearning. I am going to propose something that could be called "moral conservationism." It is based on this premise: We are born into a moral environment just as we are born into a natural environment. Just as there are basic environmental necessities, like clean air, safe food, fresh water, there are basic moral necessities. What is a society without civility, honesty, consideration, self-discipline? Without a population educated to be civil, considerate, and respectful of one another, what will we end up with? Not much. For as long as philosophers and theologians have written about ethics, they have stressed the moral basics. We live in a moral environment. We must respect and protect it. We must acquaint our children with it. We must make them aware it is precious and fragile.

I have suggestions for specific reforms. They are far from revolutionary, and indeed some are pretty obvious. They are "common sense," but unfortunately, we live in an age when common sense is becoming increasingly hard to come by.

. . . The last few decades of the twentieth century have seen a steady erosion of knowledge and a steady increase in moral relativism. This is partly due to the diffidence[32] of many teachers who are confused by all the talk about pluralism.[33] Such teachers actually believe that it is wrong to "indoctrinate" our children in our own culture and moral tradition.

Of course, there are pressing moral issues around which there is no consensus; as a modern pluralistic society we are arguing about all sorts of things. This is understandable. Moral dilemmas arise in every generation. But, long ago, we achieved consensus on many basic moral questions. Cheating, cowardice, and cruelty are wrong. As one pundit put it, "The Ten Commandments are not the Ten Highly Tentative Suggestions."

While it is true that we must debate controversial issues, we must not forget there exists a core of noncontroversial ethical issues that were settled a long time ago. We must make students aware that there is a standard of ethical ideals that all civilizations worthy of the name have discovered. We must encourage them to read the Bible, Aristotle's *Ethics*, Shakespeare's *King Lear*, the Koran, and the *Analects* of Confucius.

32. diffidence: shyness, timidity
33. pluralism: the toleration of different religious and cultural groups in a society

When they read almost any great work, they will encounter these basic moral values: integrity, respect for human life, self-control, honesty, courage, and self-sacrifice. All the world's major religions proffer some version of the Golden Rule, if only in its negative form: Do not do unto others as you would not have them do unto you.

We must teach the literary classics. We must bring the great books and the great ideas back into the core of the curriculum. We must transmit the best of our political and cultural heritage. Franz Kafka[34] once said that a great work of literature melts the "frozen sea within us." There are also any number of works of art and works of philosophy that have the same effect.

American children have a right to their moral heritage. They should know the Bible. They should be familiar with the moral truths in the tragedies of Shakespeare, in the political ideas of Jefferson, Madison, and Lincoln. They should be exposed to the exquisite moral sensibility in the novels of Jane Austen, George Eliot, and Mark Twain, to mention some of my favorites. These great works are their birthright.

This is not to say that a good literary, artistic, and philosophical education suffices to create ethical human beings; nor is it to suggest that teaching the classics is all we need to do to repair the moral ozone. What we know is that we cannot, in good conscience, allow our children to remain morally illiterate. All healthy societies pass along their moral and cultural traditions to their children.

And so I come to another basic reform: Teachers, professors, and other social critics should be encouraged to moderate their attacks on our culture and its institutions. They should be encouraged to treat great literary works as literature and not as reactionary political tracts. In many classrooms today, students only learn to "uncover" the allegedly racist, sexist, and elitist elements in the great books.

Meanwhile, pundits,[35] social critics . . . and other intellectuals . . . never seem to tire of running down our society and its institutions and traditions. We are a society overrun by determined advocacy groups that overstate the weaknesses of our society and show very little appreciation for its merits and strengths. I would urge those professors and teachers who use their classrooms to disparage America to consider the possibility that they are doing more harm than good. Their goal may be to create sensitive, critical citizens, but what they are actually doing is producing confusion and cynicism. Their goal may be to improve students' awareness of the plight of exploited peoples, but what they are actually doing is producing kids who are capable of doubting that the Holocaust took place and kids who are incapable of articulating moral objections to human sacrifice.

34. Franz Kafka: a Bohemian Jewish writer of the early twentieth century
35. pundits: political commentators, opinion-makers in the news

In my opinion, we are today not unlike those confused, scrofulous[36] hippies of the late 1960s who finally showed up at the doors of the free clinics in Haight-Ashbury to get their dose of traditional medicine. I hope we have the good sense to follow their example. We need to take an active stand against the divisive unlearning that is corrupting the integrity of our society.

William Butler Yeats[37] talked of the "center" and warned us that it is not holding. Others talk of the threats to our social fabric and tradition. But we are still a sound society; in more than one sense, we have inherited a very healthy constitution from our Founding Fathers. We know how to dispel the moral confusion and get back our bearings and our confidence. We have traditions and institutions of proven strength and efficacy, and we are still strong.

We need to bring back the great books and the great ideas. We need to transmit the best of our political and cultural heritage. We need to refrain from cynical attacks against our traditions and institutions. We need to expose the folly of all the schemes for starting from zero. We need to teach our young people to understand, respect, and protect the institutions that protect us and preserve our kindly, free, and democratic society.

This we can do. And when we engage in the Great Relearning that is so badly needed today, we will find that the lives of our morally enlightened children will be saner, safer, more dignified, and more humane.[38]

36. scrofulous: diseased
37. William Butler Yeats: an Irish poet of the early twentieth century
38. Christina Hoff Sommers, "Are We Living in a Moral Stone Age?", *Imprimis* 27, no. 3 (March 1998), https://imprimis.hillsdale.edu/are-we-living-in-a-moral-stone-age/. Reprinted by permission from IMPRIMIS, the monthly journal of Hillsdale College.

Take fifteen to twenty minutes to think and write about the following list of questions. After you have put some ideas on paper, discuss your ideas with your classmates.

1. What is Sommers's main concern for our culture and society when young people lose the ability to tell the difference between right and wrong?

   Sample answer: Sommers's main concern is that morality will break down so much that our culture and our society will fall into ruin. Young people are the future of any nation, and if it's true they're no longer learning right from wrong, the nation cannot long survive. This is because trust, safety, and decency are the glue that hold a society together.

2. In your opinion, when is it helpful to question authority and when does it become unhelpful?

   Sample answer: Probably the most helpful time to question authority is when authority is telling people to do something morally wrong. We must not allow the power of authority to blind us to issues of right and wrong. Of course, it's important—as Sommers notes—for people to have a moral center so that they know when a behavior is morally wrong.

   It becomes unhelpful to question authority when the questioning is impulsive and thoughtless, or when its aim is to tear down legitimate authority.

3. Give an example of a situation in which people should respect or accept the authority of moral truth.

   Sample answer: People should respect the authority of moral truth during heated social or political events, such as a riot. When riots happen, people often loot nearby stores, carrying off everything they can and burning businesses to the ground. It shouldn't take police officers on the scene to prevent people from stealing or burning another person's property. People in that situation should respect basic moral truth and refrain from hurting the livelihood of other people.

4. Give an example of a situation from history in which questioning authority might have been appropriate.

Sample answer: There are many examples in history of times when questioning authority, especially early in unfolding events, might have kept disaster from happening. Some examples are the Massacre of the Innocents by King Herod the Great, the Reign of Terror during the French Revolution, the Salem witch trials, the Plessy vs. Ferguson Supreme Court decision, the Holocaust, the Chinese Cultural Revolution, and the Rwandan genocide—to name a few.

5. Do you agree or disagree with Sommers's concerns? Why or why not?

Sample answer: I agree with Sommers's concerns, as I've observed moral confusion firsthand and have seen its negative consequences. I've seen online bullying that was shrugged off by students. At some schools, cheating on tests has become an epidemic. In both of those cases, the consequences of moral confusion have been harmful to someone and, ultimately, to our society. I agree with Sommers that we need "a great relearning" so that trust, goodwill, and responsibility can turn our society from this dangerous direction.

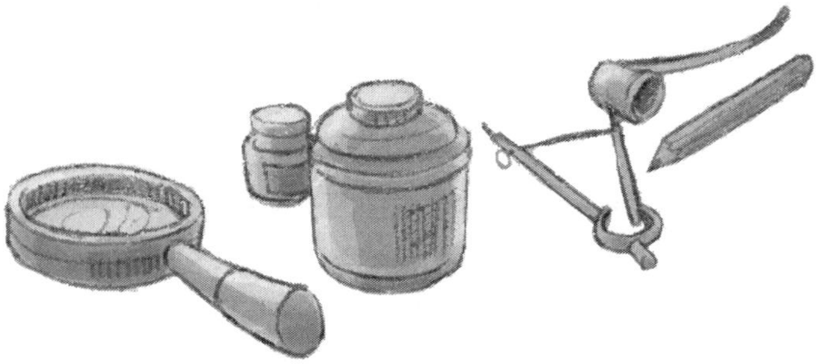

Go Deeper—

1. **DIRECT QUOTES:** In this exercise you will use excerpts from a variety of authors to practice giving context to quotes. After each passage, you will find instructions for writing a paragraph of three to five sentences that explains or analyzes the excerpt. Include at least one quote from the excerpt that supports your analysis, being sure to introduce and give context to the quote you choose. In other words, be sure to show how the quote relates to your analysis.

   Tips:

   - Try to lift a short phrase or phrases, a sentence, or at most two sentences. The idea is to keep the quotation(s) short and to the point.
   - Use the author's name and occupation as you introduce the quote, and somewhere in the paragraph include the title of the work cited. You can find the information you will need in each excerpt's title and in its footnoted citation.
   - It's helpful to your reader to know some details about the author that are relevant to the authority of the quote, but avoid any long-winded information that would submerge the quote.
   - Be sure to include an in-text citation for the quote. The information you need for citations can be found in the excerpt's title and footnoted citation.
   - Give context to the quote. In other words, explain the quote and how it relates to your analysis.
   - It is important to be fair to the author and not stretch the meaning of the quote beyond its purpose.
   - In formal writing, you should generally avoid first-person perspective: "I," "me," "my." For example, avoid using "I think," "in my opinion," and "I believe." The reader will assume that the opinions are yours already. Some writers (like Sommers in the previous exercise) use "I think" and "I believe" to soften their opinions, but this sort of moderation is only occasionally necessary.[D] TE
   - Keep in mind that different people will find different parts of the passage relevant to their explanation or analysis. In other words, you may choose a different quote than your classmate does. The key is to be certain that the quote you choose is relevant in some way.

Example:

The Two Towers

by J.R.R. Tolkien, fantasy writer

The Lord of the Rings is a David-and-Goliath story in which little people, hobbits, must save the world from a powerful evil ruler named Sauron. *The Two Towers* is the second volume in *The Lord of the Rings*. In this scene, a warrior prince named Faramir—one of the good guys—describes his hope for civilization.

> "For myself," said Faramir, "I would see the White Tree in flower again in the courts of the kings, and the Silver Crown return, and Minas Tirith[39] in peace. . . . War must be, while we defend our lives against a destroyer who would devour all; but I do not love the bright sword for its sharpness, nor the arrow for its swiftness, nor the warrior for his glory. I love only that which they defend: the City of the Men of Númenor;[40] and I would have her loved for her memory, her ancientry, her beauty, and her present wisdom."[41]

Sample analysis #1:
Write a paragraph that explains how Tolkien feels about war and weapons.

Fantasy writer J.R.R. Tolkien feels that there is not much reason to praise war and weapons. Through the words of a warrior prince, Faramir, the author of *The Two Towers* writes, "I do not love the bright sword for its sharpness, nor the arrow for its swiftness, nor the warrior for his glory. I love only that which they defend" (331). Through Faramir, Tolkien expresses that he sees little value in weapons and warriors other than their ability to guard what he truly values, the vulnerable parts of society.

39. Minas Tirith: a fictitious city whose castle courtyard was crowned by a beautiful White Tree
40. Men of Númenor: in Tolkien's mythology, a race of men who came from distant islands
41. J.R.R. Tolkien, *The Two Towers* (New York: Ballantine Books, 1982), 331. Copyright © 1954, 1965, 1966 by J.R.R. Tolkien, renewed 1982 by Christopher R. Tolkien, Michael H.R. Tolkien, John F.R. Tolkien, and Priscilla M.A.R. Tolkien; and renewed 1993, 1994 by Christopher R. Tolkien, John F.R. Tolkien, and Priscilla M.A.R. Tolkien. Reprinted by permission of Houghton Mifflin Harcourt Publishing Company (US) and HarperCollins Publishers Ltd. (UK). All rights reserved.

Sample analysis #2:
Write a paragraph that shows how Tolkien's warning about a "destroyer who would devour all" might foreshadow recent history.

In *The Two Towers*, fantasy writer J.R.R. Tolkien appears to foreshadow the rise of recent dictators such as Kim Jong-Il of North Korea, Idi Amin of Uganda, and Nicolae Ceauşescu of Romania. Tolkien's character Faramir speaks about "a destroyer who would devour all" and speaks of protecting his home, which he values for "her memory, her ancientry, her beauty, and her present wisdom," from that destroyer (331). Just as Tolkien described, these recent dictators were clearly bent on devouring everything good in civilization. One of the ways that dictators control people is by draining a culture of its memory of the past, as well as the beauty and wisdom that give it strength.

A. *The Right Stuff*

by Tom Wolfe, journalist

In this passage, Wolfe describes the bleak location of Muroc, California.[42]

Muroc was up in the high elevations of the Mojave Desert. It looked like some fossil landscape that had long since been left behind by the rest of terrestrial evolution. It was full of huge dry lake beds, the biggest being Rogers Lake. Other than sagebrush the only vegetation was Joshua trees, twisted freaks of the plant world that looked like a cross between cactus and Japanese bonsai. They had a dark petrified green color and horribly crippled branches. At dusk the Joshua trees stood out in silhouette on the fossil wasteland like some arthritic nightmare. In the summer the temperature went up to 110 degrees as a matter of course, and the dry lake beds were covered in sand, and there would be windstorms and sandstorms right out of a Foreign Legion movie. At night it would drop to near freezing, and in December it would start raining, and the dry lakes would fill up with a few inches of water, and some sort of putrid prehistoric shrimps would work their way up from out of the ooze.[43]

42. The settlement of Muroc no longer exists. It has been absorbed into the large tracts of Edwards Air Force Base.
43. Tom Wolfe, "The High Desert," in *The Right Stuff* (New York: Picador, 1979), 35. Copyright © 1979 by Tom Wolfe. Reprinted by permission of Farrar, Straus and Giroux (US) and The Random House Group Ltd. © 1980 (UK).

Write a paragraph that explains what Tom Wolfe is saying about Muroc in the Mojave Desert. Remember to include at least one quotation from the excerpt to support your topic.

Sample answer: In his novel *The Right Stuff*, journalist Tom Wolfe describes Muroc as a desolate location that does not seem fit for human habitation. He says that it is "full of huge dry lake beds" and "twisted freaks of the plant world," and there are "windstorms and sandstorms" as well as extremely hot and cold temperatures (35). Any place that looks like that would certainly seem strange and unwelcoming, and human beings certainly can't thrive in such extremes.

B. *R.U.R. (Rossum's Universal Robots)*

by Karel Čapek, Czech playwright

R.U.R. was a groundbreaking science fiction play in the 1920s. It popularized the use of the word "robot" and also the idea that artificial intelligence might take control of the world. The subtitle to the play reads, "Robots of the world! The power of man has fallen! A new world has arisen: the Rule of the Robots! March!" In this excerpt, the engineers of a robot manufacturing company, R.U.R., are explaining the "wonders" of robotry to a visitor.

Act I-9 **Domin:** To manufacture artificial workers is the same thing as to manufacture gasoline motors. The process must be of the simplest, and the product of the best from a practical point of view. What sort of worker do you think is the best from a practical point of view? . . . [Not the one who is most honest and hardworking.] No; the one that is the cheapest. The one whose requirements are the smallest. Young Rossum invented a worker with the minimum amount of requirements. He had to simplify him. He rejected everything that did not contribute directly to the progress of work!—everything that makes man more expensive. In fact, he rejected man and made the Robot. . . . The Robots are not people. Mechanically they are more perfect than we are, they have an enormously developed intelligence, but they have no soul. . . . Act I-21 You can say whatever you like to them. You can read the Bible, recite the multiplication table, whatever you please. You can even preach to them about human rights. . . .

Act I-22 **Fabry:** . . . One Robot can replace two and a half workmen. The human machine . . . was terribly imperfect. It had to be removed sooner or later.

Busman: It was too expensive.

Fabry: It was not effective. It no longer answers the requirements of modern engineering. Nature has no idea of keeping pace with modern labor. For example: from a technical point of view, the whole of childhood is a sheer absurdity. So much time lost.[44]

Write a paragraph that explains why the author of *R.U.R.* thinks that robots may replace human beings in many jobs. Remember to include at least one quotation from the excerpt to support your topic.

Sample answer: Czech playwright Karel Čapek, who popularized the word "robot" in his play *R.U.R.*, tells his audience that robots may replace human workers because they can do more and they demand less than a human worker. He says that they are "worker[s] with the minimum amount of requirements" (I-9). According to Čapek, a robot is cheaper than a person, it can replace two and a half workmen, and it doesn't require the lengthy growth and education of childhood. What's more terrifying, a robot is intelligent but lacks a soul and, by extension, a conscience—it will do any job. These qualities make a robot more efficient and less needy than a human worker, which makes the robot the more desirable worker.

C. *Gifted Hands*

by Ben Carson, MD, neurosurgeon

In this passage, brain surgeon Ben Carson describes what happens as a young girl is wheeled out of brain surgery.

Finally we were finished [with the operation]. Maranda's skull was carefully sewed back in place with strong sutures. . . . We didn't know if the seizures would stop. We didn't know if Maranda would ever walk or talk again. We could do only one thing—wait and see. . . . I followed Maranda's gurney out of surgery. She looked small and vulnerable under the pale green sheet as the orderly wheeled her down the hall toward the pediatric intensive care unit. An IV bottle hung from a pole on the gurney. Her eyes were swollen from being under anesthesia for 10 hours. Major fluid shifts in her body had altered the working of her lymph system, causing swell-

44. Adapted from Karel Čapek, *R.U.R. (Rossum's Universal Robots)*, trans. Paul Selver and Nigel Playfair, World Library, accessed July 13, 2018, http://uploads.worldlibrary.org/uploads/pdf/201106180331rur.pdf.

ing. Having the respirator tube down her throat for 10 hours had puffed her lips badly, and her face looked grotesque.

The Franciscos, alert to every sound, heard the gurney creaking down the hallway and ran to meet us. "Wait!" Terry [Maranda's mother] called softly. Her eyes were red-rimmed, her face pale. She went to the gurney, bent down, and kissed her daughter.

Maranda's eyes fluttered open for a second. "I love you, Mommy and Daddy," she said.

Terry burst into joyful tears, and Luis brushed his hand across his eyes.

"She talked!" a nurse squealed. "She talked!"

I just stood there, amazed and excited, as I silently shared in that incredible moment.[45]

Write a paragraph that explains what the author is demonstrating about modern medicine. Remember to include at least one quotation from the excerpt to support your topic.

Sample answer: In his book *Gifted Hands*, neurosurgeon Ben Carson illustrates just how amazing modern medicine can be by telling the story of a girl named Maranda who was suffering from seizures. After brain surgery that might have left her speechless or unable to walk, Maranda responded to a kiss by saying, "I love you, Mommy and Daddy" (148). Even the surgeon seems awestruck by this moment. That a child could speak intelligibly a few short hours after her brain was opened up seems nothing short of miraculous.

D. *How to Cook a Wolf*

by M.F.K. Fisher, food writer and chef

In this excerpt, M.F.K. (Mary Frances Kennedy) Fisher explains the joy of baking bread.

Perhaps this war[46] will make it simpler for us to go back to some of the old ways we knew before we came over to this land and made the Big Money. Perhaps, even, we will remember how to make good bread again.

It does not cost much. It is pleasant: one of those almost hypnotic businesses, like a dance from some ancient ceremony. It leaves you filled with peace, and the house filled with one of the world's sweetest smells. But it takes a lot of time. If you can find that, the

45. Ben Carson, *Gifted Hands* (Grand Rapids, MI: Zondervan, 2008), 148. Copyright © 1990 by Ben Carson. Used by permission of Zondervan, www.zondervan.com.
46. *How to Cook a Wolf* was written during World War II.

rest is easy. And if you cannot rightly find it, make it, for probably there is no chiropractic treatment, no Yoga exercise, no hour of meditation in a music-throbbing chapel, that will leave you emptier of bad thoughts than this homely ceremony of making bread.[47]

Write a paragraph that explains how the author feels about the act of baking bread. Remember to include at least one quotation from the excerpt to support your topic.

Sample answer: Food writer, chef, and author of *How to Cook a Wolf*, M.F.K. Fisher finds contentment and joy in the process of baking homemade bread. She describes the process as taking "a lot of time," but one that is pleasant and "leaves you filled with peace" (74). Her simple description makes plain her feelings about this traditional act.

E. *Hiroshima*

by John Hersey, journalist

Shortly after the atomic bomb blast over the Japanese city of Hiroshima, John Hersey interviewed a number of survivors. The resulting book, *Hiroshima*, chronicles the story of six of those survivors and the horrors they witnessed, including radiation poisoning and burns.

> He was the only person making his way into the city; he met hundreds and hundreds who were fleeing, and every one of them seemed to be hurt in some way. The eyebrows of some were burned off and skin hung from their faces and hands. Others, because of pain, held their arms up as if carrying something in both hands. Some were vomiting as they walked. Many were naked or in shreds of clothing. On some undressed bodies, the burns had made patterns—of undershirt straps and suspenders and, on the skin of some women (since white repelled the heat from the bomb and dark clothes absorbed it and conducted it to the skin), the shapes of flowers they had had on their kimonos. Many, although injured themselves, supported relatives who were worse off. Almost all had their heads bowed, looked straight ahead, were silent, and showed no expression whatsoever.[48]

47. M.F.K. Fisher, *How to Cook a Wolf* (New York: North Point Press, 1954), 74.
48. John Hersey, *Hiroshima* (New York: Vintage Books, 1973), 29. Copyright © 1946, 1985, copyright renewed 1973 by John Hersey. Used by permission of Alfred A. Knopf, an imprint of the Knopf Doubleday Publishing Group, a division of Penguin Random House LLC (US), and Penguin Books Ltd. (UK). All rights reserved. Any third party use of this material, outside of this publication, is prohibited. Interested parties must apply directly to Penguin Random House LLC for permission.

Write a paragraph that explains what the author is illustrating in his writing. Remember to include at least one quotation from the excerpt to support your topic.

Sample answer: In his book *Hiroshima*, journalist John Hersey describes the nightmare experienced by the survivors of the atomic blast over the Japanese city. An eyewitness sees people with eyebrows "burned off" and with skin hanging "from their faces and hands" and with burns that "had made patterns" on their skin (29). Such descriptions clearly depict the pain and horror that is associated with the atom bomb.

2. **PARAPHRASE:** In this exercise, you will put quotations into your own words—paraphrase them—in order to summarize, or condense, them. Keep your paraphrases to no more than two sentences in length. Remember that when you paraphrase you still need to introduce the author of the original text. You may want to include the author's occupation and the title of the work cited in your introduction. Be sure to also include an in-text citation for your source. The information you need for your introductions and citations can be found in the excerpts' titles and footnoted citations.

Example:

"A Bad Day for Sales"

by Fritz Leiber, fantasy and science fiction writer

Robie was still a novelty. Robie was fun. For a little while yet, he could steal the show. But the attention did not make Robie proud. He had no emotions. . . . Robie the robot was the logical conclusion of the development of vending machines. All the earlier machines had stood in one place, on a floor or hanging on a wall, and blankly delivered merchandise in return for coins, whereas Robie searched for customers. He was the demonstration model of a line of sales robots to be manufactured by Shuler Vending Machines.[49]

49. Adapted from Fritz Leiber, "A Bad Day for Sales," *Galaxy Science Fiction*, July 1953, Project Gutenberg, http://www.gutenberg.org/files/50819/50819-h/50819-h.htm.

Paraphrase:

In his short story "A Bad Day for Sales," Fritz Leiber introduces a sales robot named Robie, a vending machine that actively searches for customers. People find him fun and refreshingly different, but since he is a robot, a machine, he doesn't really care what they think of him. E TE

A. *Black Boy*

by Richard Wright, novelist and essayist

[As a young man,] I hungered for books, new ways of looking and seeing. It was not a matter of believing or disbelieving what I read, but of feeling something new, of being affected by something that made the world look different. As dawn broke, I ate my pork and beans, feeling dopey, sleepy. I went to work, but the mood of the book would not die; it lingered, coloring everything I saw, heard, did. . . . Reading was like a drug, a dope. The novels created moods in which I lived for days.[50]

Paraphrase:

Sample answer: When he was a young man, novelist Richard Wright went through a phase where he craved books. They so inflamed his imagination and emotions that they became a part of the way he saw the world (249–50).

B. *Into Thin Air*

by Jon Krakauer, outdoorsman and writer

Straddling the top of the world, one foot in China and the other in Nepal, I cleared the ice from my oxygen mask, hunched a shoulder against the wind, and stared absently down at the vastness of Tibet. I understood on some dim, detached level that the sweep of earth beneath my feet was a spectacular sight. I'd been fantasizing about this moment, and the release of emotion that would accompany it, for many months.

50. Richard Wright, *Black Boy* (New York: Harper Perennial, 1945), 249–50. Copyright 1937, 1942, 1944, 1945 by Richard Wright; renewed © 1973 by Ellen Wright. Reprinted by permission of HarperCollins Publishers (US) and John Hawkins and Associates, Inc. (UK).

But now that I was finally here, actually standing on the summit of Mount Everest, I just couldn't summon the energy to care. . . . I hadn't slept in fifty-seven hours. The only food I had been able to force down over the preceding three days was a bowl of ramen noodles and a handful of peanut M&Ms. Weeks of violent coughing had left me with two separated ribs that made ordinary breathing an excruciating trial.[51]

Paraphrase:

Sample answer: In his book *Into Thin Air*, Krakauer, an outdoorsman and writer, describes his listless, detached emotions on top of Mount Everest. Although he'd always dreamed about summiting the mountain, he finds himself too exhausted to care that he actually made it (7).

c. *A Grief Observed*

by C.S. Lewis, university professor and writer

No one ever told me that grief felt so like fear. I am not afraid, but the sensation is like being afraid. The same fluttering in the stomach, the same restlessness, the yawning. I keep on swallowing.

At other times it feels like being mildly drunk, or concussed. There is a sort of invisible blanket between the world and me. I find it hard to take in what anyone says. Or perhaps, hard to want to take it in. It is so uninteresting. Yet I want the others to be about me. I dread the moments when the house is empty. If only they would talk to one another and not to me.[52]

Paraphrase:

Sample answer: Professor and writer C.S. Lewis tells us that his experience with grief gave him some of the same symptoms as being afraid or brain injured. In addition, he wanted people to be around him, but not interacting with him (3).

51. Jon Krakauer, *Into Thin Air: A Personal Account of the Mount Everest Disaster* (New York: Anchor Books, 1997), 7. Copyright © 1997 by Jon Krakauer. Used by permission of Villard Books, an imprint of Random House, a division of Penguin Random House LLC (US), and by permission of the Licensor through PSClear (UK). All rights reserved. Any third party use of this material, outside of this publication, is prohibited. Interested parties must apply directly to Penguin Random House LLC for permission.

52. C.S. Lewis, *A Grief Observed* (New York: HarperCollins, 1996), 3. Copyright © CS Lewis Pte Ltd 1961. Used by permission of the C.S. Lewis Company Ltd.

3. **ALLUSION:** Remember that an allusion makes reference to a well-known idea, often found in a story, speech, or poem, either by hinting at it indirectly or by borrowing its words directly. In this exercise you will write allusions that could be used to start a speech. For each of the following well-known phrases or sayings, use the information and instructions provided to create an allusion to the saying. Determine who your audience is and then write your allusion in a complete sentence in the space provided.

Example:

Saying: "blood, toil, tears, and sweat"

Origin: Winston Churchill coined this saying in his speech to the British Parliament in 1940 as the nation was preparing for war with Germany. He said, "I say to the House as I said to ministers who have joined this government, I have nothing to offer but blood, toil, tears, and sweat."[53] The phrase itself alludes to the agony of a martyr dying for an important cause.

Instruction: Use the phrase to begin a speech to workers who face a difficult task.

Audience: relief workers

Allusion: No reward is waiting for any of you in the disaster zone except blood, toil, tears, and sweat.

A. Saying: "We hold these truths to be self-evident."

Origin: This saying is from the Declaration of Independence, which was written by Thomas Jefferson. Jefferson is saying that an idea such as "all men are created equal" is so obvious that it doesn't need to be pointed out.

Instruction: Use the phrase to begin a speech by a scientist addressing an important concern for the environment.

Audience: Sample answer: other scientists concerned about pollution

Allusion: Sample answer: We hold these truths to be self-evident: that all people should refrain from fouling the very water they drink and that they shouldn't pollute the very air they breathe.

53. Winston Churchill, "Blood, Toil, Tears and Sweat" (speech), House of Commons, May 13, 1940, London, England, National Churchill Museum, transcript, https://www.nationalchurchillmuseum.org/blood-toil-tears-and-sweat.html.

B. Saying: "Borrow Cupid's wings"

Origin: This saying is from *Romeo and Juliet* by William Shakespeare. It is from Mercutio's line to heavy-hearted Romeo: "Borrow Cupid's wings / And soar with them above a common bound." It means that Romeo should draw upon Cupid's winged power to rise above the heaviness of his feelings.

Instruction: Use this allusion to begin a speech to people who feel sad or frightened.

Audience: Sample answer: college students who are homesick

Allusion: Sample answer: Freshmen students, I urge you to borrow Cupid's wings and make some new friends while you are here at school.

C. Saying: "You have to kiss a lot of frogs to find a prince."

Origin: This saying is from "The Frog Prince" by the Brothers Grimm. It expresses the idea that a lot of trial and error must happen before something worthwhile is discovered.

Instruction: Use this allusion to begin a speech that encourages the audience to be persistent.

Audience: Sample answer: used-car buyers

Allusion: Sample answer: Sure some of these cars look like junk, but take a few for a drive; you have to kiss a lot of frogs to find a prince.

Lesson 6: How to Be Appealing: Ethos, the Appeal to Authority

Tell It Back—Summary

Sample important ideas:

- An authority is a highly respected source of information.
- In addition to trustworthiness, moral authority is an important part of ethos.
- Direct quotes are an important appeal to authority, but they should be kept short and used sparingly.
- When you give context, you are telling the reader how the quote or paraphrase connects to your thesis and how it's important in making your point.
- To avoid plagiarism, it is important to cite one's sources.

Talk About It—

1. Goodwill is essential to trust. A speaker who isn't on the side of humanity, wishing people evil instead of good, may lead an audience astray, and therefore can't be trusted. If a speaker doesn't have an audience's confidence, she will not be able to persuade it. No one who openly tells her audience to do or think something that is harmful or destructive to it can be truly convincing.
2. I am put off by the actor's hypocrisy, which damages his ethos and makes me less likely to heed his message. It causes me to question the actor's character so much that his words and expertise do not seem authoritative to me. Hypocrisy and deceit have the power to damage the credibility of many sincere and potentially helpful causes. In addition, I would question whether an actor should be considered an authority on global warming in the first place. I would be more likely to trust climate scientists who have data on climate change.

Write & Discuss—

[B]Although this article contains some complex ideas, it can be broken down into chunks that are fairly easy to understand. If you think your students might struggle with the article, try reading it out loud, checking for comprehension after each section. Here are summaries of each section:

1. Introduction: The beginning of the article laments the moral confusion experienced by many young people in America today.
2. Conceptual Moral Chaos: Sommers discusses how many young people do good with their lives but have little ability or even desire to express what is meant by "right" or "wrong." They would find it difficult to take a stand against the Holocaust or human sacrifice.
3. The Loss of Truth: These paragraphs describe the loss of objective truth as handed down by history and blame current education as a major cause of moral confusion.
4. The Great Relearning: Sommers compares the problem of lost morality to the hippies' rejection of traditional hygiene in the Haight-Ashbury neighborhood of San Francisco. Just as the hippies fell prey to skin diseases, so too this generation of insecure, rootless young people can fall prey to dangerous ideas. Sommers proposes a "great relearning" as the way to reclaim the moral tradition of the west.

TE

[C]Rhetorical Analysis

As you read through this thesis essay with students, you may want to point out some of its rhetorical strength. Sommers is careful to take a balanced, gentle approach with her subject. She doesn't sound accusatory or condemning of young people, but manages to say kind things about them: "There is a great deal of simple good-heartedness, instinctive fair-mindedness, and spontaneous generosity of spirit in them." Because she is generous, she is able to express her concerns and come off as caring rather than harsh and smug. Also, Sommers does a good job building her ethos. She establishes her role as a confidant of students and shows herself to be articulate and well informed, quoting both current events and Immanuel Kant. The thesis of the piece is clear and well supported: "Schools at all levels can do a lot to improve the moral climate of our society. They can help restore civility and community if they commit themselves and if they have the courage to act." Although her article follows a somewhat different format, Sommers uses many of the features of the thesis essay including confirmation, antithesis, and defense.

Go Deeper—

[D]Although certain conventions are often followed in formal writing, it's important that the student experience is not diminished as a result of following those conventions. For example, asking students to avoid using the first-person perspective does not mean that students should remove their opinions from their writing. Charlotte Mason, an important educator in the early 1900s in England, liked to say that "children are born persons,"[1] meaning that children are already endowed with a personality, with affections, with experiences. They are more than their schooling and the information they store in their heads. Hence, students should still be invited to bring their perspectives, their joys and sorrows, and their experiences to their writing—even if they avoid "I," "me," and "my," which might distract from the authoritative position they are taking. In the end, writing should awaken wonderment and the love of learning that is the inheritance of every child. As educator Marva Collins said to her students at Westside Preparatory School in Chicago, "I want you to read and write so you will never be bored again."[2]

Teachers should help students understand that, even when avoiding the use of the first person, a persuasive thesis is an opinion and thus it is a statement of belief. In our culture we often dismiss a conviction by saying, "It's just what I believe," rather than taking the time and energy to offer evidence and engage other thinkers in our persuasive case. Part of the work of academic writing is to make our opinion so full of observation, support, and analysis that it becomes persuasive to someone else. This supported and developed opinion is not separate from our experience nor from argumentation: All that we have lived and experienced contributes to the thesis statements we write and develop into arguments.

[E]You may want to point out to students that this is an example of a paraphrase whose source does not have page numbers. In this particular case, MLA style suggests that no alternate locator should be used in place of page numbers, and since the source's title and author are already in the text, no parenthetical citation is needed.

1. Charlotte Mason, *Towards a Philosophy of Education*, AmblesideOnline, accessed July 10, 2018, https://www.amblesideonline.org/CM/vol6complete.html#033.
2. *The Marva Collins Story*, directed by Peter Levin, written by Clifford Campion (Studio City, CA: Hallmark Hall of Fame Productions, 1981), film, 100 mins.

The purpose of this lesson is for students to write a thesis essay analyzing a short story. In this lesson, students will practice:

- annotating a story for character, tension, and conflict; plot twists; and significant words and images
- oral summary of a story plot
- character summary in one sentence
- critical thinking
- plot prediction
- changing infinitive verbs to participles
- changing passive voice to active voice
- examining a text and lifting supporting quotes from it
- following an outline
- writing a thesis essay including an introduction, body paragraphs, and a conclusion
- writing a complex thesis
- impromptu speaking
- reducing redundancy and padding
- revision and proofreading

Lesson 7

First Thesis Essay: Analysis of a Short Story

You may remember reading in lesson 1 about narcissism, or excessive self-love (see page 5). In this lesson I'd like to introduce you to a fictional narcissist, someone who thinks of herself more highly than she should. Her name is Madame Mathilde Loisel, and she lives in a short story called "The Necklace"[1] by French writer Guy de Maupassant. In this lesson, you'll carefully read Madame Loisel's story and write a thesis essay about it. This particular thesis essay will be a **literary analysis**.

What is a literary analysis? It is an essay that examines a written work, whether fiction or nonfiction, and creates an argument about some aspect of the work—its themes, for example, or its symbolism or how its characters change. We can assume that an author makes deliberate choices and that those choices are fair game for the reader to study and interpret. You may write about what the author intends by her plot or how to interpret her metaphors or why she uses certain words and phrases. The purpose of literary analysis is to take you deeper in your understanding of the written work.

Now, listen: I must confess that when I was an English major in college, writing literary analyses just about killed the pleasure of reading for me. You see, I love books, especially poetry

1. This story is also known as "The Diamond Necklace."

and fiction, and my imagination has been lastingly shaped by authors such as Leo Tolstoy, Langston Hughes, P.G. Wodehouse, and the Brontë sisters. I could never understand why my professors wanted to ruin a perfectly good story or poem by asking me to take it apart and look at its pieces: its plot, for example, or its setting. It was like basking in a beautiful landscape and then ripping it apart stone by stone, tree by tree. In other words, I felt that a literary analysis tore the life out of everything I read.

Looking back, however, I see the lasting benefits of doing literary analysis. I learned to examine critically the messages embedded in my favorite books. There were different layers of meaning that I could excavate in order to gain a deeper understanding of the story and the author's intentions. I learned the different elements that made literature rich, and I can now see these elements at play in every book I read, swirling like the iridescent colors in soap bubbles. In other words, I can delight in literature more because I labored with literary analysis. I hope you will consider this as you work on the analysis in this lesson. Taking a deeper look at the story can help you to enjoy it even more.

With that in mind, when you read "The Necklace" for the first time, read it for pure enjoyment. Then read it a second time, and as you read, look at the story more closely by annotating it with different colors of highlighter markers. Highlight the following:

- any descriptions of major characters
- the point where any major character changes in some way
- sentences that show tension and conflict
- points where the plot takes any sudden turn (plot twists)
- any significant words or images that recur throughout the text

Annotating the important aspects of the story will make it easier for you to locate them when you get down to writing your essay.

The Necklace

—by Guy de Maupassant

The girl was one of those pretty and charming young creatures who sometimes are born, as if by a slip of fate, into a family of clerks. She had no dowry, no expectations, no way of being known, understood, loved, married by any rich and distinguished man; so she let herself be married to a little clerk of the Ministry of Public Instruction.[2]

She dressed plainly because she could not dress well, but she was unhappy as if she had really fallen from a higher station; since with women there is neither caste nor rank, for beauty, grace and charm take the place of family and birth. Natural ingenuity, instinct for what is elegant, a supple mind are their sole hierarchy, and often make of women of the people the equals of the very greatest ladies.

2. clerk of the Ministry of Public Instruction: a lowly office worker in the Department of Education

Mathilde suffered ceaselessly, feeling herself born to enjoy all delicacies and all luxuries. She was distressed at the poverty of her dwelling, at the bareness of the walls, at the shabby chairs, the ugliness of the curtains. All those things, of which another woman of her rank would never even have been conscious, tortured her and made her angry. The sight of the little Breton peasant[3] who did her humble housework aroused in her despairing regrets and bewildering dreams. She thought of silent antechambers hung with Oriental tapestry, illumined by tall bronze candelabra, and of two great footmen in knee breeches who sleep in the big armchairs, made drowsy by the oppressive heat of the stove. She thought of long reception halls hung with ancient silk, of the dainty cabinets containing priceless curiosities and of the little coquettish perfumed reception rooms made for chatting at five o'clock with intimate friends, with men famous and sought after, whom all women envy and whose attention they all desire.

When she sat down to dinner, before the round table covered with a tablecloth in use three days, opposite her husband, who uncovered the soup tureen and declared with a delighted air, "Ah, the good soup! I don't know anything better than that," she thought of dainty dinners, of shining silverware, of tapestry that peopled the walls with ancient personages and with strange birds flying in the midst of a fairy forest; and she thought of delicious dishes served on marvellous plates and of the whispered gallantries to which you listen with a sphinxlike smile while you are eating the pink meat of a trout or the wings of a quail.

She had no gowns, no jewels, nothing. And she loved nothing but that. She felt made for that. She would have liked so much to please, to be envied, to be charming, to be sought after.

She had a friend, a former schoolmate at the convent, who was rich, and whom she did not like to go to see any more because she felt so sad when she came home.

But one evening her husband reached home with a triumphant air and holding a large envelope in his hand.

"There," said he, "there is something for you."

She tore the paper quickly and drew out a printed card which bore these words:

> *The Minister of Public Instruction and Madame Georges Ramponneau request the honor of M. and Madame Loisel's company at the palace of the Ministry on Monday evening, January 18th.*

Instead of being delighted, as her husband had hoped, she threw the invitation on the table crossly, muttering:

"What do you wish me to do with that?"

"Why, my dear, I thought you would be glad. You never go out, and this is such a fine opportunity. I had great trouble to get it. Every one wants to go; it is very select, and they are not giving many invitations to clerks. The whole official world will be there."

She looked at him with an irritated glance and said impatiently:

"And what do you wish me to put on my back?"

He had not thought of that. He stammered:

"Why, the gown you go to the theatre in. It looks very well to me."

---

3. Breton peasant: a poor farm girl from the province of Brittany in France

He stopped, distracted, seeing that his wife was weeping. Two great tears ran slowly from the corners of her eyes toward the corners of her mouth.

"What's the matter? What's the matter?" he answered.

By a violent effort she conquered her grief and replied in a calm voice, while she wiped her wet cheeks:

"Nothing. Only I have no gown, and, therefore, I can't go to this ball. Give your card to some colleague whose wife is better equipped than I am."

He was in despair. He resumed:

"Come, let us see, Mathilde. How much would it cost, a suitable gown, which you could use on other occasions—something very simple?"

She reflected several seconds, making her calculations and wondering also what sum she could ask without drawing on herself an immediate refusal and a frightened exclamation from the economical clerk.

Finally she replied hesitating:

"I don't know exactly, but I think I could manage it with four hundred francs."

He grew a little pale, because he was laying aside just that amount to buy a gun and treat himself to a little shooting next summer on the plain of Nanterre, with several friends who went to shoot larks there of a Sunday.

But he said:

"Very well. I will give you four hundred francs. And try to have a pretty gown."

The day of the ball drew near and Madame Loisel seemed sad, uneasy, anxious. Her frock was ready, however. Her husband said to her one evening:

"What is the matter? Come, you have seemed very queer these last three days."

And she answered:

"It annoys me not to have a single piece of jewelry, not a single ornament, nothing to put on. I shall look poverty-stricken. I would almost rather not go at all."

"You might wear natural flowers," said her husband. "They're very stylish at this time of year. For ten francs you can get two or three magnificent roses."

She was not convinced.

"No; there's nothing more humiliating than to look poor among other women who are rich."

"How stupid you are!" her husband cried. "Go look up your friend, Madame Forestier, and ask her to lend you some jewels. You're intimate enough with her to do that."

She uttered a cry of joy:

"True! I never thought of it."

The next day she went to her friend and told her of her distress.

Madame Forestier went to a wardrobe with a mirror, took out a large jewel box, brought it back, opened it and said to Madame Loisel:

"Choose, my dear."

She saw first some bracelets, then a pearl necklace, then a Venetian gold cross set with precious stones, of admirable workmanship. She tried on the ornaments before the mirror, hesitated and could not make up her mind to part with them, to give them back. She kept asking:

"Haven't you anymore?"

"Why, yes. Look further; I don't know what you like."

Suddenly she discovered, in a black satin box, a superb diamond necklace, and her heart throbbed with an immoderate desire. Her hands trembled as she took it. She fastened it round her throat, outside her high-necked waist,[4] and was lost in ecstasy at her reflection in the mirror.

Then she asked, hesitating, filled with anxious doubt:

"Will you lend me this, only this?"

"Why, yes, certainly."

She threw her arms round her friend's neck, kissed her passionately, then fled with her treasure.

▲ Late nineteenth-century fashion is noted for its beautiful, shimmering ball gowns. Note that instead of wearing jewelry, this woman is wearing flowers in her hair, as Monsieur Loisel suggested to his wife.

The night of the ball arrived. Madame Loisel was a great success. She was prettier than any other woman present, elegant, graceful, smiling and wild with joy. All the men looked at her, asked her name, sought to be introduced. All the attachés[5] of the Cabinet wished to waltz with her. She was remarked by the minister himself.

She danced with rapture, with passion, intoxicated by pleasure, forgetting all in the triumph of her beauty, in the glory of her success, in a sort of cloud of happiness comprised of all this homage, admiration, these awakened desires and of that sense of triumph which is so sweet to woman's heart.

She left the ball about four o'clock in the morning. Her husband had been sleeping since midnight in a little deserted anteroom with three other gentlemen whose wives were enjoying the ball.

He threw over her shoulders the wraps he had brought, the modest wraps of common life, the poverty of which contrasted with the elegance of the ball dress. She felt this and wished to escape so as not to be remarked by the other women, who were enveloping themselves in costly furs.

Loisel held her back, saying: "Wait a bit. You will catch cold outside. I will call a cab."

But she did not listen to him and rapidly descended the stairs. When they reached the street they could not find a carriage and began to look for one, shouting after the cabmen passing at a distance.

4. waist: also called a shirtwaist; a button-down blouse or bodice that is often decorated with lace and embroidery
5. attaché: a high-ranking man within the Ministry of Public Instruction; a diplomat

They went toward the Seine[6] in despair, shivering with cold. At last they found on the quay[7] one of those ancient night cabs which, as though they were ashamed to show their shabbiness during the day, are never seen round Paris until after dark.

▲ A horse-drawn cab, also known as a hackney carriage.

It took them to their dwelling in the Rue des Martyrs, and sadly they mounted the stairs to their flat. All was ended for her. As to him, he reflected that he must be at the ministry at ten o'clock that morning.

She removed her wraps before the glass so as to see herself once more in all her glory. But suddenly she uttered a cry. She no longer had the necklace around her neck!

"What is the matter with you?" demanded her husband, already half undressed.

She turned distractedly toward him.

"I have—I have—I've lost Madame Forestier's necklace," she cried.

He stood up, bewildered.

"What!—how? Impossible!"

They looked among the folds of her skirt, of her cloak, in her pockets, everywhere, but did not find it.

"You're sure you had it on when you left the ball?" he asked.

"Yes, I felt it in the vestibule of the minister's house."

"But if you had lost it in the street we should have heard it fall. It must be in the cab."

"Yes, probably. Did you take his number?"

"No. And you—didn't you notice it?"

"No."

They looked, thunderstruck, at each other. At last Loisel put on his clothes.

"I shall go back on foot," said he, "over the whole route, to see whether I can find it."

He went out. She sat waiting on a chair in her ball dress, without strength to go to bed, overwhelmed, without any fire, without a thought.

Her husband returned about seven o'clock. He had found nothing.

He went to police headquarters, to the newspaper offices to offer a reward; he went to the cab companies—everywhere, in fact, whither he was urged by the least spark of hope.

She waited all day, in the same condition of mad fear before this terrible calamity.

Loisel returned at night with a hollow, pale face. He had discovered nothing.

"You must write to your friend," said he, "that you have broken the clasp of her necklace and that you are having it mended. That will give us time to turn round."

She wrote at his dictation.

At the end of a week they had lost all hope. Loisel, who had aged five years, declared:

"We must consider how to replace that ornament."

6. Seine: the main river in Paris
7. quay: a landing place along the water's edge

The next day they took the box that had contained it and went to the jeweler whose name was found within. He consulted his books.

"It was not I, madame, who sold that necklace; I must simply have furnished the case."

Then they went from jeweler to jeweler, searching for a necklace like the other, trying to recall it, both sick with chagrin and grief.

They found, in a shop at the Palais Royal,[8] a string of diamonds that seemed to them exactly like the one they had lost. It was worth forty thousand francs. They could have it for thirty-six.

So they begged the jeweler not to sell it for three days yet. And they made a bargain that he should buy it back for thirty-four thousand francs, in case they should find the lost necklace before the end of February.

Loisel possessed eighteen thousand francs which his father had left him. He would borrow the rest.

He did borrow, asking a thousand francs of one, five hundred of another, five louis here, three louis there. He gave notes, took up ruinous obligations, dealt with usurers[9] and all the race of lenders. He compromised all the rest of his life, risked signing a note without even knowing whether he could meet it; and, frightened by the trouble yet to come, by the black misery that was about to fall upon him, by the prospect of all the physical privations and moral tortures that he was to suffer, he went to get the new necklace, laying upon the jeweler's counter thirty-six thousand francs.

When Madame Loisel took back the necklace Madame Forestier said to her with a chilly manner:

"You should have returned it sooner; I might have needed it."

She did not open the case, as her friend had so much feared. If she had detected the substitution, what would she have thought, what would she have said? Would she not have taken Madame Loisel for a thief?

Thereafter Madame Loisel knew the horrible existence of the needy. She bore her part, however, with sudden heroism. That dreadful debt must be paid. She would pay it. They dismissed their servant; they changed their lodgings; they rented a garret under the roof.

She came to know what heavy housework meant and the odious cares of the kitchen. She washed the dishes, using her dainty fingers and rosy nails on greasy pots and pans. She washed the soiled linen, the shirts and the dishcloths, which she dried upon a line; she carried the slops down to the street every morning and carried up the water, stopping for breath at every landing. And dressed like a woman of the people, she went to the fruiterer, the grocer, the butcher, a basket on her arm, bargaining, meeting with impertinence, defending her miserable money, sou by sou.[10]

Every month they had to meet some notes, renew others, obtain more time.

Her husband worked evenings, making up a tradesman's accounts, and late at night he often copied manuscript for five sous a page.

This life lasted ten years.

At the end of ten years they had paid everything, everything, with the rates of usury and the accumulations of the compound interest.

8. Palais Royal: a shopping and theater district in Paris near the palace of the Duke of Orleans
9. usurer: a person who lends money at criminally high interest rates
10. sou: French money of low denomination; "sou by sou" would be like "penny by penny"

Madame Loisel looked old now. She had become the woman of impoverished households—strong and hard and rough. With frowsy hair, skirts askew and red hands, she talked loud while washing the floor with great swishes of water. But sometimes, when her husband was at the office, she sat down near the window and she thought of that gay evening of long ago, of that ball where she had been so beautiful and so admired.

What would have happened if she had not lost that necklace? Who knows? who knows? How strange and changeful is life! How small a thing is needed to make or ruin us!

But one Sunday, having gone to take a walk in the Champs Elysees to refresh herself after the labors of the week, she suddenly perceived a woman who was leading a child. It was Madame Forestier, still young, still beautiful, still charming.

Madame Loisel felt moved. Should she speak to her? Yes, certainly. And now that she had paid, she would tell her all about it. Why not?

She went up.

"Good-day, Jeanne."

The other, astonished to be familiarly addressed by this plain good-wife, did not recognize her at all and stammered:

"But—madame!—I do not know—You must have mistaken."

"No. I am Mathilde Loisel."

Her friend uttered a cry.

"Oh, my poor Mathilde! How you are changed!"

"Yes, I have had a pretty hard life, since I last saw you, and great poverty—and that because of you!"

"Of me! How so?"

"Do you remember that diamond necklace you lent me to wear at the ministerial ball?"

"Yes. Well?"

"Well, I lost it."

"What do you mean? You brought it back."

"I brought you back another exactly like it. And it has taken us ten years to pay for it. You can understand that it was not easy for us, for us who had nothing. At last it is ended, and I am very glad."

Madame Forestier had stopped.

"You say that you bought a necklace of diamonds to replace mine?"

"Yes. You never noticed it, then! They were very similar."

And she smiled with a joy that was at once proud and ingenuous.

Madame Forestier, deeply moved, took her hands.

"Oh, my poor Mathilde! Why, my necklace was [fake]![11] It was worth at most only five hundred francs!"[12][13]

---

11. The original text says "paste" rather than "fake." Paste diamonds were not true diamonds, but rather glass and lead molded to look like diamonds.
12. five hundred francs: about one hundred dollars
13. Guy de Maupassant, "The Diamond Necklace," in *The Entire Original Maupassant Short Stories*, trans. Albert McMaster, A.E. Henderson, Mme. Quesada, et al. (Project Gutenberg, 2004), vol. 4., http://www.gutenberg.org/files/3090/3090-h/3090-h.htm.

Tell It Back—**Summary**

TE

Summarize the plot of "The Necklace" aloud, being sure to include important character names. Then, in the space provided, write one well-crafted sentence that explains how the character of Mathilde Loisel changes throughout the story. Begin the sentence with the phrase "at first."

At first Sample answer: At first Madame Loisel is peevish about not having pretty things and a fashionable life, but after she loses the necklace she accepts the hard and rough life of a common working woman.

Talk About It—

TE 1. When Mathilde Loisel first beheld the necklace, "her heart throbbed with an immoderate desire. Her hands trembled as she took it. She fastened it round her throat, outside her high-necked waist, and was lost in ecstasy at her reflection in the mirror." What does the diamond necklace mean to Madame Loisel? What does it symbolize in the story? Why do you suppose Madame Loisel takes only this one item of jewelry?

TE 2. Similar to a fable, does "The Necklace" have a moral lesson? If so, what might the moral be?

TE 3. Did the Loisels do the right thing when they discovered the missing necklace? What could they have done differently?

TE 4. If the story had continued, what do you think would have happened after Madame Forestier revealed that the necklace was an inexpensive fake?

TE 5. Maupassant tells us that Mathilde Loisel "danced with rapture, with passion, intoxicated by pleasure, forgetting all in the triumph of her beauty, in the glory of her success, in a sort of cloud of happiness comprised of all this homage, admiration, these awakened desires and of that sense of triumph which is so sweet to woman's heart." Is it generally true that "triumph of beauty" and homage and admiration are "sweet to woman's heart"? Can this be generally true for men as well? Where else in this story does Maupassant make general statements about women?

Writing Time—

1. **COPIOUSNESS:** Teachers of rhetoric from ancient times till now believe that the best writers can express the same idea any number of ways. This age-old stretching exercise is known as copiousness (or *copia* in Latin). Renaissance rhetorician Desiderius Erasmus demonstrated copiousness by writing the sentence "Your letter pleased me greatly" in 150 variations.[14] Wow!

   By developing copiousness, writers can adapt their words to better meet the needs of their audience. They can be more skillful at clarifying, summarizing, amplifying, and paraphrasing. They can write variations of a basic sentence and pick the variation that seems most clear, most precise, most interesting, and even most powerful.

   There are many ways to practice and develop copiousness, and you have seen a number of them in previous books in this series. In this exercise, you will learn a couple of tricks for rephrasing a sentence.

   A. *Change the* ***infinitive verb*** *to a participle.* The infinitive form of a verb is its basic form, and it typically starts with "to": to leap, to fly, to soar. You can sometimes change an infinitive verb to a present participle (verb + *-ing*: leaping, flying, soaring) to give your sentence more variety and a slightly less formal sound.

      Author Guy de Maupassant uses the participial form of the verb "to be" in the following example: "She had no dowry, no expectations, no way of being known, understood, loved." Maupassant could have used the infinitive "to be" instead of "being," but the sentence sounds less stilted the way it is written.

      Change the underlined infinitive verb in each of the following sentences to a participle, and write your new sentence in the space provided. You may need to tweak the wording or punctuation slightly so that the sentence makes sense with the new verb form.

      Examples:

      To receive an invitation to a ball was a cause of much happiness in Victorian homes.
      Change to: Receiving an invitation to a ball was a cause of much happiness in Victorian homes.

      Women would try to decorate their hair with flowers, feathers, or a small jewel.
      Change to: Women would try decorating their hair with flowers, feathers, or a small jewel.

14. These variations are found in Erasmus's book *Copia: Foundations of the Abundant Style*.

a. Single men and women attended balls as a way to meet one another.

Sample answer: Single men and women attended balls as a way of meeting one another.

b. Young men sometimes took a few minutes to muster their courage before they attempted to ask young women to dance.

Sample answer: Young men sometimes took a few minutes mustering their courage before asking young women to dance.

c. To refuse an invitation to dance was considered impolite unless the young woman already had a partner.

Sample answer: Refusing an invitation to dance was considered impolite unless the young woman already had a partner.

d. A young man often attempted to bow before he introduced himself to a young woman.

Sample answer: A young man often attempted bowing before he introduced himself to a young woman.

e. A gentleman also liked to escort his partner to and from the dance floor.

Sample answer: A gentleman also liked escorting his partner to and from the dance floor.

f. Dance music lasted until midnight, and only then would the servants of the house begin to serve supper.

Sample answer: Dance music lasted until midnight, and only then would the servants of the house begin serving supper.

g. The light of dawn helped to disband the all-night party.

Sample answer: The light of dawn helped with disbanding the all-night party.

▲ This Spanish couple is clearly fatigued after dancing through the night.

B. *Change passive voice to active voice.* Although passive voice is not strictly wrong from a grammatical perspective, it can make for lame writing. Active voice is sizzling. Passive voice is lukewarm. Active voice is a firm handshake, a slap on the back, a chin-up. Passive voice is a dead-fish handshake, a half-hearted hug, a thumb war. So what is passive voice? It is wording in which the subject of a sentence fails to do the acting and instead is acted upon. In practical terms, passive voice means a slow-moving sentence with excess words. Here are two examples of passive voice:

- The diamonds were shaped by a gem cutter.
- My headache was relieved with peppermint oil.

Notice that "diamonds" and "headache" are the subjects of the sentences. In both cases, the subjects are not doing the acting. Rather, the diamond is acted upon by a gem cutter, and the headache is acted upon with peppermint oil. Passive voice can be remedied by making the actor—the gem cutter or the peppermint oil—into the subject. Here goes:

- A gem cutter shaped the diamonds.
- Peppermint oil relieved my headache.

The sentences in this exercise are inspired by Honoré de Balzac's short story "A Passion in the Desert." In this tale, a French soldier is captured by Arab nomads and carried deep into the Egyptian desert. He escapes his captors and hides in a cave, only to find it occupied by a dangerous panther. For each sentence, change the passive voice to active voice and write your new sentence in the space provided.

Examples:

The desert spring was overshadowed by palm trees.

Change to: Palm trees overshadowed the desert spring.

As his captors fell asleep one by one, it was determined by the French soldier that he should run away.

Change to: As his captors fell asleep one by one, the French soldier determined that he should run away.

a. The soldier was awakened by the sun, and an intolerable heat was produced by its pitiless rays. (2 changes)

Sample answer: The sun awakened the soldier, and its pitiless rays produced an intolerable heat.

b. A huge animal was beheld by him in the cave, lying but two steps from him. (1 change)

Sample answer: He beheld a huge animal in the cave, lying but two steps from him.

c. He was troubled by the panther's sinister appearance. (1 change)

Sample answer: The panther's sinister appearance troubled him.

d. All of her secrets were revealed to him by solitude. (1 change)

Sample answer: Solitude revealed all of her secrets to him.

e. He was drawn by the panther from the quicksand as if by magic. (1 change)

Sample answer: The panther drew him from the quicksand as if by magic.

f. The knife was plunged into the panther's throat by the soldier, and a great groan was given by the beast. (2 changes)

Sample answer: The soldier plunged the knife into the panther's throat, and the beast gave a great groan.

2. **THESIS ESSAY: LITERARY ANALYSIS**—Guy de Maupassant asks the question, "What would have happened if she had not lost that necklace? Who knows? who knows? How strange and changeful is life! How small a thing is needed to make or ruin us!" What would Mathilde Loisel's life have been like if she hadn't lost the necklace? While no one can say for sure, we can speculate what might have happened—and that's where you come in. You are going to write an essay that strives to answer that speculative question.[A] Since this is going to be a thesis essay, you want to persuade your audience (if you can) to agree with your answer, your thesis statement.

[A]If you desire for your class to produce different essays, here are two additional speculative questions for students to consider:

- Would Mathilde Loisel be happy if she had been born to a higher class and more money?
- How does Mathilde Loisel change after the necklace is lost, and is her change for the better?

Here are some important literary terms you can use in your thesis essay:

- character: a person who has a role to play in a story; can be imaginary, as in fiction, or a real person, as in nonfiction
  - flat character (also known as a static character): a simple character who is easy to define and who does not change in the course of a narrative. Sherlock Holmes in the detective stories by Arthur Conan Doyle, Sancho Panza in *Don Quixote* by Miguel de Cervantes, and the Wicked Witch of the West in *The Wonderful Wizard of Oz* by L. Frank Baum are examples of flat characters.
  - round character (also known as a dynamic character): a character who is complex and who changes in the course of a narrative. Jean Valjean in *Les Misérables* by Victor Hugo, the rabbit Hazel in *Watership Down* by Richard Adams, and Lucy Pevensie in The Chronicles of Narnia by C.S. Lewis are examples of round characters. In "The Necklace," Mathilde Loisel is a round character.
- plot: the plan of action and events in a story
- **setting**: the physical location and historical time of a literary work. Panem, a fictional nation, is the physical location in *The Hunger Games* by Suzanne Collins. World War II is the historical time of *The Book Thief* by Markus Zusak.
- **symbol**: a person, place, sign, or other object that represents something in addition to its literal meaning. Rivers are a symbol of eternity in Langston Hughes's poem "The Negro Speaks of Rivers." The ring in *The Lord of the Rings* by J.R.R. Tolkien is a symbol for evil and a thirst for power.
- **theme**: an important idea or topic that is repeated throughout a literary work. Social inequality and growing up are themes in *To Kill a Mockingbird* by Harper Lee.

Types of evidence:
- details
- examples
- facts

Evidence can be presented as:
- quotations
- paraphrases
- summaries

Examining the Text: As you consider your answer to the question "What would Mathilde Loisel's life have been like if she hadn't lost the necklace?", you should have a firm grasp of what happened in the story as it exists. By thinking through the actual story, you can imagine how things might have turned out differently if Madame Loisel had not lost the necklace.

Use your annotations to review the story, locating important aspects such as character changes, conflict, plot twists, and repeated ideas and images. Then answer the following questions and provide textual evidence for your responses in the form of a short quote or two from the story.

 This icon indicates where you will be doing prewriting.

What were Madame Loisel's hopes and dreams before she lost the necklace?

Sample answer: Madame Loisel hoped to be a fashionable woman and dreamed of being celebrated by society men and women.

Supporting quote(s):

Sample answer: "She thought of . . . little coquettish perfumed reception rooms made for chatting at five o'clock with intimate friends, with men famous and sought after, whom all women envy and whose attention they all desire."

How did the loss of the necklace make Madame Loisel a round, or dynamic, character? In other words, what was her character like before the necklace was lost, and how did the years of hardship change her? How did she remain the same?

Sample answer: The loss of the necklace caused Madame Loisel to change from a starry-eyed, self-absorbed young woman into a woman who was at least willing to work hard—sacrifice all comfort—to repay a debt. She did stay somewhat prideful, even at the end, because she felt obliged to announce to Madame Forestier how she had repaid her debt.

Supporting quote(s): ______________________

Sample answers: "She would have liked so much to please, to be envied, to be charming, to be sought after."

"Madame Loisel knew the horrible existence of the needy. She bore her part, however, with sudden heroism."

"And she smiled with a joy that was at once proud and ingenuous."

What was Madame Loisel's relationship with her husband before she lost the necklace?

Sample answer: Madame Loisel considered her husband unworthy of her and felt ungrateful for his devotion.

Supporting quote(s): ______________________

Sample answer: "She looked at him with an irritated glance and said impatiently: 'And what do you wish me to put on my back?' "

Based on your examination of the text, do you think the loss of the necklace changed Madame Loisel's relationship with her husband, or did the relationship remain about the same?

Sample answer: It's hard to imagine that the loss of the necklace didn't change their relationship. The story is unclear whether Madame Loisel becomes any more grateful to her husband or learns to respect him, and it is possible that he continues to be a "nobody" to her, since the author abruptly ceases to mention him. However, there is a hint that they form a common bond in their misery and work closely together to overcome their debts, which could have made their relationship stronger and closer. The fact that Madame Loisel uses a term of togetherness—"us"—in her conversation with Madame Forestier leads me to believe that the Loisels did draw closer as a result of the loss of the necklace.

Supporting quote(s): ______________________

Sample answer: "Every month they had to meet some notes, renew others, obtain more time."

"You can understand that it was not easy for us, for us who had nothing."

Considering Audience: Think about your audience for a moment. For example:

- Has your audience read the short story before? That will determine how much of the story background you need to include in your essay.
- Is your audience already interested in a literary analysis, or is it disinterested and likely to require a strong hook to become engaged?
- What about your purpose for writing the essay? Do you want to encourage your audience by giving a hopeful, rosy answer to the speculative question? Or do you want to caution your audience by showing that Madame Loisel's selfish nature would have gotten worse if she hadn't lost the necklace?

Jot down some notes about your audience here. (If you need a refresher on considering your audience, please flip back to lesson 3.)

Who is my audience? ______________________________

Sample answer: My audience is my teacher and my classmates. They have read the story before and do not require a full recap of the story.

What is my audience's disposition (friendly, neutral, hostile, etc.)? ______________

Sample answer: My audience is neutral. My teacher will be interested in my literary analysis, but I'm not so sure my classmates will be, so I think a strong hook is important.

What is my purpose in writing to my audience (to inform, challenge, delight, awaken, encourage, warn, etc.)? ______________________________

Sample answer: My purpose is to influence my audience. I want the audience to know that sometimes pain and hardship can improve our character. It may be worse to lose our virtue than to lose material things.

Outline: Before you get started, here is the six-paragraph outline you will follow for your thesis essay. A sample completed essay is available at the back of the book.

- I. Introduction
    - A. hook and transition to thesis
    - B. thesis
    - C. explanation of thesis
    - D. transition to next paragraph
- II. Body Paragraph 1: Confirmation/Support
    - A. topic sentence
    - B. explanation of the confirmation
    - C. appeal to authority (evidence in the form of a quote or paraphrase)[A]
- III. Body Paragraph 2: Confirmation/Support
    - A. topic sentence
    - B. explanation of the confirmation
    - C. appeal to authority (evidence in the form of a quote or paraphrase)
- IV. Body Paragraph 3: Refutation/Antithesis
    - A. antithesis (as topic sentence)
    - B. explanation of the antithesis
    - C. refutation of antithesis/defense of thesis
    - D. appeal to authority (evidence in the form of a quote or paraphrase)
- V. Body Paragraph 4: Refutation/Antithesis
    - A. antithesis (as topic sentence)
    - B. explanation of the antithesis
    - C. refutation of antithesis/defense of thesis
    - D. appeal to authority (evidence in the form of a quote or paraphrase)
- VI. Conclusion
    - A. thesis restated
    - B. why the topic is important
    - C. call to action (optional)

[A]You may have noticed that this outline departs slightly from the Aphthonius essay "Should One Marry?" that you saw in lessons 4 and 5. In the marriage essay, Aphthonius does not appeal to authority quite so often as we are requesting here. This is because the essay format we use in this book is designed to conform with the modern thesis essay, which requires more evidence. In these essays you will want to quote or paraphrase the text in each of the body paragraphs.

While this first essay may feel a little daunting, please shrug off those worries. Once you get the hang of the essay form, it'll be a breeze—or at least not a tempest. We're going to walk you through it, every step of the way.

Use the following prompts for each paragraph to help you sketch out your ideas. You can use lists, phrases, or complete sentences for your answers. Then compose your full essay on a separate paper or on a computer.[B] Remember that each paragraph has a job to do in defending the thesis.

The paragraphs you write after going through these steps will be your first draft, or your first version of the essay. Assume that your first draft will need some rewriting to make it the best essay it can be.

[B]If students are struggling with portions of the prewriting or the complete essay, you may want to show them the sample answers in the Teacher's Edition to help them see how the author has accomplished the task.

Thesis Wheel

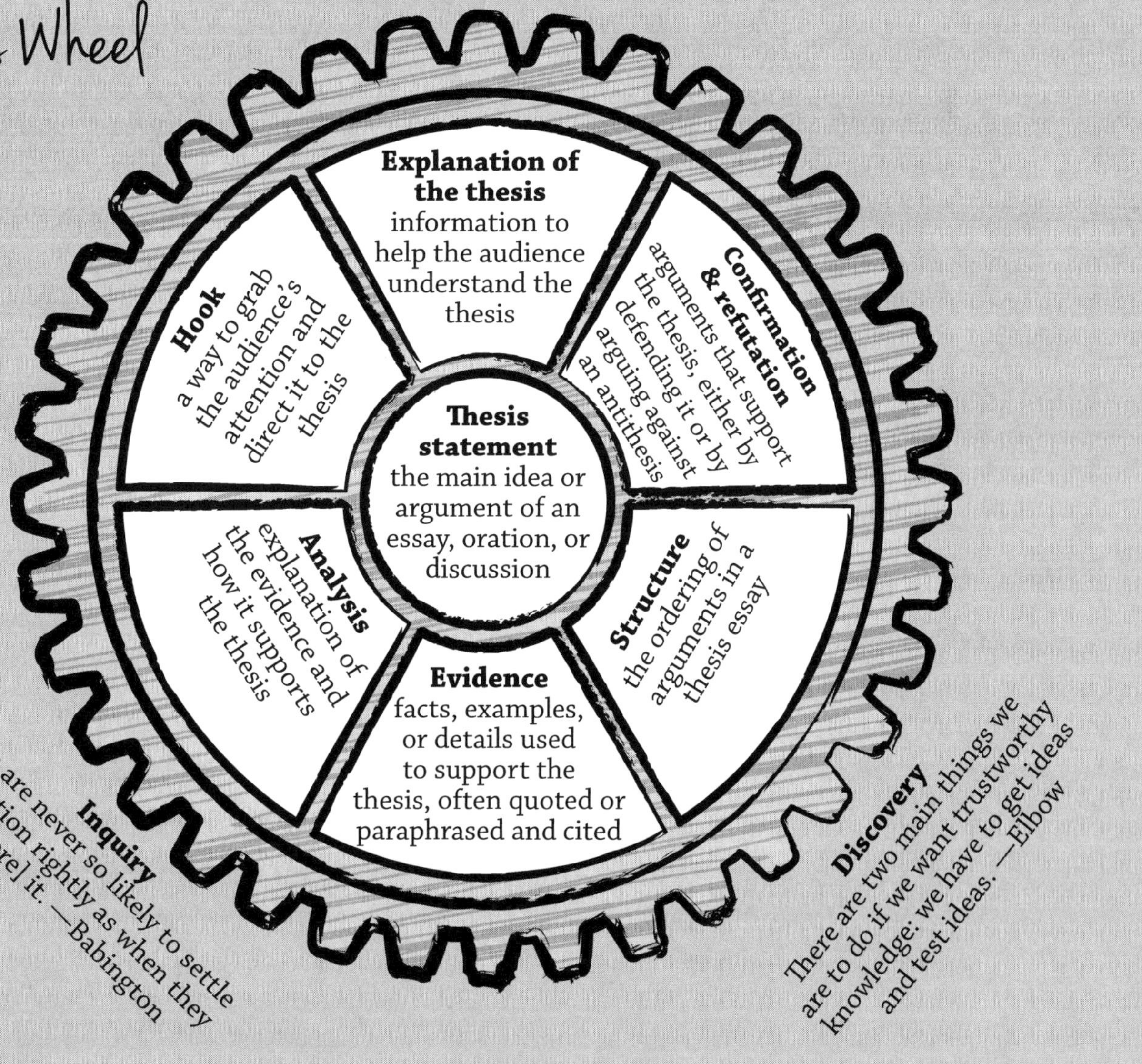

Based on the Essay Wheel developed by the Messiah College writing program.

Paragraph 1 (Introduction): The purpose of the introduction paragraph is to orient your reader and to reveal the point you plan argue. You'll want to be sure to identify the name of the story, "The Necklace," and its author, Guy de Maupassant, somewhere in your introduction: hook, thesis statement, or the explanation following the thesis.

What Goes Around Comes Around

Ripple effect on water, July 2009. Image courtesy of Sergiu Bacioiu on Flickr, https://commons.wikimedia.org/wiki/File:Ripple_effect_on_water.jpg.

Once you finish writing the body of this essay, you might want to return to your introduction and sharpen your thesis. And when you change your thesis, that may cause ripples throughout your paper. The writing process will test your thinking, and it is natural to go back and refine your words, your defenses, and sometimes (gasp!) even your entire paper. It can get messy as we explore our thoughts on paper, but that's one of the best ways to figure out what we believe. In the words of T.S. Eliot, "We shall not cease from exploration, and the end of all our exploring will be to arrive where we started and know the place for the first time."[15]

Writing the thesis is the first step in a thesis essay although you will actually place it *after* the hook when you write your introduction paragraph. Your thesis should answer the speculative question: What would Mathilde Loisel's life have been like if she hadn't lost the necklace? Here are some questions that may guide you to a thesis:

- Would she have lived a happy life after the grand ball?
- Would she have been contented with the little clerk from the Ministry of Public Instruction?
- How would the ball have changed her life, if at all, had she not lost the necklace?

Take another look at your annotations. The text of the short story should give you clues about how to answer these questions.

15. T.S. Eliot, *Four Quartets* (New York: Harvest Books, 1971), 240.

Write your thesis statement in the space provided. Remember that a thesis is the main argument of a persuasive paper. A good thesis is open to debate, is clear and specific (not too broad), and can be supported by evidence. In this essay, the thesis statement should also mention the two supporting arguments that you will expand on in your confirmation paragraphs.[B]

[B]Here is an example of a thesis statement that includes a main argument and also mentions two supporting arguments:

Simple Thesis — "Children younger than thirteen should not own cell phones

supporting argument 1 — because they impair learning

supporting argument 2 — and cause addiction."

If you need to refresh your memory on this type of thesis statement, flip back to lesson 2.

Thesis statement: ______________________________

Sample answer: Had she not lost the necklace and become a poor working woman, Mathilde Loisel would have faced even more serious calamity, because she would have grown more selfish and destructive.[C]

[C]If you feel students need additional examples of a thesis statement for this essay, the following are some other possibilities:

- If Mathilde Loisel hadn't lost the necklace, the pursuit of riches and popularity would have caused her selfishness to increase.
- Had Mathilde Loisel not lost the necklace, her dissatisfaction would have increased because she would not be satisfied by riches and dishonorable relationships.
- If she hadn't lost the necklace, Mathilde Loisel would have led a happier life: happier with the memories of the ball, and happier with a higher status.

Now, in one sentence, explain your thesis. You will expand on this explanation in your confirmation paragraphs.

Explanation of thesis: ______________________________

Sample answer: She would have squandered her husband's meager income to keep up the false image of a rich lady, and she probably would have treated "the little clerk" faithlessly.

____

Now write a transition sentence that takes the reader from the thesis explanation to the first confirmation paragraph. Remember that a transition forms a bridge from one paragraph to another. One side of the "bridge" will be made by referencing the topic of your first paragraph and the other side of the bridge will hint at what comes next.

Transition sentence: ______________________________

Sample answer: Mathilde Loisel was heading for trouble no matter what because she was self-centered and grasping.

____

____

Next, go back and think about the very beginning of your introduction paragraph, the hook. Decide on a way to hook your audience that will lead naturally to your thesis. You can choose from narratives (fables, parables, anecdotes, jokes, news flashes, summaries), questions, descriptions, illustrations, proverbs, sayings, quotations, provocative statements, statistics, or facts. For example, you could use a well-known fable that has a moral similar to that of "The Necklace." ("The Goose That Laid the Golden Egg" and "The Dog and

His Reflection" by Aesop come to mind.) You could choose a parallel story from the Bible (e.g., "The Parable of the Rich Fool") or a cautionary tale about riches and misery that is taken from history (e.g., the story of Howard Hughes, Joan Crawford, or Michael Jackson). You could describe the sparkle and allure of a famous jewel (e.g., the Hope Diamond, the Koh-i-Noor, the Star of India, or the Sunrise Ruby) or describe an extravagant ball gown. There are too many possibilities to name them all.

Ideas for a hook: ______________________________

Sample answer:

- "Be careful what you wish for, because you might just get it."
- "The Necklace" is similar to "The Sausage," "The Fisherman and His Wife," and "The Monkey's Paw"
- shows that not everything we think we want is good for us, how we can learn from the consequences of our desire

In order to move from your hook to your thesis, you will need some sort of transition. In his essay on marriage, Aphthonius summarized his hook in order to lead in to his thesis.[C] Other transitions may include giving a plot summary of the text you are analyzing or putting forth the speculative question you are answering. You may even use more than one element to make your transition. However you do it, you should make a smooth connection between your hook and the argument you will be presenting.

[C] Aphthonius's Model

Transition: "From one marriage, then, came gods and goddesses and the Roman people. The gift of life isn't the only reason to praise marriage, either."

Thesis: "Marriage is worthy of praise because it gives men and women great courage and self-control."

Transition from the hook to the thesis: ______________________________

- summary of story, to show how it relates to the moral in the hook
- present speculative question

____

When you write your full introduction paragraph, remember that even though in your prewriting you started with the thesis and then worked back to the hook, your completed paragraph should follow the order of hook (with transition), thesis, transition.

Paragraph 2 (First Confirmation): Each confirmation paragraph will explain and justify your thesis in depth from a different angle. In other words, each paragraph will set out one confirming argument that shows why your thesis is true. Start the paragraph with a topic sentence, which tells the main idea of the paragraph—what your confirmation argument will be.

Topic sentence: Sample answer: Without the loss of the necklace, Madame Loisel would have become even more selfish because she would have wanted more and more of the things she desired.

Follow the topic sentence by explaining it and giving supporting evidence. In order to appeal to authority, be sure to quote or paraphrase an idea from the story. Your quote or paraphrase should support (confirm) or clarify your argument. Remember that your quote will need to be introduced and then explained, and be sure to cite your source.[D]

Quotation or paraphrase from the text:

Sample answer: "She danced with rapture, with passion, intoxicated by pleasure, forgetting all in the triumph of her beauty, in the glory of her success, in a sort of cloud of happiness comprised of all this homage, admiration, these awakened desires and of that sense of triumph which is so sweet to woman's heart" (Maupassant).

[D]If your students need a refresher on using quotations and paraphrase to provide evidence, please refer them to lesson 6.

Paragraph 3 (Second Confirmation): Start with a topic sentence, which tells the main idea of the paragraph—what your confirmation argument will be.

Topic sentence:

Sample answer: As Mathilde Loisel's need for homage, admiration, and triumph increased, she would have undoubtedly proved unfaithful to her husband as well, pursuing dishonorable relationships with other men and causing the destruction of her reputation and character.

Follow the topic sentence by explaining it and giving supporting evidence. In order to appeal to authority, be sure to quote or paraphrase an idea from the story. Your quote or paraphrase should support (confirm) or clarify your argument. Remember that your quote will need to be introduced and then explained, and be sure to cite your source.

Quotation or paraphrase from the text: ______________________________

Sample answer: "All the men looked at her, asked her name, sought to be introduced. All the attachés of the Cabinet wished to waltz with her" (Maupassant).

____

____

Paragraph 4 (First Refutation): Each refutation paragraph will explain and refute an antithesis, a disagreement with your thesis. In other words, each paragraph will set out one antithesis and then show why it is untrue. Start the paragraph with the antithesis, which will serve as the topic sentence or main idea of the paragraph. You should lead into the antithesis with a phrase such as "Some readers might argue that . . .".

- Tip: Consider your audience as you work on your antitheses. What objections might your teacher or classmates have to your thesis? You may even want to ask them.

Antithesis: ______________________________

Sample answer: Some readers might say that, if she had not lost the necklace, the ball would have satisfied Madame Loisel's longings and she would have lived, if not happily ever after, then at least with more contentment.

____

Follow the antithesis by explaining it. To help you think through your explanation, consider listing some supporting arguments for the antithesis before you start to write.

Next, defend the thesis by telling why the antithesis is wrong. Appeal to authority with textual evidence by using a quote or paraphrase from the story that supports or clarifies your defense. Remember that your quote will need to be introduced and then explained, and be sure to cite your source.

Defense: ______________________________

Sample answer: Madame Loisel's head was too stuffed with dreams of pleasure and riches to ever be satisfied by a single ball.

____

____

Quotation or paraphrase from the text: ______________________________

> Sample answer: "She was unhappy as if she had really fallen from a higher station; since with women there is neither caste nor rank, for beauty, grace and charm take the place of family and birth" (Maupassant).

____

Paragraph 5 (Second Refutation): Start with the antithesis, which will serve as the topic sentence or main idea of the paragraph. You should lead into the second antithesis with a phrase such as "Other readers might argue that . . .".

Antithesis: ______________________________

> Sample answer: Others might say that Madame Loisel's selfish and destructive nature would have improved had she not lost the necklace, because she would have left her dull husband, the ball and chain in her life.

____

Follow the antithesis by explaining it. To help you think through your explanation, consider listing some supporting arguments for the antithesis before you start to write.

Next, defend the thesis by telling why the antithesis is wrong. Appeal to authority with textual evidence by using a quote or paraphrase from the story that supports or clarifies your defense. Remember that your quote will need to be introduced and then explained, and be sure to cite your source.

Defense: ______________________________

> Sample answer:
> - The problem was not her husband, but her lack of character.
> - If anything, Monsieur Loisel was a positive influence.

____

Quotation or paraphrase from the text: ______________________________

> Sample answer: "He compromised all the rest of his life, risked signing a note without even knowing whether he could meet it; and, frightened by the trouble yet to come, by the black misery that was about to fall upon him, by the prospect of all the physical privations and moral tortures that he was to suffer, he went to get the new necklace, laying upon the jeweler's counter thirty-six thousand francs" (Maupassant).

____

Paragraph 6 (Conclusion): In your conclusion, you will make your case one last time by restating your thesis. For the prewriting stage, jot down a new version of the thesis using fresh language.

Restatement of the thesis: ______________________________

Sample answer: If she hadn't lost the necklace, she would have declined in her moral character and possibly encountered far more disastrous consequences as a result of her desires.

When you come back to this prompt to write your full paragraph, consider what you have learned from supporting your thesis in the previous paragraphs. Your final restatement should express a fuller and more complete understanding of the thesis now that you have tested your ideas in the body of the paper.

Example:

- Original thesis: "Students should spend time outdoors to improve their quality of life and overall health."
- Restated thesis: "By spending time outdoors, students will reduce stress and boost their overall happiness, as well as get physical exercise and experience improved sleep."

Notice how the restatement presents the thesis with more precision and insight, demonstrating the deeper understanding that was gained through the process of writing the essay. Rework your restated thesis as needed to express this deeper understanding.

Next, tell why your topic is important. In other words, how can this topic be applied to real life or change the reader's outlook?

Why your topic is important: ______________________________

Sample answers:

- can help us to examine our own vanity and self-centeredness
- hardship can work as a kind of grace in our lives and help us to be less morally debased
- promotes humility as a virtue

You can also look carefully at your body paragraphs and emphasize any points that best support your thesis. Another possibility is to urge your readers to take heed of the moral lesson in "The Necklace" or to take some sort of concrete action.

Call to action (optional): ______________________________

Sample answer: We ought to look at our own troubles and what they are teaching us that success would not be able to teach.

Once you have completed your prewriting, go through these instructions again and write your paragraphs based on the prompts.

Speak It—

This icon points to more tips on elocution at the back of the book.

This icon means that you can also use a recording device for this exercise.

1. **STUMP SPEECH GAME:** Not so long ago, people who wanted to make an impromptu speech would jump up on a tree stump in a public place and use it as a stage. The speaker, now taller than most people in the crowd, would then address some political or moral topic. In this public-speaking exercise, you will deliver a speech from your own classroom "stump."

   A taped area on the floor or a sturdy chair or crate can serve as the stump. One student at a time will stand on the stump and deliver an impromptu speech on a particular position. The topic of the speech can be drawn from a hat or assigned by your teacher.

   You will be given one and a half minutes for your speech. For the first forty-five seconds you must speak in favor of the position, and for the second forty-five seconds you must speak against the position. Be sure to give reasons why you are "for" or "against" the position. (Please note: Because the time is so short, this exercise is not designed for debating significant, weighty issues, but only for practicing speaking in front of a group.)

   Sample positions include:

   - Ballroom dancing should be the mainstay at high school dances.
   - It's possible to care too much about your appearance.
   - Tarantulas make excellent pets.
   - Peaches are the best fruit.
   - Winter is a beautiful season.
   - The school week should be three days long.
   - Roller coasters must be avoided.
   - ________ is the most impressive superhero.

2. **PARTNER FEEDBACK:** With a student partner (or your teacher), take turns reading the rough drafts of your thesis essays. You and your partner should give each other comments about what is more or less effective about your writing. Use the following rubric to help you get ideas for your comments. (Don't worry about awarding points to your classmate. Scoring an essay is your teacher's job.) Try to say two positive things about your partner's essay, and then come up with at least two suggestions for editing or revising the essay.[E]

[E]At this stage, students can give each other thoughtful feedback. The thesis rubric can serve as their guide for constructive comments and notes. Students will likely need to hear a teacher say that feedback is a way for writers to help each other and that every professional writer depends on the input of others, hence it's important that feedback comes with a healthy dose of respect and encouragement. Make sure to allow enough time between drafts so that students can receive help from classmates and the teacher.

Please note that this rubric is a simplified version of the more detailed rubric found at the back of this book. Your teacher may choose to use the detailed rubric to assess your essay.

Thesis Essay Rubric

Name: ______________________________ Date of Assignment: ____________________

Content _________/72

Paragraph 1: Introduction ________/12 __________
- Does the introduction contain a hook, a complex thesis, and an explanation of the thesis?

Paragraph 2: First Confirmation ________/12 __________
- Does the paragraph begin with a topic sentence?
- Is this confirmation clearly explained and supported by evidence?

Paragraph 3: Second Confirmation ________/12 __________
- Does the paragraph begin with a topic sentence?
- Is this confirmation clearly explained and supported by evidence?

Paragraph 4: First Refutation ________/12 __________
- Does the paragraph begin with a topic sentence that states an antithesis to the thesis? Is the antithesis fully explained?
- Does the paragraph clearly refute the antithesis and provide evidence for the refutation?

Paragraph 5: Second Refutation ________/12 __________
- Does the paragraph begin with a topic sentence that states an antithesis to the thesis? Is the antithesis fully explained?
- Does the paragraph clearly refute the antithesis and provide evidence for the refutation?

Paragraph 6: Conclusion ________/12 __________
- Is the thesis restated in new words that express a fuller understanding?
- Does the author tell why the topic is important?

Style _________/8

Does the author include a creative title that reflects the heart of the essay? (2 points) __________

Has the author written the essay with consideration of the audience's makeup, disposition, and needs? (2 points) __________

Has the author consistently used formal language (with third-person perspective) throughout the essay? (4 points) __________

Form _________/20

Title, header, spacing, indentation, and font are formatted correctly and consistently (2 points) __________

In-text citations are included and formatted correctly (4 points) __________

Sentence variety __________

Many varied sentences: 4 points	Good sentence variety: 3 points
Some sentence variety: 2 points	Little or no sentence variety: 0 points

Grammar and usage __________

Few or no grammar errors: 4 points	Occasional grammar errors: 3 points
Some grammar errors: 2 points	Many grammar errors: 0 points

Number of spelling, punctuation, and capitalization errors __________

2 or fewer per page: 6 points	3 per page: 5 points
4 per page: 4 points	5 or more per page: 0 points

Total: _________/100

Ask each other:

- Does my hook capture your interest?
- Is my thesis clear, specific, and debatable?
- Does each confirmation paragraph clearly support the thesis?
- Does each antithesis clearly argue against the thesis?
- Does each defense (refutation) paragraph clearly refute its antithesis and support the thesis?
- Do I introduce and explain credible evidence, and do I include a source citation for every quote or paraphrase?

If you are constructively honest with your partner, your comments will really help him or her.

Revise It—

1. **STYLISTIC VICE: WORDINESS—**In this lesson and in lessons 8 and 10, we will be pointing out some vices in writing. Vices are flaws that should be weeded out of your work during the process of revision. Today's vices are—ta da!—redundancy and padding, or the excess use of words.

Redundancy is the unnecessary repetition of ideas. Even if you use different words to create the repetition, they just add flab to your sentences. Take the expression "basic necessities." The noun "necessities" already carries the idea of "basic" and "essential." The adjective "basic" does nothing useful, so including it is redundant.

Although repetition sometimes can be used to forcefully reinforce an idea, you should stay away from common redundancies that add nothing in the way of rhetorical power. Examples of common redundancies are:

- bouquet of flowers

  Since in most cases a bouquet refers to flowers, this phrase is unnecessarily repetitive. It can be said more efficiently as, simply, "bouquet."
- frozen ice

  Ice is by definition frozen water, so describing ice as frozen is unnecessary. This should simply be "ice."
- clenched fist

  A fist is a clenched hand, so the adjective "clenched" is unnecessary and repetitive. Instead, simply use "fist."
- "I'd like to score <u>at least</u> ten points <u>or more</u>."

  The phrases "at least" and "or more" both imply that ten points is the minimum score desired. Since both phrases mean the same thing, one of them should be deleted.

[F] From p. 171: Please keep in mind that there is a subjective element to identifying redundancies and padding. Be prepared to discuss students' answers and the answers marked in the TE, as some students may not readily see a concern until it is explained to them.

- "I counted each and every jellybean in the jar."

  "Each and every" is a common redundant expression used for emphasis. Either "each" or "every" can be deleted without losing the meaning of the sentence.
- "Let me tell you, this rain is never going to stop."

  The speaker does not need to say, "Let me tell you . . ." because the listener already understands that she is being told something.
- "The merry, happy child did a little dance."

  The adjectives "merry" and "happy" essentially mean the same thing, and only one is necessary in this sentence.

Padding is any empty word, phrase, or sentence that is used to make writing look longer, usually to fill out a page or paragraph requirement. A word to the wise: Teachers can spot padding a mile away! It would be far better for you to do the right thing and think about ways to develop your ideas more fully. You can always define, explain, or describe your topic as well as qualify or amplify it—anything to avoid meaningless words!

Cross out any redundancies (10) or padding (2) in the following paragraphs. **F**

The Supper Room after a Ball

—adapted from *The Scarlet Pimpernel* by Baroness Orczy

When the French agent reached the supper room, it was ~~empty and~~ deserted. It had that woebegone, ~~sad,~~ tawdry appearance, which reminds one so much of a ball dress the morning after. Half-empty~~, half-full~~ glasses littered the table, and unfolded napkins lay about. The chairs—gathered ~~together~~ in groups of twos and threes—stood in ~~close~~ proximity to one another—in the far corners of the room, most likely the scene of recent whispered flirtations, over cold game-pie and ~~sparkling~~ champagne. There were sets of three and four chairs that recalled pleasant, animated discussions over the latest scandal. There were chairs straight up in a row that still looked starchy, critical, acid, like antiquated ~~old~~ ladies. There were a few ~~isolated,~~ single chairs, close to the table, that spoke of gourmets intent on the most cherished dishes, and others overturned on the floor, that spoke volumes on an excess amount of wine. ~~In short, the supper room was a bit of a mess.~~

It was a ghostlike replica, ~~in point of fact,~~ of that fashionable gathering upstairs; a ghost that haunts every house where balls and good suppers are given; a picture drawn with white chalk on gray cardboard, ~~dull and colorless,~~ now that the bright silk dresses and gorgeously embroidered coats had disappeared ~~from sight,~~ and now that the candles flickered sleepily in their sockets.[16]

16. Baroness Orczy, *The Scarlet Pimpernel* (New York: Signet Classics, 1974), 136.

2. **REWRITING:** Follow these steps to turn your ugly-duckling first draft into a lovely swan.
    a. Get feedback. Use comments from your student partners (or from your teacher) to strengthen and improve your paper.
    b. Wait a day or two before you rewrite your paper. The time away from it will help you to see its problems more clearly.
    c. Read the paper aloud to yourself. This is often the best way to catch mistakes—grammar errors, as well as words that don't work well—because you will be using two senses—seeing and hearing—instead of one. If something sounds wrong, it probably is.

REC

Once you are ready to rewrite, use the following steps to aid with your revision:

a. *Find your thesis and underline it.* There also should be a restatement of the thesis in your conclusion. This restatement should show a fuller and more complete understanding of the thesis.
b. *Find the topic sentence for each body paragraph and highlight it.* Each body paragraph should begin with a topic sentence stating the main idea of the paragraph. The topic sentence for a confirmation paragraph should confirm some aspect of the thesis. The topic sentence for a refutation paragraph should introduce an antithesis, which opposes the thesis.
c. *Find the evidence (appeal to authority) in each body paragraph and highlight it.* Did you choose the best quote or paraphrase to make your point? Make sure that all evidence is properly introduced and explained and has source citations.
d. *Make sure each paragraph gets the job done.* Remember that each paragraph has a special purpose in supporting your thesis through analysis and evidence. Does each paragraph successfully accomplish this goal?
e. *Make sure you have consistently considered audience.* Have you written your essay based on your understanding of the audience's makeup, disposition, and needs? Have you carefully considered possible objections to your thesis?
f. *Find and fix grammar mistakes.* Make sure all your nouns and verbs agree and that your writing is clear. Fix any fragments or run-ons. In other words, make sure you are writing complete sentences.
g. *Strengthen phrasing.* Are your word choices specific instead of vague? Do you use strong nouns and verbs? Do you vary your sentences and occasionally begin them with a prepositional phrase or a participial phrase? Weed out passive voice and excess adjectives. Use compound sentences, appositives, adverb phrases, and questions to make your writing more interesting. Transition smoothly between ideas and paragraphs using transition words.
h. *Proofread.* Look for any punctuation, spelling, or capitalization errors. Then fix them!
i. *Retype* the draft with the corrections you have made.

Lesson 7: First Thesis Essay: Analysis of a Short Story

Tell It Back—Summary

Sample oral summary: Although Mathilde Loisel lives a comfortable life with her clerk husband, she dreams of great riches and the attention of fabulously wealthy men. When her husband receives an invitation to his office ball, Madame Loisel despairs of looking the part of a beautiful society woman. Her despair quickly turns to joy when her husband buys her a shimmering ball gown and her rich friend, Madame Forestier, lends her a diamond necklace. Madame Loisel is a great success at the ball and the night is everything she dreamed it to be—but then disaster strikes. When the Loisels return home, they discover that the diamond necklace has fallen from Madame Loisel's throat and has vanished somewhere in Paris. Days of hopeless searching follow. The couple finally decides to replace the necklace with a matching diamond necklace at an astronomical price, never letting Madame Forestier know that it was replaced. It takes the Loisels ten long years of struggle and poverty to pay off the necklace, and during that time they lose their youthful bloom. In the end, Madame Loisel approaches her rich friend to boast about having purchased a new necklace to replace the lost one, only to learn that the original necklace was fake.

Talk About It—

1. Answers will vary. Sample answer: For Madame Loisel, the necklace means climbing above her lowly station in life to the higher class where she feels she belongs. She craves the look of the upper-class women, including their jewelry, because she thinks it will bring her the love and attention of handsome men, and the admiration and envy of fashionable women.

   The necklace symbolizes Madame Loisel's dreams of wealth and status, which prove false and ruinous to her in the end, just as the diamonds are themselves false.

   Madame Loisel took only the diamond necklace because she did not want to appear greedy and to be refused by her friend, Madame Forestier. She picked the one ornament she believed would make her look the most beautiful.

2. Answers will vary.

   Sample answer 1: Yes, I think "The Necklace" has a moral lesson. It is: Be contented and grateful for the good things already in your life.

   Sample answer 2: Yes, I think "The Necklace" has a moral lesson. It is: The road to ruin is paved with dissatisfaction and greed.

TE

3. Answers will vary. Sample answer: When they first discovered the necklace was missing, the Loisels did the right thing. Monsieur Loisel retraced their steps and looked for the necklace. He placed an ad in the newspaper and offered a reward. These were reasonable steps for recovering lost property. But when the Loisels were unsuccessful at finding the necklace, they began to try to cover up the loss, which was not the right thing to do. The further they went, finding a new necklace and going deep into debt, the less reasonable their actions were. It was foolish to destroy ten years of their lives paying back debt without telling the truth to Madame Forestier. What they could have done differently was to throw themselves at Madame Forestier's mercy. If the diamonds had been worth a fortune, they may have been forgiven. If the diamonds were fake, they could have easily paid her back.
4. Answers will vary. Sample answer: Madame Loisel was probably stunned by the revelation that the diamonds were fake. I would assume that out of friendship, Madame Forestier would return the real diamonds to Madame Loisel and let her sell them for cash. That way the Loisels would at least have something more to live on. Perhaps circumstances for the Loisels would improve and they would be wiser in how they live, not foolishly chasing after unattainable wealth and status.
5. Answers will vary. Sample answer: While many women find homage and admiration about their beauty sweet to their hearts, this statement is not true for every woman. Some women prefer to gain respect solely from their character or from their accomplishments.

   Men also can be motivated, probably just as much as women, by the desire to be admired for their good looks and can enjoy the triumph that their looks can bring in a social setting.

   Maupassant also makes some general statements about women in the beginning of the story when he says, "With women there is neither caste nor rank, for beauty, grace and charm take the place of family and birth. Natural ingenuity, instinct for what is elegant, a supple mind are their sole hierarchy, and often make of women of the people the equals of the very greatest ladies."

Sample Essay

The sample essay that you would typically find in these teacher pages has instead been printed as an appendix for student reference and imitation. Feel free to refer your students to that sample if they are struggling with writing any particular paragraph. The rest of the essay-writing lessons will include the full sample essay in the teacher pages as usual.

The purpose of this lesson is for students to write a thesis essay analyzing an autobiography for theme.

In this lesson, students will practice:

- annotating a personal narrative for thematic elements
- oral summary of a chapter
- description of a setting and its role in two sentences
- providing evidence for important themes
- critical thinking
- using the Rule of Three to build copiousness and rhetorical strength
- examining a text and lifting supporting quotes from it
- following an outline
- assessing the most significant theme
- writing a thesis essay, including an introduction, body paragraphs, and a conclusion
- writing a complex thesis
- distinguishing between proper and improper grammar
- editing for a more formal tone
- revision and proofreading

Lesson 8

Second Thesis Essay: Analysis of an Autobiography

The reading that you analyzed in the previous lesson was narrative fiction. In this lesson you will be analyzing narrative nonfiction, which is a story based on fact. *Survive to Live* is the autobiography of a young man named Jonathan Orozco, who escaped from a notorious shantytown[1] in Guatemala to make the perilous journey to the United States. You will be reading from "La Limonada," the first chapter in Orozco's story, which tells about his life in the shantytown.

Before you begin the reading, I want to make you aware of a literary concept called theme. A theme is an important idea that keeps cropping up throughout a work of literature. Similar to a theme in music, which is a melody or rhythm that forms a recognizable pattern, a literary theme repeats itself throughout the narrative. It is not usually stated explicitly by the author—he doesn't write, "I'm going to tell you about love"—but is advanced through the characters' thoughts and actions. Love is indeed a common theme in literature, as is courage, hope, revenge, struggle, hardship, and sacrifice. In the last lesson, you saw themes of envy and pride in "The Necklace." (Check out the sidebar on the next page to see how Maupassant made a pattern of quotes, words, and images to develop the theme of pride.)

1. shantytown: a poor section of a city with crudely built houses

Whether young or old, all of us have plenty of experience with some of the big concerns of life: growing up, for instance, and overcoming obstacles, the joy of victory, the sorrow of defeat, the pursuit of happiness, and the downfall of pride. We've encountered embarrassment, heroism, cowardice, sorrow, greed, and generosity. These are all universal aspects of the human experience, all things that you and I and everyone else on this planet will bump into time and time again if we live long enough. For a writer of fiction or nonfiction, these common human experiences are a gold mine—a rich vein of interesting topics to explore and develop. These are the themes of literature.

Examples of Theme from Guy de Maupassant's "The Necklace"

You may have noticed some themes popping up in "The Necklace" in lesson 7. For example, the theme of Mathilde Loisel's pride is laced throughout the story. Here are a few sentences from the story that bring this idea to the fore:

- "Mathilde suffered ceaselessly, feeling herself born to enjoy all delicacies and all luxuries."
- "It annoys me not to have a single piece of jewelry, not a single ornament, nothing to put on. I shall look poverty-stricken."
- "There's nothing more humiliating than to look poor among other women who are rich."
- "She danced with rapture . . . forgetting all in the triumph of her beauty, in the glory of her success, in a sort of cloud of happiness comprised of all this homage, admiration, these awakened desires and of that sense of triumph which is so sweet to woman's heart."
- "She smiled with a joy that was at once proud and ingenuous."
- Notice that the author uses the word "proud" only once, but the other sentences also strongly develop this theme.
- Images and word choices can also be used to create the patterns of a theme.
- The image of a dress or gown—a poor dress and, in contrast, a costly gown—appears ten times. The poor dress is connected to Mathilde's feelings of envy, whereas the costly gown is connected to her feelings of pride and success.
- Words for money (franc) and expense ("cost" and "price") appear twelve times. The lack of money is connected to Mathilde's envy, and later to the financial ruin caused by her pride.

The repetition of these images and words hints that money and riches are connected to themes of envy and pride and the destruction they can cause.

[A] Some suggestions for highlighting are marked with a dotted line. Feel free to allow students to see the suggestions before they begin their own highlighting if you feel it would be helpful to them.

Go ahead and read the first chapter of Orozco's autobiography once just to get acquainted with the author and his story. Then read the chapter a second time, and be on the lookout for the themes Orozco develops. When you start to see themes emerge, mark the words, images, actions, and sentences that tip you off to a pattern. Use a different color of highlighter for each theme.[A] Look for:

- repeated words and ideas such as "violence," "hope," "fear," "dreams," and "family"
- repeated actions such as stealing, fighting, and running
- repeated images such as images of light, dark, weapons, poverty, and prosperity

You won't be able to highlight all of them, so you will need to decide which themes strike you as most important. Have fun!

La Limonada (The Lemonade)

—adapted from *Survive to Live* by Jonathan Orozco

page 3
"Help! Help!"

The scream sliced through the clamor of women shrieking, the slamming and bolting of doors, the pounding of bare feet on the dirt. It was a voice I knew all too well. Doña Toña,[2] the local *chismosa*,[3] was broadcasting my neighborhood's late-breaking news. For anyone without a TV, she was the closest thing we had to a local anchor, but this time there was an extra sense of urgency in her voice. "Someone stop this fight!" she yelled.

Naturally curious, I followed the crowd, running towards the old church where a bunch of my neighbors were watching two men fighting. I could sense that this was much more serious than a typical drunken fistfight—many bystanders were running *away* from the conflict. They nearly knocked me over as they fled past me, their eyes wide open in panic, their faces twisted with fear. It could only mean one thing: it was a fight to the death.

I jostled close enough to see the two combatants in the center of the onlookers who had decided not to run away. One of them held a long, ugly machete in his hand. It was already dripping with blood. His opponent clutched his slashed page 4 abdomen with his left hand while he kept swinging with his right fist. He stumbled and swayed while blood continued to gush through his fingers grabbing at his wounded gut. Finally, staggering badly, he crumbled to the ground.

Machete appears here as a weapon of aggression, later as a defensive weapon.

"I *told* you not to mess with me!" sneered the man with the machete. He took off, running through the crowd to avoid being caught. I took a good look at the face of the defeated man. I recognized him immediately. He was a well-known thief and

2. Doña Toña: Old Lady Toña
3. *chismosa*: gossiper

drug addict who liked to hide out in our ravine. When this guy was high—which was all the time—he did and said crazy things that made people afraid. Apparently, the man who had just dissected his belly in broad daylight didn't feel like putting up with him anymore.

Doña Toña, silent for once in her life, approached the fallen man and helped him to his feet. As he began to stand up, I cringed in horror when I looked down and saw him holding his own bloody intestines in his left hand!

The crowd parted, clearing a path to let him escape. I resisted the urge to throw up as I watched him limp his way out of the ravine, cradling his guts and leaving a trail of blood behind him. Incredibly, I saw him a few weeks later, stitched up and seemingly good as new, swapping stories and sniffing glue with some fellow thugs on the corner like nothing had happened.

Terror, fascination, and blood in the dirt—just another ordinary day in La Limonada.

The word "blood" appears four times. The liquid images of blood, river, and sewer may create a thematic pattern of life's essence tainted by pollution and violence.

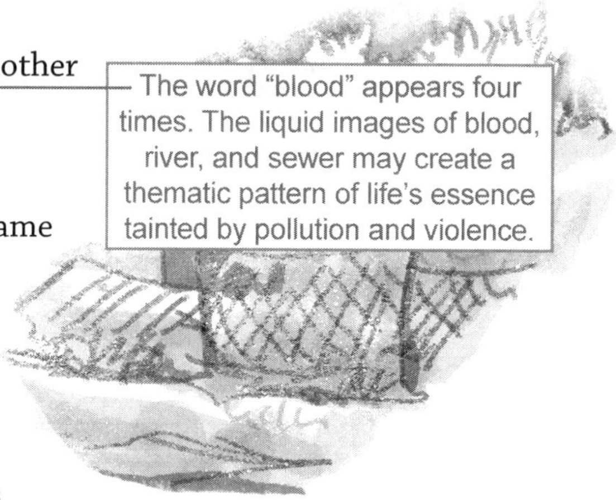

The ravine was better known as La Limonada, a name coined by somebody with a sick sense of humor.[4] This place was a terrible accident of architecture. An inward-slanting jumble of corrugated tin roofs and thin plaster walls a mile long, my *colonia*[5] defied gravity. It was balanced around the edges of what was once considered an uninhabitable ravine near Guatemala City, and it looked like a strong wind might easily blow everything down. Amazingly, it withstood the rain and the sometimes harsh climate.

La Limonada was a *barrio*, a slum, a shantytown. Here, simple squabbles often ended in bloodshed. It was a place where thieves, rapists, drug dealers, and gangs

page 5

planted themselves in the soil of disorder the *colonia* offered them, reaping a never-ending harvest of the bitter fruits of sin. The ravine was infamous throughout the whole country, all of Central America, and even all of Latin America for its sheer savagery. Yet to call it home carried with it a warped sense of pride, a kind of badge—not of honor, but of toughness. It was a members-only survival code that said, *Hey, don't mess with me . . . I'm from La Limonada*. Everyone who lived there enjoyed this harsh self-importance, which was one of the very few good things La Limonada had to offer.

4. Orozco probably means that the name "lemonade" is ironic. Lemonade is sweet and refreshing, but the shantytown is rarely that. More often life in La Limonada seems sour, bitter, and even poisonous. (footnote added)

5. *colonia*: neighborhood

Everyone in La Limonada was poor; some were just poorer than others. It was seventy thousand Pedros robbing Pablos to pay Juan, and so on—a twisted, ongoing Guatemalan Robin Hood tale. The poor stole from the poor to survive. It was both ridiculous and sad, but it was here, in La Limonada, where I took my first steps, where I grew up, where I spent so many years . . . a place where life could never be normal. The words of a local saying nailed it: "Whoever enters here will leave robbed of everything, even their socks and their smile."

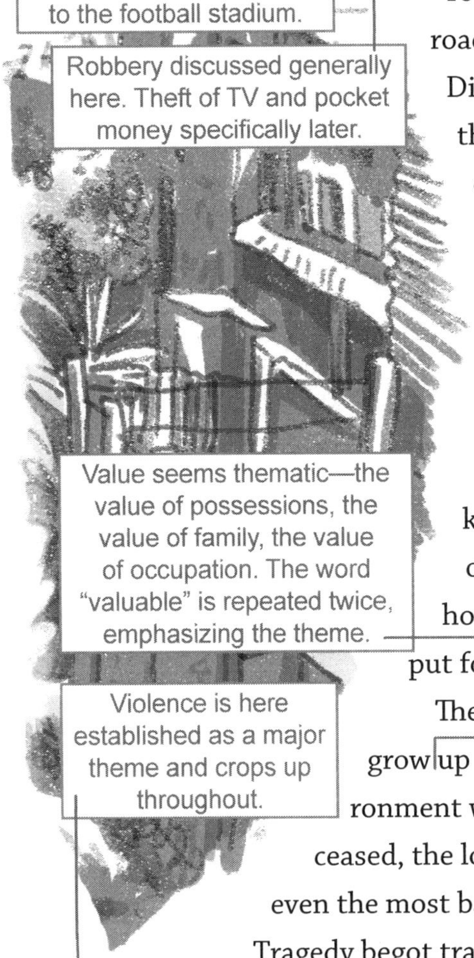

Poverty as a theme, developed later in contrast to the football stadium.

Robbery discussed generally here. Theft of TV and pocket money specifically later.

To enter and leave La Limonada was a test in itself. Narrow roads were the only way in and out, paved only by foot traffic. Dirt paths dug by generations of inhabitants led the way through winding rows of *covachas*.[6] We struggled up and down these paths, slipping on the mud in the winter and choking on dust in the summer. To add spice to the experience, a river of sewer water ran beside the main roads, flowing northward for miles upon miles. The people of La Limonada had no choice but to build their public restrooms directly beside the river.

Value seems thematic—the value of possessions, the value of family, the value of occupation. The word "valuable" is repeated twice, emphasizing the theme.

As hard as it may be to believe, to some of La Limonada's kids, that dirty river was a potential gold mine. At great risk to our lives, we would trudge into the grimy, waist-deep water in hopes of finding something valuable that we could sell to help put food on the table.

Violence is here established as a major theme and crops up throughout.

page 6

The fact was that although most parents wanted their kids to grow up with good manners and get a decent education, the environment was simply too unstable. Besides, even if all crime magically ceased, the local school facilities were crumbling and understaffed, lacking even the most basic necessities.

Tragedy begot tragedy every day in La Limonada. There was no peace on this part of the earth. Every night was rattled by gunshots and the screams of those who'd been hurt by switchblades, bullets, and fists. The stench of the sewer-river was everywhere in my *barrio*, but the aura of violence was more so—and far less predictable. The authorities had abandoned us to our collective fate as well. To them, we did not exist! They were too cowardly even to set foot in La Limonada. Naturally, criminals took the absence of the police as an invitation to take up residence among us and steal what they could, when they could.

6. *covachas*: shacks

The word "God" is mentioned five times, each time in a hopeful way.

But in the alleys of La Limonada, these opportunists met their match in hardy residents determined to hang on to what few possessions they had. In the words of my optimistic mother, La Limonada was *our* place, *our* home. Mom viewed our ravine through the hopeful lens of her faith, insisting that our *colonia* was a beautiful place under God's watch. She never stopped believing that someday, somehow, things would get better and all would be well. Eventually, she proved to be right.

How could a place be so bad? Easy. Generation upon generation knew nothing else. La Limonada was embedded in our DNA from our first moment in the womb, binding unborn souls in defeat before they were ever allowed to dream.

The words "defeat" and "dream" appear ten times. These opposing ideas create a thematic contrast.

My brothers and I feared that it was just a matter of time before one of us became a target, just like so many neighbors and acquaintances from our *colonia* whose lives had been ruined by violence. The worst thing would be to lose one another, to find ourselves alone in that brutal place. While there were a hundred excuses for throwing in the towel, staying here was the ultimate failure. Survival was a consolation prize, but getting out of La Limonada was hitting the jackpot.

page 7

The idea of winning or scoring seems thematic. Words connected to this concept are "gold," "stealing," "victory," and "getting out."

That was what I wanted: to hit the jackpot and leave. I knew I had to leave, but it wouldn't be easy. Night after night I woke up drained from a night of worry, sucked dry of energy before the day had even begun. But my thoughts and dreams all flew beyond the ravine, far and free. I knew there was something else out there—I had *seen* it on our little black-and-white television set! Images of serene palm trees waving in the wind flickered on the screen, dotting the beaches in a faraway place called California. This was matched by a city named Los Angeles, where everybody just basked in the sunlight on Santa Monica beach all day without a care in the world. Sometimes I would stand in the doorway of my *covacha* gazing up at the sky above La Limonada, picturing the surreal majesty of Los Angeles, and I wished that this paradise would one day descend from the sky to become the new backdrop for my life.

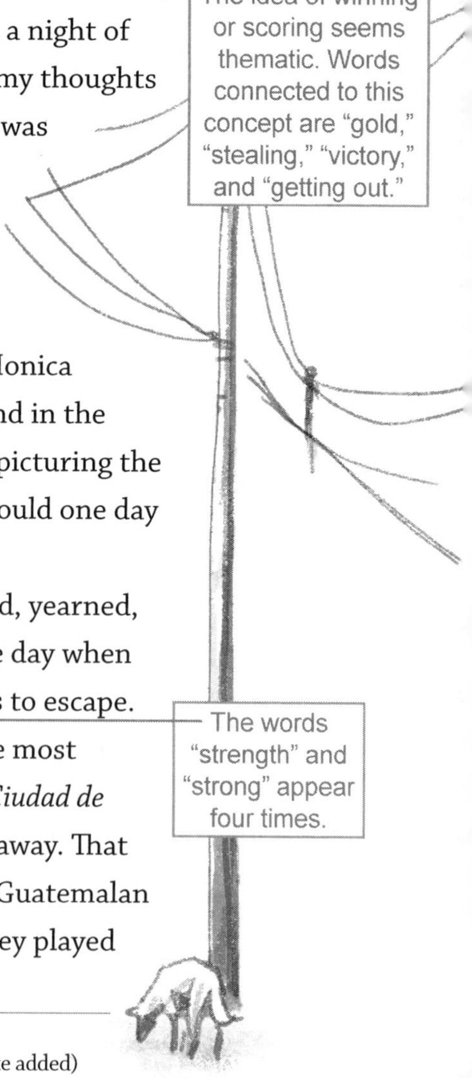

La Limonada was not the place I wanted to die in. No. I longed, yearned, to be released. I had a will to survive. And I looked forward to the day when somehow I would gather the superhuman strength and resources to escape. Of all the injustices that framed the daily grind of our *colonia*, the most ironic thing was that the famous Mateo Flores stadium and the *Ciudad de los Deportes*[7] was *right outside* the ravine, just a few hundred feet away. That stadium was La Limonada's singular claim to fame. The national Guatemalan team[8] played there, as they still do to this day. One year, when they played

The words "strength" and "strong" appear four times.

7. *Ciudad de los Deportes*: Sports Complex
8. This refers to a football team, or what we would call a soccer team in the United States. (footnote added)

a qualifying match for the World Cup at Mateo Flores stadium, excitement swept through the heart of every kid in La Limonada. Instead of sitting at home, listening to the radio or gluing our eyes to the TV as usual, I followed everyone to the stadium to try to catch a glimpse of the game with my own two eyes. After walking only a few minutes from my front door, there was the glorious temple of soccer awaiting us, rising as tall and broad as dreams.

Of course, we had all entertained plenty of fantasies about playing on Guatemala's national team one day, and now the team was *here*! We laid our hands on the walls of the stadium, as if they could give weight to our grand *fútbol* illusions. I still remember [it] like it was yesterday. We heard the shout of "*¡Goooooool!*" but, was it a goal for us, the blue and white? Frantic and hopeful, we all talked amongst ourselves, asking, "Whose was it? Who scored?" It took a few minutes to find out, since La Limonada kids didn't have the *quetzales*[9] to buy tickets to see the game for ourselves. Still, it was a moment of patriotism in our *barrio*. Time stopped across Guatemala when our national team played, and hanging outside the stadium made us participants in the excitement! In those brief moments, it was almost as if every person in La Limonada was actually family. Every one of us—the working class, the sick, the elderly, the children—felt unified by the same thrill. I didn't care so much that I couldn't see the game. I could hear it and feel it in my bones.

page 8

In response, we would rush to a tiny plot of land in our neighborhood with wooden goals set up on either end. No money for nets, but we were good at improvising and imagining. It was there that kids, teenagers, and grown-ups would come and scrimmage together. As a joke, we called that field *Maracaná*, named after a huge soccer stadium in Brazil. Maracaná stadium was where the world-champion Brazilian team suffered a memorable loss against Uruguay in the 1950s with the whole country watching. So, when the local team would lose those pick-up games in La Limonada, people would rub it in our faces by saying, "You got hit by the *maracanazo*!"[10]

One morning, I woke up wanting to watch some cartoons on our little television, but the TV set had disappeared. My family wondered how the thieves had taken the TV from our *covacha* without waking any of us up. Annoyed, my father began a nightly ritual of locking up the house more tightly than ever before.

"Did you already lock the door?" my father shouted from across the room.

The word "family" appears eleven times. The idea of sticking together is first developed here, but more obviously when Orozco describes his own family.

9. *quetzales*: Guatemalan money
10. *maracanazo*: the overwhelming shame of losing the game on their home field like the Brazilians did

"*¡Sí!*" I nodded. How could I forget? My job was to lock the front door, and I did

page 9

it the same way every night. One by one, I would turn several makeshift deadbolts into that useless doorframe and then secure it with an iron bar. When my father went to sleep, he kept a machete under his mattress just in case. My father was a fearsome match for any thief. Although short in stature, he was a man of great physical strength. His face was broad and square-jawed, his skin burnt brown by the sun. His black hair and equally black eyes gave him a fierce look that made those planning to cross him think twice. He had a stiff military walk and carried himself with pride, too. He always considered it a matter of great importance that his sons learn to fight for their survival, just as he had, so sometimes he would gather us together for a fighting lesson. We would shove the furniture away from the center of the room to clear a space, watching in awe as our father pulled his shirt up over his head. He must have known that the mere sight of his muscles both inspired and intimidated us. *Someday*, I thought, *I want to be strong like that. Strong and fearless.* He shifted around us like a caged tiger as my brothers and I all assumed a fighting stance, trying to impress him.

"Always intimidate your opponent with your gaze," he said, his eyes meeting each of ours. If I looked down or away, he corrected me. "No. Do not look down. Don't ever look down. If you look down, you lose your advantage. Your odds of winning the fight go down fifty percent." I tried to stand still as my father's eyes looked into mine, inspiring a cold shudder that rippled through my entire body. That look of his could bring down a man twice his size.

He came over to me and demonstrated what to do. "Stand like this." He puffed out his chest and gazed directly forward, straightening his shoulders.

"Yes, like that," he said when I kept my eyes level, and his praise was like a warm blanket. He never showed me or my brothers any affection, so a single word of praise from my father was like getting a championship trophy.

"The first fight you have to win is the psychological fight. Then comes the physical one. Remember, the winner may not be the biggest man, but always the smartest one."

Lined up in front of him, my brothers and I followed every move he made.

page 10

"Left, right! Punch! Punch as hard as you can! Go for the weak parts of the body." He would watch us, correcting our stance or the angle of our thrusting arms.

I tried to imagine an enemy standing there before me, sensing that someday I would need to do this for real. With my father's instruction, I understood that it was necessary to fight like this.

"Don't ever let anyone put you down. This life is about surviving." That was his mantra.

The ideas of learning to fight and survival are strongly developed in this story.

I respected and admired my father so much for his strength. Being strong was part of being an Orozco. My father (Francisco) had four brothers and one sister: Mario, Conrado, Jorge, Tono and Tía Naty. The five Orozco brothers never really had a childhood—they had worked their entire lives. They worked so hard because they believed in surviving with honor and dignity. My father loved to tell us how he made his living shining shoes in Concordia Park and carrying grocery bags for the housewives returning home from the market. He never gave up working, believing that someday he would be able to leave La Limonada behind. He had clipped a picture of his dream house out of a magazine and taped it to the back of the door, sneaking glances at it in his many moments of discouragement.

He led my family in dreaming of other tempting possibilities on the other side of the ravine. Just outside La Limonada, in Guatemala City, things were better. There was more space, more room to spread out, to make progress, to fulfill dreams. It was one of those things we did not dare discuss very often, but all of us shared the idea that someday we would free ourselves from this place. Years later, my family did finally escape, but not before La Limonada had taken her share.

Just like me, my father had been born and raised in La Limonada. His parents, lacking the means to live anywhere better, had settled here back in the 1950s. My grandparents cobbled together a *covacha* out of tin, wood scraps, and cardboard, and began to work hard and hope for the best. Back then, La Limonada wasn't nearly as crowded, but as the years went by and their sons grew into men, more and more families kept arriving. Not every family was poor but noble like my grandparents were, though, and our family's best defense against evil was to stick together. As a way to seal their bond of brotherly unity, my father and his four brothers all built themselves homes on my grandparents' plot of land and settled with their respective wives and children. My sister and brothers and I, along with my cousins Abel, Jorge, Mynor, Oralia, and Diana were the second Orozco generation to grow up in La Limonada. As one of the longest-established and largest families, there was a certain local prestige surrounding our page 11 family. We were important enough that Doña Toña made sure to keep us informed of all the latest developments in La Limonada's rumor mill.

Besides our family's solidarity, faith in God was also important. My father, his brother Jorge, and his mother Carlota attended the neighborhood evangelical Christian church faithfully every week. My *abuelita*[11] believed it was her duty to set a good example for us by how she lived her life. She had a copy of the Bible that she kept by her bedside, never missing an opportunity to speak to her children and grandchildren about God. That little church was where my father met Noemi, my

11. *abuelita*: grandmother

mother, who was the daughter of a Christian minister. My mom's glowing fair skin, sweet eyes, and curly hair set her apart, as did her beautiful soul. My father found her irresistible! Their relationship progressed rapidly towards marriage, and in time they brought five children into the world.

Each one of us had a unique personality. Libni was the baby, always curious. He asked me so many questions that it would drive me crazy! He was constantly running around the house playing with toy guns, pretending he was a soldier. Francis was the clown of the family, always making us laugh with his funny faces. Sometimes he would put on a show for us, setting up a little stage with a curtain and making puppets out of socks and old rags. Werner . . . liked to manage his money carefully. He was a saver, wise beyond his years, always talking about how he wanted to open his own business. Zully was the *nena*[12] of the house. As the only girl in the page 12 family, she had four brothers to contend with, so she secretly watched my father give us boys those fighting lessons to help her hold her own in our household. She had a defiant, independent streak that often got her in trouble, but she was also a daddy's girl, able to tug at my father's heartstrings and avoid the harsh style of discipline he used with his sons when they misbehaved.

My father, who knew all too well what a dangerous place this was to raise his children, viewed discipline as his best weapon against the bad influences in the streets. It galled him that some of my cousins fell in with the wrong crowd and ended up getting killed while running with the local gangs. My father would have none of this for his children, saying, "If I ever catch you smoking or hanging around with any riffraff, every inch of your back is going to meet my belt."

I, as his oldest son, had to be especially careful, knowing I was setting the example for all his children. I was a creative child, always memorizing poetry and dreaming of being a famous singer. I wanted to learn how to play an instrument, although of course my family couldn't afford to buy one for me. The ever-present perils of La Limonada did not look kindly upon a dreamer like me. Inspired by Mom's ceaseless optimism and my own tendency to daydream, I had a naïve outlook that got me in trouble when I chose to trust the wrong people. I was a gullible kid who was an easy target for pranksters and pickpockets. Whenever I was tricked into losing anything valuable, I knew I'd be in for it when I got home. Let's just say that my back and my father's belt became well-acquainted over the years.

My father devised his own trademark tortures to set me straight. Sometimes he would force me to kneel on hard corn kernels while holding a large tree branch as he beat me. I sometimes wondered where he got the inspiration for these punishments, but asking never seemed like a good idea. When they were over, trying to erase the

12. *nena*: baby girl

pain was my first and only priority, since his strictness meant that all too often there was another beating soon to follow.

One morning, Mom sent me to the store to buy some groceries as she often did. I was used to doing what was asked of me and for the most part my parents were able to trust me. "Jonathan, I need page 13 you to do this quickly," Mom said, "Your father will be home soon and you know how cranky he can be if his lunch is not ready."

She handed me a paper with a short list of groceries and a few bills with which to buy them. As I headed out the door she called, "Put the money in your pocket before you lose it. And don't forget to hurry!"

I set out on my way. As I neared the store, I spotted a group of my friends shooting marbles in the middle of a dusty alley. I was a sociable kid and loved to make friends with other kids, whether they had good or bad reputations. I thought it was best to be equally friendly with everyone. I smiled and went over to say hello to them.

One of the kids looked up at me, blocking the sun from his eyes. "Well, look who got out of the cage," he said sarcastically as I approached.

I took his mocking in stride.

"I bet Mommy and Daddy told you to hurry right back home, didn't they, mama's boy?" He grinned as this got a few laughs from the boys around him.

"Shut up. I'm not no mama's boy," I countered, although I had to admit to myself that he was right: Mom had been clear that I needed to be quick about this errand. *But how would she know if I stopped for five minutes?* I thought. *Would it really make a difference?*

I sat down with the rest of the kids. The game of marbles started heating up and we were all laughing and shouting. It was only a moment before I was lost in the game and forgot about the time. The sun was high at my back and suddenly I felt its warmth vanish. A huge shadow fell across the ground, covering our game. The rest of the boys went silent. I turned around, but the sun was at the person's back and I couldn't see who it was that stood behind me. Suddenly, the familiar lash of a belt identified the shadow as my father. I screamed.

I stood up as quickly as I could. "I'm sorry, *papa*! I'll never do it again, I promise!"

He didn't respond. Instead, he grabbed my arm and marched me home. When he pushed me through the door of our house, the first thing I saw was my mom's face. It was a mix of worry and relief.

page 14

"Where were you?" she cried, a note of fear cutting through her gentle voice. "I thought something had happened to you. What took you so long?"

As usual, Mom was concerned about my well-being while my father was concerned with how best to discipline me and make sure I didn't forget myself again. I put my head down, ashamed to have worried her.

"You didn't even get the groceries?" she asked, half-surprised. "Well, at least give me the money back. We'll have to go to the store later." She held out her hand.

I dug into my pockets. The money was not where I put it. One of the boys must have stolen it right out of my pocket while I played marbles! How could I have been so stupid? I stood there mad at myself and in dread of my father: the missing money guaranteed me an awful whipping. . . .

page 16 I knew it was a parent's job to discipline children who misbehaved, but there were times when my father would violently beat Mom in full view of his five children, and there was no way that my mind could come up with any way to justify his abusive behavior. As we all watched our mom suffer, a seething hatred mushroomed within me that spilled over and left its mark not just on my body, but on my mind and soul. The rage I felt towards my father became a self-propelled motor within me that only the power of God would be able to still.

Yet even while I despised his mistreatment, I had plenty of respect for him, too. My feelings towards my father were hopelessly conflicted. I hated him and loved him at the same time. How can I explain such a thing? Way down deep, I understood that he worked hard every day, making sacrifices while trying to feed his wife and five children. Not an easy task for a man who had no special skills or training and no prospects for a steady job. His frustration was our cross to bear.

Mom tried several times to escape from our father by bringing us to live with my maternal grandparents, Gabino and Ruth, who lived in a much better area just outside of the ravine. Here, we breathed easy for a few days, but it never lasted, since my father always convinced Mom to return to him. In her mind, it was right to honor the vows of marriage, even if it meant she had to suffer pain. Although no one would have blamed her for leaving an abusive husband, she wouldn't do it because she wanted her children to grow up with a father figure. Mom's commitment to both her kids and her marriage held the family together. Even the worst moments could not strip her of her relentless optimism.

Mom was always making the best of things with that big smile of hers. She taught us that we just have to enjoy life the best we can and that we should always look on the bright side. Her smile made us feel loved and safe page 17 even at the moments when life seemed like hell. More than anyone else, she was the one who gave us hope.

Besides the endless inspiration I got from my mom, I found my own hope that remained constant throughout my years in La Limonada. A presence of a mysterious nature was reaching out to me at the dawn's first light—a signal from God. Each day, the earliest light of dawn would poke through the rusted metal rooftops of our neighborhood, giving me the strength to face whatever challenges the coming day held for me. That light from above would sneak in through a little hole in our roof, and it would touch my face, as if it were trying to wake me up. "We need to patch that hole in the roof," we would always say, but somehow it never got repaired.

Sometimes, when I was daydreaming, I would think about that light and what it was trying to tell me. Was it letting me know ahead of time that something greater was in store for my life? It seemed so, but I could never be sure. In any case, that enigmatic beam of light was a very welcome guest in my *covacha*. I wondered to myself how long it might be—days, weeks, maybe even years—until that little light's prediction about my life would be fulfilled.[13]

Jonathan Orozco is a writer, music leader, and motivational speaker. Having survived childhood in a notorious slum in Guatemala, immigration to the United States, and his experiences with abuse, poverty, drug addiction, and gangs, he now shares a story of transformation for the encouragement and inspiration of others. To read more of the life and story of Jonathan Orozco, check out *Survive to Live* at https://amzn.to/2MtD89E or ask at your local library. You can get involved with helping kids in La Limonada with a group called Lemonade International (https://www.lemonadeinternational.org).

13. Jonathan Orozco, "La Limonada," in *Survive to Live* (self-pub., CreateSpace, 2017). Used by permission of the author.

Tell It Back—Summary

TE

1. Summarize “La Limonada” aloud, being sure to include important characters such as Jonathan Orozco’s father and mother, and incidents such as hanging out at the football stadium, the fighting lesson, and so on. Then, in the space provided, write two well-crafted sentences that describe the shantytown and the role it plays in the author’s life. The first sentence should begin with the phrase “A place of terror and fascination. . . .”

A place of terror and fascination ______________________________

Sample answer: A place of terror and fascination, La Limonada is a shantytown on the outskirts of Guatemala City and the childhood home of Jonathan Orozco. It was here that he learned the hard lessons of survival: how to fight and how to find hope.

TE

2. Look over the words, actions, and images that you highlighted in your reading of “La Limonada.” What important themes emerged as you read? Remember that a theme is an important idea that is repeated throughout a work of literature. Write down three different themes from the story and for each one offer at least two quotes as evidence of the theme.

   a. Theme:

   Sample answer: the struggle to survive

   Supporting quotes:

   Sample answers:

   “We struggled up and down these paths, slipping on the mud in the winter and choking on dust in the summer.”

   “The poor stole from the poor to survive.”

   b. Theme:

   Sample answer: violence

   Supporting quotes:

   Sample answers:

   “It was a place where thieves, rapists, drug dealers, and gangs planted themselves in the soil of disorder the *colonia* offered them, reaping a never-ending harvest of the bitter fruits of sin.”

   “When my father went to sleep, he kept a machete under his mattress just in case.”

c. Theme:

Sample answer: hope

Supporting quotes:

Sample answers: "I looked forward to the day when somehow I would gather the superhuman strength and resources to escape."

"He had clipped a picture of his dream house out of a magazine and taped it to the back of the door, sneaking glances at it in his many moments of discouragement."

"Sometimes, when I was daydreaming, I would think about that light and what it was trying to tell me. Was it letting me know ahead of time that something greater was in store for my life?"

Talk About It—

TE

1. What are some of the things that make life hard in a shantytown such as La Limonada?
2. Would it be possible to find anything beautiful or hopeful in a place such as La Limonada? Where would you look for beauty or hope? What aspects of Orozco's personality help him to stay positive?

Writing Time—

1. **COPIOUSNESS:** In the previous book in this series, *Description & Impersonation*, we introduced the idea of the Rule of Three as a great way to develop copiousness in your writing. We defined it as a writing technique that uses three repeated elements—including words, phrases, clauses, and sentences—that often are parallel in structure. Jonathan Orozco uses the rule in this sentence:

   Terror, fascination, and blood in the dirt—just another ordinary day in La Limonada.

   Here he lists two nouns and a noun phrase that describe an "ordinary day" in La Limonada. He does something similar in the following sentence, in which he uses three noun phrases to shape the identity of his community:

   La Limonada was a barrio, a slum, a shantytown.

   The Rule of Three is a valuable way of expressing your ideas because it establishes a pattern that helps to emphasize a point or improve the flow of your writing—all with the reader's understanding or pleasure as your goal. Although the Rule of Three involves a repetition of ideas, it is not the same as the stylistic vice of wordiness or redundancy that you saw in lesson 7. Redundancy is the *unnecessary* repetition of ideas, which adds excess to a sentence rather than rhetorical energy.

The Rule of Three is also known as the tricolon, and it is a rhetorical device with a long and illustrious career. The following are some excellent examples of how the rule has been used in a variety of settings.

- To rouse the citizens of Athens to action against the Macedonian conqueror Philip, Demosthenes uses tricolon:

  If you will consent to become your own masters, and if each man will cease to expect that his neighbor will do everything for him, then, God willing, you will recover your own, you will restore what has been frittered away, and you will turn the tables upon Philip.[14]

- In the movie *The Wizard of Oz*, the Wizard uses tricolon to brag on himself:

  You are talking to a man who has laughed in the face of death, sneered at doom, and chuckled at catastrophe.[15]

- President Barack Obama uses the tricolon frequently in his first inaugural address to celebrate the people of America:

  It has been the risk-takers, the doers, the makers of things—some celebrated, but more often men and women obscure in their labor—who have carried us up the long rugged path towards prosperity and freedom.

  For us, they packed up their few worldly possessions and traveled across oceans in search of a new life. For us, they toiled in sweatshops, and settled the West, endured the lash of the whip, and plowed the hard earth. For us, they fought and died in places like Concord and Gettysburg, Normandy and Khe Sanh.[16]

  Time and again these men and women struggled and sacrificed and worked till their hands were raw so that we might live a better life. They saw America as bigger than the sum of our individual ambitions, greater than all the differences of birth or wealth or faction.[17]

Notice how these examples demonstrate that the Rule of Three (or tricolon) isn't limited to using nouns or noun phrases. As noted in our definition of this rhetorical device, tricolon can make use of parallel words (such as verbs and adjectives), phrases, clauses, and whole sentences.

14. Adapted from Demosthenes, "The First Philippic," The Latin Library, accessed November 15, 2018, http://www.thelatinlibrary.com/imperialism/readings/demosthenes.html.
15. *The Wizard of Oz*, directed by Victor Fleming, written by Noel Langley, Florence Ryerson, and Edgar Allan Woolf (Culver City, CA: Metro-Goldwyn-Mayer, 1939), film, 102 mins.
16. These are important battles in American history: Concord during the American Revolution, Gettysburg during the Civil War, Normandy during World War II, and Khe Sanh during the Vietnamese War.
17. Barack Obama, Inaugural Address, The White House, January 20, 2009, Washington, DC, transcript, https://obamawhitehouse.archives.gov/blog/2009/01/21/president-barack-obamas-inaugural-address.

In this exercise you will try your hand at the Rule of Three as you take a closer look at the country of Guatemala, where author Jonathan Orozco lived as a child. Each of the following paragraphs provides information about Guatemala. After reading the paragraph, follow the instructions for creating several tricola (plural for tricolon) in the space provided.

Example:

Volcán de Agua

The land of Guatemala is mountainous and contains numerous volcanoes, several of which are active to this day. Although no longer spitting fire, the second highest volcano is Volcán de Agua, meaning "Volcano of Water" for the floods it has caused historically. The volcano forms a giant cone over the towns of Antigua and Santa María de Jesús. Its lower slopes are green with coffee trees, nurtured by a soil of ash and fertile volcanic dust. Coffee grown in volcanic soil is unrivalled in strength and flavor. Meanwhile, the bluish upper slopes of Volcán de Agua are often hidden by thick, gray clouds and rain.

▲ Volcan de Agua taken from "Cerro de la Cruz" in Antigua, July 2004. Image courtesy of Gusjer on Flickr, https://commons.wikimedia.org/wiki/File:Volcan_de_Agua_2004.jpg.

a. Create a complete sentence that includes a tricolon of adjectives that describe Volcán de Agua.

Above the towns of Antigua and Santa María looms giant, cone-shaped, colorful Volcán de Agua.

b. Create a complete sentence that includes a tricolon of nouns or noun phrases that describe Volcán de Agua.

Volcán de Agua is a giant, a tower of many colors, a watery peak of clouds and rain.

c. Create a complete sentence that includes a tricolon of parallel verbs that describe what Volcán de Agua does.

Volcán de Agua looms like a giant, nurtures like a mother, and hides like an assassin behind mist and rain.

d. Create a tricolon of parallel sentences to describe Volcán de Agua.

The Volcán de Agua resides among mountains. It rises above towns. It stands strong in the clouds.

A. Lake Atitlán

▲ View of Lake Atitlan and the Tolimán (right) and San Pedro volcanoes, February 2012. Image courtesy of Murray Foubister on Flickr, https://commons.wikimedia.org/wiki/File:Lake_Atitlan_%26_Volcanoes_from_the_East_(6996008535).jpg.

Lake Atitlán is the deepest lake in Central America, over 1,000 feet deep in one location. It shines like a blue jewel in the mountainous highlands of Guatemala. The lake itself was formed when a volcano collapsed and left behind an enormous caldera.[18] Around the shores of Lake Atitlán sit age-old villages in which Mayan culture is still strong. The villagers wear colorful Mayan dress, and often make a living from coffee bean and avocado growing or from fishing for bass and tilapia. Ancient Mayan ruins have been found on the shores and hidden in the waters of the lake. One of the most interesting aspects of the lake is a sudden strong wind that blows across the water at midday, a wind called Xocomil (show-koh-MEEL). According to Mayan legends, the wind carries sin away in its strong gusts. Some people say Lake Atitlán is the most beautiful lake in the world, and when you see it with the volcanoes of San Pedro and Tolimán off in the distance, you might agree.

a. Create a complete sentence that includes a tricolon of adjectives that describe Lake Atitlán.

Sample answer: The deepest, bluest, windiest lake in Guatemala is Lake Atitlán, which is surrounded by Mayan villages.

b. Create a complete sentence that includes a tricolon of nouns or noun phrases that describe Lake Atitlán.

Sample answer: Lake Atitlán is Guatemala's jewel of the mountains, her queen of fisheries, her keeper of history.

18. caldera: a volcanic crater

c. Create a complete sentence that includes a tricolon of parallel verbals that describe what Lake Atitlán does.

Sample answer: Lake Atitlán sits in the mountains, shining like a jewel, sheltering Mayan culture, hiding Mayan ruins.

d. Create a tricolon of parallel sentences that tell a tourist why she should visit Lake Atitlán.

Sample answer: Visit Lake Atitlán because it is beautiful. Stay there because Mayan culture remains alive on its shores. Return again and again because your fascination will only grow.

B. City of Panajachel

▲ Panajachel Docks, July 2009. Image courtesy of Francisco Anzola on Flickr, https://commons.wikimedia.org/wiki/File:Panajachel_Docks_(3746411153).jpg.

Tourists are drawn to Panajachel, a city on the shores of Lake Atitlán. Here in this Spanish-style town, visitors can charter boats for bass fishing or stroll down Calle Santander, a bustling market street lined with vendors selling local crafts. At midday the Xocomil winds blow off the lake, bringing a cooling breeze to siesta time—the time after lunch for taking a luxurious afternoon nap. At night, the Church of Saint Francis, a beautiful colonial church in the heart of the old city, resembles a castle as it glows in the floodlights. Religious pilgrims come to Saint Francis from all over the world to participate in the Lenten procession. Lovely hotels with high balconies overlook Lake Atitlán, and visitors stay out late dining on pumpkin soup and Pepián (a tomato, meat, and pepper stew). Tamales and empanadas (potato pastries) are also popular dishes, and you can wash them down with a cup of superb coffee or a papaya shake. But don't drink the coffee late at night or the caffeine will keep you awake till dawn.

a. Create a complete sentence that includes a tricolon of adjectives that describe the city of Panajachel.

Sample answer: Busy, bustling, beautiful Panajachel is the city I most want to visit.

b. Create a complete sentence that includes a tricolon of nouns or noun phrases that describe the city of Panajachel.

Sample answer: Let's stay forever in Panajachel, city of fishermen, city of tourists, city of pilgrims.

c. Create a complete sentence that includes a tricolon of parallel verbs that tell what visitors can do in the city of Panajachel.

Sample answer: In Panajachel, an adventurous tourist can feed her stomach, fill her shopping bag, and find her way to a famous church.

d. Create a tricolon of parallel sentences, joined by semicolons, that describe the city of Panajachel.

Sample answer: It bustles in the morning; it sleeps at midday; it glows at night.

Here are some important literary terms you can use in your thesis essay:

- autobiography: the nonfiction description or story of someone's life that is written by the person himself, usually in the first-person point of view
- character: a person who has a role to play in a story; can be imaginary, as in fiction, or a real person, as in nonfiction
  - flat character (also known as a static character): a simple character who is easy to define and who does not change in the course of a narrative
  - round character (also known as a dynamic character): a character who is complex and who changes in the course of a narrative. In the case of an autobiography, the narrator typically aims to present herself as a round character.
- fiction: literary prose that is imaginative and, even when based on historical people or events, fanciful rather than actual; includes novels and short stories
- first person: uses the pronouns "I," "me," "my"; the narrator takes part in the story
- nonfiction: literary prose that is based on actual events; includes biography, history, and essays
- setting: the physical location and historical time of a literary work
- theme: an important idea or topic that is repeated throughout a literary work

2. **THESIS ESSAY: LITERARY ANALYSIS**—The shantytown in "La Limonada" is a place of violence, terror, poverty, and disorder. At the same time, the story's author takes pains to show that hope still shines in the darkness, that family and dreams moor us to life. These ideas are all themes found in Jonathan Orozco's story, and there are more themes besides these: good versus evil, dark versus light, chaos versus order, and so on.

Think about the themes you listed in the Tell It Back section of this lesson. What do you think is the most meaningful theme in "La Limonada" and why? In other words, what central idea explored in this autobiography is most significant? You may want to answer the question by stating which theme is most significant to you, the reader, or you may want to answer by stating what theme you think is most significant to the characters or plot of the story. This speculative question has no single answer. You may answer one way and a classmate may answer a different way. But you are going to write an essay that strives to give *your* answer to this speculative question.[B] Since this is going to be a thesis essay, you want to persuade your audience (if you can) to agree with your answer, your thesis statement.

Types of evidence:
- details
- examples
- facts

Evidence can be presented as:
- quotations
- paraphrases
- summaries

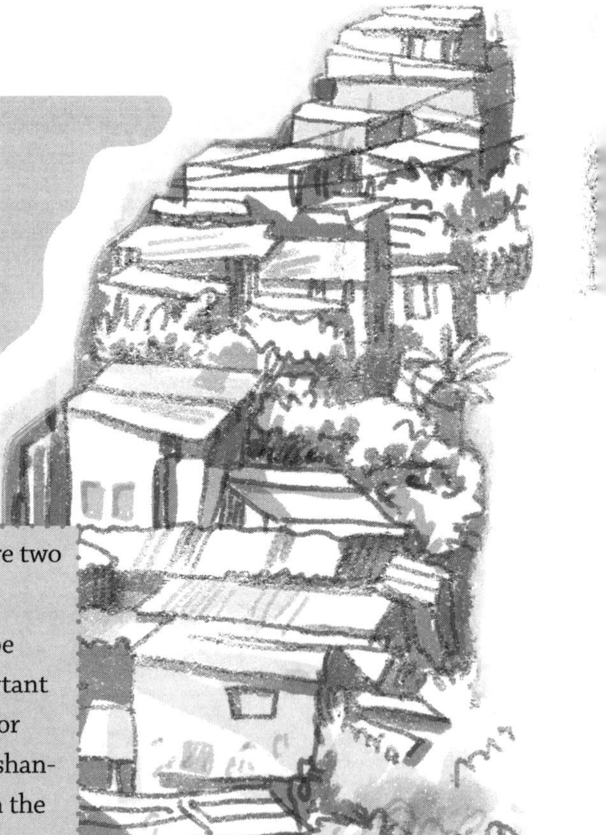

[B]If you desire for your class to produce different essays, here are two additional speculative questions for students to consider:

- Such a powerful setting as La Limonada will inevitably shape the character of the people who live there. Choose an important character from the story—Papa or the author (Jonathan), for example. How has this character been shaped by life in the shantytown, and how do you think it will change his character in the future for better or worse?
- How does the character of Papa, Mama, or the author (Jonathan) contribute to the important themes of survival and hope?

Examining the Text: As you consider your answer to the question "What do you think is the most meaningful theme in 'La Limonada' and why?" you should have a firm grasp of what happened in the story. By thinking through the story's ups and downs, you can think about what big ideas seem most important.

Use your annotations to review the story, making note of the repeated words, ideas, and images that you highlighted—elements that can all point to theme. Then answer the following questions and provide textual evidence for your responses in the form of a short quote or two from the story.

What causes the residents of La Limonada to feel despair, fear, and sorrow?

Sample answer: The ugly, unhealthy, poverty-stricken surroundings contribute to feelings of despair and sorrow. The seemingly inescapable violence—happening daily—probably contributes the most to fear.

Supporting quote(s):

Sample answers: "The fact was that although most parents wanted their kids to grow up with good manners and get a decent education, the environment was simply too unstable. Besides, even if all crime magically ceased, the local school facilities were crumbling and understaffed, lacking even the most basic necessities."

"Here, simple squabbles often ended in bloodshed."

"A river of sewer water ran beside the main roads, flowing northward for miles upon miles. The people of La Limonada had no choice but to build their public restrooms directly beside the river."

What causes the residents of La Limonada to feel happy or hopeful?

Sample answer: Football games played by the national team in a nearby stadium give the residents some sense of happiness, and even a simple game of marbles makes the children happy. Even more important, however, are moments of family love and natural beauty.

Supporting quote(s):

Sample answers: "We had all entertained plenty of fantasies about playing on Guatemala's national team one day, and now the team was *here*!"

"[Mom's] smile made us feel loved and safe even at the moments when life seemed like hell. More than anyone else, she was the one who gave us hope."

"I found my own hope that remained constant throughout my years in La Limonada. A presence of a mysterious nature was reaching out to me at the dawn's first light—a signal from God. Each day, the earliest light of dawn would poke through the rusted metal rooftops of our neighborhood, giving me the strength to face whatever challenges the coming day held for me."

How do you think La Limonada affects the main character of the story (Jonathan Orozco) for better or worse?

Sample answer: The main character of the story is a sensitive boy who likes to dream big. La Limonada is probably causing him to be hardened, to be more inclined to suspicion, violence, and ferocity, but conceivably his dreams and his sense of hope can help him to overcome these tendencies.

Supporting quote(s):

Sample answers: "The ever-present perils of La Limonada did not look kindly upon a dreamer like me. Inspired by Mom's ceaseless optimism and my own tendency to daydream, I had a naïve outlook that got me in trouble when I chose to trust the wrong people."

"My brothers and I feared that it was just a matter of time before one of us became a target, just like so many neighbors and acquaintances from our *colonia* whose lives had been ruined by violence."

"*Someday*, I thought, *I want to be strong like that. Strong and fearless.* He shifted around us like a caged tiger as my brothers and I all assumed a fighting stance, trying to impress him."

Considering Audience: Think about your audience for a moment. For example:

- Has your audience read Orozco's autobiography before? That will determine how much of the story background you need to include in your essay.
- Is your audience already interested in a nonfiction analysis, or is it disinterested and likely to require a strong hook to become engaged?
- What about your purpose for writing the essay? When you answer the speculative question, what point do you want to make? Do you want to caution your audience with themes of darkness, violence, or abuse so it better understands the harmful side of human nature? On the other hand, do you want to inspire your audience with a theme of hope or courage or resilience? The theme you pick can impact your audience to make it wiser or more compassionate, more suspicious or more hopeful.

Jot down some notes about your audience here. (If you need a refresher on considering your audience, please flip back to lesson 3.)

Who is my audience?

Sample answer: My audience is my teacher and my classmates. They have read the chapter before and do not require a full recap of the story.

What is my audience's disposition (friendly, neutral, hostile, etc.)?

Sample answer: My audience is friendly. My teacher and classmates will be interested in my nonfiction analysis, and eager to see what theme I think is most significant. Although my audience is friendly, I will want to engage them with the best evidence possible so that my ethos is solid and my understanding is seen as reasonable.

What is my purpose in writing to my audience (to inform, challenge, delight, awaken, encourage, warn, etc.)?

Sample answer: My purpose is to awaken my audience to the strength of the human spirit, which is hopeful even when surrounded by horrors and darkness. I want the audience to know that sometimes pain and hardship can improve our character.

Outline: Before you get started, here is the six-paragraph outline you will follow for your thesis essay. A sample of a completed thesis essay is available in the appendix (page 285).

I. Introduction
- A. hook and transition to thesis
- B. thesis
- C. explanation of thesis
- D. transition to next paragraph

II. Body Paragraph 1: Confirmation/Support
- A. topic sentence
- B. explanation of the confirmation
- C. appeal to authority (evidence in the form of a quote or paraphrase)

III. Body Paragraph 2: Confirmation/Support
- A. topic sentence
- B. explanation of the confirmation
- C. appeal to authority (evidence in the form of a quote or paraphrase)

IV. Body Paragraph 3: Refutation/Antithesis
- A. antithesis (as topic sentence)
- B. explanation of the antithesis
- C. refutation of antithesis/defense of thesis
- D. appeal to authority (evidence in the form of a quote or paraphrase)

V. Body Paragraph 4: Refutation/Antithesis
- A. antithesis (as topic sentence)
- B. explanation of the antithesis

C. refutation of antithesis/defense of thesis
D. appeal to authority (evidence in the form of a quote or paraphrase)

VI. Conclusion
A. thesis restated
B. why the topic is important
C. call to action (optional)

[C]If students are struggling with portions of the prewriting or the complete essay, you may want to show them the sample answers in the Teacher's Edition to help them see how the author has accomplished the task.

Use the following prompts for each paragraph to help you sketch out your ideas. You can use lists, phrases, or complete sentences for your answers. Then compose your full essay on a separate paper or on a computer.[C] Remember that each paragraph has a job to do in defending the thesis.

The paragraphs you write after going through these steps will be your first draft, or your first version of the essay. Assume that your first draft will need some rewriting to make it the best essay it can be.

Thesis Wheel

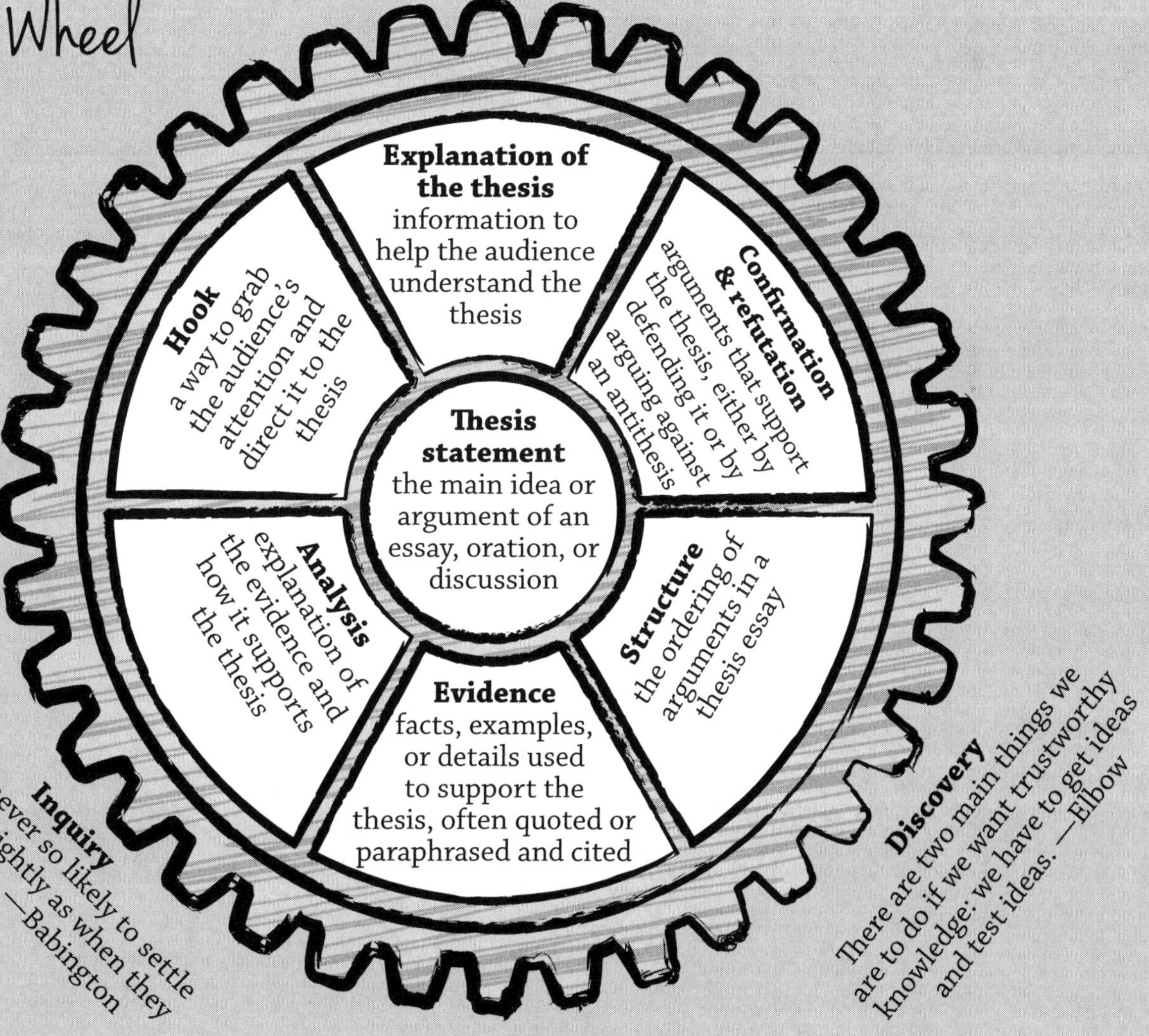

Based on the Essay Wheel developed by the Messiah College writing program.

Paragraph 1 (Introduction): The purpose of the introduction paragraph is to orient your reader and to reveal the point you plan to argue. You'll want to be sure to identify the name of the story, "La Limonada," and its author, Jonathan Orozco, somewhere in your introduction: hook, thesis statement, or the explanation following the thesis.

Writing the thesis is the first step in a thesis essay although you will actually place it *after* the hook when your write your introduction paragraph. Your thesis should answer the speculative question: What do you think is the most meaningful theme in "La Limonada" and why? Here are some questions that may guide you to a thesis:

- How should I determine what theme is most meaningful? Think in terms of what makes any aspect of life important and meaningful: Does the theme have a significant impact on the main character of the story? Does the theme reveal an important understanding of the human experience or human nature? Does the theme teach a lesson or provide inspiration?
- What idea seems to be repeated most often?
- What is the author's intention? Why did he write this autobiography? What message do you think he is trying to get across to his readers?
- As you consider your answer to the speculative question, look over your highlighter markings in the reading selection and gauge how much evidence you have to support your claim. You are trying to persuade your audience that your answer is correct. Therefore, the more evidence you can muster from the text to prove your point, the better.

Write your thesis statement in the space provided. Remember that a thesis is the main argument of a persuasive paper. A good thesis is open to debate, is clear and specific (not too broad), and can be supported by evidence. In this essay, the thesis statement should also mention the two supporting arguments that you will expand on in your confirmation paragraphs.[A]

[A]Here is an example of a thesis statement that includes a main argument and also mentions two supporting arguments:

simple thesis — "Children younger than thirteen should not own cell phones

supporting argument 1 — because they impair learning

supporting argument 2 — and cause addiction."

If you need to refresh your memory on this type of thesis statement, flip back to lesson 2.

Confidence Booster

Keep in mind that your thesis is an informed opinion. You have read the story carefully, taken notes, tracked words, and noted and discussed different themes. You are ready to have an opinion that really counts. Don't worry about having "the one true opinion." Rather, find a theme that you are eager to analyze and interpret for your audience. You are well prepared for this task. You've got this!

Thesis statement: Sample answer: Despite the violence and terror that appear to reign supreme in the shantytown, the most meaningful theme in Orozco's chapter "La Limonada" is hope, because it remained constant in his childhood through his mother's love and through the sunlight that shone through his roof.

Now, in one sentence, explain your thesis. You will expand on this explanation in your confirmation paragraphs.

Explanation of thesis: Sample answer: Because this hope returned again and again to lift Orozco's spirits and outshine difficulties, it was more significant than the other elements of life in La Limonada.

Now write a transition sentence that takes the reader from the thesis explanation to the first confirmation paragraph. Remember that a transition forms a bridge from one paragraph to another. One side of the "bridge" will be made by referencing the topic of your first paragraph and the other side of the bridge will hint at what comes next.

Transition sentence: Sample answer: Even when life in the shantytown was grim, hope showed up and overcame in a variety of ways.

Next, go back and think about the very beginning of your introduction paragraph, the hook. Decide on a way to hook your audience that will lead naturally to your thesis. You can choose from narratives (fables, parables, anecdotes, jokes, news flashes, summaries), questions, descriptions, illustrations, proverbs, sayings, quotations, provocative statements, statistics, or facts.

Ideas for a hook: ______ Sample answer:

- Cicero: "When there's life, there's hope."
- Cicero never travelled to La Limonada. Can there really be hope there?

In order to move from your hook to your thesis, you will need some sort of transition. You might summarize your hook or the plot of the text you are analyzing, or put forth the speculative question you are answering. You may even use more than one element to make your transition. However you do it, you should make a smooth connection between your hook and the argument you will be presenting.

Transition from the hook to the thesis: ______

Sample answer:

- summary of the story
- show how the story relates to the question asked in the hook

When you write your full introduction paragraph, remember that even though in your prewriting you started with the thesis and then worked back to the hook, your completed paragraph should follow the order of hook (with transition), thesis, transition.

Paragraph 2 (First Confirmation): Each confirmation paragraph will explain and justify your thesis in depth from a different angle. In other words, each paragraph will set out one confirming argument that shows why your thesis is true. Start the paragraph with a topic sentence, which tells the main idea of the paragraph—what your confirmation argument will be.

Topic sentence: ______ Sample answer: One way that Orozco constantly saw hope in his early days was through the faith and love of his mother.

Follow the topic sentence by explaining it and give supporting evidence. In order to appeal to authority, be sure to quote or paraphrase an idea from the story. Your quote or paraphrase should support (confirm) or clarify your argument. Remember that your quote will need to be introduced and then explained, and be sure to cite your source.[D]

[D]If your students need a refresher on using quotations and paraphrase to provide evidence, please refer them to lesson 6.

Quotation or paraphrase from the text: ______________________________

Sample answer: "She never stopped believing that someday, somehow, things would get better and all would be well. Eventually, she proved to be right" (Orozco, 6).

Paragraph 3 (Second Confirmation): Start with a topic sentence, which tells the main idea of the paragraph—what your confirmation argument will be.

Topic sentence: ______________________________

Sample answer: The light of dawn that touched Orozco's face each morning was another expression of hope's constant presence in his life.

Follow the topic sentence by explaining it and giving supporting evidence. In order to appeal to authority, be sure to quote or paraphrase an idea from the story. Your quote or paraphrase should support (confirm) or clarify your argument. Remember that your quote will need to be introduced and then explained, and be sure to cite your source.

Quotation or paraphrase from the text: ______________________________

Sample answer: "I found my own hope that remained constant throughout my years in La Limonada. A presence of a mysterious nature was reaching out to me . . . giving me the strength to face whatever challenges the coming day held for me" (Orozco, 17).

Paragraph 4 (First Refutation): Each refutation paragraph will explain and refute an antithesis, a disagreement with your thesis. In other words, each paragraph will set out one antithesis and then show why it is untrue. Start the paragraph with the antithesis, which will serve as the topic sentence or main idea of the paragraph. You should lead into the antithesis with a phrase such as "Some readers might argue that . . .".

- Tip: Consider your audience as you work on your antitheses. What objections might your teacher or classmates have to your thesis? You may even want to ask them.

Antithesis: Sample answer: Some readers of *Survive to Live* might argue that survival is the most meaningful theme of "La Limonada."

Follow the antithesis by explaining it. To help you think through your explanation, consider listing some supporting arguments for the antithesis before you start to write.

Next, defend the thesis by telling why the antithesis is wrong. Appeal to authority with textual evidence by using a quote or paraphrase from the story that supports or clarifies your defense. Remember that your quote will need to be introduced and then explained, and be sure to cite your source.

Defense: Sample answer: Orozco had bigger dreams than survival. He wanted a better, happier life for himself and for his family.

Quotation or paraphrase from the text:

Sample answer: "La Limonada was not the place I wanted to die in. No. I longed, yearned, to be released. I had a will to survive. And I looked forward to the day when somehow I would gather the superhuman strength and resources to escape" (Orozco, 7).

Paragraph 5 (Second Refutation): Start with the antithesis, which will serve as the topic sentence or main idea of the paragraph. You should lead into the second antithesis with a phrase such as "Other readers might argue that . . .".

Antithesis:

Sample answer: Other readers might see despair, not hope, as the primary theme of "La Limonada."

Follow the antithesis by explaining it. To help you think through your explanation, consider listing some supporting arguments for the antithesis before you start to write.

Next, defend the thesis by telling why the antithesis is wrong. Appeal to authority with textual evidence by using a quote or paraphrase from the story that supports or clarifies your defense. Remember that your quote will need to be introduced and then explained, and be sure to cite your source.

Defense:

Sample answer: If the residents of La Limonada had been more despairing than hopeful, would they have tried to protect their possessions and families?

Quotation or paraphrase from the text: ______________________________

> Sample answer: "But in the alleys of La Limonada, these opportunists met their match in hardy residents determined to hang on to what few possessions they had. In the words of my optimistic mother, La Limonada was *our* place, *our* home" (Orozco, 6).

Paragraph 6 (Conclusion): In your conclusion, you should make your case one last time by restating your thesis. For the prewriting stage, jot down a new version of the thesis using fresh language.

Restatement of the thesis: ______________________________

> Sample answer: Although at times only a glimmer, the light of hope was the strongest theme in Jonathan Orozco's story because it was always present, showing up through people, circumstances, and nature, remarkably triumphant in the worst of situations.

When you come back to this prompt to write your full paragraph, consider what you have learned from supporting your thesis in the previous paragraphs. Your final restatement should express a fuller and more complete understanding of the thesis now that you have tested your ideas in the body of the paper.

Example:

- Original thesis: "Students should spend time outdoors to improve their quality of life and overall health."
- Restated thesis: "By spending time outdoors, students will reduce stress and boost their overall happiness, as well as get physical exercise and experience improved sleep."

Notice how the restatement presents the thesis with more precision and insight, demonstrating the deeper understanding that was gained through the process of writing the essay. Rework your restated thesis as needed to express this deeper understanding.

Next, tell why your topic is important. In other words, how can this topic be applied to real life or change the reader's outlook?

Why your topic is important: ______________________________

> Sample answer: It's important to realize that hope can be found even in a place such as La Limonada. Orozco's optimistic outlook, even in the worst of circumstances, proves that darkness and despair do not have the last word.

You can also look carefully at your body paragraphs and emphasize any points that best support your thesis. Another possibility is to urge your readers take some sort of concrete action.

Call to action (optional): ______________________________

Sample answer: Few of us have obstacles as big as Orozco's. His story shows that we should take a positive outlook and determine to push through the hardships in our lives.

Once you have completed your prewriting, go through these instructions again and write your paragraphs based on the prompts.

[E]If you want to draw out the game or make sure every student has a turn, you can require each participant to answer correctly twice before being able to hit the piñata.

Speak It—

1. **GRAMMAR PIÑATA:** It doesn't have to be someone's birthday party for you to bash a piñata. In this game, hang a piñata or two from a tree branch or basketball hoop. Individual students will be given two sentences written on card stock, one with correct grammar and the other with incorrect grammar. The student must choose the sentence with correct grammar. If she chooses correctly, she wins the chance to wear a blindfold and swing a stick at the piñata. (Another possibility is to draw a piñata on the board and make X marks upon it for correct answers. After twenty marks, it "bursts open.")[E]

▲ The burro is a common shape for a piñata in Latin America.

Piñata in San Diego, California, September 2007. Image courtesy of Paul Sapiano on Flickr, https://commons.wikimedia.org/wiki/File:Pi%C3%B1ata_in_San_Diego.jpg.

For instance, the cards might say, "I was deeply effected by the play" and "I was deeply affected by the play." Given the context of the sentence, "affect" is the proper word. The blindfolded student would choose the proper card and say, "I was deeply affected by the play. 'Affect' with an A." She would then take a swing at the piñata. If she gets the answer wrong, she must yield the turn to the next student in line.

Here are some grammatical concepts you could practice with this game:

- accept and except
  - "Accept" is a verb meaning "to receive willingly or admit as true." For example: "I accept this award on behalf of my whole team." "We accept your explanation."
  - "Except" can be a preposition, a conjunction, or occasionally a verb. As a preposition, it means "excluding, not including, or apart from." For example: "We have nothing to fear except fear itself." As a conjunction, it can take the place of "but." For example: "I tried to call you, except your ringer was off." As a verb, it means "to leave out or exclude." For example: "It would be wrong to except children from this restaurant." "All dentists are terrifying, present company excepted."

- affect and effect
    - "Affect" as a verb means "to have an influence on" or "to change somehow." For example: "The Supreme Court ruling will affect this nation for generations." "Are you affected much by the medicine?"
    - "Effect" as a noun means "outcome" or "result." It can also mean "the impression or appearance of something." For example: "The effect of the stock market crash was financial ruin." "The actor paused for dramatic effect."
- farther and further
    - "Farther" can be used as an adverb meaning "a greater distance" when referring to a physical distance. For example: "My legs will collapse if we go much farther." It can also be an adjective meaning "more distant." For example: "We will row to the farther island."
    - "Further" is an adverb that can mean "a greater distance" when referring to a figurative, nonphysical distance. For example: "You must go further in providing evidence for your thesis." It can also be an adjective meaning "additional" or "more." For example: "I don't have any further questions, your honor."
- fewer and less
    - "Fewer" is a useful adjective when you are talking about multiple items that can be counted. For example: "We see fewer butterflies in our garden than last year."
    - The adjective "less" is used when you are talking about a singular or abstract noun that can't be counted. For example: "This year there has been less rain than usual." "The less greed the better."
- lay and lie
    - "Lay" and "lie" are busy verbs with many meanings. In the present tense, "lay" is a transitive verb (needs an object) that means "to put something or someone down." For example, "I lay down the book." In the present tense, "lie" in an intransitive verb (no object needed) that means "to recline or be in a horizontal position." For example: "I lie down whenever I need a nap." An easy way to remember the difference between the two words is: "You lay something down, and people lie down on their own."
- if and whether
    - "If" is a conjunction generally used to introduce a condition. For example: "If it rains, the picnic will be cancelled." "I won't eat the toast if you've used marmalade."
    - "Whether" is also a conjunction, but it is mostly used to show two alternatives. For example: "I've been wondering whether [or not] to grow a mustache." "You should study hard whether the test is easy or difficult."

- which and that
  - "Which" can be used as a pronoun to introduce a **nonrestrictive clause**, a clause that can be deleted without changing the meaning of the sentence. For example: "The train, which blows its horn every night, is fun to watch from the bridge." "I want to learn to play every instrument in the orchestra, which is the only reason I want to live for two hundred years."
  - "That" can be used as a pronoun to introduce a **restrictive clause**, a clause that can't be deleted without changing the meaning of the sentence. For example: "Brazil is the team that has won the World Cup the most times." "The Earth is the only planet that sustains life as far as we know."

A variation of this game can be done with spelling and vocabulary words. For example, a teacher would say, "Spell 'onomatopoeia' for a chance to whack the piñata." Or the teacher would say, "In which sentence is the word 'onomatopoeia' used correctly and why?" and then give two alternative sentences.

2. **PARTNER FEEDBACK:** With a student partner (or your teacher), take turns reading the rough drafts of your thesis essays. You and your partner should give each other comments about what is more or less effective about your writing. Use the rubric at the back of the book to help you get ideas for your comments. (Don't worry about awarding points to your classmate. Scoring an essay is your teacher's job.) Try to say two positive things about your partner's essay, and then come up with at least two suggestions for editing or revising the essay.[F]

Ask each other:

- Does my hook capture your interest?
- Is my thesis clear, specific, and debatable?
- Does each confirmation paragraph clearly support the thesis?
- Does each antithesis clearly argue against the thesis?
- Does each defense (refutation) paragraph clearly refute its antithesis and support the thesis?
- Do I introduce and explain credible evidence, and do I include a source citation for every quote or paraphrase?

If you are constructively honest with your partner, your comments will really help him or her.

[F]At this stage, students can give each other thoughtful feedback. The thesis rubric can serve as their guide for constructive comments and notes. Students will likely need to hear a teacher say that feedback is a way for writers to help each other and that every professional writer depends on the input of others, hence it's important that feedback comes with a healthy dose of respect and encouragement. Make sure to allow enough time between drafts so that students can receive help from classmates and the teacher.

Revise It—

1. **STYLISTIC VICE:** Mixing Formal and Informal Language—**Formal language** is wording that takes a more serious, objective, or impersonal tone. It is appropriate for academic writing, the kind of writing you are most likely to do in school. You also typically want to be formal when applying for a job or whenever you want your writing to sound elevated or professional. **Informal language**, which is more casual and personal, is fine in most other situations, especially when you want to share your feelings, entertain your audience, or sound more relaxed and conversational.

   Of course, when writing persuasively, you need to take your audience into consideration. Some audiences may be moved by formal language while others may be moved by informal language. What doesn't work so well (unless you have a legitimate stylistic reason) is when you bounce between formal and informal. When your tone is inconsistent, you're likely to give your audience a case of stylistic motion sickness. It won't likely know how to take you.

   For the thesis essays in this book, you will take a formal tone. Here are some basic rules for sounding more formal:

▲ Just as this young woman is dressed in a formal, fancy gown for her quinceañera, the celebration of her fifteenth birthday, you should be ready to use formal language in a thesis essay.

Quinceañera, April 2011. Image courtesy of Eneas De Troya on Flickr, https://commons.wikimedia.org/wiki/File:Quincea%C3%B1eras_2012_-_Ma%C3%B1ana,_todo_el_d%C3%ADa_(7119927199).jpg.

- *Use a more precise vocabulary.* Precise words show that you have put thought into your writing, and that you are not simply thinking "off the cuff."

  Examples:
  - Instead of the word "good," use "honorable," "merciful," "considerate," "polite," and so on.
  - Instead of the word "scary," use "intimidating," "abhorrent," "spooky," "alarming," and so on.
- *Use interesting sentence structures, including compound and complex sentences, in addition to simple sentences.* Formal writing seeks to capture more sustained and complex ideas.

  Examples:
  - Give me your tired, your poor, your huddled masses yearning to breathe free. —from "The New Colossus" by Emma Lazarus[19]

19. Emma Lazarus, "The New Colossus," in *Emma Lazarus: Selected Poems and Other Writings*, ed. Gregory Eiselein (Ontario: Broadview Press, 2002), Poetry Foundation, https://www.poetryfoundation.org/poems/46550/the-new-colossus.

- With malice toward none, with charity for all, with firmness in the right as God gives us to see the right, let us strive on to finish the work we are in, to bind up the nation's wounds, to care for him who shall have borne the battle and for his widow and his orphan, to do all which may achieve and cherish a just and lasting peace among ourselves and with all nations. —from Abraham Lincoln's second inaugural address[20]

- *Avoid* **colloquialisms**, which are informal or slang expressions. Unintentional use of colloquialisms can make a writer seem careless.

  Examples:
  - Instead of "chill," use "relax."
  - Instead of "gonna," use "going to."
  - Instead of "blue," use "sad."
  - Instead of "ain't," use "am not," "is not," "are not," "has not," or "have not."
  - Instead of "kid," use "child."

- *Avoid the first and second person (I, me, my/you, you, your). Prefer third person (he, she, it, one/they, them, their).* Formal writing seeks an objective tone. Use of first-person and second-person point of view can make the sentence more personal and subjective.[21] **G**

  Tip: Use the words "people," "one," "someone/somebody," etc., to take the place of "you," or rearrange the sentence and avoid the personal reference altogether.

  Examples:
  - *Informal:* Poison ivy rash really causes you to itch badly.
  - *Formal:* Poison ivy causes a rash and significant discomfort for anyone allergic to its oils.
  - *Informal:* You should understand the importance of bees and pollination.
  - *Formal:* Everyone should understand the importance of bees and pollination.

GPlease understand that eliminating first and second person takes some practice and discussion, but eventually students become more adept at finding substitutions and learn to self-correct. As pointed out in the footnote, some writers can successfully use first- and second-person point of view in formal writing. However, it is best for young writers to stick with the third person while learning to handle evidence and argument. Once they have gotten a firm grasp on thesis writing, they can return to the challenge of writing formally in the first or second person.

HPlease note that identifying informalities is somewhat subjective and your students may make different choices and leave some things unchanged. The idea of this exercise is not to require identical answers from person to person, but to grow awareness that language has formal and informal registers and that these registers are appropriate and inappropriate depending on the context. Feel free to show students the sample corrections in the Teacher's Edition and discuss what is different and how the differences affect the reading.

20. Abraham Lincoln, Second Inaugural Address, April 10, 1865, Washington, DC, Our Documents, transcript, https://www.ourdocuments.gov/doc.php?flash=true&doc=38&page=transcript.
21. As with many writing rules, skillful writers sometimes break this rule for a desired effect. In this case, some writers can succeed in sounding formal even when using the first- and second-person point of view.

The following excerpt is adapted from *Guatemala, The Country of the Future* by Charles Melville Pepper, a special trade agent and journalist. He is likely writing to business people and diplomats who want a serious, sober assessment of Guatemala's resources. We have altered some of Pepper's formal language to include the informalities of imprecise vocabulary, too many simple sentences together, colloquialisms, and first- and second-person point of view. Correct the excerpt so that the language is consistently formal. Feel free to delete, substitute, or rearrange words and phrases, or to leave them alone if they sound formal enough. **H**

Use the following proofreader's marks to mark up the text.

≡ capitalize

/ lowercase

delete letter, word, or punctuation

^ insert letter, word, or punctuation

Guatemala, the Country of the Future

The Republic of Guatemala, which name is derived from the Indian word "Quanhitemallan," signifying "land covered with trees," has been described as the ~~best~~ privileged zone of Central America. This is because of its resources, ~~It is also because of~~ its climate, And its accessibility, ~~helps as well. You can get to~~ the country ~~super fast~~ is easily reached from all directions through its seaports on both the Pacific and Atlantic Oceans and through its system of railways, which is ~~breaking out and~~ growing rapidly. From California, from the neighboring ports of other Central American countries, and from Panama, ~~you can hitch a ride using~~ it's possible to take the regular and reliable steamship service on the Pacific coast. On the Atlantic or Gulf side from New York, New Orleans, Galveston, and Mobile, there is steamship service ~~most~~ all the time. ~~And that isn't all, not by a long shot~~.[I] The steamers on the Pacific coast

[I] Please note that students may recognize this statement as redundancy, which they learned about in lesson 7. It is both a redundancy and informal language.

~~totally~~ connect at San José with the Guatemala Central Railway, which makes it ~~a piece of cake~~ easy to arrive at the capital city and the great coffee-raising districts.

In its physical aspects Guatemala is a country of mountains~~, It's got~~. tropical forests~~, It's got~~. lakes and rivers~~,~~. ~~And, of course, we shouldn't forget the~~ coastal plains. ~~I've heard it~~ It has been described as extremely fertile and well cultivated, and ~~it's my opinion~~ this description holds ~~good~~ today. ~~You will find that~~ Guatemala [City], the capital, is the largest city in Central America. The location is ~~awfully~~ very healthy, being 5,000 feet above sea level. The city is laid out on a~~n almighty~~ splendid scale with many fine avenues, not to mention parks.

The soil of Guatemala is remarkable in its ~~big~~ vast extent and ~~nice~~ abundant variety of two classes of products, which are unusual within the same degrees of latitude. That is, it produces both tropical and temperate staples of agriculture in great profusion. The soil grows coffee, sugar-cane, cacao, bananas, tobacco, cotton, rubber, vanilla, sarsaparilla, and ~~loads of~~ other products ~~stuff as well~~. ~~Never mind~~ It also produces a long list of medicinal plants, while it likewise produces the cereals, wheat, and Indian corn, which are only found in temperate regions, giving two and in some places three crops of these annually. There are also~~,~~ ~~if I may say so,~~ endless kinds of good hardwood, mahogany, rosewood, ebony, cedar, and the like, which ~~you can call~~ are called tropical timber, and at the same time pine and oak exist in the mountain regions of the interior.

▲ The coffee fruit looks like a red cherry.

Coffee berries March 2011. Image courtesy of Stanislaw Szydlo on Flickr, https://commons.wikimedia.org/wiki/File:Coffee_berries_1.jpg.

As ~~you should~~ many people know, Guatemala's best regarded agricultural product is coffee. The fame of Guatemalan coffee is worldwide, and it commands the highest prices.[22]

22. Adapted from Charles M. Pepper, *Guatemala, the Country of the Future* (Washington, DC, 1906; Project Gutenberg, 2011), https://www.gutenberg.org/files/38264/38264-h/38264-h.htm.

2. **REWRITING:** Follow these steps to improve your first draft.

   a. Get feedback. Use comments from your student partners (or from your teacher) to strengthen and improve your paper.

   b. Wait a day or two before you rewrite your paper. The time away from it will help you to see its problems more clearly.

   c. Read the paper aloud to yourself. This is often the best way to catch mistakes—grammar errors, as well as words that don't work well—because you will be using two senses—seeing and hearing—instead of one. If something sounds wrong, it probably is.

The following is the original formal language of author Charles M. Pepper. Feel free to read the excerpt to your students after they have completed the Revise It exercise. By listening to the original, young people may be better able to discern the more serious, objective tone of formal writing.

> The Republic of Guatemala, which name is derived from the Indian word "Quanhitemallan," signifying "land covered with trees," has been described as the privileged zone of Central America. This is because of its resources, its climate, and its accessibility. The country is easily reached from all directions through its seaports on both the Pacific and Atlantic Oceans and through its rapidly growing system of railways. From California, from the neighboring ports of other Central American countries and from Panama, there is regular and reliable steamship service on the Pacific coast. On the Atlantic or Gulf side from New York, New Orleans, Galveston and Mobile there is frequent steamship service. The steamers on the Pacific coast connect at San José with the Guatemala Central Railway, which affords easy means of arriving at the capital city and the great coffee-raising districts.
>
> In its physical aspects Guatemala is a country of mountains, tropical forests, lakes and rivers and coastal plains. It has been described as extremely fertile and well cultivated, and this description holds good to-day. Guatemala [City], the capital, is the largest city in Central America. The location is unusually healthy, being 5,000 feet above sea level. The city is laid out on a splendid scale with many fine avenues and parks.
>
> The soil of Guatemala is remarkable in the vast extent and great variety of two classes of products which are unusual within the same degrees of latitude, that is, it produces both tropical and temperate staples of agriculture in great profusion. The soil grows coffee, sugar-cane, cacao, bananas, tobacco, cotton, rubber, vanilla, sarsaparilla, and a long list of medicinal plants, while it likewise produces the cereals, wheat and Indian corn which are only found in temperate regions, giving two and in some places three crops of these annually. There are also endless kinds of valuable hardwood, mahogany, rosewood, ebony, cedar and the like, which are especially tropical timber, and at the same time pine and oak exist in the mountain regions of the interior.
>
> As is well known, Guatemala's most valuable agricultural product is coffee. The fame of Guatemalan coffee is worldwide and it commands the highest prices.

Once you are ready to rewrite, use the following steps to aid with your revision:

a. *Find your thesis and underline it.* There also should be a restatement of the thesis in your conclusion. This restatement should show a fuller and more complete understanding of the thesis.
b. *Find the topic sentence for each body paragraph and highlight it.* Each body paragraph should begin with a topic sentence stating the main idea of the paragraph. The topic sentence for a confirmation paragraph should confirm some aspect of the thesis. The topic sentence for a refutation paragraph should introduce an antithesis, which opposes the thesis.
c. *Find the evidence (appeal to authority) in each body paragraph and highlight it.* Did you choose the best quote or paraphrase to make your point? Make sure that all evidence is properly introduced and explained and has source citations.
d. *Make sure each paragraph gets the job done.* Remember that each paragraph has a special purpose in supporting your thesis through analysis and evidence. Does each paragraph successfully accomplish this goal?
e. *Make sure you have consistently considered audience.* Have you written your essay based on your understanding of the audience's makeup, disposition, and needs? Have you carefully considered possible objections to your thesis?
f. *Make sure you have kept a formal tone throughout the essay.* Have you eliminated informalities of writing such as too many simple sentences, imprecise vocabulary, first- and second-person pronouns, and colloquialisms?
g. *Find and fix grammar mistakes.* Make sure all your nouns and verbs agree and that your writing is clear. Fix any fragments or run-ons. In other words, make sure you are writing complete sentences.
h. *Strengthen phrasing.* Are your word choices specific instead of vague? Do you use strong nouns and verbs? Do you vary your sentences and occasionally begin them with a prepositional phrase or a participial phrase? Weed out passive voice and excess adjectives. Use compound sentences, appositives, adverb phrases, and questions to make your writing more interesting. Transition smoothly between ideas and paragraphs using transition words.
i. *Proofread.* Look for any punctuation, spelling, or capitalization errors. Then fix them!
j. *Retype* the draft with the corrections you have made.

Lesson 8: Second Thesis Essay: Analysis of an Autobiography

Tell It Back—Summary

1. Sample oral summary: Jonathan Orozco starts his story about life in the Guatemalan shantytown of La Limonada with the description of a dangerous knife fight between two of its more notorious residents. We learn that such violence is frequent and ordinary in this crowded barrio of ramshackle houses watered by a stream that has become a sewer. Like other kids of La Limonada, young Orozco dreams of getting out and traveling beyond the ravine that traps him in the shantytown. He and his friends hang out at the nearby national football stadium and wonder if, someday, they too can become famous players and leave. Orozco's father is a tough guy who demands that his children be tough for their survival, giving them fighting lessons and telling them never to look away from an opponent. Orozco's mother provides a gentler influence in his life and gives him the kind of love he needs to keep his dreams alive. Even when his father abuses his mother, Orozco finds comfort in a spot of light that enters through a hole in the roof and touches his face.
2. Here are two strategies students can use to identify important themes:
    - Make lists of repeating words, actions, and images. Group them in columns according to their similarity of meaning.
    - Look at words, actions, and images, as well as settings and physical descriptions, and see if patterns are created that compare or contrast these elements. For example, the purity of sunlight contrasts with the impurity of the sewer. The gentleness of the mother contrasts with the toughness of the father.

    As noted in the highlighting instructions earlier in the lesson, you will find examples of themes marked in the reading selection as well as in the following sample answers. Feel free to share the examples with your students as needed.

Talk About It—

1. The threat of violence seems to hang over every aspect of life in La Limonada. It would be very stressful and oppressive to have to face the possibility of harm (and even death) around every street corner. Another difficulty is the poverty filling the entire shantytown. The author experienced having his TV stolen from his shack while he was sleeping and having his pockets picked while shooting marbles. It seems as if no one can trust his neighbor. Anytime a resident of the shantytown has a speck of "wealth," it doesn't seem to last long before it's stolen from him. In addition, the houses seem to be falling down and the stream running through the neighborhood is a dangerous, open sewer. It would not be easy to live in conditions such as those.

2. I don't know that everyone in a slum such as La Limonada would be able to find beauty and hope, but I would like to think that beauty and hope still find their way into the cracks and crevices of life there.

   Just as Orozco found hope and beauty in a sunbeam in his home and in the smile of his mom, it might be possible to find hope and beauty in nature, and in family and friends.

   Orozco describes himself as a dreamer and a hopeful person, and these aspects of the personality can play an important role in a person's ability to find beauty and hope in difficult circumstances.

Paragraph Writing Instructions

Paragraph 1 (Introduction): Start with a hook, followed by a transition to your thesis. Then state your thesis, explain the thesis, and transition to the next paragraph.

Paragraph 2 (First Confirmation): Start with a topic sentence that makes one confirming argument showing why your thesis is true. Follow the topic sentence by explaining it and giving supporting evidence. Be sure to include a quote or paraphrase from the story.

Paragraph 3 (Second Confirmation): Start with a topic sentence that makes a second confirming argument showing why your thesis is true. Follow the topic sentence by explaining it and giving supporting evidence. Be sure to include a quote or paraphrase from the story.

Paragraph 4 (First Antithesis): Start with a topic sentence that gives one antithesis to your thesis. Explain the antithesis and then defend your thesis by telling why the antithesis is wrong. Be sure to include a quote or paraphrase from the story.

Paragraph 5 (Second Antithesis): Start with a topic sentence that gives a second antithesis to your thesis. Explain the antithesis and then defend your thesis by telling why the antithesis is wrong. Be sure to include a quote or paraphrase from the story.

Paragraph 6 (Conclusion): Restate your thesis with fresh language that shows a more complete understanding of the thesis. Then tell why your topic is important (how it applies it to real life or changes the reader's outlook). If desired, follow with a call to action.

Sample Thesis Essay: The Light of Hope

Paragraph 1: Introduction

hook

Cicero, a famous Roman statesman, once claimed, "When there's life, there's hope." But Cicero never travelled to La Limonada, a place where survival is difficult and hope seems nearly impossible. Can there be any hope in a place where drug dealers and murderers roam the streets, and a simple disagreement ends in bloodshed? Jonathan Orozco grew up in the Guatemalan shantytown of La Limonada, and he chronicled his childhood there in his gripping autobiography *Survive to Live*. He and his family wanted to escape the violence that plagued everyday existence, but this violence consistently threatened their dreams. However, despite the violence and terror that appear to reign supreme in the shantytown, the most meaningful theme in Orozco's chapter "La Limonada" is hope, because it remained constant in his childhood through his mother's love and through the sunlight that shone through his roof. Because this hope returned again and again to

Transition from hook to thesis

Thesis

Thesis explanation

lift Orozco's spirits and outshine difficulties, it was more significant than the other elements of life in La Limonada. Even when life in the shantytown was grim, hope showed up and overcame in a variety of ways.

Transition

Paragraph 2: First Confirmation

Topic sentence

Explanation and evidence

One way that Orozco constantly saw hope in his early days was through the faith and love of his mother. Although surrounded by poverty and crime from a young age, Orozco was raised by a woman of unflagging optimism. She was abused by her husband and she was forced to raise her family in a leaky shack, yet Jonathan Orozco's mother was a source of inspiration to him in the darkness of La Limonada. He writes of his mother, "She never stopped believing that someday, somehow, things would get better and all would be well" (6). He calls her "the one who gave us hope" and says that it was her smile, her commitment to her family, and her belief that God was watching over the Orozcos that so often gave her family the courage to go on (17). His mother's belief that the darkness couldn't last forever and her belief in life's possibilities helped to inspire Orozco's own hopeful dreams. Because her hope was so constant, hope became the predominant theme of Orozco's childhood, and he notes that "eventually, she proved to be right" (6).

Paragraph 3: Second Confirmation

Topic sentence

Explanation and evidence

Evidence from the text

The light of dawn that touched Orozco's face each morning was another expression of hope's constant presence in his life. Orozco saw the beam as a sign that he was destined for more than a violent, destructive life. Because the light poked through his roof at the beginning of every day, every day in La Limonada began for him with a ray of hope. It was his personal reminder each morning that someday his life would be full of light instead of darkness. Orozco remembers that through the light, "I found my own hope that remained constant throughout my years in La Limonada. A presence of a mysterious nature was reaching out to me . . . giving me the strength to face whatever challenges the coming day held for me" (17). Orozco's hopeful interpretation of the light shows that he was determined to overcome the difficulties of his childhood. He wanted to find hope, and hope found him in the form of this light. Because the light's hope "remained constant" instead of flickering or dying out, and because it gave him strength to meet each day's challenges, this hope was a constant and strong theme in the darkness of La Limonada.

Paragraph 4: First Refutation

Antithesis

Explanation of antithesis

Refutation/ defense

Some readers of *Survive to Live* might argue that survival is the most meaningful theme of "La Limonada." Not only is the word "survive" in the book's very title, but survival is the primary goal of the residents of the shantytown. Because of the high crime rate and poverty, Orozco's family and neighbors could not hope for anything more than to survive each day. Orozco may have been a dreamer, but wasn't his ultimate dream simply to stay alive? A closer look at the text reveals otherwise, however. It shows that Orozco had bigger dreams than mere survival. He not only wanted to continue living, but he also wanted a better, happier life for himself and for his family. He hoped for more than what La Limonada could offer, and this

TE

Refutation/ defense

hope transcended mere survival. He writes that "La Limonada was not the place I wanted to die in. No. I longed, yearned, to be released. I had a will to survive. And I looked forward to the day when somehow I would gather the superhuman strength and resources to escape" (7). Orozco did not want to die in La Limonada, but he also did not want to continue living there. He had hope that he would escape someday. Instead of writing that he'd escape *if* he gathered resources, he wrote that he'd escape *when* he gathered them. He was confident that escape from the darkness was coming. Survival was a high priority, but the hope of better things was more meaningful to him.

Evidence from the text

Paragraph 5: Second Refutation

Antithesis

Explanation of antithesis

Refutation/ defense

Other readers might see despair, not hope, as the primary theme of "La Limonada." The violence and mayhem in the town's streets prevented Orozco from having a safe childhood, and terror pervaded daily life for his family. Hope must have been fragile compared to the despair of having to endure those conditions. But if the residents of La Limonada had been more despairing than hopeful, would they have tried to protect their possessions and families? Despair was certainly a possibility, but the good people in La Limonada still believed that hope could prevail. After describing the thieves who prowled the streets and stole from residents, Orozco writes, "But in the alleys of La Limonada, these opportunists met their match in hardy residents determined to hang on to what few possessions they had. In the words of my optimistic mother, La Limonada was *our* place, *our* home" (6). It was hope, not despair, that characterized the inhabitants of the shantytown. Instead of giving in to violence and surrendering their possessions to thieves, some clung to what they could and still thought of La Limonada as their home. The crime was frightening and discouraging, but it could never erase these residents' belief that private property should be protected and that it was important to establish a home. This example shows that hope was more present than despair for them.

Evidence from the text

Paragraph 6: Conclusion

Restatement of thesis

Why topic is important

Although at times only a glimmer, the light of hope was the strongest theme in Jonathan Orozco's story because it was always present, showing up through people, circumstances, and nature, remarkably triumphant in the worst of situations. If hope can be found even in a place such as La Limonada, then Orozco's optimistic outlook proves that darkness and despair do not have the last word. His story shows that a positive mentality and determination to push through hardships can make even the darkest of situations lose its power over the human spirit.

Work Cited

Orozco, Jonathan. "La Limonada." *Survive to Live*. Translated by Jay Trovato, self published, printed by CreateSpace, 2017.

The purpose of this lesson is to expose students to a variety of authors who have considered the question "What is beauty?" and to inspire students' thinking about this subject.
In this lesson, students will practice:

- annotation
- written summarization
- critical thinking
- picture analysis
- recitation of poetry

Lesson 9

Feel free to be flexible with how you use this lesson. While we see value in every reading in this chapter, you can adapt the number and difficulty of the readings to fit the needs of your particular class.

Third Thesis Essay, Part I: What Is Beauty?

Have you visited an art museum recently? I have. And as often happens to me, I was astonished by the incredible, almost superhuman skill of the artists. I wish I could share with you all the beauty I saw under one roof that day, but here are several highlights:

I saw *Woman Holding a Balance* by Johannes Vermeer:

In a gallery down the hall I saw *The Last of the Buffalo* by Albert Bierstadt:

One short people-mover ride away, I found this stormy painting, *Snow in New York*, by Robert Henri:

And I was captivated by this bright, sun-drenched scene, *Open Window, Collioure*, by Henri Matisse:

The power that artists have to create beauty delighted me in gallery after gallery. Yet when it came to the modern wing of the museum, I felt that some artists had intentionally lost touch with beauty. I grew increasingly critical of the objects hanging on the walls and standing on the floor. There was a corkscrew of rusty metal that looked like wreckage from a junkyard. There were dark rubber blobs in a window that looked like tire tracks in the mud. There were paintings with blocks of color and with black scribbles that reminded me of finger paintings I had done as a fat-fingered four-year-old. I felt that some of the artists were perpetuating a kind of joke on me and the other visitors at the museum.

I know it's not very sophisticated of me to admit that I find a fair bit of modern art to be thoughtless, ridiculous, and ugly. To be clear, I've seen some modern art that I believe to be masterpieces as well. One has only to look upon the Fallingwater house of Frank Lloyd Wright or the surrealist paintings of Salvador Dalí or the abstract paintings of Makoto Fujimura or the stained glass swirling through the interior of the Cathedral of Brasília to see that the fire of beauty continues to be sustained. And yet . . . too many contemporary artists seem to have achieved celebrity status no thanks to their ability to capture beauty, but thanks to a cultural shift that celebrates the new, the fresh, the different—even the shocking. In some cases a new and controversial gimmick is easier to market, easier to publicize, than something merely beautiful.

▲ Fallingwater, southern perspective, August 15, 2016. Image courtesy of SuperAnth, https://commons.wikimedia.org/wiki/File:Fallingwater_-_Southern_perspective.jpg.

I'm not the only one who thinks this way. In his documentary *Why Beauty Matters*, philosopher Roger Scruton has this to say:

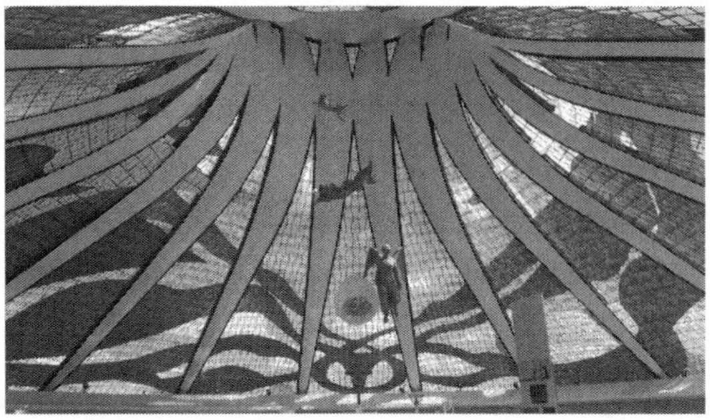

▲ Interior da Catedral Metropolitana de Brasília, May 18, 2013. Image courtesy of Setnab, https://commons.wikimedia.org/wiki/File:C%C3%BApula_da_Catedral_de_Bras%C3%ADlia_-_Setnab.jpg.

> At any time between 1750 and 1930, if you had asked educated people to describe the aim of poetry, art, or music, they would have replied, "Beauty." And if you had asked for the point of that, you would have learned that beauty is a value, as important as truth and goodness. Then in the twentieth century, beauty stopped being important. Art increasingly aimed to disturb and to break moral taboos. It was not beauty, but originality, however achieved and at whatever moral cost, that won the prizes.
>
> Not only has art made a cult of ugliness, [but] architecture, too, has become soulless and sterile. And it's not just our physical surroundings that have become ugly. Our language, our music, and our manners are increasingly raucous, self-centered, and offensive as though beauty and good taste have no real place in our lives. One word is written large on all [of] these ugly things and that word is "me"—my profits, my desires, my pleasures—and art has nothing to say in response to this except, "Yeah, go for it."
>
> I think we are losing beauty, and there is a danger that with it we will lose the meaning of life. . . . Philosophers have argued that through the pursuit of beauty, we shape the world as a home. We also come to understand our own nature as spiritual beings, but our world has turned its back on beauty and because of that we find ourselves surrounded by ugliness and alienation.[1]

But what does that word "beauty" mean? We use it as an adjective all the time. Babies, models, and mothers are all *beautiful*. That was a *beautiful* gesture, a *beautiful* song, a *beautiful* memory, a *beautiful* time, a *beautiful* place, a *beautiful* feeling. What is beauty? Many would say that modern art—the strange, the shocking, the childish—is indeed beautiful, that the culture has not shifted away from beauty in art but rather that the definition of beauty has expanded and grown more sophisticated. And who is Roger Scruton—or me or you—to sit in the seat of judgment and decide whether something is beautiful or not? Isn't beauty in the eye of the beholder? What's beautiful to me is not necessarily beautiful to you, right?

This idea that beauty is determined by each individual is known as subjective beauty. It is an idea promoted by philosophers such as David Hume and Voltaire. Hume writes, "Beauty is no quality in things themselves: It exists merely in the mind which contemplates them; and each mind

1. Excerpted from Roger Scruton, *Beauty* (New York: Oxford University Press, 2009), as used in *Why Beauty Matters*, November 28, 2009, BBC2, off-air recording, https://www.youtube.com/watch?v=bHw4MMEnmpc. Used by permission of Oxford University Press.

perceives a different beauty. One person may even perceive deformity, where another is sensible of beauty;[2] and every individual ought to acquiesce in his own sentiment, without pretending to regulate those of others."[3] Along these lines Voltaire says, "Ask a toad what beauty is. . . . He will answer you that it is his toad wife with two great round eyes issuing from her little head, a wide, flat mouth, a yellow belly, a brown back. . . . Interrogate the devil; he will tell you that beauty is a pair of horns, four claws and a tail. Consult, lastly, the philosophers, they will answer you with gibberish: they have to have something conforming to the arch-type of beauty in essence, to the *to kalon*."[4 5] Obviously Hume and Voltaire see beauty as nothing more than something that creates a response of pleasure in a person. And Hume thinks that people should "butt out" before judging anybody else's idea of beauty.

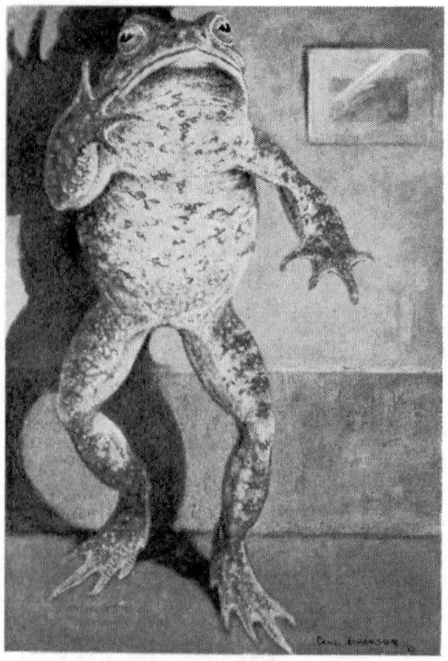

▲ "Ask a toad what beauty is. . . . He will answer you that it is his toad wife with two great round eyes issuing from her little head, a wide, flat mouth, a yellow belly, a brown back." —Voltaire

But wait a minute. Aren't these philosophers talking about taste when they discuss beauty? As we noted in lesson 2, everyone has different taste. There's no way to explain why one person prefers a red dress and another prefers a black dress. Or why someone enjoys tortilla soup instead of tom yum soup. For foodies like me, the more soup in the world, the better. Taste *is* subjective—there's no accounting for it. But just because you or I can't appreciate a particular thing—a blossoming cherry tree or rain on a windowpane, for instance—doesn't mean that the object isn't beautiful. There may be qualities to the object that make it beautiful regardless of a person's taste for it.

I think Hume and Voltaire are dodging the question, "What is beauty?" Certainly we each experience beauty differently, and there is something essential in the unique response of each individual, but beauty is something bigger than taste. If beauty were only in the eye of the beholder, a matter of taste, then everything would be beautiful and the word would have no meaning. In other words, if everything were beautiful, nothing would be beautiful. And let's face it: Some people find destructive things to be appealing to their taste. Some people have a taste for cruelty, for pornography, for racism, for being intoxicated. Is it OK to call something beautiful if it is destructive to human life and spirit? For something to be truly beautiful, doesn't it also have to be good? And what does it mean to be good? Does it mean simply good technique (e.g., skillful sculpting) or does it mean moral goodness?

2. Hume is saying that one person may see ugliness where another person sees beauty. For example, one person may see the mole on Marilyn Monroe's cheek as beautiful and someone else may see it as a deformity.
3. David Hume, "Of the Standard of Taste," in *Harvard Classics: English Essays*, ed. Charles W. Eliot, vol. 27, *From Sir Philip Sidney to Macaulay* (New York: P.F. Collier & Son Company, 1909–14; New York: Bartleby.com, 2001), http://www.bartleby.com/27/15.html.
4. *to kalon*: a Greek concept that means "an ideal beauty," which combines physical perfection and moral goodness. The idea that outer beauty comes from some inner, unseen, objective standard of beauty is shared by Plato and others in the classical world.
5. Voltaire, *The Philosophical Dictionary*, trans. H.I. Woolf (New York: Knopf, 1924; Hanover College, 1995), https://history.hanover.edu/texts/voltaire/volbeaut.html.

[A]You may need to remind students that we are not asking what is beautiful about the image itself but about the idea that is being demonstrated by the image, such as a soldier's fierce valor.

Beauty seems easy to understand until we try to define it. And many have tried: Beauty is "a red, red rose."[6] Beauty is the starry night sky, "the burning tapers"[7] of heaven. Beauty is the "Attic shape"[8] of a Grecian urn. While these images may summon up some facet of beauty, they are really just sparkles in a great, glittering diamond. We aren't any closer to defining the idea of beauty, are we? Like all abstract nouns—"truth," "goodness," and "love" among them—"beauty" can describe many things. What do a pretty face and a mountain have in common that they should both be called beautiful? How is it that we use the term "beautiful" to describe a grandfather's tender love as well as a soldier's fierce valor and a delicious meal?

Each of these images demonstrates something we might call beautiful: the fierce valor of soldiers, a grandfather's tender love, a majestic mountain, a pretty or handsome face, and a delicious meal. What do these five things have in common that might lead us to describe each of them as beautiful? **A**

▲ The fierce valor of soldiers: *The Three Servicemen* by Frederick Hart

▲ A grandfather's tender love: *The Banjo Lesson* by Henry Ossawa Tanner

▲ A majestic mountain: *Mount Fuji Seen Across a Ray* by Hiroshige

▲ A pretty or handsome face: *Pinkie* by Thomas Lawrence and *The Blue Boy* by Thomas Gainsborough

Sarah Barrett Moulton: Pinkie by Thomas Lawrence, 1794. Image courtesy of Flickr user LongLiveRock via Wikimedia Commons November 2008, https://commons.wikimedia.org/wiki/File:Pinkie_by_Thomas_Lawrence_(3051046057).jpg.

▲ A delicious meal: *Pancakes with Berries* by Herson Rodriguez

6. Robert Burns, "A Red, Red Rose."
7. William Shakespeare, *Titus Andronicus*, act 4, scene 2.
8. John Keats, "Ode on a Grecian Urn."

One possible way to unlock beauty's deeper meanings is to examine literature and consider what the poets and storytellers have to say about beauty's effect on their characters. Consider the legends of three of the most beautiful women of all time: Helen of Troy, Cleopatra of Egypt, and Xi Shi (Hsi Shih) of China.

We are told that Helen was "the fairest of her sex,"[9] with such a glorious face that her abduction sparked the Trojan War and launched a thousand ships. While the Greeks were looting Troy, her husband Menelaus went roaming through the ruins, searching for Helen to murder her and take revenge for her faithlessness. But when he found her, what happened? He was again so struck by her beauty that he sheathed his sword and swept her into his arms.

According to Shakespeare, Cleopatra's beauty "beggared all description,"[10] and Plutarch tells us: "The attraction of her person, joining with the charm of her conversation, and the character that attended all she said or did, was something bewitching."[11] She was so bewitching, in fact, that both Julius Caesar and Marc Antony fell in love with her.

> Antony was so captivated by her that . . . [leaving his troops] assembled in Mesopotamia, and ready to enter Syria, he . . . suffer[ed] himself to be carried away by her to Alexandria, there to keep holiday, like a boy, in play and diversion, squandering and fooling away [his days] in enjoyments.[12]

▲ *Cleopatra*, Michelangelo, black chalk on paper

It would be fair to say that Antony's obsession with Cleopatra's beauty caused him to lose the Roman Empire. He simply spent too much valuable time dallying in Egypt while his rival in Rome, Octavian, strengthened his power. But before we're too harsh with Antony, let's ask guys to answer honestly: Which would they rather do, fight a war in the rain and the gore and the muck, or stay in luxurious Egypt hanging out with one of the most beautiful women of all time?

As for Xi Shi, her beauty was so dazzling that it is rumored that when she gazed into a pond, the fish would forget to swim and sink to the bottom. If she looked up into the sky as a flock of birds was passing overhead, they would fall smitten to the ground. The powerful warrior king Fuchai of Wu married Xi Shi. He found her to be so beautiful that he forgot all about ruling and fighting. Instead, he spent his days building her beautiful palaces and gardens. In the end, Fuchai's kingdom was captured and he committed suicide.

9. Thomas Bulfinch, "The Trojan War," in *Bulfinch's Mythology: The Age of Fable* (Project Gutenberg, 2004), http://www.gutenberg.org/cache/epub/3327/pg3327.html.
10. William Shakespeare, *The Tragedy of Antony and Cleopatra*, 2.2.888 (Project Gutenberg, 2000), http://www.gutenberg.org/cache/epub/2268/pg2268-images.html.
11. A.H. Clough, *Plutarch's Lives* (Project Gutenberg, 1996), http://www.gutenberg.org/cache/epub/674/pg674-images.html.
12. Clough, *Plutarch's Lives*.

The common theme in each of these stories is that beauty disarms the warrior male. (Teachers may also want to point to the myth of Venus and Mars.)

▶ There's a theme running through these stories. Can you say what it is?

Despite the sorry demise of Antony and Fuchai, beauty clearly did something wonderful in the lives of these men. It gave something beyond conquest for them to aspire to and enjoy.

Lest you think that these lightning bolts of beauty happen only to men, there are plenty of examples of famous women struck by passion for the male form. Tennyson's Lady of Shalott was told she would be cursed and die if she ever looked directly out her tower window upon the castle of Camelot. But then mighty Sir Lancelot comes riding through the wood, dressed in brass armor, and he shines in "blue unclouded weather"[13] like a meteor in the sky. Of course, the Lady can't resist gazing upon the beautiful knight, and it is her joy in his beauty that leads to her death. Think of Venus's infatuation with Adonis, Hippolyta's amazement at Hercules, Atalanta's love for Hippomenes, and Bathsheba Everdeen's passion for Sergeant Troy and you see that the shoe is often on the other foot.

In the epic poem *Paradise Lost*, the character Satan is depicted by Milton as being deeply affected by the beauty of Eden. But then, feeling estranged from the beauty he desires, he determines to destroy it. Here's what Satan says when he first spies the glories of the garden:

O Earth, how like to Heav'n, if not preferred
More justly, Seat worthier of Gods, as built
With second thoughts, reforming what was old!
For what God after better worse would build?
Terrestrial Heav'n, danced round by other Heav'ns — heavn's: stars and planets
That shine, yet bear their bright officious Lamps, — officious: eager to serve
Light above Light, for thee alone, as seems,
In thee concentering all their precious beams
Of sacred influence . . .
With what delight could I have walked thee round,
If I could joy in aught, sweet interchange — aught: anything
Of Hill, and Valley, Rivers, Woods and Plains,
Now Land, now Sea, and Shores with Forest crowned,
Rocks, Dens, and Caves; but I in none of these
Find place or refuge; and the more I see
Pleasures about me, so much more I feel
Torment within me, as from the hateful siege
Of contraries; all good to me becomes
Bane, and in Heav'n much worse would be my state. — Bane: poison
But neither here seek I, no nor in Heav'n
To dwell, unless by mastering Heav'ns Supreme; — In other words, Satan can't enjoy heaven or earth if he can't conquer God.

13. Alfred, Lord Tennyson, "The Lady of Shalott," Poetry Foundation, accessed November 30, 2018, https://www.poetryfoundation.org/poems/45359/the-lady-of-shalott-1832.

Nor hope to be myself less miserable
By what I seek, but others to make such
As I, though thereby worse to me redound:
For only in destroying I find ease
To my relentless thoughts.[14]

redound: return, recoil

In Milton's epic, the beauty of nature exerts a momentarily wholesome power over even as depraved a figure as Satan. But his response is a desire to take revenge on that feeling rather than to be led by it to worship God.

A similar thing happened in real life. When the German *führer* Adolf Hitler defeated France, he took a tour of Paris, often considered to be the most beautiful city in the world. Like Satan in Milton's Eden, Hitler toured all of the city's delights: the opera house, the Eiffel Tower, the Arc de Triomphe, and the Panthéon. At the end of the tour, with glittering eyes, he told his favorite architect, "It was the dream of my life to be permitted to see Paris. I cannot say how happy I am to have that dream fulfilled today."[15] Later he said, "Wasn't Paris beautiful? But Berlin must be made far more beautiful. In the past I often considered whether we would not have to destroy Paris, but when we are finished in Berlin, Paris will only be a shadow. So why should we destroy it?"[16] Hitler likely stayed his wanton impulses because of the worthy influence of beauty. Interestingly enough, his first response was like Satan's—he wanted to destroy beauty to protect and bolster his own ego and sense of power.

In all of these cases—from Menelaus to the Lady of Shalott—we get a sense of a powerful force acting on each person. This force comes from the human form, from nature, from a city. . . . It is the force of beauty. Beauty awakens a deep longing in each person to hold on to something, to embrace it passionately, to be enfolded into it. And those who encounter beauty are somehow changed, if only temporarily. What is going on here? Can you put this effect into words? Here are some sentence starters that may help you:

- The force of beauty is like . . .
- People want to embrace beauty because . . .
- Beauty causes people to be more . . .
- Beauty causes people to be less . . .

14. John Milton, *Paradise Lost*, bk. 9, lines 99–130, The John Milton Reading Room, accessed November 5, 2018, https://www.dartmouth.edu/~milton/reading_room/pl/book_9/text.shtml. Spelling has been standardized.
15. "Hitler Tours Paris, 1940," Eyewitness to History, accessed November 5, 2018, http://www.eyewitnesstohistory.com/hitlerparis.htm.
16. "Hitler Tours Paris."

Thinking about how beauty affects people can help you develop a sense of its qualities, which can, in turn, steer you to a definition of beauty. Of course, this is only one of many ways that you can tackle the topic.

As you can see, beauty is a complex subject and it won't be easy to define and describe it. And yet that is your task. Your job will be to define and describe this mysterious power, this wonderful, fascinating force, in your thesis essay. Before you get started, however, take some time to plow through the readings in this lesson, which highlight a number of different ideas about beauty. (You will find exercises among the readings to help you think about them more deeply.) These readings tend to be philosophical in nature—that is, thoughtful and carefully reasoned—and you may find them a challenge at first. However, they are worth the effort, for they offer valuable insight to help you consider and support your thesis.

Heads Up!

To save yourself time flipping back and forth between this lesson (mainly readings) and the next lesson (mainly writing) when you write your essay, you may want to make a list of the paragraphs and pages from this lesson that you find most useful. Or, you could break out your fancy highlighters, gel pens, and sticky notes to tag quotes and inspirational passages so you can find them quickly—but don't overdo it! If you mark practically everything, you won't easily spot what you're looking for.

Although the ideas presented in these readings are challenging, the evidence you will use to support them (and your thesis) will be much more straightforward. They will come from all the lovely paintings, music, poetry, sculpture, architecture, dance, figure skating, and literature you've encountered. Think about the kindness of your friends, the coziness of your home, the courage of a police officer. You will use the things you love as examples of beauty, and these examples will support the ideas you choose from this lesson to prove your point.

Now, onward!

The Importance of Size in Beauty

—adapted from *Poetics* by Aristotle

One of the great philosophers of ancient Greece, Aristotle (c. 384–322 BC) wrote *Poetics* mainly to describe the elements of poetry and drama (comedy and tragedy). Here he takes a brief digression to describe the importance of size to beauty.

A beautiful object, whether it be a living organism or any whole composed of parts, must not only have an orderly arrangement of parts, but must also be of a certain size; for beauty depends on size and order. Hence a very small creature cannot be beautiful because it is hard to see and the view of it becomes confused. Nor, again, can any giant object be beautiful for as the eye cannot take it all in at once, the unity and sense of the whole is lost for the spectator. An example of something too large to be beautiful would be an object one thousand miles long. The size of an object must be easily embraced in one view.[17]

▲ According to Aristotle's definition of beauty, this Grecian urn and this Mughal mausoleum, the Taj Mahal, are neither too large nor too small, but just the right size to be beautiful. Greek amphorae, such as the urn, were also prized for their symmetry. If a line were drawn straight down the middle of the urn, you would see the delightful balance between the two halves. The same principle holds true for the Taj Mahal.

Taj Mahal, 2010. Image courtesy of Yann Forget, edited by Jim Carter. © Yann Forget / Wikimedia Commons / CC-BY-SA-3.0, https://commons.wikimedia.org/wiki/File:Taj_Mahal_(Edited).jpeg.

17. Adapted from Aristotle, *Poetics*, trans. S.H. Butcher (Project Gutenberg, 2008), part VII, https://www.gutenberg.org/files/1974/1974-h/1974-h.htm.

The Importance of Symmetry in Beauty

—adapted from *The Ten Books on Architecture* by Vitruvius

Marcus Vitruvius Pollio (c. first century BC) was a Roman architect and military engineer who wrote the famous handbook *On Architecture*, which stressed the importance of symmetry and proportion in architectural and human beauty.

1. The design of a temple depends on symmetry, the principles of which must be most carefully observed by the architect. They are due to proportion—in Greek ἀναλογία. Proportion is a correspondence among the measures of the members of an entire work, and of the whole to a certain part selected as standard. From this result we derive the principles of symmetry. Without symmetry and proportion there can be no principles in the design of any temple; if there is no precise relation between its members it cannot be beautiful, and the same is true for man.

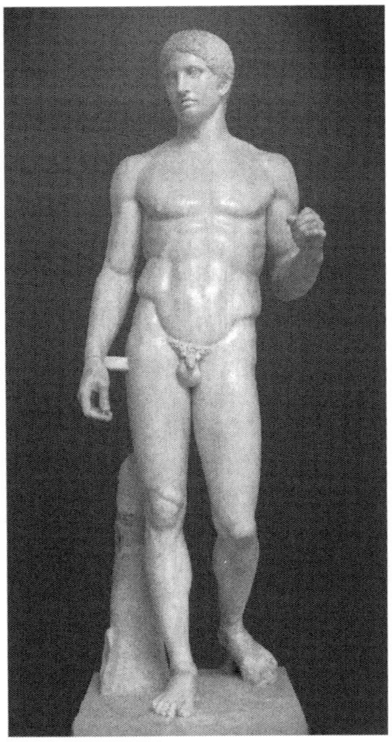

▲ The *Doryphoros*, or *Spear Bearer*, was designed by the sculptor Polykleitos to depict the perfectly proportioned man using exact mathematical measurements. Similarly, Greek architects strove to make their temples harmonious in their proportions, as demonstrated by the Parthenon in Athens.

Doryphoros from Pompeii. Image courtesy of Marie-Lan Nguyen, February 13, 2012, https://commons.wikimedia.org/wiki/File:Doryphoros_MAN_Napoli_Inv6011-2.jpg.

Parthenon, Athens, Greece, August 26, 1978. Image courtesy of Flickr user Steve Swayne via Wikimedia Commons, https://commons.wikimedia.org/wiki/File:The_Parthenon_in_Athens.jpg.

2. For the human body is so designed by nature that the face, from the chin to the top of the forehead and the lowest roots of the hair, is a tenth part of the whole height; the open hand from the wrist to the tip of the middle finger is just the same; the head from the chin to the crown is an eighth, and with the neck and shoulder from the top of the breast to the lowest roots of the hair is a sixth; from the middle of the breast to the summit of the crown is a fourth. If we take the height of the face itself, the distance from the bottom of the chin to the underside of the nostrils is one third of it; the nose from the underside of the nostrils to a line between the eyebrows is the same; from there to the lowest roots of the hair is also a third, comprising the forehead. The length of the foot is one sixth of the height of the body; of the forearm, one fourth; and the breadth of the breast is also one fourth. The other members, too, have their own symmetrical proportions, and it was by employing them that the famous painters and sculptors of antiquity attained to great and endless renown. . . .

3. Therefore, since nature has designed the human body so that its members are duly proportioned to the frame as a whole, it appears that the ancients had good reason for their rule, that in perfect buildings the different members must be in exact symmetrical relations to the whole general scheme. Hence, while transmitting to us the proper arrangements for buildings of all kinds, they were particularly careful to do so in the case of temples of the gods, buildings in which merits and faults usually last forever.[18]

18. Adapted from Vitruvius, *The Ten Books on Architecture*, trans. Morris Hicky Morgan (Cambridge, MA: Harvard University Press, 1914; Project Gutenberg, 2006), 72–73, https://www.gutenberg.org/files/20239/20239-h/20239-h.htm#Page_72.

Tell It Back—Narration

TE

According to Aristotle and Vitruvius, what are some qualities that a person should consider in order to determine if an object is beautiful?

Talk About It—

TE

Renaissance artist Leonardo Da Vinci sketched a man according to the proportions mapped out by Vitruvius, hence the name of the illustration, *The Vitruvian Man*. It illustrates the symmetry that Vitruvius believed was ideal. Look around at the objects in your classroom. What objects and patterns seem symmetrical (or balanced from one side to the other) and what objects seem asymmetrical and unbalanced? What do you like about symmetry or asymmetry? In your estimation, do symmetry and "proper proportion" make an object more beautiful? Why or why not?

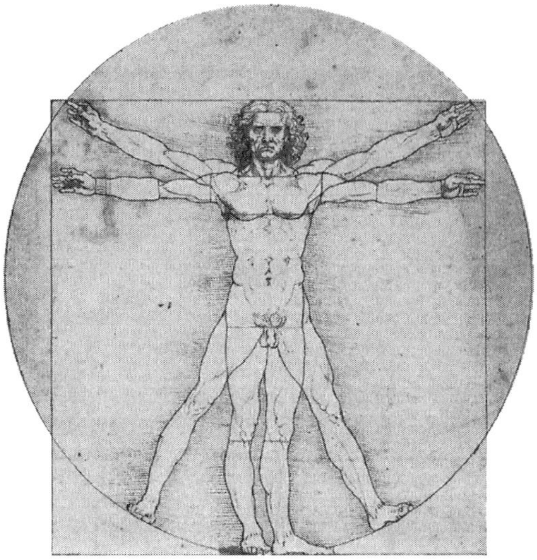

▲ *The Vitruvian Man* by Leonardo Da Vinci

Beauty Causes Something Like Love

—adapted from *A Philosophical Enquiry into the Origin of our Ideas of the Sublime and Beautiful* by Edmund Burke

Anglo-Irish philosopher Edmund Burke (1730–1797) scoffs at the idea that beauty is due to perfect proportions by giving examples of beauty that does not have harmony of parts. Instead he connects beauty to love. Beauty, he believes, is something that moves us to a form of love that is higher than brutish desires and lust.

page 169 Turning our eyes to the vegetable kingdom, we find nothing [there so beautiful as flowers; but flowers are of every sort of shape, and every sort of disposition; they are turned and fashioned into an infinite variety of forms. . . . The rose is a large flower, yet it grows upon a small shrub; the flower of the apple is very small, and it grows upon a large tree; yet the rose and the apple blossom are both page 170 beautiful. . . . The swan, confessedly a beautiful bird, has a neck longer than the rest of its body, and but a very short tail; is this a beautiful proportion? we must allow that it is. But what shall we say of the peacock, who has comparatively but a short neck, with a tail longer than the neck and the rest of the body taken together? How many birds are there that vary infinitely from each of these standards, and from every other which you can fix; with proportions different, and often directly opposite to each other! and yet many of these birds are extremely beautiful.] ?

Would a peacock or flamingo be beautiful without its coloring?

▲ *Peacock* by Japanese artist Masuyama Sessai. Burke would say that though the bird is disproportionate, it is beautiful.

page 172 There are some parts of the human body that are observed page 173 to hold certain proportions to each other. . . . These proportions are certainly to be found in handsome bodies. They are just as certainly to be found in ugly ones. . . ? Nay, the least perfectly proportioned bodies may be some of the most beautiful. [You may assign any proportions you please to every part of the human body; and I undertake that a painter shall religiously observe them all, and still produce, if he pleases, a very ugly figure. The same painter shall considerably deviate from these proportions, and produce a very beautiful one. . . .]

I wonder if any person is objectively ugly. Every person has some beauty.

page 165

Beauty is that quality, or those qualities in bodies, which cause love, or some passion similar to it. I confine this definition to the merely sensible qualities of things. . . . I likewise distinguish love from desire or lust. These are energies of the mind that compel us to try to possess certain objects. They do not affect us as beauty does, but in a way altogether different.[19]

Sample opinion: I agree that beauty can sometimes cause a reaction like love, but it's not truly love. True love can only happen between persons who care deeply for one another.

Love is caring for something unselfishly; lust is a desire to use something selfishly.

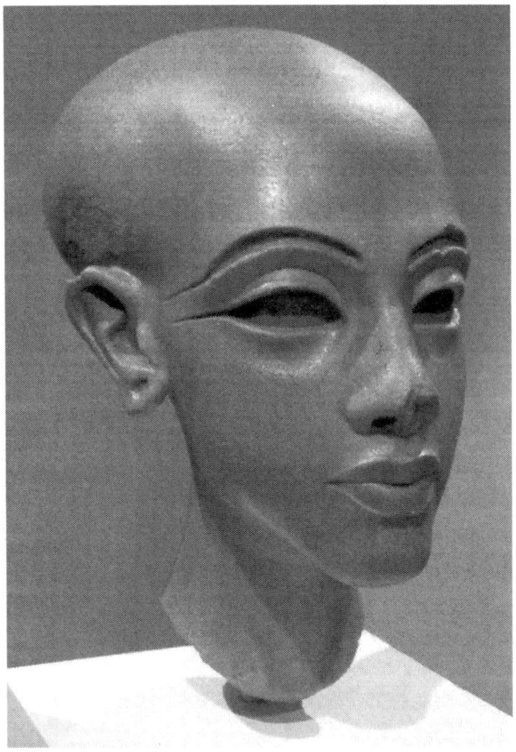

▲ *Flaming June* by Frederic Lord Leighton and *Bust of Unknown Amarna Princess*. Burke might use these figures to illustration his contention that proportionality is not required for an object to be beautiful. They contain disproportionalities—the right leg of the woman is much too long for the rest of her body; the face of the princess is stretched and her eyes are bigger than usual—yet Burke would say that their effect is still beautiful.

19. Adapted from Edmund Burke, *A Philosophical Enquiry into the Origin of Our Ideas of the Sublime and Beautiful*, in *The Works of the Right Honorable Edmund Burke* (London: John C. Nimmo, 1887; Project Gutenberg, 2005), vol. 1, https://www.gutenberg.org/files/15043/15043-h/15043-h.htm.

Behind Everything Beautiful Is the Divine

—adapted from "An Essay on the Beautiful" by Plotinus

In this essay, the Greco-Roman philosopher Plotinus (205–270) seeks to explain how different phenomena all share beauty in common and arrives at a surprising conclusion. He was inspired by Plato's ideas and believed that every physical object sprang from some invisible, divine essence just as sunbeams emanate from the sun.

Sample opinion: I might agree—but other organs (e.g., nose, tongue, skin) are also important for having the full experience of beauty (e.g., beautiful smells, tastes, and touches). Without these senses, it would be harder to fully experience beautiful sights and sounds.

For the most part, beauty appeals to the eye; but it can also enter through our ears, through the skillful arrangement of words and the harmony of sounds. If we go beyond the senses of sight and hearing into unseen regions, the realm of soul, we will see even more beauty in actions and habits, knowledge and virtue. Is anything above these, a still higher beauty? We must investigate and see if anything appears.

What is it that causes objects to appear fair to the sight, sounds beautiful to the ear, and knowledge and virtue lovely to the mind? How do these very different wonders all partake in the idea of beauty? Is beauty the same in all of them? Or is the beauty of objects one kind, and the beauty of souls another? And again, what is beauty if they are separate? Or, what is beauty if they are connected and one? . . .

Good questions for answering "What is beauty?"

Most people assume that a certain balance of parts to each other, and to the whole, creates the kind of beauty that is delight to the sight. Does that mean that only the whole is beautiful and not the parts? Surely it is necessary that a lovely whole should consist of beautiful parts, for beauty can never rise out of the ugly.[20] But from such a definition, it follows that bright colors and the light of the sun cannot be beautiful since they are simple and do not receive their beauty from proportion. What about the beauty of gold? Or the glittering of night and the glorious spectacle of the stars? In like manner, a simple musical note may not be beautiful in itself, but a beautiful song requires that all the notes in it be beautiful, as parts of the whole. And is there anything balanced or proportionate in beautiful sciences, laws or disciplines? Or is a virtue or the intellect or the soul itself symmetrical? No, beauty must come from something higher and deeper than balance of parts.

Gold is beautiful in many forms, from that of a simple nugget to something more complex, such as the burial mask of King Tut. The nugget is not as balanced and harmonious as the funeral mask, but its luster and color are still beautiful.

Sample opinion: Definitely true. There is no balance of parts in many beautiful things (e.g., the smell of baking cookies).

20. In some sense, the parts of a beautiful object must be beautiful because the whole object would be diminished or impossible if they were not. However, we would not typically respond with delight to the parts of many objects. For instance, an ear is a part of a face. Taken alone, most people would not find an ear beautiful. The organs of a face need each other in order to create a beautiful face. (footnote added)

Sample opinion: There is probably something to this idea of beautiful things communing with divine essence. Not sure I understand it fully, but there seems to be something deeper to beauty than we can catch with our senses—a recognition of something wonderful beyond us.

We must therefore repeat the question: "What is the beauty of objects?" It is something which at first view presents itself to our senses, and then the soul apprehends and eagerly embraces it, as if this beauty were allied to itself. But when the soul meets with the ugly, it hastily recoils from it and flees from its discordant nature.

What does this mean? Is there one unseen, true form for all beauty, or different unseen forms for each specific beauty?

Objects therefore become beautiful through communion with a divine essence. The soul, by an innate power, is able to discern and recognize the true form of beauty by meeting it on an unseen level.? This is why, to the good man, virtue shining forth in youth is lovely because it agrees with the true virtue which lies deep in the soul. This is also why fire surpasses many other objects in beauty, because it is intimately received by others physically and spiritually.! It imparts heat, but admits no cold, and it is ornamented with color; it beams forth exalted like some immaterial form of beauty become visible. Another example: The voices of a choir rouse the harmony latent in the soul, and opens her eye to the perception of beauty, and strike the respective senses with wonder and delight. Behind everything beautiful is the divine, and it is through our souls that we perceive it.[21]

Interesting interpretation of fire as both physical and spiritual.

Sample opinion: I think I agree. If beauty is pure and perfect, that fits the definition of divine. And how else can we know this invisible essence is there unless we have a sixth sense—something like a soul?

21. Adapted from Plotinus, "An Essay on the Beautiful," trans. Thomas Taylor (London: John M. Watkins, 1917; Project Gutenberg, 2009), https://www.gutenberg.org/files/29510/29510-h/29510-h.htm.

Tell It Back—

1. **MARK UP THE TEXT—ANNOTATION**: Read through "Beauty Causes Something Like Love" and "Behind Everything Beautiful Is the Divine" again. As you read, write in the margin of the text symbols that will help you understand it better and find important details later. In particular, seek statements that may help you to define beauty—"beauty must be this" or "beauty must be that." The following are some symbols you might use: **B**
   - Underline the main idea of the excerpt or any important point. Make a note of whether you agree or disagree with the idea and include the reason for your opinion. By wrestling with this question, you will be better prepared to make an argument in the next lesson.
   - Place brackets [ ] around any part of the text that provides an example or illustration that helps you understand the reading more clearly.
   - Put a question mark in the margin to mark any part of the excerpt you don't understand.
   - Write any questions or thoughts you have in the margin.
   - Put an exclamation point in the margin to mark any part of the story you find surprising or particularly interesting.
   - Circle any important or unfamiliar vocabulary words or proper nouns when they are first introduced. Remember, a proper noun is the name for any specific person, place, thing, or idea. How do you know which words to circle? Circle words that appear repeatedly, or words you can't understand from the context of the sentence alone. Look up any unfamiliar words in a dictionary.
2. **SUMMARY:** For each of the readings, in the space provided write one well-crafted sentence that tells the reading's main idea about beauty as best as you understand it. **C** To arrive at the main idea, ask yourself, "What is this essay trying to say about beauty?"

   Main idea for "Beauty Causes Something Like Love":

   Sample answer: Beauty does not come from proportion, but from a quality that moves a person in a way that is similar to the action of love.

   Main idea for "Behind Everything Beautiful Is the Divine":

   Sample answer: Although the senses take in beauty, we are able to recognize its divine essence on the deeper level of our souls.

Talk About It—

TE 1. Edmund Burke tells us that "beauty is that quality, or those qualities in bodies, which cause love, or some passion similar to it." He goes on to "distinguish love from desire or lust." According to Burke, what desire does lust awaken in a person? What is the difference in your mind between love and lust? Is there something beautiful in your life that you love, and how do you respond to it?

TE 2. Plotinus gives a number of examples of beautiful things that aren't balanced in their parts: the glitter of stars in the night sky, the gleam of gold, colors, and music. He also states that some things that are invisible, such as science, virtue, intelligence, and laws, are beautiful. How does Plotinus explain how it is possible for us to know that something invisible is beautiful? Can you think of other examples of invisible beauty?

[B]Note that in the Teacher's Edition sample annotations have been made in reading selections. Annotation is highly individual, and the markings on these texts are for sample purposes only. Your students may choose different words and passages to mark up.

If your students need extra support with these challenging texts, feel free to share the sample annotations from the Teacher's Edition or to make annotations with your entire class. It is especially important for your students to wrestle with the main ideas of the readings and to gauge whether or not they agree with them. Students who form an early opinion will fare better with thesis writing in the next lesson.

We recommend that you stop for discussion whenever there seems to be confusion or whenever the class is eagerly engaged. Encourage students to use their instincts—their loves, for example, or their antipathies—in responding to these ideas and to pull in ideas from their own experiences and reading.

[C]Please feel free to share the sample answers with any student who may be having trouble with writing a summary. You may also want to closely read the passage aloud with your students and ask them to share main ideas with the class.

Beauty and Goodness Are Fundamentally Identical

—adapted from *Summa Theologica* by Thomas Aquinas

In his massive book that summarizes Christian theology, medieval scholar Thomas Aquinas (c. 1224–1274) illuminates the idea that beauty and goodness are not just related, but the same thing deep down. He also explains the connection between beauty and the upright stature of human beings.

[I-II, Q. 27, Art. 1] The beautiful is the same as the good, and they differ in aspect only. Goodness is what everyone seeks, and so the idea of the good is whatever calms our desire for goodness. The notion of the beautiful is whatever calms this desire by being seen or known. And so, those senses by which we chiefly experience the beautiful are sight and hearing for we speak of beautiful sights and beautiful sounds.[22] [23]

[I, Q. 91, Art. 3] An upright stature is appropriate to human beings. The senses are given to humans, not only for the purpose of procuring the necessaries of life like other animals, but also for the purpose of knowledge. Whereas the other animals take delight in the objects of the senses only as ordered to food and sex, people alone take pleasure in the beauty of sensible objects for its own sake. Therefore, as the senses are situated chiefly in the face, other animals have the face turned to the ground, as it were for the purpose of seeking food and procuring a livelihood. Human beings have their faces erect, in order that by the senses, and chiefly by sight, which is more subtle and penetrates further into the differences of things, they may freely survey the sensible objects around them, both heavenly and earthly, so as to gather intelligible truth[24] from all things.[25]

22. In other words, goodness is a kind of beauty and beauty is a kind of goodness. We all crave good things for our lives, and the quality of goodness primarily becomes visible in beautiful things such as peacocks and friendship.
23. Adapted from Thomas Aquinas, *Summa Theologica*, parts I–II, trans. Fathers of the English Dominican Province (New York: Benzinger Brothers; Project Gutenberg, 2006), http://www.gutenberg.org/cache/epub/17897/pg17897-images.html.
24. Aquinas believed that both goodness and beauty come from truth. Think of goodness and beauty as a single flame leaping from the woodpile of truth. The flame changes color from blue (goodness) to yellow (beauty) as it rises higher, but it is still the same flame. In the same way, although we may separate the ideas of goodness and beauty in our minds, they have the same source and their essence is the same.
25. Adapted from Thomas Aquinas, *Summa Theologica*, part I, trans. Fathers of the English Dominican Province (New York: Benzinger Brothers; Project Gutenberg, 2006), http://www.gutenberg.org/cache/epub/17611/pg17611-images.html.

Tell It Back—Summary

1. In the space provided, condense Aquinas's idea about the relationship between goodness and beauty into a single, well-crafted sentence. Begin the sentence with the phrase "According to Aquinas" and use the word "whenever" as a conjunction in the middle of the sentence.

   According to Aquinas ___ Sample answer: According to Aquinas, we experience goodness whenever we sense beauty. ___ whenever ___.

2. In the space provided, condense Aquinas's idea about the upright stature of human beings into a single, well-crafted sentence. Begin the sentence with the word "because."

   Because ___ Sample answer: Because human beings go beyond simply meeting physical needs and also take pleasure in beauty, their upright posture helps them to better see and appreciate it. ___

Talk About It—

TE

Think about something you consider to be both beautiful and good. Perhaps it's the sight of a red barn in a cornfield, the feeling of mist on a sea breeze, the sound of distant bells from a church tower, or the smell of hot pizza from a corner pizzeria. In what ways is that beautiful thing also good?

[D]After students have written their own answers, it may be helpful for you to share the sample answers in the Teacher's Edition as well, to show different perspectives.

Write & Discuss—

Take fifteen minutes to answer the following questions in complete sentences in the space provided, and be sure to give clear examples. Then get together as a class or in small groups to read and discuss your answers.[D] Ask yourself if you agree with your classmates' opinions.

1. Can something that's harmful or destructive (such as brain-injuring drugs or pornography) or deadly (such as a disease-carrying mosquito, a poisonous snake, or a toxic flower) be beautiful? Why or why not?

   Sample answer 1: No, nothing that's harmful or destructive or deadly can be beautiful. I measure whether something is beautiful or not by how much good it does to people and to nature. Brain-injuring drugs and pornography may imitate or mimic things that are beautiful, but users are headed for broken minds and broken relationships. Hurricanes may seem beautiful from outer space, but not on the ground to the people whose homes and loved ones are carried away by these storms. Because these things don't do good, they can't be beautiful.

Sample answer 2: I agree with Aquinas that beauty must be good at its root, but it is possible for some harmful things to have an aspect of beauty (goodness) to them. In other words, badness and beauty can exist in the same object. For example, the most colorful, bright red and blue lakes in the world are filled with toxic chemicals, yet we find their colors beautiful. Some of the most deadly snakes and spiders have the beauty of color and symmetry of form. Even the wings on a mosquito can be seen from a certain point of view as a beautiful feat of design and engineering. However, some other things are not beautiful in any way. For example, drugs and pornography are destructive because they twist and corrupt desires that are basically beautiful or good: the desire for happiness and the desire for love. These harmful things point to beautiful things, but they are not beautiful themselves.

2. Based on Aquinas's idea of beauty, how might he define ugliness?

Sample answer 1: Aquinas might say that ugliness is anything that is ultimately harmful to human beings and the environments they inhabit.

Sample answer 2: Aquinas would probably say that ugliness is anything that is morally bad or evil deep down.

Beauty May Serve as a Sexual Charm

—from *The Descent of Man* by Charles Darwin

Charles Darwin (1809–1882) believed in a purely material and naturalistic explanation for beauty and did not see the need for a supernatural understanding. In this passage, he implies that the human enjoyment of beauty evolved from the need to select a mate. If this is true, then the appreciation of beauty comes from instinct and has no deeper meaning.

The case of the male Argus pheasant is eminently interesting, because it affords good evidence that the most refined beauty may serve as a sexual charm, and for no other purpose. We must conclude that this is the case, as the secondary and primary wing-feathers are not at all displayed, and the ball and socket ornaments are not exhibited in full perfection until the male assumes the attitude of courtship.

Sample opinion: I disagree with Darwin's point. He reduces beauty to a lever that triggers sexual instinct, an idea so limited that it explains almost nothing about our experience of it.

[The Argus pheasant does not possess brilliant colors, so that his success in love appears to depend on the great size of his plumes, and on the elaboration of the most elegant patterns.] Many will declare that it is utterly incredible that a female bird should be able to appreciate fine shading and exquisite patterns. It is undoubtedly a marvelous fact that she should possess this almost human degree of taste.? He who thinks that he can safely gauge the discrimination and taste of the lower animals may deny that the female Argus pheasant can appreciate such refined beauty; but he will then be compelled to admit that the extraordinary attitudes assumed by the male during the act of courtship, by which the wonderful beauty of his plumage is fully displayed, are purposeless; and this is a conclusion which I for one will never admit.[26]

▲ Male Argus pheasant displaying feathers to a female.

How does he arrive at this conclusion?

Sample opinion: The idea that the bird's taste is so close to a human's is a leap. In addition, humans no doubt appreciate a bird's feathers in an entirely different way—consciously vs. instinctively.

26. Charles Darwin, *The Descent of Man* (New York: Penguin Classics, 2004), 449.

A Brief Introduction to the Philosophical History of Beauty

—adapted from the *The Aesthetical and Philosophical Essays* by Friedrich Schiller

German philosopher and poet Friedrich Schiller (1759–1805) supported the idea that beauty transcended (or went beyond) natural appetites. Beauty, he believed, lifted people up and gave them freedom. He believed that the French Revolution collapsed into fearful violence because the French people were not adequately trained by a love for beauty. In this selection he goes over some important ideas about beauty.

The history of philosophy presents us with many theories on the nature of the beautiful, but we have only enough time to consider the most important among them. The coarsest of these theories defines the beautiful as that which pleases the senses. This theory turns beauty ugly by converting it into selfish desire. Pleasing the senses is narcissistic and can never be satisfied.[27]

Sample opinion: I agree that this idea is coarse if it claims that beauty merely pleases the senses. Something deeper, more spiritual, seems to affect us.

Others have thought that beauty consists in proportion, in symmetry. No doubt proportion is one of the conditions of beauty, but only one. An ill-proportioned object cannot be beautiful, but the exact correspondence of parts, as in geometrical figures, does not fully explain beauty.

Sample opinion: I disagree that ill-proportioned objects can't be beautiful. The Burke reading makes a convincing point about this.

▲ Schiller believes that beauty is something deeper than merely the surface appearance of an object. Domenico Ghirlandaio's *An Old Man and His Grandson* illustrates this idea. The young boy's symmetrical face "pleases the senses" more than the grandfather's deformity. However, the old man's tender love for his grandson is beautiful to behold, and thus we glimpse a different kind of beauty, a beauty that goes beyond our senses.

27. Schiller probably agrees that beauty pleases our senses—sight, hearing, touch, taste, and smell—but he sees this explanation as inadequate and vulgar. He sees beauty as something much more sacred than mere physical pleasure. Note that this belief directly contradicts Darwin's idea of beauty as merely a sexual charm.

A noted ancient theory makes beauty consist in the perfect suitableness of means to their end.[28] In this case the beautiful is not the useful, it is the suitable. But this theory doesn't have the true character of the beautiful. Again, order is a less mathematical idea than proportion, but it does not explain what is free and flowing in certain beauties.

Sample opinion: I disagree with this idea. A knife may be perfectly suitable for cutting someone's throat, but can it be said to be beautiful for this reason?

The most plausible theory of beauty is that beauty consists of two contrary and equally necessary elements—unity and variety.[29] [A beautiful flower has all the elements we have named; it has unity, symmetry, and variety of shades of color.]

Sample opinion: Not sure how I feel about this idea. Unity and variety only partially explain beauty.

▲ Unity, symmetry, and variety in an aster.

Aster tataricus. Image courtesy of Pascalou petit, https://commons.wikimedia.org/wiki/File:Aster_Tataricus.JPG.

There is no beauty without life, and life is movement, diversity. These elements are found in beautiful and also in sublime[30] objects. . . . In objects that our five senses can comprehend, the feeling of the beautiful comes under one class called physical beauty. But above and beyond this in the region of mind we have first intellectual beauty, including the laws that govern intelligence and the creative genius of the artist, the poet, and the philosopher. Again, [the moral world has beauty in its ideas of liberty, of virtue, of devotion, the justice of Aristides,[31] the heroism of Leonidas.][32] [33]

Sample opinion: I agree that life is necessary for beauty. Beauty requires a living being to sense and perceive it.

Sample opinion: I agree that beauty can reside in the intellect, in law, in art, in acts, and in ideas. Beauty does not need parts, per se, to be perceived as beauty.

We have now established that there is beauty and sublimity in nature, in ideas, in feelings, and in actions. After all this it might be supposed that a unity could be found amidst these different kinds of beauty. [The sight of a statue, as the Apollo of Belvedere, of a man, of Socrates expiring, are offered as producing impressions of the beautiful;] but the form cannot be a form by itself, it must be the form of

28. In other words, something that is beautiful perfectly achieves its purpose. A beautiful chair is sturdy and comfortable for sitting. A beautiful book contains wonderful and engaging writing. A hammer that effectively pounds nails would also be beautiful by this definition.
29. In other words, the various parts of a beautiful object create a unified whole. Think about the bold brushstrokes of color used by the Impressionist painters. When we stand back from the canvas, we see the variety of colors and strokes blend together into a beautiful whole.
30. sublime: majestic, unsurpassed, glorious, and sometimes invisible. The word "sublime" also includes the idea of moral or spiritual goodness and excellence.
31. Aristides (530–468 BC): an Athenian commander and statesman
32. Leonidas (c. 540–480 BC): a warrior king of Sparta who died defending Greece at the Battle of Thermopylae
33. Schiller is agreeing with Plotinus that beauty goes beyond what the five senses can discern.

something. Physical beauty is the sign of an interior beauty,[34] a spiritual and moral beauty which is the basis, the principle, and the unity of the beautiful.[35]

- Physical beauty is an envelope to intellectual and to moral beauty.
- Intellectual beauty, the splendor of the true, can only have for principle that of all truth.

Moral beauty comprehends two distinct elements, equally beautiful, justice and charity.[36] Thus God is the principle of the three orders of beauty: physical, intellectual, and moral. He also construes the two great powers distributed over the three orders, the beautiful and the sublime. God is beauty par excellence; He is therefore perfectly beautiful; He is equally sublime. He is to us the type and sense of the two great forms of beauty. In short, the Absolute Being as absolute unity and absolute variety is necessarily the ultimate principle, the extreme basis, the finished ideal of all beauty. This was the marvelous beauty which Diotimus had seen, and which is described in the Banquet of Socrates.[37]

Tell It Back—

1. **MARK UP THE TEXT—ANNOTATION:** Read through "Beauty May Serve as a Sexual Charm" and "A Brief Introduction to the Philosophical History of Beauty" again. As you read, write in the margin of the text symbols that will help you understand it better and find important details later. The following are some symbols you might use: **E**
   - Underline the main idea of the excerpt or any important point. Make a note of whether you agree or disagree with the idea and include the reason for your opinion. By wrestling with this question, you will be better prepared to make an argument in the next lesson.
   - Place brackets [ ] around any part of the text that provides an example or illustration that helps you understand the reading more clearly.
   - Put a question mark in the margin to mark any part of the excerpt you don't understand.
   - Write any questions or thoughts you have in the margin.
   - Put an exclamation point in the margin to mark any part of the story you find surprising or particularly interesting.
   - Circle any important or unfamiliar vocabulary words or proper nouns when they are first introduced. Remember, a proper noun is the name for any specific person, place, thing, or idea. How do you know which words to circle? Circle words that appear repeatedly, or words you can't understand from the context of the sentence alone. Look up any unfamiliar words in a dictionary.

34. The idea that physical beauty is a sign of interior beauty is widely disputed today, except in the Platonic sense that the beauty we see represents an unseen ideal.
35. Schiller agrees with Aquinas that beauty must have the moral quality of goodness and that goodness is what all beautiful things have in common.
36. According to Schiller, all beauty, including moral beauty, is composed of two elements—unity and diversity. Additionally, moral beauty also consists of the two elements of justice and charity (or mercy).
37. Adapted from Friedrich Schiller, "Introduction," in *The Aesthetical and Philosophical Essays* (Project Gutenberg, 2006), https://www.gutenberg.org/files/6798/6798-h/6798-h.htm.

2. **SUMMARY:** In the space provided, write one well-crafted sentence that tells the Darwin reading's main idea about beauty as best as you understand it.[F] To arrive at the main idea, ask yourself, "What is this essay trying to say about beauty?"

Main idea for "Beauty May Serve as a Sexual Charm":

Sample answer: As illustrated by the mating behavior of the Argus pheasant, the purpose of beauty may be solely to serve as a sexual charm.

In the space provided, write down two important ideas from the Schiller reading. Tell each idea in a well-crafted sentence.

Two important ideas from "A Brief Introduction to the Philosophical History of Beauty":

a. Sample answer: The most valid theory about beauty is that it consists of both unity and variety.

b. Sample answer: Beauty can be found in many things visible and invisible, including virtue, actions, nature, intellect, morality, and ideas.

[E]Note that in the Teacher's Edition sample annotations have been made in reading selections. Annotation is highly individual, and the markings on these texts are for sample purposes only. Your students may choose different words and passages to mark up.

If your students need extra support with these challenging texts, feel free to share the sample annotations from the Teacher's Edition or to make annotations with your entire class. It is especially important for your students to wrestle with the main ideas of the readings and to gauge whether or not they agree with them. Students who form an early opinion will fare better with thesis writing in the next lesson.

We recommend that you stop for discussion whenever there seems to be confusion or whenever the class is eagerly engaged. Encourage students to use their instincts—their loves, for example, or their antipathies—in responding to these ideas and to pull in ideas from their own experiences and reading.

[F]Please feel free to share the sample answers with any student who may be having trouble with writing a summary. You may also want to closely read the passage aloud with your students and ask them to share main ideas with the class.

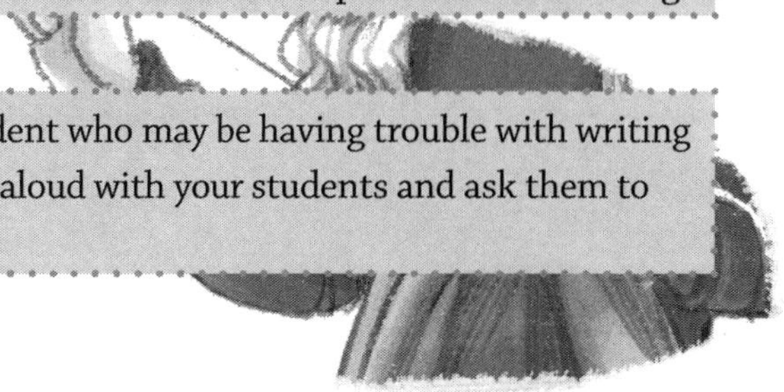

Now We Have a Cult of Ugliness

—from *Why Beauty Matters* by Roger Scruton

This reading is a continuation of the excerpt by philosopher Roger Scruton (1944–) found at the beginning of this lesson. Here Scruton continues to build his case for the importance of beauty and notes what trends have diminished beauty in our culture.

Beauty matters. . . . It is not just a subjective thing, but a universal need of human beings. If we ignore this need we find ourselves in a spiritual desert. . . .

Sample opinion: I agree that beauty is a universal human need. Without beauty, people would die from despair and depression.

The great artists of the past were aware that human life is full of chaos and suffering, but they had a remedy for this, and the name of that remedy was beauty. The beautiful work of art brings consolation in sorrow and affirmation in joy. It shows human life to be worthwhile. Many modern artists have become weary of this sacred task. The randomness of modern life, they think, could not be redeemed by art. Instead, it should be displayed.? The pattern was set nearly a century ago by the French artist Marcel Duchamp, who signed a urinal with a fictitious signature "R Mutt" and entered it for an exhibition.

Sample opinion: Agreed. Art can function to cheer the downcast and delight the joyful. Why? Because beauty touches our emotions directly.

Sample opinion: I agree that some modern artists want to show the randomness of life, rather than beauty, but I don't think that's always the case. Some art captures human folly as a lesson for society to grow in wisdom.

Might there be value in showing the randomness of life, or is this just plain cynical?

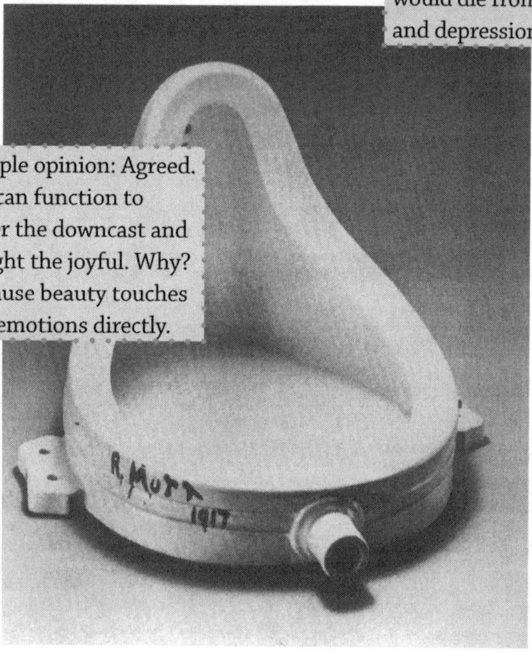

▲ A joke has turned into a way of doing art: *Fountain* by Marcel Duchamp.

His gesture was satirical, designed to mock the world of art, and the snobberies that go with it, but it has been interpreted in another way, as showing that anything can be art. [Like a light going on and off. A can of excrement. Or even a pile of bricks.] No longer does art have a sacred status, no longer does it raise us to a higher moral or spiritual plane. It is just one human gesture among others, no more meaningful than a laugh or a shout. . . .

Sample opinion: Scruton is right that, in today's art world, anything can be art. I've seen trash and rotting fruit displayed as art. Art has lost its meaning as something beautiful or sublime.

I both agree and disagree. This is a very general statement that leaves out artists who pursue beauty. Too many artists do seem to wallow in the mud, however.

Art once made a cult of beauty. Now we have a cult of ugliness instead. Since the world is disturbing, art should be disturbing too. Those who look for beauty in art are just out of touch with modern realities. Sometimes the intention is to shock us, but what is shocking first time 'round is boring and vacuous when repeated. This makes art into an elaborate joke, though one that by now has ceased to be funny. Yet the critics go on endorsing it, afraid to say that the emperor has no clothes. . . .

Sample opinion: I don't agree that critics lack courage. Rather, they can profit by endorsing popular art. Greed may be a stronger motive than fear.

Maybe people have lost their faith in beauty because they have lost their belief in ideals. All there is, they are tempted to think, is the world of appetite.[38] There are no values other than utilitarian ones. Something has a value if it has a use. And what's the use of beauty? "All art is absolutely useless," wrote Oscar Wilde, who intended his remark as praise. For Wilde, beauty was a value higher than usefulness. People need useless things just as much as, even more than, they need things with a use. Just think of it, what is the use of love? Of friendship? Of worship? None whatsoever, and the same goes for beauty.

Sample opinion: I disagree with Scruton that people need useless things. People only *need* useful things. However, there is nothing useless about love or friendship or worship or beauty. If something is beautiful, it is useful in the sense that it uplifts our spirits and keeps us from despair.

? Not sure what this means.

Our consumer society puts usefulness first, and beauty is no better than a side effect. Since art is useless, it doesn't matter what you read, what you look at, what you listen to. We are besieged by messages on every side, titillated, tempted by appetite never addressed and that is one reason why beauty is disappearing from our world. . . .

▲ Damien Hirst at his exhibition *Damien Hirst: The Complete Spot Paintings 1986–2011*. Hirst is one of those artists who Scruton would say profits from the "cult of ugliness."

Damien Hirst at the exhibition *Damien Hirst The Complete Spot Paintings 1986–2011*, Gagosian Gallery, NYC, photographed by Andrew Russeth, January 11, 2012. Image courtesy of Flickr user 16 Miles of String via Wikimedia Commons, https://commons.wikimedia.org/wiki/File:Damien_Hirst_(6712600369).jpg.

▲ *Death Denied* by Damien Hirst. The tiger shark is immersed in a bath of formaldehyde to keep its corpse preserved.

Death Denied by Damien Hirst, 2008. Image courtesy of Agent001, https://commons.wikimedia.org/wiki/File:Shark84.JPG.

38. Note that Scruton indirectly challenges Darwin's idea of beauty as solely a means to find a sexual mate. He is saying that there is more to life than the appetites (e.g., the appetite for sex or for food) and that beauty has a separate and higher value.

Sample opinion: I agree that ugliness and usefulness have hurt the pursuit of beauty in art. Many hungry artists will create works that boost their reputation, even if they must reject beauty.

Beauty is assailed from two directions: by the cult of ugliness in the arts and by the cult of utility in everyday life. [These two cults come together in the world of modern architecture. At the turn of the twentieth century, architects, like artists, began to be impatient with beauty and to put utility in its place. The American architect Louis Sullivan expressed the credo of the modernists when he said that "form follows function." In other words, stop thinking about the way a building looks and think instead about what it does. Sullivan's doctrine has been used to justify the greatest crime against beauty that the world has yet seen and that is the crime of modern architecture.]

Tour Montparnasse from Eiffel Tower, May 23, 2013. Image courtesy of Panoramio user Rodrigo Pereira da S... via Wikimedia Commons, https://commons.wikimedia.org/wiki/File:Tour_Montparnasse_from_Eiffel_Tower_-_panoramio.jpg.

Leaning Tower of Pisa, August 8, 2005. Image courtesy of Johann H. Addicks, https://commons.wikimedia.org/wiki/File:Pisa_-_Campo_Santo_-_Campanile_1_-_2005-08-08_10-15_4638.JPG.

Caltrans District 7 Headquarters in Downtown Los Angeles, November 10, 2006. Image courtesy of Geographer, https://commons.wikimedia.org/wiki/File:Cal_Trans_District7_HD.jpg.

Kinkaku-ji / Golden Temple in Kyoto, November 28, 2013. Image courtesy of Jaycangel, https://commons.wikimedia.org/wiki/File:Kinkaku-ji_the_Golden_Temple_in_Kyoto_overlooking_the_lake_-_high_rez.JPG.

▲ Form follows function: Too many unlovely modern buildings create unloved spaces. Top: Tour Montparnasse in Paris, France, versus the Leaning Tower of Pisa in Pisa, Italy. Bottom: The Caltrans District 7 Headquarters in California versus the Temple of the Golden Pavilion (Deer Garden Temple) in Kyoto, Japan.

▲ Form that is both beautiful and functional: These two modern buildings illustrate the fact that new buildings don't have to be ugly if the architect, in fact, strives for beauty.

Thorncrown Chapel in Eureka Springs, Arkansas, September 2, 2006. Image courtesy of Bobak Ha'Eri, https://commons.wikimedia.org/wiki/File:09-02-06-ThorncrownChapel1.jpg.

[I grew up near Reading, which was a charming Victorian town with terraced streets and Gothic churches, crowned by elegant public buildings and smart hotels. But in the 1960s, things began to change. Here, in the center, the homely streets were demolished, to make way for office blocks, a bus station, and car parks, all designed without consideration for beauty, and the result proves, as clearly as can be, that if you consider only utility, the things you build will soon be useless. This building is boarded up because nobody has a use for it. Nobody has a use for it because nobody wants to be in it. Nobody wants to be in it because the thing is so damned ugly.] Everywhere you turn there is ugliness and mutilation. . . . Everything has been vandalized, but we shouldn't blame the vandals. This place was built by vandals, and those who added the graffiti merely finished the job. Most of our towns and cities have areas like this in which buildings erected merely for their utility have rapidly become useless. . . . This returns me to Oscar Wilde's remark that all art is absolutely useless. Put usefulness first and you lose it. Put beauty first and what you do will be useful forever.[39]

▲ Ugliness and mutilation exist in cities because of unbeautiful architecture, according to Scruton. He says, "Those who added the graffiti merely finished the job."

Bridge Woman Graffiti, October 27, 2013. Image courtesy of Sascha Kohlmann, https://commons.wikimedia.org/wiki/File:Bridge_Women_Graffiti_(51568700).jpeg.

39. Excerpted from Roger Scruton, *Beauty* (New York: Oxford University Press, 2009), as used in *Why Beauty Matters*, November 28, 2009, BBC2, off-air recording, https://www.youtube.com/watch?v=bHw4MMEnmpc. Used by permission of Oxford University Press.

The Vocabulary of Beauty Continues to Expand

—by Christine Perrin

Christine Perrin (1969–) is a poet as well as teacher and director of writing at Messiah College. She has been privileged to think about poetry's relationship to visual art, especially in her teaching in the Gordon in Orvieto program in Orvieto, Italy.

Sample opinion: I agree that every culture and time creates a vocabulary within its art. We see evidence of this in works ranging from cave paintings to the art of today. It is not the case, however, that every culture has equally beneficial things to say: The level of merit depends on the goodness of a culture.

Albrecht Dürer: "I know not what beauty is, but she has many garbs and many cloaks."

Art reflects, is shaped by, and shapes the culture that produces it. What happens to a culture in history and technology is expressed in its art. For example, the broken brushstrokes of French impressionist paintings reflect the break with tradition that occurred in the French Revolution. Each culture and time period finds a vocabulary, within its art, for what it needs to say.

Although this vocabulary may differ in each culture and time period, the art of the past is always informing the art of the present. All great artists are in dialogue with the art of the past—sometimes directly referencing it in their work and sometimes simply responding to it. Michelangelo, for example, was greatly influenced by the ancient Greek sculptors. His statue of David borrows its pose and style from statues of the Greek gods. Thus the new builds on the old and expands the overall vocabulary.!

Fascinating thought! We are heirs of all the past.

Each new artistic expression that takes hold, even for a short time, offers more resources for future artists to draw from as they create. Today's artists may fear that they will have nothing new left to create,? that they will find that everything has already been created. But because of the multitude of inspirations from the past and the resulting multitude of ways to express our ideas artistically, there is always room for something new to spring from what came before.

I wonder: How true is this feeling among artists?

We can see evidence of the ever-expanding vocabulary of artistic expression when we consider the art of today. Some modern art lacks obvious or traditional beauty, which may cause us to quickly dismiss it as worthless or question its identity as art. However, art that isn't immediately pleasing to the eye can still serve an important (and beautiful) purpose—it can reflect and respond to a moment in time that itself is ugly and difficult.

Sample opinion: I agree that art's purpose can be beautiful despite the ugliness of its subject. Some pop art, for instance, may not be beautiful but serves a beautiful purpose by showing the pitfalls of consumerism.

▲ An example of Dadaist art: *Shirt Front and Fork* by Jean Arp.

Shirt Front and Fork by Jean Arp. Photograph taken May 31, 2010. Image courtesy of AgnosticPreachersKid, https://commons.wikimedia.org/wiki/File:Shirt_Front_and_Fork.JPG.

▶ An example of Cubism: *Girl with a Mandolin* by Pablo Picasso.

An example of this response is Dadaism, an artistic and literary movement that began in Zurich, Switzerland, and gave rise to other movements later in the twentieth century (such as Cubism, Futurism, Constructivism, and Expressionism). Dadaism began as a reaction to the catastrophic First World War and to other atrocities in the bloody twentieth century. It provided a way for artists to say something about the terrible destruction and absurdity of their time. Dada artists wanted their work to stand in opposition to art that was traditionally considered beautiful, because traditionally beautiful art often emerged out of peaceful and happy ideas. Instead of employing traditional methods and materials, they often used found or "ready-made" objects as art. Duchamp's toilet (*Fountain*) is one such example.[40]

40. Perrin notes that some people find "ready-made" objects pleasing and beautiful despite Scruton's dismissal of Duchamp's urinal as a joke.

By expanding the idea of art, the Dadaists also created a broader vocabulary for what is beautiful. Change in art is inevitable and necessary to culture because it responds to the realities of its time—whether they be war, religious reform, or political turmoil. Each work of art plays a role in developing a dialogue that has gone on throughout the centuries.? We are glad when art captures something true and specific to the period in which it was made, because it makes plain for us what was being "said" at that time. So while it is certainly valuable to attempt to establish a stable definition of beauty and to decide what makes a piece beautiful, we might also ask what kind of art we need today to respond to and manifest what is happening in the world. There are other beauties than the ones that meet the eye and other questions that must be asked to enlarge our understanding of art.

Is this true for all art or just what the culture remembers as "good" art?

I, too, appreciate the beautiful. As someone who loves medieval art, I prefer art that is beautiful for its skill and craft rather than for a meaning or an idea. I judge Duchamp's *Fountain* to be very poor art. However, I am glad that ideas about art and beauty continue to expand. When we wonder what is beautiful, we have to see that beauty has dimensions.! It is a beautiful thing, on some level, to tell about destruction with art that shows what it was like to live through devastation. As our vocabulary continues to expand, we are richer for it.[41]

Very true! After reading these excerpts, I now see beauty as very complex.

[G]Note that in the Teacher's Edition sample annotations have been made in reading selections. Annotation is highly individual, and the markings on these texts are for sample purposes only. Your students may choose different words and passages to mark up.

If your students need extra support with these challenging texts, feel free to share the sample annotations from the Teacher's Edition or to make annotations with your entire class. It is especially important for your students to wrestle with the main ideas of the readings and to gauge whether or not they agree with them. Students who form an early opinion will fare better with thesis writing in the next lesson.

We recommend that you stop for discussion whenever there seems to be confusion or whenever the class is eagerly engaged. Encourage students to use their instincts—their loves, for example, or their antipathies—in responding to these ideas and to pull in ideas from their own experiences and reading.

41. Christine Perrin, "The Vocabulary of Beauty Continues to Expand" (working paper, Classical Academic Press, Camp Hill, PA, 2018).

Tell It Back—

1. **MARK UP THE TEXT—ANNOTATION:** Read through "Now We Have a Cult of Ugliness" and "The Vocabulary of Beauty Continues to Expand" again. As you read, write in the margin of the text symbols that will help you understand it better and find important details later. The following are some symbols you might use:**G**
   - Underline the main idea of the excerpt or any important point. Make a note of whether you agree or disagree with the idea and include the reason for your opinion. By wrestling with this question, you will be better prepared to make an argument in the next lesson.
   - Place brackets [ ] around any part of the text that provides an example or illustration that helps you understand the reading more clearly.
   - Put a question mark in the margin to mark any part of the excerpt you don't understand.
   - Write any questions or thoughts you have in the margin.
   - Put an exclamation point in the margin to mark any part of the story you find surprising or particularly interesting.
   - Circle any important or unfamiliar vocabulary words or proper nouns when they are first introduced. Remember, a proper noun is the name for any specific person, place, thing, or idea. How do you know which words to circle? Circle words that appear repeatedly, or words you can't understand from the context of the sentence alone. Look up any unfamiliar words in a dictionary.

2. **SUMMARY:** In the space provided, write in a single, well-crafted sentence the idea you consider the most important from "Now We Have a Cult of Ugliness." Begin the sentence with the phrase "Of all the ideas found in . . .".

Of all the ideas found in ______________________________

Sample answer 1: Of all the ideas found in "Now We Have a Cult of Ugliness," the most important is that people need "useless," beautiful things to inspire and delight them.

Sample answer 2: Of all the ideas found in "Now We Have a Cult of Ugliness," the most important is that use cannot be the only standard for making an object, or we actually render it less useful.

In the space provided, write in a single, well-crafted sentence an idea you consider important from "The Vocabulary of Beauty Continues to Expand." Begin the sentence with the phrase "No doubt" or "Without question."

No doubt/Without question ____

Sample answer 1: No doubt some art is ugly but serves a beautiful purpose.

Sample answer 2: Without question, beauty has many dimensions.

____

Talk About It—

TE 1. Philosopher Roger Scruton believes that many modern artists and consumers are participating in a "cult of ugliness." The word "cult" can be defined positively or negatively. In the positive sense, "cult" can mean "great devotion to a person or an idea by a group of admirers." In the negative sense, "cult" can be defined as "an extreme group that blindly follows obscure and harmful ideas." In which sense is Scruton using the word "cult"? Explain your answer.

TE 2. Scruton seems to hold many modern buildings in contempt—not because they are new, but for other reasons. What reasons does he give for his dislike of them? Do you have a modern building in your town that stands out? Do you like or dislike it, and why? Do you prefer or not prefer older buildings, and why?

TE 3. Christine Perrin prefers medieval art to modern art, but she is nonetheless encouraged by recent artistic developments. What are some of her reasons for being encouraged?

TE 4. There are many examples of "ugly" modern art, ranging from mundane paintings of soup cans and photos of twisted plumbing pipes to dirty mattresses, fake vomit, and cans of excrement. Does ugliness have a power to attract people? Why or why not? Are there any valid reasons for an artist to create ugly art?

The Beauty of Nature

—loosely adapted from *Nature* by Ralph Waldo Emerson

Essayist and poet Ralph Waldo Emerson (1803–1882) made his mark on the youthful United States with his keen intelligence and his ability to write beautifully. In writing his essay *Nature*, he created a genre of nature journaling that would be imitated by later naturalists such as Henry David Thoreau, John Muir, and Annie Dillard.

Crossing a bare field, in snow puddles, at twilight, under a clouded sky, I have enjoyed a perfect exhilaration. . . . In the woods too, a man casts off his years, as the snake sloughs off his skin, and at whatever period of life, is always a child. In the woods is perpetual youth. Within these plantations of God, beauty and sanctity reign, a perennial festival is dressed, and the guest sees not how he should tire of them in a thousand years. In the woods, we return to reason and faith. There I feel that nothing can befall me in life—no disgrace, no calamity—which nature cannot repair. Standing on the bare ground—my head bathed by the blithe air, and uplifted into infinite space—all mean egotism[42] vanishes. I become a transparent eye-ball; I am nothing; I see all; the currents of the Universal Being circulate through me; I am part or particle of God. . . . I am the lover of uncontained and immortal beauty. In the wilderness, I find something more dear and harmonious than in streets or villages. In the tranquil landscape, and especially in the distant line of the horizon, man beholds somewhat as beautiful as his own nature. . . .

The eye is the best of artists. . . . The simple perception of natural forms is a delight. The influence of the forms and actions in nature is so needful to man. . . . Nature satisfies by its loveliness. . . . I see the spectacle of morning from the hill-top over against my house, from day-break to sun-rise, with emotions which an angel might share. The long slender bars of cloud float like fishes in the sea of crimson light. From the earth, as a shore, I look out into that silent sea. . . .

Not less excellent was the charm, last evening, of a January sunset. The western clouds divided and subdivided themselves into pink flakes modulated with tints of unspeakable softness; and the air had so much life and sweetness, that it was a pain to come within doors.

The inhabitants of cities suppose that the country landscape is pleasant only half the year. I please myself with the graces of the winter scenery and believe that we are as much touched by it as by the genial[43] influences of summer. To the attentive

42. egotism: self-centeredness
43. genial: friendly

eye, each moment of the year has its own beauty, and in the same field, it beholds, every hour, a picture which was never seen before, and which shall never be seen again. The heavens change every moment, and reflect their glory or gloom on the plains beneath. The state of the crop in the surrounding farms alters the expression of the earth from week to week. The succession of native plants in the pastures and roadsides, which makes the silent clock by which time tells the summer hours, will make even the divisions of the day sensible to a keen observer. The tribes of birds and insects, like the plants punctual to their time, follow each other, and the year has room for all. . . .

But this beauty of Nature is just part of its value. The shows of day, the dewy morning, the rainbow, mountains, orchards in blossom, stars, moonlight, shadows in still water, and the like, if too eagerly hunted, become decorations merely. Go out of the house to see the moon, and it is mere tinsel. . . . In order to grasp the fullness of Nature's goodness, the seeker must sense the presence of a higher, spiritual element, which is essential to Nature's perfection. The high and divine beauty which can be loved is found in combination with the human will. Beauty is the mark God sets upon virtue. Every natural action is grace-filled. Every heroic act is also beautiful and causes the place and the bystanders to shine. We are taught by great actions that the universe is the property of every individual in it. Every rational creature has all Nature for his dowry and estate. . . .

The world thus exists to the soul to satisfy the desire of beauty. . . . Beauty, in its largest and profoundest sense, is one expression for the universe. God is the all-fair. Truth, and goodness, and beauty, are but different faces of the same All.[44]

44. Ralph Waldo Emerson, "Beauty," in *Nature* (Boston & Cambridge: James Munroe and Company, 1849; Project Gutenberg, 2009), http://www.gutenberg.org/files/29433/29433-h/29433-h.htm#3.

Tell It Back—Narration

Based on Emerson's essay, what might be some reasons people enjoy the beauty of nature? What makes nature beautiful? In the space provided, summarize your answer in four or five sentences.

Sample answer: People enjoy the beauty of nature because, as Emerson says, it gives nature's "guests" exhilaration, which is a feeling of great happiness. Nature's beauty also helps her visitors to feel youthful and to experience wonder like a child, and returns a man to faith and reason. There is a sense that no calamity or disgrace in human society can touch man in nature. Ultimately Emerson believes that the world, including nature, exists to satisfy a deep longing in people—the desire for beauty. Nature is beautiful because it is good: a tranquil, harmonious, and grace-filled gift bestowed upon humanity by the universe.

Talk About It—

TE 1. Do you agree with Emerson that "each moment of the year has its own beauty," every season, every day? Or do you feel that nature is more beautiful in certain times and seasons? Give examples of your favorite times or seasons in nature.

TE 2. Emerson writes, "In the wilderness, I find something more dear and harmonious than in streets or villages." Would you say that it is difficult to stay in touch with natural beauty in a city? Why or why not?

TE

3. Look at the two paintings of natural scenes. The first is a painting of Schroon Lake, New York, by Thomas Cole, and the second is a painting of a lily pond and Japanese bridge by Claude Monet. What are the elements of the paintings that you find beautiful? Elements may include objects in the frame and how these objects are balanced, as well as the contrast between light and dark. Do you prefer the scene from the wilderness or the scene from a garden? Why?

▶ Schroon Lake by Thomas Cole

◀ The Japanese Bridge by Claude Monet

A Thing of Beauty Is a Joy Forever: Poems about Beautiful Things

Philosophers are not the only ones to have their say about beauty. Poets have plenty to say as well. The poetry in this section provides perspectives that are complementary to the other readings in this lesson, and it is also highly quotable. As you read through these poems, note the imagery they use to develop the idea of beauty. Just as you might use the examples of art and architecture throughout this lesson, you can use the poetry here to illustrate your claims about beauty in your thesis essay.

Two Poems about Romantic Love by Paul Laurence Dunbar

An African American poet from Ohio, Dunbar (1872–1906) died young of the lung disease tuberculosis. Like John Keats, another poet who died young of tuberculosis, Dunbar deems romantic love the most beautiful thing of all.

In an English Garden

In this old garden, fair, I walk to-day
Heart-charmed with all the beauty of the scene:
The rich, luxuriant grasses' cooling green,
The wall's environ, ivy-decked and gray,
The waving branches with the wind at play,
The slight and tremulous blooms that show between,
Sweet all: and yet my yearning heart doth lean
Toward Love's Egyptian fleshpots far away.

Beside the wall, the slim Laburnum grows
And flings its golden flow'rs to every breeze.
But e'en among such soothing sights as these,
I pant and nurse my soul-devouring woes.
Of all the longings that our hearts wot of,
There is no hunger like the want of love![45]

45. Paul Laurence Dunbar, "In an English Garden," in *The Complete Poems of Paul Laurence Dunbar* (New York: Dodd, Mead and Company, 1922; Project Gutenberg, 2006), 111, http://www.gutenberg.org/files/18338/18338-h/18338-h.htm.

Roses and Pearls

▲ Head of a Negro by John Singleton Copley

Your spoken words are roses fine and sweet,
The songs you sing are perfect pearls of sound.
How lavish nature is about your feet,
To scatter flowers and jewels both around.

Blushing the stream of petal beauty flows,
Softly the white strings trickle down and shine.
Oh! speak to me, my love, I crave a rose.
Sing me a song, for I would pearls were mine.[46]

Two Poems on the Beauty of Human Beings

She Walks in Beauty

—by George Gordon, Lord Byron

In this poem, English poet Lord Byron (1788–1824) describes the loveliness of a beautiful woman who is made more beautiful by her goodness and innocence.

She walks in beauty, like the night
Of cloudless climes and starry skies;
And all that's best of dark and bright
Meet in her aspect and her eyes;
Thus mellowed to that tender light
Which heaven to gaudy day denies.

One shade the more, one ray the less,
Had half impaired the nameless grace
Which waves in every raven tress,
Or softly lightens o'er her face;
Where thoughts serenely sweet express,
How pure, how dear their dwelling-place.

▲ *Juliet* by John William Waterhouse

And on that cheek, and o'er that brow,
So soft, so calm, yet eloquent,
The smiles that win, the tints that glow,
But tell of days in goodness spent,
A mind at peace with all below,
A heart whose love is innocent![47]

46. Paul Laurence Dunbar, "Roses and Pearls," in *The Complete Poems of Paul Laurence Dunbar* (New York: Dodd, Mead and Company, 1922; Project Gutenberg, 2006), 270, http://www.gutenberg.org/files/18338/18338-h/18338-h.htm.
47. George Gordon, Lord Byron, "She Walks in Beauty," Poetry Foundation, accessed November 30, 2018, https://www.poetryfoundation.org/poems/43844/she-walks-in-beauty.

My Beloved

—from Song of Solomon in the Hebrew scriptures

Song of Solomon is one of the finest love poems of the ancient world. In this portion of the poem, a beautiful woman from Shulem describes her beloved husband, a handsome and dashing man.

Friends
How is your beloved better than others,
most beautiful of women?
How is your beloved better than others,
that you so charge us?

She
My beloved is radiant and ruddy,
outstanding among ten thousand.
His head is purest gold;
his hair is wavy
and black as a raven.
His eyes are like doves
by the water streams,
washed in milk,
mounted like jewels.
His cheeks are like beds of spice
yielding perfume.
His lips are like lilies
dripping with myrrh.
His arms are rods of gold
set with topaz.
His body is like polished ivory
decorated with lapis lazuli.
His legs are pillars of marble
set on bases of pure gold.
His appearance is like Lebanon,
choice as its cedars.
His mouth is sweetness itself;
he is altogether lovely.
This is my beloved, this is my friend,
daughters of Jerusalem.[48]

▲ Fayum mummy portrait, c. 50 BC–AD 200.

48. Song of Solomon 5:9–16 (NIV).

A Poem on the Enduring Nature of Beauty

Endymion

—by John Keats

In his "Ode on a Grecian Urn," Keats (1795–1821) famously wrote, "Beauty is truth, truth beauty." In this portion of his lengthy poem *Endymion*, he claims that something beautiful belongs to eternity.

A thing of beauty is a joy forever:
Its loveliness increases; it will never
Pass into nothingness; but still will keep
A bower quiet for us, and a sleep
Full of sweet dreams, and health, and quiet breathing.
Therefore, on every morrow, are we wreathing
A flowery band to bind us to the earth,
Spite of despondence, of the inhuman dearth
Of noble natures, of the gloomy days,
Of all the unhealthy and o'er-darkened ways
Made for our searching: yes, in spite of all,
Some shape of beauty moves away the pall
From our dark spirits. Such the sun, the moon,
Trees old and young, sprouting a shady boon
For simple sheep; and such are daffodils
With the green world they live in; and clear rills
That for themselves a cooling covert make
'Gainst the hot season; the mid forest brake,
Rich with a sprinkling of fair musk-rose blooms:
And such too is the grandeur of the dooms
We have imagined for the mighty dead;
All lovely tales that we have heard or read:
An endless fountain of immortal drink,
Pouring unto us from the heaven's brink.[49]

49. John Keats, *Endymion*, bk.1, lines 1–24, "From *Endymion*," Poetry Foundation, accessed November 30, 2018, https://www.poetryfoundation.org/poems/44469/endymion-56d2239287ca5.

Three Poems about the Beauty of Nature

Poetry covers the gamut of things that are beautiful, including things in nature. The starry night sky, among other natural beauties, can be found in these poems.

Flowers and Moonlight on the Spring River

—by Yang-ti

The evening river is level and motionless—
The spring colors just open to their full.
Suddenly a wave carries the moon away
And the tidal water comes with its freight of stars.[50]

Haiku

—by Matsuo Basho

Seas are wild tonight . . .
stretching over
Sado Island
Silent clouds of stars[51]

▲ *The Starry Night* by Vincent van Gogh

I Hear the Stars Still Singing

—by James Weldon Johnson

I hear the stars still singing
To the beautiful, silent night,
As they speed with noiseless winging
Their ever westward flight.
I hear the waves still falling
On the stretch of lonely shore,
But the sound of a sweet voice calling
I shall hear, alas! no more.[52]

50. Yang-ti, "Flowers and Moonlight on the Spring River," in *A Hundred and Seventy Chinese Poems*, trans. Arthur Waley (London: Constable and Company, 1918; Project Gutenberg, 2013), 92, https://www.gutenberg.org/files/42290/42290-h/42290-h.htm.
51. Matsuo Basho, "Haiku," Haiku of Basho, The Gold Scales, accessed November 5, 2018, http://oaks.nvg.org/basho.html.
52. James Weldon Johnson, "I Hear the Stars Still Singing," James Weldon Johnson, Poemhunter.com, accessed November 5, 2018, https://www.poemhunter.com/poem/i-hear-the-stars-still-singing/.

Tell It Back—

In the space provided, list three images from the previous poems that strike you as particularly beautiful. (Your answers don't have to be in complete sentences.) Then, in one well-crafted sentence, try to summarize what beautiful quality or qualities these three images have in common.

Image 1: Sample answer: a mind at peace with all below

Image 2: Sample answer: sweet dreams, and health, and quiet breathing

Image 3: Sample answer: silent clouds of stars

Quality the three images have in common:

Sample answer: These three images have in common a sense of the sweetness of serenity and the beautiful peace that comes before rest or sleep.

Talk About It—

TE 1. The poems in this section identified romance, a beloved person, and stars as beautiful things. Now it's your turn. Name and describe something beautiful and tell why it is so. Try to explain what qualities—physical, emotional, moral—make it beautiful to you. Consider a particular marvel of nature or the weather, a flower, a poem, a story, a painting, a dance, a sculpture, a piece of music, a pattern in figure skating, a movie, a play, a kindness, a fragrance, a spiral galaxy, or something else.

TE 2. What are some of the things the poets in this section are saying about beauty?

TE 3. Each of these poets experienced beauty so clearly or so powerfully that they wanted to share their thoughts and experiences with others. Why do you think beauty is important for individuals, groups, and even a whole nation to experience? What effect do you think beauty can have on people?

Speak It—

1. Memorize one of the poems in this lesson and recite it to your class using good volume, inflection, and pacing.

TE 2. With your class or with a partner, take turns describing aloud a painting, building, or sculpture that is particularly beautiful, or describe an image you see in this lesson. Give details about the object's foreground, middle ground, and background, and note anything particularly striking: shapes, lines, colors, textures, or motion.

Lesson 9: Third Thesis Essay, Part 1: What Is Beauty?

The Importance of Symmetry in Beauty

Tell It Back—Narration

According to Aristotle, "a beautiful object, whether it be a living organism or any whole composed of parts, must not only have an orderly arrangement of parts, but must also be of a certain size." Order and size are therefore important aspects of beauty to Aristotle. Vitruvius tells us, "The design of a temple depends on symmetry, the principles of which must be most carefully observed by the architect." According to Vitruvius, what's true for temples is also true for human beings: Symmetry is essential to a beautiful object.

Talk About It—

In my classroom, I'm looking at chairs and desks, a violin on the wall, a stapler, a lamp with a shade, and a book case, and all of these objects seem balanced between their two halves. I can also see random blotches on the ceiling from a one-time water leak, and I can see the books on my shelves, which lack any balance, as well as a stubby tree that is lopsided and misshapen.

I like the sense of predictability and orderliness in the symmetrical objects, how their parts are like mirror images of one another and how their lines run parallel. The asymmetrical objects are pleasant in their uniqueness—sometimes strange and sometimes amusing.

The symmetrical objects do seem more beautiful to me. At the same time, I find the asymmetrical objects to be more interesting. It seems to me that the symmetrical objects are more pleasing to look at because the shapes give me a feeling of peace and their regularity makes them predictable in a positive way. The odd-shaped objects are interesting because they are so unpredictable and varied.

Behind Everything Beautiful Is the Divine

Talk About It—

1. Burke tells us that lust awakens the desire to possess something, and we can assume he means to possess selfishly.

   In my mind, love and lust are opposites. Love is caring for something—the desire to nurture and cherish it—even if you get no benefit in return. Lust is the desire to use something without truly caring for it.

I love beautiful mountain vistas. I love to be on top of a mountain with a wide view of this amazing world. The beauty of those vistas makes me want to care for the environment so that the mountain views can continue to inspire human beings for generations to come.

2. Plotinus explains that every beautiful thing has some kind of divine nature that is detectable by the senses, but also by the human divine nature. Because of this, our souls can detect the essence of beauty in anything, whether visible or invisible.

   Invisible beauties would include the aroma of baking bread, the purring of a cat, love, courage, friendship, and the warmth from a mug of coffee.

Beauty and Goodness Are Fundamentally Identical

Talk About It—

Answers will vary. Sample answer: I'm thinking of the smell of fried chicken, biscuits, and gravy. Smell enhances the pleasure of taste, and taste is good for increasing pleasure in the act of eating, which is essential to survival and existence. Both pleasure and the act of nourishment are good, and therefore that beautiful smell is good, because it leads to pleasure and nourishment. More than that, however, the smell of fried chicken, biscuits, and gravy reminds me of family reunions and my grandma's home cooking, and it is both a pleasure and a joy to remember times of family love. These memories help to strengthen my connection to people who depend on me and I on them. Thus, another reason the smell is good is that it leads to those memories, which are good.

The Vocabulary of Beauty Continues to Expand

Talk About It—

1. Scruton is using "cult" in the negative sense, referring to blind followers of obscure and harmful ideas. He makes his meaning clear through the wording he uses and the statements he makes about "ugly" modern art. At one point, he calls some modern architects vandals, which implies they are doing harm. Scruton believes that artists no longer believe in beauty, but have—in essence—gone over to "the dark side" in only capturing the randomness and ugliness of the human experience, and he talks about the harm that may be caused by this shift.

2. Scruton dislikes many modern buildings because they were built for utility without considering the need for beauty. He seems especially resentful that sections of his hometown were demolished to put up buildings of "ugliness and mutilation."

   There is nothing very special about most of the modern buildings in my town of Indianapolis. Most of them are made of steel and glass, and they are unimaginatively rectangular, like so many other modern buildings in other towns. The two buildings that stand out in a positive way are the Eiteljorg Museum of American Indians and Western Art and The Pyramids office buildings. The Eiteljorg Museum building is modeled after the Southwest architectural style of the Anasazi Indians, and the Pyramids office buildings suggest the three main pyramids of the Giza burial complex in Egypt.

I like these modern buildings because they capture something of the style and mystery of ancient architecture.

I prefer older buildings such as Tabernacle Presbyterian Church, a neo-Gothic building, and the Morris-Butler House, built in the Second Empire style of the nineteenth century. Both of these buildings are stately and elegant, and they help me to imagine life in a more romantic time.

3. Perrin is encouraged by modern artistic developments because she believes that they are part of the process by which the "vocabulary" of art and beauty continues to expand. This expansion means that today's artists have many more ways to express themselves than did artists of the past. Perrin also believes that there is beauty in the ability of art to respond to what is happening in the world, even if it must point out ugliness and absurdity.

4. We have only to see how many people are drawn to the scene of a car accident or to a horror movie filled with gore to see the power of ugliness. Ugliness does have a power to attract people, but in a different way than beauty does. Some "ugly" things—Duchamp's *Fountain*, for example—can be ridiculous, and we laugh at them. Sometimes "ugly" things—a pug dog, for example—can be charming, and we find them endearing. Mostly, though, we are fascinated when ugliness breaks the taboos of ordinary life and we are confronted with things that would usually not be public or "out in the open." Examples would be a broken leg or parasitic worms in a piece of fish. These unpleasant things fill us with disgust, but despite the revulsion, we have a hard time not being fascinated by them.

   Valid reasons for creating ugly art would be those that have thoughtful intentions: to make a statement about the human condition, for example, or to avoid clichés and sentimentality.

The Beauty of Nature

Talk About It—

1. I agree with Emerson that every season and day has some beauty, but I have strong preferences for certain seasons and certain days. I like autumn best for its frosty weather, for apple and chestnut picking, and for the turning of leaves. Autumn is an in-between season with cool temperatures that make for carefree hiking and picnicking, and her bright, sunny days are invigorating. On the other hand, I also love the stormy, rainy days of summer. When the sky turns black and there's the sizzle of lightning in the air, I feel the most exhilarated. I love to splash through puddles with an umbrella in hand, and I take delight in watching raindrops streak across the windowpanes of my sunroom.

2. I do find it difficult to stay in touch with natural beauty in the city because everywhere we are surrounded by man-made objects and man-made sensations. The lights of the city block out the stars and turn the sky into a murky ceiling overhead. The drone of the freeway and the noise of lawnmowers block out the chatter of squirrels and the song of birds. I find that I must look much harder to find nature in the cracks in the sidewalk and in the weeds of empty lots. Even our parks are often overrun with noisy, exuberant people.

3. In Cole's painting, the distant mountain and the lake, glowing in the soft light, are beautiful. I like how the serenity of the scene seems broken by the buck swimming across the water. There's a beautiful balance in the frame between the gnarled tree on the right and the mountain on the left. In Monet's painting, the Japanese bridge creates a harmonious arch across the lily pond. The bright flowers floating on the darker water seem to float off the canvas. Both scenes are beautiful and inviting, and I think that I should be happy to experience both of them. I have a slight preference for the wilderness scene because nature is so bold there, so untamed and giant.

A Thing of Beauty Is a Joy Forever: Poems about Beautiful Things

Talk About It—

1. Snowflakes are beautiful. When they land on our coats and gloves, we've been graced with miniature masterpieces falling from the sky. Snowflakes are formed when water crystalizes into six-sided, symmetrical arrangements, and their order and symmetry is part of what makes them beautiful. In addition, each flake is uniquely individual, never to be repeated in the history of the earth. That individuality is part of their beauty, as is the fleeting nature of their existence. We appreciate the few seconds we have with a snowflake because it lasts for such a short time. Snowflakes are also beautiful because they can point us to goodness. When we take the time to appreciate a snowy day, we can see snowflakes as messengers of peace and reflection to a world that is too hurried.
2. Dunbar's poems celebrate romantic love and the beauty of being in love. "She Walks in Beauty" and "Song of Solomon" rejoice in the physical beauty of the beloved. These poems seem to be saying that we find beauty most fully in the love of another human being. Keats tells us that beauty has an everlasting, undying quality. Last, the poems about nature remind us to open our eyes to the world around us—sky and sea—because natural beauty literally surrounds us, whether we see it or not.
3. We are unique among the creatures of Earth in our appreciation of beauty and our consciousness of it. Beauty is important to individuals because it inspires us to be better human beings—more caring human beings. When we discover something beautiful—such as a work of art or a shady grove—the effect on us is powerful. We want to take care of it and nurture it. The process of nurturing beauty can also prompt us to nurture and uplift other people by sharing beauty with them. Beauty also affects individuals by giving meaning to their lives. We can make it our life's mission to share beauty and even to create it. Almost everyone wants to leave a legacy in the world, and the legacy of beauty is a deep motivator. Some groups of people in particular are affected by this quality of beauty. Parents want to leave behind children who are morally beautiful and artists want to leave behind masterworks that will be admired by the ages. And, in fact, an entire nation can be affected by beauty's ability to give meaning to life. Without meaning, people can be aimless, confused, and fearful, and these negatives can create misunderstanding, anger, and cruelty. Beauty is important to a healthy society because without it, a vacuum is created in the human heart that can breed selfishness, misery, and hatred. Beauty can help a whole nation by inspiring the positive qualities that help it to thrive.

Speak It—

2. Answers will vary. Sample answer: The Temple of the Golden Pavilion in Kyoto, Japan, must be one of the most beautiful buildings in the world. When photographed from across its pond, it seems almost like a bright water lily floating on the water. Two dark, curved roofs rest on top of three square levels of the building, each side perfectly symmetrical, almost like the layers of a wedding cake. The upper two levels are painted in bright gold, and it makes a shimmering reflection on the dark water, which is shaded green by tall trees in the background. Perhaps the most inviting aspect of the architecture is the levels of golden balconies surrounding the entire building. One can picture a Buddhist monk standing on a balcony watching the fish jump or listening for deer in the surrounding forest.

Notes

Notes

The purpose of this lesson is for students to write a thesis essay answering the speculative and philosophical question, "What is beauty?"

In this lesson, students will practice:

- brainstorming ideas with others
- prewriting by creating a list
- assessing the main ideas of other writers
- critical thinking
- following an outline
- writing a thesis essay, including an introduction, body paragraphs, and a conclusion
- writing a complex thesis
- writing descriptively
- examining a text and lifting supporting quotes from it
- dramatic reading
- formal discussion
- editing dangling modifiers and faulty predication
- revision and proofreading

Lesson 10

Third Thesis Essay, Part 2: What Is Beauty?

In the previous lesson, you read and considered the work of a slew of thinkers and writers as they discussed beauty and its meaning. Some of these thinkers agreed with each other, some disagreed, and many borrowed ideas from people in the past and extended those ideas in a new direction. The dialogue between thinkers through the ages has been dubbed "the Great Conversation," and it certainly does seem that these thinkers are speaking to one another, reacting to each other, even over many centuries and long distances.

So now, guess what? You knew this was coming—it's your turn to add your voice to the Great Conversation!

Admittedly, you are young and probably you don't have much experience reasoning in the public square with other philosophers. Maybe this is your first dive into philosophy. When confronted with the question "What is beauty," many of my students tell me, "Mr. K., I know beauty when I see it. . . . But I can't tell you what it is!"

Believe it or not, that is a terrific place to begin. The philosopher Socrates believed that learning takes place only when you acknowledge that you are ignorant. A humble self-opinion is always a good place to begin learning. In Plato's *Apology*, Socrates[1] tells a story about meeting a man whom crowds of people considered super bright and wise. In fact, the man believed the rumors himself and went around Athens with a big head. Here's what happened when Socrates met up with him:

> When I began to talk with him, I could not help thinking that he was not really wise, although he was thought wise by many, and still wiser by himself. I tried to explain to him that he thought himself wise, but was not really wise; and the consequence was that he hated me. . . . So I left him, saying to myself, as I went away: Well, although I do not suppose that either of us knows anything really beautiful and good, I am better off than he is, for he knows nothing, and thinks that he knows; I neither know nor think that I know. In this latter particular, then, I seem to have slightly the advantage of him.[2]

▲ Sculpture of Socrates in the Louvre. Image courtesy of CherryX, https://commons.wikimedia.org/wiki/File:Louvre,_Socrates-Sculpture.jpg.

So Socrates begins with the premise of ignorance—"I neither know nor think that I know"—and that is where we all begin with any subject.

Thinking with Others—

Now, if I were going to tackle an abstract subject such as beauty, I would first have conversations with the people around me. I call this process "thinking with others," and it's an ideal way to begin brainstorming (or prewriting) your essay. You can't very well have a game of tennis by yourself, and you can't do your best thinking without sooner or later bouncing your ideas off of other people. Here are some of the ways you can think with others:

- **Agree/Disagree:** Pick a reading from the previous lesson and locate its thesis. Ask yourself whether you agree or disagree with the thesis (or whether you land somewhere in-between). Try to put your agreement or disagreement clearly into words. Next, have a conversation with a classmate or teacher and see where she stands on the same reading. Where do you agree? Where do you disagree?
- **Compare/Contrast:** With a classmate, locate the theses of two readings. Next, try to put into words where the authors' perspectives are similar and where they are different. How would the authors regard something that you or your classmate considers beautiful? Which author do you resonate with best? What about your classmate?

1. Plato was a student of Socrates. In the works of Plato, Socrates is usually the principal character.
2. Adapted from Plato, *Apology*, trans. Benjamin Jowett (Project Gutenberg, 2008), https://www.gutenberg.org/files/1656/1656-h/1656-h.htm.

Types of evidence:

- details
- examples
- facts

Evidence can be presented as:

- quotations
- paraphrases
- summaries

- **Getting and Testing Ideas:** Take a thesis or idea that you like from one of the readings and expand on it by providing your own arguments and examples for it. For example, Schiller writes, “Physical beauty is an envelope to intellectual and to moral beauty.” You could test this idea by coming up with examples that show how it might be true, false, or both true and false. For instance, the example of a gold watch might prove the statement true: The craftsmanship (physical beauty) of the watch and its measure of invisible time reveal a deeper beauty, the intellect of the human mind. Check your examples with a classmate. Does the thesis or idea hold up as you try to run with it, or does it fall apart?
- **Socratic Dialogue:** Have a conversation in a question-and-answer format, with one person asking questions and the other person answering. This is what it would look like: The first person asserts a thesis about beauty based on one of the readings. The second person asks a question about the thesis. The first person answers the question. The second person then asks a new question based on the first person’s response. And so on. The idea is to expose assumptions and open up new ideas on the topic. (An example of Socratic dialogue can be found in the Speak It section of this lesson.)

Thinking with others in these ways will help you shape your ideas as you begin this venture into philosophy.

Whatever your answer to the question “What is beauty?” let me assure you that it won’t be the final word on the subject. Your ideas will likely change with time. Even so, what you think about now is meaningful, because your reflections shape the person you will become. As the poet William Wordsworth said, “The child is the father of the man.” Your life as a young person fathers forth (or mothers forth) the person you become as an adult. What we reflect upon, what we grow to love, what we find beautiful makes us who we are. So take seriously this effort to reflect upon beauty. You’ll be glad you did—and maybe this dive into philosophy will become a lifelong love for you!

Writing Time—Thesis Essay: What Is Beauty?

In this essay, you will strive to answer the speculative question "What is beauty?" To answer this deep question, you will be borrowing ideas about beauty from other thinkers and turning those ideas into something that belongs to you—your idea of beauty. Since this is going to be a thesis essay, you want to persuade your audience (if you can) to agree with your answer, your thesis statement.

Examining the Text: In *A Philosophical Enquiry into the Origin of Our Ideas of the Sublime and Beautiful*, Edmond Burke writes, "Beauty is that quality, or those qualities in bodies, which cause love, or some passion similar to it."[3] Burke's statement strikes me as true as far as it goes. Beyond the bodies of things such as bright-feathered birds, muscular athletes, or a nebula seen through a telescope, I would also include things without typical bodies, such as music, the voice of a loved one, the smell of a bakery or a fragrant lilac, and a host of other things besides. When we first hear a sweet melody, when we are first captured by a gorgeous idea, when we first stand on a beach before the mighty ocean, doesn't it feel something like falling in love—however brief and fleeting?

Whether you personally agree with Burke or not, let's assume for a moment that you do. To get you thinking about beauty, consider this: What is it that you love? What do you find beautiful? In the space provided, write down some of the things that move your heart to joy. Be specific, and include a brief description or reason for your answer.

Examples:

- Mount Whitney in California is a beautiful mountain. Its summit is a snowy spire of rock that reflects the dawning light in vivid colors.
- The cha-cha from Cuba and the step dance from Ireland are beautiful, athletic dances. Each dance requires precise steps and spins to a brisk, intense rhythm.
- My grandmother's crisp, good-humored voice and her sunshiny laugh have the beautiful power to lift people's spirits.
- The miniature working parts of mosquitoes, and the delicacy of their wings, are oddly beautiful to behold.
- Malvin Gray Johnson's *Self-Portrait* beautifully captures a look of creative confidence in a colorful world of the artist's own imagination.

▲ *Self-Portrait* by Malvin Gray Johnson

3. Adapted from Edmund Burke, *A Philosophical Enquiry into the Origin of Our Ideas of the Sublime and Beautiful*, in *The Works of the Right Honorable Edmund Burke* (London: John C. Nimmo, 1887; Project Gutenberg, 2005), vol. 1, https://www.gutenberg.org/files/15043/15043-h/15043-h.htm#Page_165.

What I find beautiful:

Sample answer: I find the ghostly light of the full moon beautiful, especially as it illuminates winding footpaths of sand across the grassy high dunes of Lake Michigan. The quality of light on the glowing sand is a rare, otherworldly sight.

Now consider some of the important ideas from the readings in the previous lesson. As you look over the following list, choose four of the ideas that interest you the most. Then write down your thoughts about those ideas in the space provided. (You don't need to write anything in the spaces for the remaining ideas.) What do you find about each reading's central idea(s) to be valuable? What examples from art and architecture, literature and human action, support this idea?

- Aristotle: "Beauty depends on size and order": a certain size and an orderly arrangement of parts.

- Vitruvius: Beauty in architecture and people requires symmetry and due proportion.

- Edmund Burke: Beauty is not due to proportion, but is a quality that causes love.

- Plotinus: Behind everything beautiful is a divine essence, which our souls perceive.

Sample answer: Makes sense to me. Beautiful things have a mysterious quality that is hard to define, but easy to recognize. This is especially true for things that lack a beautiful appearance but have a beautiful quality, such as an ugly dog that has the qualities of faithfulness or an affectionate nature. Plotinus's idea is valuable because it gives some common foundation for all the things we call beautiful.

- Thomas Aquinas: Goodness is what every person desires, and beauty is the form of goodness that our senses can observe. Beauty and goodness are the same things deep down below the level of the senses.

- Charles Darwin: The instinct to mate has given people their appreciation for beauty.

- Friedrich Schiller: The idea that beauty is anything that pleases the senses is a "coarse" understanding.

Sample answer: Although Schiller says this is a coarse or crude understanding of beauty, I think that pleasure must be part of the equation. Pleasure is a universal response that people feel in the presence of beauty. For example, many people feel great pleasure when surrounded by the stained glass of Saint Chapelle or the rock walls of Yosemite National Park. While it is important to acknowledge the pleasure that beauty causes, what's valuable about Schiller's idea is the reminder that beauty is about more than pleasure alone.

- Friedrich Schiller: The most plausible ancient definition of beauty is that it consists of two contrary and equally necessary elements—unity and variety.

- Friedrich Schiller: "Physical beauty is an envelope to intellectual and to moral beauty."

Sample answer: This idea reminds me of Plotinus, who says that there's a divine essence in everything beautiful. Intelligence seems to be an aspect of beauty—that is, there is an intelligence behind everything people find beautiful, whether a handsome rooster or a frosted root beer float. Beautiful things seem beautiful by design. Schiller's idea is valuable because it confirms the idea that there is a deeper essence to beauty.

- Roger Scruton: Beauty "is not just a subjective thing, but a universal need of human beings."

____

____

____

- Christine Perrin: "Beauty has dimensions." Beauty can be found in the act of properly representing certain kinds of unbeautiful experiences.

Sample answer: This idea resonates with me when I think of paintings such as Pablo Picasso's *Guernica* and Edvard Munch's *The Scream*. There's beauty in both paintings in terms of a high level of skill, but the subject matter is horrifying and disturbing. It's possible that the painting of these subjects helped to purge bad experiences, and there is something beautiful about using art in that way. Perrin's idea is valuable because it causes us to consider expanding traditional ideas of what beauty may be.

- Ralph Waldo Emerson: "Beauty, in its largest and profoundest sense, is one expression for the universe."

____

____

____

Considering Audience: Think about your audience for a moment. For example:

- Has your audience considered defining beauty before? That will determine how much of the philosophical background you need to include in your essay.
- Is your audience already interested in understanding beauty better, or is it disinterested and likely to require a strong hook to become engaged?
- What about your purpose for writing the essay? Do you want to inspire your audience and help them to see beauty differently? Or do you want to caution your audience against a shallow understanding of beauty that can harm our culture?

Jot down some notes about your audience here. (If you need a refresher on considering your audience, please flip back to lesson 3.) **A**

Who is my audience?

Sample answer: My audience is my social media friends from camp. They haven't considered philosophical ideas about beauty before and will need me to be crystal clear.

[A]Note that the sample answers for this exercise are written as if the teacher has instructed students to write for an audience outside of their classroom. If you feel it is appropriate for your students, you may want to stretch their writing skills by having them write to an audience that consists of someone other than their classmates.

What is my audience's disposition (friendly, neutral, hostile, etc.)?

Sample answer: My audience is probably a bit hostile. They won't necessarily agree with me that for something to be truly beautiful, it also needs to be good. They may even attack me for sounding preachy.

What is my purpose in writing to my audience (to inform, challenge, delight, awaken, encourage, warn, etc.)?

Sample answer: My purpose is to influence my audience. I want my friends to pursue what is good and beautiful, rather than what is destructive and shallow.

Outline: Before you get started, here is the six-paragraph outline you will follow for your thesis essay. A sample of a completed thesis essay is available at the back of the book.

I. Introduction
- A. hook and transition to thesis
- B. thesis
- C. explanation of thesis
- D. transition to next paragraph

II. Body Paragraph 1: Confirmation/Support
- A. topic sentence
- B. explanation of the confirmation
- C. appeal to authority (evidence in the form of a quote or paraphrase)

III. Body Paragraph 2: Confirmation/Support
- A. topic sentence
- B. explanation of the confirmation
- C. appeal to authority (evidence in the form of a quote or paraphrase)

IV. Body Paragraph 3: Refutation/Antithesis
- A. antithesis (as topic sentence)
- B. explanation of the antithesis
- C. refutation of antithesis/defense of thesis
- D. appeal to authority (evidence in the form of a quote or paraphrase)

V. Body Paragraph 4: Refutation/Antithesis
- A. antithesis (as topic sentence)
- B. explanation of the antithesis
- C. refutation of antithesis/defense of thesis
- D. appeal to authority (evidence in the form of a quote or paraphrase)

VI. Conclusion

A. thesis restated

B. why the topic is important

C. call to action (optional)

[B]If students are struggling with portions of the prewriting or the complete essay, you may want to show them the sample answers in the Teacher's Edition to help them see how the author has accomplished the task.

Use the following prompts for each paragraph to help you sketch out your ideas. You can use lists, phrases, or complete sentences for your answers. Then compose your full essay on a separate paper or on a computer.[B] Remember that each paragraph has a job to do in defending the thesis.

The paragraphs you write after going through these steps will be your first draft, or your first version of the essay. Assume that your first draft will need some rewriting to make it the best essay it can be.

Thesis Wheel

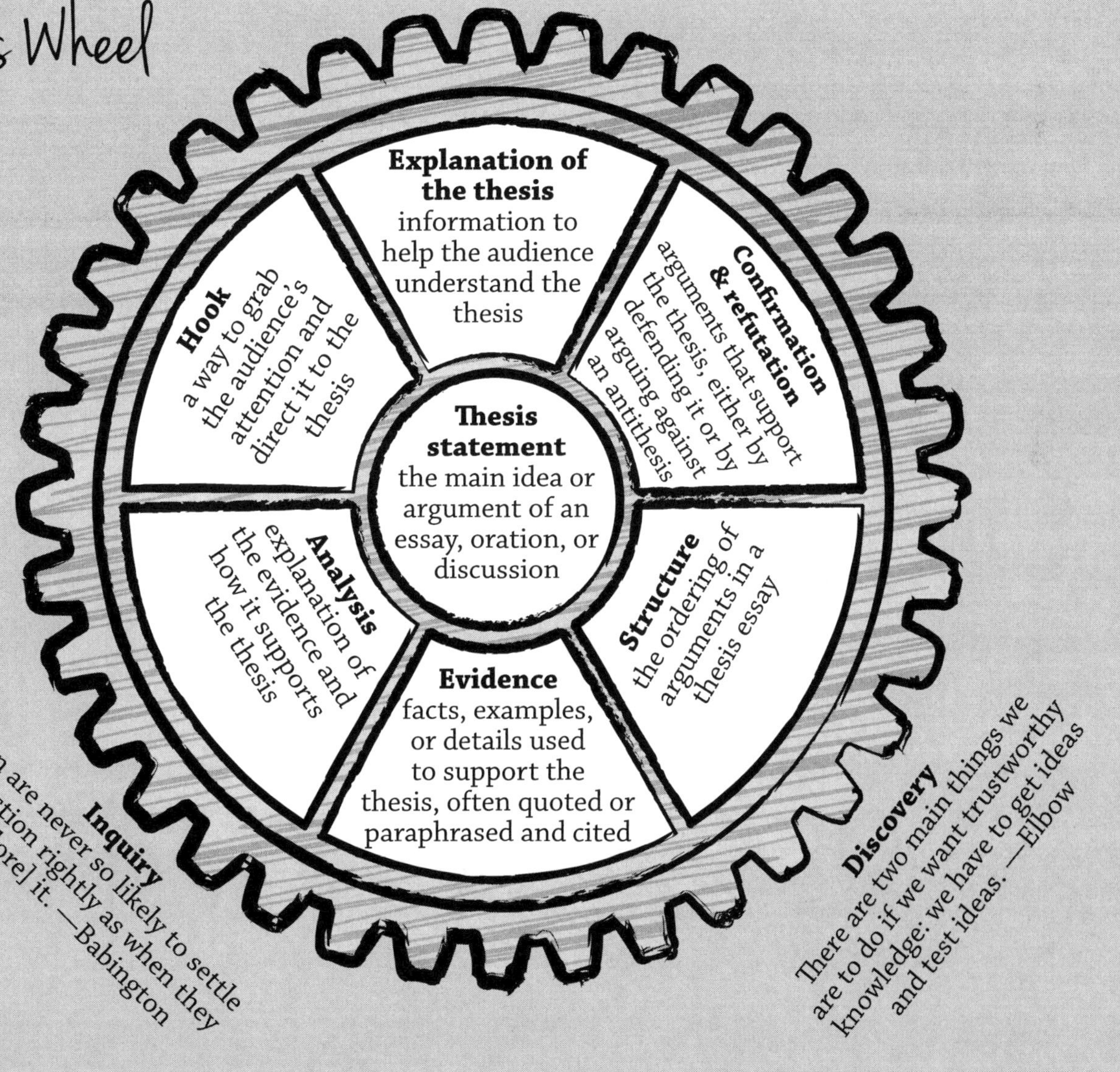

Based on the Essay Wheel developed by the Messiah College writing program.

Paragraph 1 (Introduction): The purpose of the introduction paragraph is to orient your reader and to reveal the point you plan to argue.

Writing the thesis is the first step in a thesis essay although you will actually place it *after* the hook when you write your introduction paragraph. Your thesis should answer the speculative question: What is beauty? Although your thesis statement will essentially be a definition of beauty, avoid consulting the dictionary! Dictionary definitions of beauty are incomplete at best and lack personal insight. Here are some questions that may guide you to a thesis:

- Are things uniquely beautiful, and not related to one another, or do they all have a quality of beauty that unites them? If the latter, what is that quality?
- What is the reaction that people often have when they experience something beautiful?
- How does beauty make a difference in life?

Take another look at your annotations and the exercises in the last lesson. The texts of the various philosophers and writers should give you some ideas to consider as you think about how to answer these questions, but you will have to choose among them. Perhaps you also gained some good insights from the last lesson's introductory text or when you were "thinking with others" earlier in this lesson.

Write your thesis statement in the space provided. Remember that a thesis is the main argument of a persuasive paper. A good thesis is open to debate, is clear and specific (not too broad), and can be supported by evidence. In this essay, the thesis statement should also mention the two supporting arguments that you will expand on in your confirmation paragraphs.[A]

[A]Here is an example of a thesis statement that includes a main argument and also mentions two supporting arguments:

Simple Thesis — "Children younger than thirteen should not own cell phones

supporting argument 1 — because they impair learning

supporting argument 2 — and cause addiction."

If you need to refresh your memory on the type of thesis statements you will write in this book, flip back to lesson 2.

Thesis statement: ____________________

Sample answer: Beauty is goodness in a tangible, detectable form, as seen in the way it enhances life and arouses wonder and pleasure.

Now, in one sentence, explain your thesis. You will expand on this explanation in your confirmation paragraphs.

Explanation of thesis: ____________________

Sample answer: Since these effects are the products of goodness, it is clear that any "visible" experience of beauty is a reflection of the invisible quality of goodness.

Now write a transition sentence that takes the reader from the thesis explanation to the first confirmation paragraph. Remember that a transition forms a bridge from one paragraph to another. One side of the "bridge" will be made by referencing the topic of your first paragraph and the other side of the bridge will hint at what comes next.

Transition sentence: ____________________

Sample answer: One can find evidence of how beauty, an exterior quality, reflects a deeper inner quality by looking at the effect it has on people.

Next, go back and think about the very beginning of your introduction paragraph, the hook. In this lesson, you will be provided with some specific instructions for the examples you use to support your thesis, to aid you in this more challenging writing task. For the hook, begin with a rich description of a specific natural setting or something else that you find particularly beautiful.[4] Use vivid words, details, and metaphors or similes. Here is an example:

> As the snorkeler slides under the water of Hanauma Bay, Oahu, an azure world of corals and fishes opens before his eyes, as clear and bright as the air above. He floats for a moment to get his bearings and enjoys the sound of water sluicing in his ears, the sound of steady breathing through his snorkel, the feeling of liquid from head to foot. Then he kicks gently and off he floats, bobbing over a bustling city of fantastically colored creatures: red and white wrasses, black and gold Moorish idols, yellow

4. For more detail about describing nature, please see *Writing & Rhetoric Book 9: Description & Impersonation*.

tangs, silver-blue needlefish, and green surgeonfish. He feels as though he is swimming through the bands of a rainbow with the colors darting and swirling around him. He is immersed in beauty. In the poem *Endymion*, John Keats says that "A thing of beauty is a joy forever; its loveliness increases," and this is true of a swim and a dive in Hanauma Bay. A beautiful experience grows lovelier with time, and, in its essence, beauty is . . .

Here is another example written by an eighth-grade student:

The sun is suspended low over a faraway hill and the fog begins to settle over the landscape below. Perched on a boulder above the valley, a russet sparrow watches the sprawling vegetation turn into splashes of brown and green, blurred as if painted with watercolor. A dilapidated wooden fence cuts through the brush. The auburn-tinted rays of the fading sun brighten the stalks of prairie grass that thrive on the rocky fields. Behind the boulders, the forest is dark, deep, silent, and still. The battlefield of Gettysburg seems to be brooding over the young men whose lives ended in blasts of cannon fire on its soil. The peace that now abides in this valley is startling. Crickets begin chirping. Clouds bunch up in an effort to cover the last rays of the golden sun that are peeping over the hills. The effect is stunning. It makes a person wonder, what makes something so beautiful? What unites music, art, nature, people, and poetry under the category of beauty? What is beauty? Beauty is . . .[5]

Ideas for a hook: ______________________________

Sample answer:

- twilight in the Galilee region, rolling hills and lush vineyards
- on a wooden boat, Sea of Galilee, at sunset
- city lights like diamonds, colors in the sky over black horizon
- flock of seagulls, cool air, lapping water

In order to move from your hook to your thesis, you will need a transition. Notice how the writer of the first hook example transitions from a specific experience in nature to a general quotation about beauty and then to his thesis statement. That's one way to do it. The writer of the second example uses a series of questions at the end of the description to transition to her thesis. You will need to decide how you want to use your description to lead to your thesis. You can transition directly to your thesis, or you can use another type of hook—a question, a proverb, a quotation, a provocative statement, a statistic, or a fact—to make the transi-

5. Adapted from a thesis essay submitted by Clara Malek, a student at The Oaks Academy, Indianapolis, Indiana, 2018. Used with permission.

tion. However you do it, you should make a smooth connection between your hook and the argument you will be presenting.

Transition from the hook to the thesis: ______________________________

Sample answer: question/wondering about the nature of beauty

____

When you write your full introduction paragraph, remember that even though in your prewriting you started with the thesis and then worked back to the hook, your completed paragraph should follow the order of hook (with transition), thesis, transition.

Paragraph 2 (First Confirmation): Each confirmation paragraph will explain and justify your thesis in depth from a different angle. In other words, each paragraph will set out one confirming argument that shows why your thesis is true. Start the paragraph with a topic sentence, which tells the main idea of the paragraph—what your confirmation argument will be.

Topic sentence: ______________________________

Sample answer: The essence of beauty is unseen goodness, and this is demonstrated in the way that beauty gives or enhances life.

____

Follow the topic sentence by explaining it and giving supporting evidence. Use a specific work of art or literature with which you are intimately acquainted—a painting, a sculpture, a building, a piece of music, a ballet, and so on—as an example to illustrate your topic sentence.

Illustration from art or literature: ______________________________

Sample answer:
- statue of Aphrodite found in Milos
- the fable of "The Crow and the Pitcher"
- Borodin's Second Symphony

____

In order to appeal to authority, be sure to quote or paraphrase an idea from one of the readings in lesson 9, or from the examples in that lesson's introduction. Your quote or paraphrase should support (confirm) or clarify your argument. Remember that your quote will need to be introduced and then explained, and be sure to cite your source.[C]

Quotation or paraphrase from the text: ______________

[C]If your students need a refresher on using quotations and paraphrase to provide evidence, please refer them to lesson 6.

Sample answer:

And on that cheek, and o'er that brow,
So soft, so calm, yet eloquent,
The smiles that win, the tints that glow,
But tell of days in goodness spent,
A mind at peace with all below,
A heart whose love is innocent! (Byron)

Paragraph 3 (Second Confirmation): Start with a topic sentence, which tells the main idea of the paragraph—what your confirmation argument will be.

Topic sentence: ______________

Sample answer: Another way that beauty brings the light of goodness to the world is by producing wonder and pleasure.

Follow the topic sentence by explaining it and giving supporting evidence. Use a beautiful human action from history or literature as an example to illustrate your topic sentence. For instance:

- From history: As a young lawyer in Alabama, Bryan Stevenson fought to save prisoners who were unjustly imprisoned or sentenced with the death penalty.
- From literature: In the book *To Kill a Mockingbird*, lawyer Atticus Finch fights to save a man who was imprisoned for a crime he did not commit.

Illustration of a beautiful human action from history or literature: ______________

Sample answer: During World War II, army medic Desmond Doss risked his life in the Battle of Okinawa to save seventy-five wounded soldiers, all without carrying a gun or shooting at the enemy.

In order to appeal to authority, be sure to quote or paraphrase an idea from one of the readings in lesson 9, or from the examples in that lesson's introduction. Your quote or paraphrase should support (confirm) or clarify your argument. Remember that your quote will need to be introduced and then explained, and be sure to cite your source.

Quotation or paraphrase from the text: ______

Sample answer: "Beauty is the quality, or those qualities in bodies, which cause love, or some passion similar to it" (Burke 165).

Paragraph 4 (First Refutation): Each refutation paragraph will explain and refute an antithesis, a disagreement with your thesis. In other words, each paragraph will set out one antithesis and then show why it is untrue. Start the paragraph with the antithesis, which will serve as the topic sentence or main idea of the paragraph. You should lead into the antithesis with a phrase such as "Some might argue that . . .".

- Tip: Consider your audience as you work on your antitheses. What objections might your teacher or classmates have to your thesis? You may even want to ask them.

Antithesis: ______

Sample answer: Some might argue that goodness and beauty do not always go hand in hand.

Follow the antithesis by explaining it. To help you think through your explanation, consider listing some supporting arguments for the antithesis before you start to write.

Next, defend the thesis by telling why the antithesis is wrong. Appeal to authority with textual evidence by using a quote or paraphrase from the readings in lesson 9, or from the examples in that lesson's introduction, that supports or clarifies your defense. Remember that your quote will need to be introduced and then explained, and be sure to cite your source.

Defense: ______

Sample answer:

- Beauty in a person or thing is still good even if other aspects of the person or thing are not.
- When something beautiful is used for bad purposes, it is not the case that its beauty lacks goodness but that the beautiful thing is being misused or corrupted.

Quotation or paraphrase from the text: ______________________________

Sample answer:
- "mastering Heav'ns Supreme" (Milton 9.125)
- "sweet interchange of Hill, and Valley, Rivers, Woods and Plains" (Milton 9.115–16)

Paragraph 5 (Second Refutation): Start with the antithesis, which will serve as the topic sentence or main idea of the paragraph. You should lead into the second antithesis with a phrase such as "Others might argue that . . .".

Antithesis: ______________________________

Sample answer: Others might argue that something can be beautiful without inspiring wonder and pleasure.

Follow the antithesis by explaining it. To help you think through your explanation, consider listing some supporting arguments for the antithesis before you start to write.

Next, defend the thesis by telling why the antithesis is wrong. Appeal to authority with textual evidence by using a quote or paraphrase from the readings in lesson 9, or from the examples in that lesson's introduction, that supports or clarifies your defense. Remember that your quote will need to be introduced and then explained, and be sure to cite your source.

Defense: ______________________________

Sample answer: Just because someone isn't capable of experiencing inspiration from beauty doesn't mean the inspiration doesn't exist at all.

Quotation or paraphrase from the text: ______________________________

Sample answer: "The voices of a choir rouse the harmony latent in the soul, and open her eye to the perception of beauty, and strike the respective senses with wonder and delight" (Plotinus).

Paragraph 6 (Conclusion): In your conclusion, you will make your case one last time by restating your thesis. For the prewriting stage, jot down a new version of the thesis using fresh language.

Restatement of the thesis: ______________________________

Sample answer: Beauty is the reflection of goodness, a tangible reality that, by its effects, reveals the invisible good that sustains and improves life.

____

When you come back to this prompt to write your full paragraph, consider what you have learned from supporting your thesis in the previous paragraphs. Your final restatement should express a fuller and more complete understanding of the thesis now that you have tested your ideas in the body of the paper.

Example:

- Original thesis: "Students should spend time outdoors to improve their quality of life and overall health."
- Restated thesis: "By spending time outdoors, students will reduce stress and boost their overall happiness, as well as get physical exercise and experience improved sleep."

Notice how the restatement presents the thesis with more precision and insight, demonstrating the deeper understanding that was gained through the process of writing the essay. Rework your restated thesis as needed to express this deeper understanding.

Next, tell why your topic is important. In other words, how can this topic be applied to real life or change the reader's outlook?

Why your topic is important: ______________________________

Sample answer: By pondering what beauty is, and how it relates to goodness, people can distinguish between things that are beautiful and worthwhile to experience and things that are not, or whose goodness has been spoiled.

____

____

You can also look carefully at your body paragraphs and emphasize any points that best support your thesis. Another possibility is to urge your readers to take heed of the importance of beauty in shaping a person's life and character or to take some sort of concrete action.

Call to action (optional): ____________________

Sample answer: It's important to stop to smell the roses and listen to the song of birds. True beauty should be embraced.

D If your students are struggling with understanding this particular dialogue, you may want to point them to the SparkNotes summary, which is available at https://www.sparknotes.com/philosophy/symposium/. Be careful when using online summaries, however, as some students may choose to default to these and avoid reading the actual books.

Once you have completed your prewriting, go through these instructions again and write your paragraphs based on the prompts.

Speak It—

1. **SOCRATIC DIALOGUE:** One of the aims of the Speak It section is to improve elocution and speaking skill. While that is a worthy goal in itself, we also find that in speaking ideas aloud, we develop new ways of thinking about them. Speaking holds a prism up to the invisible white light of an idea and splits it into a spectrum of "visible" thoughts.

   As you learned in the introduction to this lesson, a Socratic dialogue is a conversation in which the speakers ask and answer questions about an idea, their goal being to think more deeply about the topic. In the following conversation, loosely based on *Symposium*[6] by Plato, the character Socrates seeks to get at the invisible nature of love and beauty.[7] The philosopher finds that love desires beauty, which is another way of saying love desires what is good. **D**

   Stage a dramatic reading of the conversation, with one person reading the part of Socrates, the philosopher interviewer, and another person reading the part of Agathon, a playwright and poet who acts as the interviewee.

SOCRATES: When we speak of Love, are we saying that love is of something or of nothing? But wait! Let me explain myself. I do not want you to say that Love is the love of something, such as the love of a father for a child or the love of a mother for a child. That would be too easy. Rather, I want to know what is it that defines Love. Please answer as you would if I were to ask you, "Is a father a father of something?" to which you would find no difficulty in replying, "A father is a father of a son or daughter." That would be the right answer.

AGATHON: Very true.

SOCRATES: And you would say the same of a mother: The mother is a mother of a son or daughter?

AGATHON: Of course.

6. symposium: a meeting for the purpose of discussing a topic
7. Keep in mind that Plato is the author of this text, but he often used Socrates as his starring character and put his ideas into the mouth of Socrates.

SOCRATES: OK. . . . Let me ask you one more question in order to illustrate my meaning: Isn't a brother to be regarded essentially as a brother of something?

AGATHON: Certainly. A brother is only a brother if he has a brother or a sister.

SOCRATES: Good. So now let me now ask you about Love. Is Love of something or of nothing?

AGATHON: Of something, surely.

SOCRATES: Keep in mind what this something is. Tell me what I want to know—does Love desire what Love already is?[8]

AGATHON: Yes, surely.

SOCRATES: Really? So Love desires what it already possesses. And does the person possess, or does he not possess, that which he loves and desires?

AGATHON: Hmm. Probably not, I should say.

SOCRATES: Do you mean probably not, or *necessarily* not? Doesn't a person who desires something lack that something? Doesn't a person who desires nothing have everything he needs? To me, Agathon, desire necessarily means that a person lacks something. What do you think?

AGATHON: All right, I agree with you. A person *necessarily* does not possess that which he loves and desires.

SOCRATES: Very good. Would he who is great, desire to be great, or he who is strong, desire to be strong?

AGATHON: Obviously not. That would be inconsistent with what we've just established.

SOCRATES: True. For he who is something cannot wish to be something he already is?

AGATHON: Very true.

SOCRATES: And so, if a man being strong desired to be strong, or being swift desired to be swift, or being healthy desired to be healthy, in that case he might be thought to desire something that he already has or is. I give these examples in order that we may avoid misunderstanding. For the possessors of these qualities, Agathon, must be supposed to have their respective advantages—strength, speed, health—at the time, whether they choose or not. And who can desire what he already has? Therefore, when a person says, "I am well and wish to be well," or "I am rich and wish to be rich," and "I desire simply to have what already I have"—to him we should say: "You, my friend, already have wealth and health and strength, and yet you want to have the continuance of them. At this moment, whether you choose or not, you have those things. And when you say, 'I desire what I already have and nothing else,' isn't your meaning that you want to have what you now have in the future?" This person must agree with us—isn't that so?

AGATHON: Yes, that's right.

SOCRATES: Then this person desires that what he has in the present time may be preserved for him in the future. Basically he's saying that he desires something which is nonexistent to him, and which he has not gotten yet. Right?

8. This idea that Love must desire something may seem strange to modern students. One of the Greek words for love, *Eros*, means "desire." So Socrates is really asking, "Does Desire want what Desire already has?" In other words, a word that means "desire" must actually desire something. A lover desires the object of her love, something she's lacking. A sick person desires (loves) health. A poor person desires (loves) money.

AGATHON: True. Go on.

SOCRATES: Then this person, and everyone who desires, desires something he doesn't have already, something that is future and not present, and that he doesn't have and that he lacks. These are the sort of things which Love and desire seek?

AGATHON: I see your point. Go on.

SOCRATES: Then now, let us recapitulate the argument. First, isn't Love of something, and of something too that is wanting to a man?

AGATHON: Yes.

SOCRATES: Remember also what you said in your speech, or if you do not remember I will remind you: You said that the love of the beautiful set in order the empire of the gods, for that of deformed things there is no love. Didn't you say something of that kind?

AGATHON: I admit I did.

SOCRATES: Yes, my friend. And if this is true, Love is the love of beauty and not of deformity?

AGATHON: OK.

SOCRATES: And the admission has been already made that Love is of something that a person wants, but doesn't have?

AGATHON: True.

SOCRATES: Then Love wants beauty, and the desire means it doesn't have beauty?

AGATHON: Certainly.

SOCRATES: And would you call something beautiful that lacks and does not possess beauty?

AGATHON: Certainly not.

SOCRATES: Then would you still say that Love is beautiful? If Love desires the beautiful, how can it already possess the beautiful?

AGATHON: I fear that I did not understand what I was saying.

SOCRATES: You made a very good speech, Agathon, but there is yet one small question which I would dare ask: Isn't the good also the beautiful?

AGATHON: Yes.

SOCRATES: Then in desiring the beautiful, Love also desires the good?

AGATHON: I can't refute you, Socrates. Let's assume that what you say is true.

SOCRATES: Say rather, beloved Agathon, that you cannot refute the truth, for Socrates is easily refuted.[9]

▲ According to Socrates, love longs for the beautiful, which is also the good. Here the Hunchback of Notre Dame longs for the beautiful and good gypsy girl Esmeralda. Because he can't have what he desires, he asks the gargoyles, "Why was I not made of stone, like thee?"[10]

9. Loosely adapted from Plato, *Symposium*, trans. Benjamin Jowett (Project Gutenberg, 2008), https://www.gutenberg.org/files/1600/1600-h/1600-h.htm.

10. *The Hunchback of Notre Dame*, directed by William Dieterle, written by Sonya Levien, Bruno Frank, and Victor Hugo (Los Angeles: RKO Radio Pictures, 1939), film, 117 minutes.

2. **FORMAL DISCUSSION:** Your teacher may instruct you to have a formal discussion. This sort of discussion is not a debate. Rather, it is an opportunity for your class to have a conversation around an open question or a controversial topic. Discussion is a great way to hear other people's ideas and to learn to express your own thoughts well. You can take sides as in a debate, but you are also free to agree with one another, enhancing each other's arguments. Usually a teacher will not participate in a formal discussion; instead she stands aside and listens in.[E] **TE**

Here's how it works: Your teacher will assign you a topic. She might allow you to prepare for the discussion as homework, or she may give you time in class to jot down your thoughts. Either way, you will probably be permitted to keep your notes with you as you discuss. You will then have a conversation about the topic; this conversation usually lasts for fifteen to twenty minutes. Be sure to let everyone have a chance to speak, and if some people are being quiet, feel free to draw them into the conversation by asking them direct questions. If you can support your ideas by quoting a text, so much the better! In the end, your teacher may assign you a score based on the scoring guidelines included with this exercise.

Formal Discussion Scoring Guidelines

Award points based on the following criteria:

- taking a stand by clearly stating an argument (thesis) +2
- providing evidence for the argument +2
- making an analogy +2
- making a relevant comment +1
- restating someone else's point accurately in order to agree or disagree +1
- asking a clarifying question +1
- inviting another student to participate +1
- interrupting -1
- monopolizing the conversation -2
- making personal attacks -2
- distracting the audience -2

Each student's participation in a formal discussion can be evaluated based on a point system such as the one found in this score chart. Be aware of whether or not scoring creates a healthy dynamic in your classroom. Some students may refrain from speaking if there is too much pressure to perform.

3. **PARTNER FEEDBACK:** With a student partner (or your teacher), take turns reading the rough drafts of your thesis essays. You and your partner should give each other comments about what is more or less effective about your writing. Use the rubric at the back of the book to help you get ideas for your comments. (Don't worry about awarding points to your classmate. Scoring an essay is your teacher's job.) Try to say two positive things about your partner's essay, and then come up with at least two suggestions for editing or revising the essay.[F] **TE**

Ask each other:

- Does my hook capture your interest?
- Is my thesis clear, specific, and debatable?
- Does each confirmation paragraph clearly support the thesis?
- Does each antithesis clearly argue against the thesis?
- Does each defense (refutation) paragraph clearly refute its antithesis and support the thesis?
- Do I introduce and explain credible evidence, and do I include a source citation for every quote or paraphrase?

If you are constructively honest with your partner, your comments will really help him or her.

Revise It—

1. **GRAMMATICAL VICES:** Dangling Modifiers and Faulty Predication—Drum roll, please! Today's vices are—*bah-dah boom*—dangling modifiers and faulty predication. Both of these vices interfere with the logic of a sentence and must be eliminated.

Dangling modifiers: A **modifier** is a word, phrase, or clause that describes another word or phrase. Here is a sentence showing the proper use of a modifier:

> Fangs gleaming, the tiger eyed the unsuspecting deer.

"Fangs gleaming" is used to describe "the tiger," which is the subject of the sentence.

Now here is a sentence using the same modifier, but in this sentence it's not used properly:

> Fangs gleaming, the deer was completely unsuspecting of the tiger.

In this sentence, the deer seems to have the gleaming fangs rather than the tiger. The phrase "fangs gleaming" isn't properly connected to what it's modifying: the tiger. Instead, it is dangling in space.

Here's another example:

> After snapping photos of the waterfall, the bus pulled away from the curb with the tourists on board.

Is that a proper modifier or a dangling modifier? Hopefully it's obvious to you that the modifier is dangling. The bus did not snap photos of the waterfall!

Patricia T. O'Conner gives us this tip in her book *Woe Is I*:

> Always suspect an *ing* word of dangling if it's near the front of a sentence: consider it guilty until proved innocent. To find the culprit, ask yourself whodunit. Who's doing the *walking, talking, singing,* or whatever? You may be surprised by the answer.[11]

11. Patricia T. O'Conner, *Woe Is I: The Grammarphobe's Guide to Better English in Plain English*, 4th ed. (New York: Riverhead Books, 2019), 191. Used by permission of the author.

We should note, however, that dangling modifiers aren't limited to *-ing* words. Here's an example with two adjectives that dangle:

Stinky and putrid, Reggie took out the garbage.

In this sentence, the garbage is more likely to be stinky and putrid than Reggie.

In order to fix a dangling modifier, you will need to cut, change, or rearrange the words in a sentence. For example:

Reggie took out the stinky and putrid garbage.

Faulty predication: Faulty predication makes as little sense in a sentence as a dangling modifier. Faulty predication happens when the subject and verb of a sentence don't logically fit together. Here's a sentence with faulty predication:

The golfer's day was distressed when he drove a ball through the windowpane.

The subject "day" does not go with the verb "to be distressed." A day can't feel emotion such as distress. Here are two possible fixes:

- The golfer was distressed when he drove a ball through the windowpane.
- The day was spoiled when the golfer drove a ball through the windowpane.

Faulty predication can also happen when "is when" and "is where" are used. For example:

The purpose of painting is when a painter tries to capture beauty on canvas.

The subject of this sentence is "purpose," and purpose doesn't go with a particular time as implied by the word "when." This sentence can be improved thus:

The purpose of painting is to capture beauty on canvas.

Here's another example using "is where":

The mystery of the *Mona Lisa* is where you will see many numbers hidden in the picture.

The subject of this sentence is "mystery," and mystery is not a place as implied by the word "where." Here's a better sentence:

The mystery of the *Mona Lisa* is the many numbers hidden in the picture.

Read the following paragraph, and as you read, underline any dangling modifiers or faulty predication. Then, in the spaces provided, rewrite the incorrect sentences so that they make sense. There are three dangling modifiers and three faulty predications.

Famous Leaning Towers

The Leaning Tower of Pisa is a beautiful Romanesque bell tower in Italy that is known for its tilt. Built on soft ground in the twelfth century, time has caused the tower to tip by as much as 5.5 degrees. Only the reconstruction of the tower's foundation in the 1990s, led by a team of architects, kept it from collapsing. Now, the tower declares that it will remain standing for three hundred years more. Another famous leaning tower is the Minaret of Jam, located in the province of Ghor, Afghanistan. Standing at two hundred feet tall, the river Jam continues to erode the foundation of the great tower. Without immediate firming at its base, the beautiful tan-brick building could collapse at any time, but for now it still stands. Another leaning tower, the famous "hunchbacked" minaret of Mosul, was not so lucky. In 2017, one shame of the Iraq War was where terrorists blew up the tower, as well as the entire Mosque of al-Nuri. Who knows if it can ever be rebuilt? Meanwhile in China, the tipsy Giant Wild Goose Pagoda stands seven stories above the city of Xi'an. When walking through the rooms of the pagoda, the statue of a Buddhist monk sits in a lotus position near the stairs. The beauty of a pagoda is when each story of the building gets progressively narrower toward the top.

▲ Leaning Tower of Pisa, August 8, 2005. Image courtesy of Johann H. Addicks, https://commons.wikimedia.org/wiki/File:Pisa_-_Campo_Santo_-_Campanile_1_-_2005-08-08_10-15_4638.JPG.

▲ Minaret of Jam, January 7, 2011.

▲ Giant Wild Goose Pagoda, October 17, 2006. Image courtesy of Alex Kwok, https://commons.wikimedia.org/wiki/File:Giant_Wild_Goose_Pagoda.jpg.

a. Sample answer: Built on soft ground in the twelfth century, the tower has tipped by as much as 5.5 degrees over time.

b. Sample answer: Now, the tower will remain standing for three hundred years more.

c. Sample answer: The river Jam continues to erode the foundation of the two-hundred-foot-tall minaret.

d. Sample answer: In 2017, terrorists shamefully blew up the tower, as well as the entire Mosque of Al-Nuri.

e. Sample answer: When walking through the rooms of the pagoda, visitors can see the statue of a Buddhist monk sitting in a lotus position near the stairs.

f. Sample answer: A pagoda's beauty comes from the narrowing of each story as the building rises to the top.

2. **REWRITING:** Follow these steps to turn your doughnut of a first draft into a three-layer chocolate cake!
   a. Get feedback. Use comments from your student partners (or from your teacher) to strengthen and improve your paper.
   b. Wait a day or two before you rewrite your paper. The time away from it will help you to see its problems more clearly.
   c. Read the paper aloud to yourself. This is often the best way to catch mistakes—grammar errors, as well as words that don't work well—because you will be using two senses—seeing and hearing—instead of one. If something sounds wrong, it probably is.

REC

Once you are ready to rewrite, use the following steps to aid with your revision:

a. *Find your thesis and underline it.* There also should be a restatement of the thesis in your conclusion. This restatement should show a fuller and more complete understanding of the thesis.

b. *Find the topic sentence for each body paragraph and highlight it.* Each body paragraph should begin with a topic sentence stating the main idea of the paragraph. The topic sentence for a confirmation paragraph should confirm some aspect of the thesis. The topic sentence for a refutation paragraph should introduce an antithesis, which refutes the thesis.

c. *Find the evidence (appeal to authority) in each body paragraph and highlight it.* Did you choose the best quote or paraphrase to make your point? Make sure that all evidence is properly introduced and explained and has source citations.

d. *Make sure each paragraph gets the job done.* Remember that each paragraph has a special purpose in supporting your thesis through analysis and evidence. Does each paragraph successfully accomplish this goal?

e. *Make sure you have consistently considered audience.* Have you written your essay based on your understanding of the audience's makeup, disposition, and needs? Have you carefully considered possible objections to your thesis?
f. *Make sure you have kept a formal tone throughout the essay.* Have you eliminated informalities of writing such as too many simple sentences, imprecise vocabulary, first- and second-person pronouns, and colloquialisms?
g. *Find and fix grammar mistakes.* Make sure all your nouns and verbs agree and that your writing is clear. Fix any fragments or run-ons. In other words, make sure you are writing complete sentences.
h. *Strengthen phrasing.* Are your word choices specific instead of vague? Do you use strong nouns and verbs? Do you vary your sentences and occasionally begin them with a prepositional phrase or a participial phrase? Weed out passive voice and excess adjectives. Use compound sentences, appositives, adverb phrases, and questions to make your writing more interesting. Transition smoothly between ideas and paragraphs using transition words.
i. *Proofread.* Look for any punctuation, spelling, or capitalization errors. Then fix them!
j. *Retype* the draft with the corrections you have made.

Lesson 10: Third Thesis Essay, Part 2: What Is Beauty?

Speak It—

2. **FORMAL DISCUSSION:**

[E]Generally, in a classroom setting, a formal discussion works best with only five or six students, who have prepared in advance for the conversation, carrying out the discussion in front of the class. You may want to give students a time limit of 15–20 minutes for the discussion. After the discussion they can either take turns critiquing each other, or you can both facilitate and critique the discussion. You can also invite the remainder of the class to add their comments at the end of the discussion, or you can follow through with your own comments.

Two of the "thinking with others" ideas in the introduction of this lesson are ideal for generating topics for a formal discussion:

- Agree/Disagree: Choose one reading to discuss as a group. Each student must take a stand on the reading's thesis. Do you agree or disagree with it, or partially agree, and why? Defend your answers.
- Compare/Contrast: As a group, choose two of the readings and discuss how their ideas are similar and different. Why are these similarities and differences important? Defend your answers.

The following are some other ideas that a group of students can respond to in a formal discussion:

- What are the qualities that make a person beautiful? Explain your answer.
- Nineteenth-century author Théophile Gautier said, "There is nothing truly beautiful but that which can never be of any use whatsoever; everything useful is ugly." Art critic John Ruskin said something similar: "Remember that the most beautiful things in the world are the most useless: peacocks and lilies, for instance." Do you agree or disagree that beautiful things are useless, and why?
- According to Greek myth, the nine Muses or goddesses of inspiration were Calliope (epic poetry), Clio (history), Euterpe (music and lyric poetry), Thalia (comedy and pastoral poetry), Melpomene (tragedy), Terpsichore (dance), Erato (love poetry), Polyhymnia (sacred poetry), and Urania (astronomy). These arts were considered the most important by the ancient Greeks, but modern people would most likely expand this list. What arts do you think should be added to the list? What art do you believe is the most vital and significant to humanity today, and why?

You may want to follow up a formal discussion with additional writing. You can ask students to write down a thesis statement that sums up a certain position that emerged during the discussion and then bullet point important evidence from the discussion that supports the position. Or you can have students write about the process of the discussion itself: What comments and behavior created and extended a healthy discussion and what caused it to wane or degenerate?

3. **PARTNER FEEDBACK:**

F At this stage, students can give each other thoughtful feedback. The thesis rubric can serve as their guide for constructive comments and notes. Students will likely need to hear a teacher say that feedback is a way for writers to help each other and that every professional writer depends on the input of others, hence it's important that feedback comes with a healthy dose of respect and encouragement. Make sure to allow enough time between drafts so that students can receive help from classmates and the teacher.

Paragraph Writing Instructions

Paragraph 1 (Introduction): Start with a hook, followed by a transition to your thesis. Then state your thesis, explain the thesis, and transition to the next paragraph.

Paragraph 2 (First Confirmation): Start with a topic sentence that makes one confirming argument showing why your thesis is true. Follow the topic sentence by explaining it and giving supporting evidence. Be sure to include a quote or paraphrase from the texts in lesson 9.

Paragraph 3 (Second Confirmation): Start with a topic sentence that makes a second confirming argument showing why your thesis is true. Follow the topic sentence by explaining it and giving supporting evidence. Be sure to include a quote or paraphrase from the texts in lesson 9.

Paragraph 4 (First Antithesis): Start with a topic sentence that gives one antithesis to your thesis. Explain the antithesis and then defend your thesis by telling why the antithesis is wrong. Be sure to include a quote or paraphrase from the texts in lesson 9.

Paragraph 5 (Second Antithesis): Start with a topic sentence that gives a second antithesis to your thesis. Explain the antithesis and then defend your thesis by telling why the antithesis is wrong. Be sure to include a quote or paraphrase from the texts in lesson 9.

Paragraph 6 (Conclusion): Restate your thesis with fresh language that shows a more complete understanding of the thesis. Then tell why your topic is important (how it applies to real life or changes the reader's outlook). If desired, follow with a call to action.

Sample Thesis Essay: The Essence of Beauty

Paragraph 1: Introduction

hook

It is twilight in the Galilee region, nicknamed the "Tuscany of Israel" for its rolling hills and lush vineyards. The first thing the visitor notices as she steps onto the wooden boat is the breeze dancing across her face. The boat moves out onto the lake just as the sun begins to set over the city of Tiberias. The lights of the city, nestled away across the water, twinkle from the other side, as if they were hook

diamonds adorning the darkness of the hills. The sky is navy above, and as the visitor's eyes travel toward the horizon the navy becomes a bright orange, then a red as dark as blood. The boldly colored expanse holds the glowing orb of the sun as it sinks steadily toward the black outline of the hills. Just as the sun dips out of view, a flock of seagulls swoops in front of the boat, their cries piercing the night. The visitor's thirsty spirit drinks in this moment—the cool of the evening, the rush of wings past her face, the lapping of water against the wood underneath her feet. Sailing across the Sea of Galilee, she revels in the beauty of nature. And she wonders, what is beauty itself? Beauty is easy to experience but difficult to define. It is goodness in a tangible, detectable form, as seen in the way it enhances life and arouses wonder and pleasure. Beautiful things, both manmade and natural, have the power to amaze people, fill them with joy, and inspire them to be better human beings. Since these effects are the products of goodness, it is clear that any "visible" experience of beauty is a reflection of the invisible quality of goodness. One can find evidence of how beauty, an exterior quality, reflects a deeper inner quality by looking at the effect it has on people.

Transition from hook to thesis

Thesis

Thesis explanation

Transition

Paragraph 2: First Confirmation

Topic sentence

Explanation and evidence

The essence of beauty is unseen goodness, and this is demonstrated in the way that beauty gives or enhances life. Whenever goodness materializes as beauty it affects people positively or sparks a desire in them to enjoy life more, to be more joy-filled, to be more generous and loving. A mother's love for her child is beautiful, and in that love a child's life is nurtured. A heroic act, such as a fire-fighter rescuing a child from a burning building, is beautiful, and it gives new life to someone on the verge of death. A beautiful work of art, such as the statue of Aphrodite found in Milos, celebrates the living human form and in turn elevates the minds of some who might otherwise debase the human body. A beautiful literary work such as the fable of "The Crow and the Pitcher" teaches its viewers an important lesson about life. A beautiful composition of music, such as Borodin's Second Symphony, stirs the listener's soul and inspires him to live a better life. These beautiful things all accomplish something good in bettering life. They are detectable forms of invisible goodness. In turn, it is their goodness that makes each of these things beautiful. Their beauty seems to flow from their goodness, just as water flows from an artesian well. The poet George Gordon, Lord Byron, captures this idea in the poem "She Walks in Beauty." In it he describes a beautiful woman, and her beauty emanates from her goodness:

> And on that cheek, and o'er that brow,
> So soft, so calm, yet eloquent,
> The smiles that win, the tints that glow,
> But tell of days in goodness spent,
> A mind at peace with all below,
> A heart whose love is innocent! (Byron)

Evidence from the text

Byron describes someone whose actions, character, and physical features are all discernible aspects of goodness, and these aspects are in harmony with one

TE

Explanation and evidence

another. The woman's beauty flows from and reflects goodness. Wherever it is discerned, beauty enhances and gives life, making it easy to see that beauty is a form of goodness.

Paragraph 3: Second Confirmation

Topic sentence

Explanation and evidence

Evidence from the text

Another way that beauty brings the light of goodness to the world is by producing wonder and pleasure. Just seeing a beautiful object fills people with amazement and their senses are enchanted. A garden in bloom renews the wonder of childhood in people—"How could so many kinds of flowers exist? What causes their bright colors?" And it fills them with pleasure—"They have so many whimsical shapes and fragrances. I'd like to pluck a few and make a bouquet." When people experience the beauty of another person's self-sacrifice, they experience a sense of amazement and joy at the capacity of people to be good. For example, during World War II, army medic Desmond Doss risked his life repeatedly during the Battle of Okinawa to save seventy-five wounded soldiers. Each of these soldiers was literally given life anew by the beauty of Doss's actions, and people who hear Doss's story respond with wonder and pleasure. Edmund Burke compares the individual's reaction upon experiencing something beautiful to falling in love, writing that "beauty is the quality, or those qualities in bodies, which cause love, or some passion similar to it" (165). Beauty can lead people from a reaction of their senses to a deeper experience such as love. Just as falling in love engages all of the senses, experiencing something beautiful likewise engages the senses and intoxicates people with delight. The crescendo in a musical piece such as Beethoven's Egmont Overture or the kind words of a friend can move people to tears. The twirling of a ballerina onstage or the magic of softly falling snow can mesmerize individuals. When people experience beauty, whether through sacrificial deeds or through physical enchantments, they understand that something good has happened to them. This goodness brings joy, which is one of the deepest needs of life.

Paragraph 4: First Refutation

Antithesis

Explanation of antithesis

Refutation/ defense

Evidence from the text

Some might argue that goodness and beauty do not always go hand in hand. An evil person may have a beautiful face, and beauty can disguise an evil or unwholesome character. For example, in photos Jesse James and John Dillinger are quite handsome, but these real-life outlaws were quick to shoot anyone who got in their way. Just because something inspires pleasure and wonder does not mean it is necessarily good. This may be true, but the beauty in a person or thing is still good even if other aspects of the person or thing are not. For example, a person's body—the ears, the nose, the hand, the toes—supports the life of a person and is amazing and wonderful to reflect upon in its intricacy and its function. In this sense, everyone partakes in the beauty and goodness of being human, and that beauty remains the same, remains good, even if a person does things that are bad. In addition, everything was designed for a proper purpose, and the misuse of a thing does not argue against its proper use. The figure of Satan in Milton's *Paradise Lost* demonstrates how a beautiful thing can be designed for goodness and yet be corrupted by misuse. Satan can't take delight in earth's beauty, as it reminds him of God's goodness, and he longs for

Refutation/ defense

what he thinks would be best: "mastering Heav'ns Supreme" (Milton 9.125). He believes that if he is installed in power over all, he will then be able to enjoy "sweet interchange of Hill, and Valley, Rivers, Woods and Plains" (Milton 9.115–16). His longing for power points to what is actually good—the proper rule or stewardship of the universe—but in Satan that idea is corrupted. Satan's misuse of a beautiful thing, however, does not take away that it was designed for good. Likewise, a beautiful person was designed for good, just as all people were designed to be good to one another. If a person chooses to do evil, then he has deviated from who he was made to be, but the design for goodness still exists. Beauty is always a reflection of goodness.

Paragraph 5: Second Refutation

Antithesis

Explanation of antithesis

Refutation/ defense

Evidence from the text

Others might argue that something can be beautiful without inspiring wonder and pleasure. Someone might hear a beautiful symphony and think that it is dull or too long. Someone might see a beautiful building and think that it is too ornate or not ornate enough. People experience beauty differently and therefore something can be beautiful yet fail to inspire wonder or pleasure. This argument is true as far as it goes, but it does not take the full scope of beauty into account. No one is able to appreciate all forms of beauty just as not every ear can hear certain wavelengths of sound. Just because one person isn't capable of experiencing inspiration from beauty doesn't mean the inspiration doesn't exist at all. Plotinus uses the example of a choir when describing beauty: "The voices of a choir rouse the harmony latent in the soul, and open her eye to the perception of beauty, and strike the respective senses with wonder and delight." He notes that a soul's eyes must be "open" to receive the wonder and delight of beauty. This implies that some souls have not yet awakened to certain kinds of beauty. Not all people who experience beauty have the correct mind-set or motivations to appreciate it. Not everyone has a receptive spirit or can easily recognize what is beautiful. Sometimes the appreciation of beauty needs to be cultivated before it can bring an upwelling of wonder and pleasure. Yet Plotinus's example still assumes the power of beauty to inspire. The fact that beauty sometimes goes unappreciated does not mean that the beauty doesn't exist or doesn't inspire.

Paragraph 6: Conclusion

Restatement of thesis

Why topic is important

Call to action

Beauty is the reflection of goodness, a tangible reality that, by its effects, reveals the invisible good that sustains and improves life. By pondering what beauty is, and how it relates to goodness, people can distinguish between things that are beautiful and worthwhile to experience and things that are not, or whose goodness has been spoiled. For example, if something is appealing to the senses but harmful to human life, such as recreational drugs or pornography, then that thing is a corruption of what was designed to be beautiful and good and ought to be avoided. An understanding of true beauty, which is good, will not only enhance a person's life, but also protect him from dangerous counterfeits. Truly unspoiled beauty brings goodness and joy to life. It can take people outside of themselves and lift their spirits, inspiring them to act virtuously toward other people and allowing them to step away from the busyness of life. Because of this, it's important to stop to smell the roses and listen to the song of birds. True beauty should be embraced.

TE

Works Cited

Burke, Edmund. *A Philosophical Enquiry into the Origin of Our Ideas of the Sublime and Beautiful. The Works of the Right Honorable Edmund Burke*, vol. 1. London, John C. Nimmo, 1887. *Project Gutenberg*, 2005, https://www.gutenberg.org/files/15043/15043-h/15043-h.htm#Page_165.

Gordon, George, Lord Byron. "She Walks in Beauty." *The Poetry Foundation*. The Poetry Foundation, https://www.poetryfoundation.org/poems/43844/she-walks-in-beauty. Accessed November 27, 2018.

Milton, John. *Paradise Lost*. *The John Milton Reading Room*. Trustees of Dartmouth College, https://www.dartmouth.edu/~milton/reading_room/pl/book_9/text.shtml. Accessed November 5, 2018.

Plotinus. "An Essay on the Beautiful." Translated by Thomas Taylor, London, John M. Watkins, 1917. *Project Gutenberg*, 2009, https://www.gutenberg.org/files/29510/29510-h/29510-h.htm.

Appendix

Sample Thesis Essay

If you're having trouble writing your thesis essay, feel free to consult this sample for inspiration. Once you get the picture, make sure you go back to the writing prompts in the lesson and compose your essay on your own. This will help you avoid the temptation to copy someone else's ideas or wording.

Paragraph Writing Instructions

Paragraph 1 (Introduction): Start with a hook, followed by a transition to your thesis. Then state your thesis, explain the thesis, and transition to the next paragraph.

Paragraph 2 (First Confirmation): Start with a topic sentence that makes one confirming argument showing why your thesis is true. Follow the topic sentence by explaining it and giving supporting evidence. Be sure to include a quote or paraphrase from the story.

Paragraph 3 (Second Confirmation): Start with a topic sentence that makes a second confirming argument showing why your thesis is true. Follow the topic sentence by explaining it and giving supporting evidence. Be sure to include a quote or paraphrase from the story.

Paragraph 4 (First Antithesis): Start with a topic sentence that gives one antithesis to your thesis. Explain the antithesis and then defend your thesis by telling why the antithesis is wrong. Be sure to include a quote or paraphrase from the story.

Paragraph 5 (Second Antithesis): Start with a topic sentence that gives a second antithesis to your thesis. Explain the antithesis and then defend your thesis by telling why the antithesis is wrong. Be sure to include a quote or paraphrase from the story.

Paragraph 6 (Conclusion): Restate your thesis with fresh language that shows a more complete understanding of the thesis. Then tell why your topic is important (how it applies to real life or changes the reader's outlook). If desired, follow with a call to action.

Sample Thesis Essay: The Consequences of Desire in "The Necklace"

Paragraph 1: Introduction

Hook

"Be careful what you wish for, because you might just get it." This saying would make a fitting moral for Guy de Maupassant's "The Necklace." Like other wishing stories—"The Sausage," "The Fisherman and His Wife," and "The Monkey's Paw"—"The Necklace" shows that not everything we crave is either attainable or good for us. In each story, however, the characters have an opportunity to live a life of contentment if they will only learn from the disasters that befall them.

Transition from hook to thesis

The main character of "The Necklace," Madame Mathilde Loisel, is essentially granted three wishes: an invitation to a ball, a lovely diamond necklace, and the admiration of all the partygoers. When she loses the necklace, however, the consequences of her desires catch up with her. The comfortable life she has enjoyed is dashed and she suffers a life of hardship and poverty—yet those very consequences may have taught her something and saved her from a more disastrous ending. What would Madame Loisel's life have been like if she hadn't lost the necklace?

Thesis

Had she not lost the necklace and become a poor working woman, Mathilde Loisel would have faced even more serious calamity, because she would have grown more selfish and destructive.

Thesis explanation

She would have squandered her husband's meager income to keep up the false image of a rich lady, and she probably would have treated "the little clerk" faithlessly.

Transition

Madame Loisel was heading for trouble no matter what because she was self-centered and grasping.

Paragraph 2: First Confirmation

Topic sentence

Without the loss of the necklace, Madame Loisel would have become even more selfish because she would have wanted more and more of the things she desired, and the consequences would be disastrous.

Explanation and evidence

Once her passion to be the center of attention was intensified by the Ministry of Public Instruction ball, there would have been no satisfying her. She would have craved more dances, more parties, more praise and attention. New social events would demand new dresses, new jewelry, manicurists, and hair stylists. We get a glimpse of how all-consuming Madame Loisel's passion is in Maupassant's description of her spinning on the dance floor. He writes, "She danced with rapture, with passion, intoxicated by pleasure, forgetting all in the triumph of her beauty, in the glory of her success, in a sort of cloud of happiness comprised of all this homage, admiration, these awakened desires and of that sense of triumph which is so sweet to woman's heart." This picture of her danc-

Evidence from the text

Explanation and evidence

ing "intoxicated by pleasure" shows that she is becoming more compulsive in her vanity, not less. It is not reasonable to assume that she who dreamed of balls and servants, palaces and rich foods before the ball, would be satisfied by one simple ball sponsored by a government educational organization. No, she would fancy herself to be truly deserving of new attentions and new social engagements and put all of her energy into satisfying herself. Ultimately this would result in an even greater tragedy, as both her bank account and her character would be impoverished.

Evidence from the text

Paragraph 3: Second Confirmation

Topic sentence

As Madame Loisel's need for homage, admiration, and triumph increased, she would have undoubtedly proved unfaithful to her husband as well, pursuing dishonorable relationships with other men and causing the destruction of her reputation and character.

Explanation and evidence

We catch a glimpse of how superfluous her husband is to her when he retires to the anteroom for a nap while she dances the night away with other men. Maupassant tells us that Madame Loisel is universally admired by the men at the ball: "All the men looked at her, asked her name, sought to be introduced. All the attachés of the Cabinet wished to waltz with her." With so much male attention, all of which Madame Loisel encourages, can it be doubted that she would soon be looking for better prospects than her "little clerk": a handsomer man, a richer man, a man with title or position? What would there be to restrain her from pursuing these attentions? She doesn't seem to be grounded by any sense of high purpose about marriage or any religious obligation. In addition, since it's questionable whether Madame Loisel would be able to remarry to a man of higher position—her "caste" and fortune are too low for that—it's likely that her pursuit of other men would have an even more sordid result than the abandonment of one husband for another. She might well have become a rich man's girlfriend and led a double life, causing her lover to also commit infidelities. This increasingly destructive behavior would create a much greater tragedy in her life than the honorable hardship she experienced when she worked to replace the necklace.

Evidence from the text

Paragraph 4: First Refutation

Antithesis

Some readers might say that, if she had not lost the necklace, the ball would have satisfied Madame Loisel's longings and she would have lived, if not happily ever after, then at least with more contentment.

Explanation of antithesis

She would have the wonderful memory of the dance to keep her going and perhaps dreams of a new ball in the future, and any selfish or destructive impulses would be put to rest.

Refutation/defense

But how realistic is this idea given her dissatisfied character? Life is long compared with one dreamy event. It's doubtful that Madame Loisel would have been satisfied with one night of wish fulfillment. Her head was too stuffed with dreams of pleasure and riches to ever be satisfied by a single ball. Maupassant tells us, "She was unhappy as if she had really fallen from a higher station; since with women there is neither caste nor rank, for beauty, grace and charm take

Evidence from the text

Refutation/ defense

the place of family and birth." Clearly Madame Loisel fancies herself royalty of sorts, a princess in disguise, deserving better than her lot in life. Even when she looks at herself longingly in the mirror after the ball, we sense that this wistfulness will soon become unhappiness all over again. Her perpetual dissatisfaction is a theme of the story. It even shows itself when her husband is gone at the office and she—now a coarse and disheveled woman after the loss of the necklace—thinks wistfully of the ball long ago.

Paragraph 5: Second Refutation

Antithesis

Explanation of antithesis

Refutation/ defense

Evidence from the text

Others might say that Madame Loisel's selfish and destructive nature would have improved had she not lost the necklace, because she would have left her dull husband, the ball and chain in her life. Setting herself free to be the lively and flirtatious beauty she was meant to be would have enabled her to be a better person. But even if the lost necklace hadn't completely diverted her life in another direction, Madame Loisel would have remained vain, shallow, and hungry for attention. The problem was not her husband, but her lack of character. If anything, Monsieur Loisel was a positive influence, helping to anchor Madame Loisel to reality, and his faithfulness to her possibly helped her to grow in gratitude and affection. He gave up his own dreams of a happy, comfortable future to be her partner in paying off the debt of the necklace. Maupassant tells us, "He compromised all the rest of his life, risked signing a note without even knowing whether he could meet it; and, frightened by the trouble yet to come, by the black misery that was about to fall upon him, by the prospect of all the physical privations and moral tortures that he was to suffer, he went to get the new necklace, laying upon the jeweler's counter thirty-six thousand francs." This moving picture of a man who loves his wife enough to sacrifice his happiness for her shows how likely it is that Monsieur Loisel was a positive influence on his wife. If she were to leave her husband and his influence, Madame Loisel's flawed character may well have grown worse, leading to more serious calamity.

Paragraph 6: Conclusion

Restatement of thesis

Why topic is important

In the end, the lost necklace turned out to be a blessing in disguise for Mathilde Loisel. If she hadn't lost the necklace, she would have declined in her moral character and possibly encountered far more disastrous consequences as a result of her desires. "The Necklace" shines a shimmering light on vanity and leaves the reader feeling uncomfortable—for what person is not at least a little vain? It is a powerful reminder to keep our harmful desires in check—yet it also helps us to see how hardship can be a kind of grace to save us from ourselves.

Work Cited

De Maupassant, Guy. "The Diamond Necklace." *The Entire Original Maupassant Short Stories*. Translated by Albert McMaster, A.E. Henderson, Mme. Quesada, et al., *Project Gutenberg*, 2004, http://www.gutenberg.org/files/3090/3090-h/3090-h.htm.

Please note that this rubric is a simplified version of the more detailed rubric found later in this appendix. Your teacher may choose to use the detailed rubric to assess your essay.

Thesis Essay Rubric (Simplified)

Name: ______________________ Date of Assignment: ______________________

Content ________/72

Paragraph 1: Introduction ________/12 ________
- Does the introduction contain a hook, a complex thesis, and an explanation of the thesis?

Paragraph 2: First Confirmation ________/12 ________
- Does the paragraph begin with a topic sentence?
- Is this confirmation clearly explained and supported by evidence?

Paragraph 3: Second Confirmation ________/12 ________
- Does the paragraph begin with a topic sentence?
- Is this confirmation clearly explained and supported by evidence?

Paragraph 4: First Refutation ________/12 ________
- Does the paragraph begin with a topic sentence that states an antithesis to the thesis? Is the antithesis fully explained?
- Does the paragraph clearly refute the antithesis and provide evidence for the refutation?

Paragraph 5: Second Refutation ________/12 ________
- Does the paragraph begin with a topic sentence that states an antithesis to the thesis? Is the antithesis fully explained?
- Does the paragraph clearly refute the antithesis and provide evidence for the refutation?

Paragraph 6: Conclusion ________/12 ________
- Is the thesis restated in new words that express a fuller understanding?
- Does the author tell why the topic is important?

Style ________/8

Does the author include a creative title that reflects the heart of the essay? (2 points) ________

Has the author written the essay with consideration of the audience's makeup, disposition, and needs? (2 points) ________

Has the author consistently used formal language (with third-person perspective) throughout the essay? (4 points) ________

Form ________/20

Title, header, spacing, indentation, and font are formatted correctly and consistently (2 points) ________

In-text citations are included and formatted correctly (4 points) ________

Sentence variety ________

Many varied sentences: 4 points | Good sentence variety: 3 points
Some sentence variety: 2 points | Little or no sentence variety: 0 points

Grammar and usage ________

Few or no grammar errors: 4 points | Occasional grammar errors: 3 points
Some grammar errors: 2 points | Many grammar errors: 0 points

Number of spelling, punctuation, and capitalization errors ________

2 or fewer per page: 6 points | 3 per page: 5 points
4 per page: 4 points | 5 or more per page: 0 points

Total: ________/100

Thesis Essay Rubric (Detailed)

Name: ______________________________ Date of Assignment: ____________________

Content ________ /72

Paragraph 1: Introduction ______ /12

- Does the hook captivate the reader's attention? (4 points) ______
- Is there a transition from the hook to the thesis? (1 point) ______
- Does the thesis clearly and specifically present an argument? Does it make a main argument and also mention two supporting arguments? (4 points) ______
- Does the explanation of the thesis make clear the meaning of the thesis? (2 points) ______
- Is there a transition between the introduction and paragraph 2? (1 point) ______

Paragraph 2: First Confirmation ______ /12 ______

- Does the paragraph begin with a topic sentence that clearly makes a supporting argument in defense of the thesis? (4 points) ______
- Is the confirmation thoroughly and clearly explained? (2 points) ______
- Does the author use evidence (examples, quotes, details) to support the confirmation? Does the author use at least one quote or paraphrase (properly introduced and given context) as evidence? (6 points) ______

Paragraph 3: Second Confirmation ______ /12 ______

- Does the paragraph begin with a topic sentence that clearly makes a supporting argument in defense of the thesis? (4 points) ______
- Is the confirmation thoroughly and clearly explained? (2 points) ______
- Does the author use evidence (examples, quotes, details) to support the confirmation? Does the author use at least one quote or paraphrase (properly introduced and given context) as evidence? (6 points) ______

Paragraph 4: First Refutation ______ /12 ______

- Does the paragraph begin with a topic sentence that clearly states an antithesis to the thesis? (4 points) ______
- Does the paragraph include a clear explanation of the antithesis? (2 points) ______
- Does the paragraph include a clear refutation of the antithesis? (2 points) ______
- Does the author use evidence (examples, quotes, details) to support the refutation? Does the author use at least one quote or paraphrase (properly introduced and given context) as evidence? (4 points) ______

This rubric intentionally covers the many details of thesis writing found in this book. If you feel that it is too complex for your purposes, please consider using the simplified version of this rubric or creating a rubric that targets the specific needs of your students.

Content *(continued)*

Paragraph 5: Second Refutation ________/12 ________

- Does the paragraph begin with a topic sentence that clearly states an antithesis to the thesis? (4 points) ________
- Does the paragraph include a clear explanation of the antithesis? (2 points) ________
- Does the paragraph include a clear refutation of the antithesis? (2 points) ________
- Does the author use evidence (examples, quotes, details) to support the refutation? Does the author use at least one quote or paraphrase (properly introduced and given context) as evidence? (4 points) ________

Paragraph 6: Conclusion ________/12 ________

- Is the thesis restated in new words? Does the restatement express a fuller understanding of the thesis based on insight gained from the body paragraphs? (6 points) ________
- Does the author tell why the topic is important? (6 points) ________

Style ________/8

- Does the author include a creative title that reflects the heart of the essay? (2 points) ________
- Does the author use specific and natural language that helps to clarify ideas throughout the essay? (2 points) ________
- Has the author written the essay with consideration of the audience's makeup, disposition, and needs? (2 points) ________
- Has the author consistently used formal language (with third-person perspective) throughout the essay? (2 points) ________

Form ________/20

- Title, header, spacing, indentation, and font are formatted correctly and consistently (2 points) ________
- In-text citations are included and formatted correctly (4 points) ________
- Sentence variety ________
  Many varied sentences: 4 points | Good sentence variety: 3 points
  Some sentence variety: 2 points | Little or no sentence variety: 0 points
- Grammar and usage ________
  Few or no grammar errors: 4 points | Occasional grammar errors: 3 points
  Some grammar errors: 2 points | Many grammar errors: 0 points
- Number of spelling, punctuation, and capitalization errors ________
  2 or fewer per page: 6 points | 3 per page: 5 points
  4 per page: 4 points | 5 or more per page: 0 points

Total: ________/100

Get to the Point: Tips for Summarizing

Every morning the president of the United States receives a daily brief on his desk. The brief contains a summary of the most important happenings in the world and the biggest threats to the nation's security. It's the king of all summaries. It's the whole world shrunk down to a few pages.

Many reasons exist for summarizing, and they mostly boil down to a matter of time and the need for simplicity. While the president wishes to be informed about world events, he doesn't have time to read about every detail every morning. In the same way, your audience doesn't have endless hours to devote to your speech or essay. Sometimes you will want your work to include information from another source, but what if that information is too detailed to share in full? By summarizing, you can share the main idea of the information without overwhelming your audience.

Do you need to communicate only the most important facts? Summarize! Do you need to tell a long story in just a few words? Summarize! Do you need to hold your audience's attention and not bore it to death? Summarize! As an added bonus, summarizing can help you to understand something better because it forces you to focus on the most essential details.

Here's a list of tips to help you summarize:

1. Ask yourself, "Is a summary necessary?"
   - Is the information too detailed to include without summarizing?
   - Do you need to retell a longer story in shortened form?
   - Do you want to avoid using a quotation by using your own words instead?

   You might want to include a summary of an article or story in your essay if it:
   - engages the emotions of your audience (pathos).
   - helps you to have better credibility with your audience (ethos).
   - supports the logic of your paper's topic (logos).
2. Read the article or story you intend to retell very carefully. Note the main points. If you want to summarize something lengthy, it can be helpful to create an outline first.
3. Eliminate unnecessary description, dialogue, or less important ideas. By doing this, you are making sure that your summary contains only the most significant parts of the story.
4. Put the important parts of the article or story into your own words. This is called paraphrasing. When you summarize, it's your turn to tell the story. How would you retell the story so that it makes the most sense to you? Give yourself a reasonable number of sentences with which to summarize and try to stick to that number.
5. Keep in mind that summaries require authors to be careful and fair in how they portray somebody else's work. You don't want to misrepresent your source or pretend that the person said something she didn't.
6. Finally, cite the source of your summary.

The following passage is adapted from *A Good Man Is Hard to Find*, a short story by Flannery O'Connor. The author uses description and dialogue to create an amusing portrait of a talkative, pain-in-the-neck grandmother who is going on a trip with her son and his family. Read the passage and then look at the example of a good summary that follows.

> The next morning the grandmother was the first one in the car, ready to go. She had her big black valise that looked like the head of a hippopotamus in one corner. . . . [She] had on a navy blue straw sailor hat with a bunch of white violets on the brim and a navy blue dress with a small white dot in the print. Her collars and cuffs were white organdy trimmed with lace. . . . In case of an accident, anyone seeing her dead on the highway would know at once that she was a lady.
>
> She said she thought it was going to be a good day for driving, neither too hot nor too cold, and she cautioned Bailey, [her son], that the speed limit was fifty-five miles an hour and that the patrolmen hid themselves behind billboards and small clumps of trees and sped out after you before you had a chance to slow down. She pointed out interesting details of the scenery: Stone Mountain; the blue granite that in some places came up to both sides of the highway; the brilliant red clay banks slightly streaked with purple; and the various crops that made rows of green lace-work on the ground. . . .
>
> "Let's go through Georgia fast so we won't have to look at it much," John Wesley, [her grandson], said.
>
> "If I were a little boy," said the grandmother, "I wouldn't talk about my native state that way. Tennessee has the mountains and Georgia has the hills."
>
> "Tennessee is just a hillbilly dumping ground," John Wesley said, "and Georgia is a lousy state too."
>
> "You said it," June Star, [her granddaughter], said.
>
> "In my time," said the grandmother, folding her thin veined fingers, "children were more respectful of their native states and their parents and everything else."

Summary (of this portion of the story):

> In the short story *A Good Man Is Hard to Find*, Flannery O'Connor creates the portrait of a grandmother who likes to control everything and everyone. She wants to control how her son drives, how she'll be seen if she should die in an accident, and what her grandchildren say when she feels that they aren't being "respectful of their native states" (O'Connor, 1–2).[1]

1. It is important to cite (or give credit to) the source of your information, and this is an example of a citation. For an additional resource on MLA style, we recommend the *MLA Handbook for Writers of Research Papers* by the Modern Language Association. Purdue's Online Writing Lab (OWL) can also be helpful: https://owl.english.purdue.edu/owl/section/2/11/.

Outlines: Your Very Own Story Maps

Have you ever been lost? When I was a kid, I wandered into the toy department of a huge store without telling my parents. Next thing I knew, my parents were gone and I was racing madly through the store trying to find them. Come to think of it, I got lost a lot—in flea markets, in parades, and in the woods. I always wished I had a map or a GPS for finding my parents.

When you're somewhere you don't know very well, a map is an essential tool to help you understand where you are. Similarly, an outline is your very own "map" of what you read. When you create an outline, you are drawing a map that helps you navigate the different parts of a story or essay. Important points in the essay and important events in the story are like landmarks that stand out and can be seen from miles around. Smaller points are the streets and back alleys you explore as you move through a story.

Writing an Outline

Outlines are summaries of a story that look like organized lists. To create an outline, use Roman numerals (*I, II, III, IV, V*, etc.) to list the biggest, most important points. Then, list the next important points using the letters of the alphabet (*A, B, C, D, E*). Next, use numbers for even smaller points that help to establish the larger points by telling more about them (*1, 2, 3, 4, 5*). Note, however, that some outlines may not need all these levels of detail. Your teacher will set a standard for the level of detail required in your classroom.

The following famous Arabian story was retold by American writer W. Somerset Maugham and is adapted here. Take a look:

> There was a wealthy merchant in Baghdad who sent his servant to the bazaar to buy fresh fruits and vegetables. In a little while, the servant came back with his bags empty. He was trembling with fear, and said, "Master, just now when I was in the bazaar, I was bumped by a woman in the crowd. When I turned around, I saw it was Death who had bumped into me, and she gave me a threatening look! Now, let me borrow your horse, and I will ride away from this city and avoid dying. I will flee to Samarra, and in that city Death won't find me." The merchant let him borrow his horse, and the servant jumped upon it, and he dug his heels in its flanks. He rode away as fast as the horse could gallop. Then the merchant went down to the bazaar and he saw Death standing in the crowd. He marched up to Death and said angrily, "Why did you give my servant a threatening look when you saw him this morning?" "That was not a threatening look," Death said. "It was merely a start of surprise. I was astonished to see him in Baghdad, for I had an appointment with him tonight in Samarra."[1]

1. Adapted from *Sheppey*, a play by W. Somerset Maugham (copyright 1933 by W. Somerset Maugham), published in 1933 by William Heinemann Ltd., London.

Now here is an outline based on the story:

I. The servant of a merchant was bumped by Death in a Baghdad bazaar.
    A. Death gave him a threatening look.
    B. The servant returned to his master, terribly frightened.
II. The servant fled to Samarra in fear.
    A. He begged for a horse to get away from Baghdad.
    B. He told the merchant his destination was Samarra.
    C. The merchant lent him a horse.
        1. The servant dug his heels into the horse's flanks.
        2. The horse galloped fast.
III. The merchant confronted Death.
    A. He found her in the bazaar.
    B. He demanded to know why Death gave a threatening look to his servant.
    C. Death assured the merchant that she had not given a threatening look, but had merely been startled to see the servant there.
IV. Death told the merchant she was surprised because she had expected to meet the servant that night in Samarra.

> Although outlining is not specifically practiced in this book, it has been used regularly throughout the series. If you feel continued practice would benefit your students, you are free to assign outlining exercises as you wish. In that case, students who have followed this series throughout may find these instructions helpful as a refresher, and students who are new to the series will want to take a look at them before beginning the exercise.

Elocution Electrifies

Elocution is the skill of clear and powerful public speaking. Elocution is the way you thrill your audience with your words and make them sit up and pay attention. You might call it the current of electricity in a speech that gives everyone listening a lovely jolt.

Elocution has always been a vital part of rhetoric. In fact, it is really a combination of two of the five laws of rhetoric: *memoria* (memory) and *actio* (delivery). When you deliver a speech or a dramatic reading, you rely heavily on your memory and on the way you speak (delivery) to make a good impression on your audience.

Almost all public speaking is rehearsed ahead of time, so whether or not you actually learn a speech by heart, memory is still very important. You have to try to remember when to use gestures or when to change the emotion in your voice. When you read from a script, you want to remember the script well enough to look up and make eye contact with your audience.

Delivery involves a number of different skills: breathing, articulation, posture, eye contact, expression, and gestures. Take a quick look at each one of these.

- **Breathing:** To make your voice sound loud or soft, and to give it emotion, you will need to have a good volume of breath in your lungs. Empty your lungs of air and then try to speak with force and expression—it can't be done! Now fill your lungs with air and listen to all the wonderful things you can do with your voice. Make sure you draw full breaths as you are speaking.
- **Articulation:** In delivering your speech, you want to speak each word clearly and crisply so that your audience understands you. You must avoid mumbling or slurring your words together. Audiences have a hard time understanding mumbling, even with a microphone to amplify the voice. Enunciate each and every word, and you will surely sound like you know what you're talking about.
- **Posture:** You can't hope to avoid mumbling if you are hunched over while you recite. When you stand erect, straight and tall, you can fill your lungs more easily. You can speak with greater power and articulation. When you square your shoulders and keep your chin up, you will feel confident that you have something important to share. Your audience will also feel confident that something extraordinary is about to happen.
- **Eye contact:** Making eye contact is like having good posture for your eyes. You don't want your eyes to "stoop" any more than your shoulders. Unless you are saying something very sad or shy, keep your eyes off the floor and on the faces of the people in your audience. People like to feel as if you are speaking to them. It helps them to feel as if you recognize them and like them. If looking people in the eye is difficult at first, go ahead and look at their foreheads or at their ears. People won't know that you aren't peering directly into their eyes.

- **Expression:** In previous Writing & Rhetoric books, you've learned that you need to use your voice to convey emotion to the audience. Tone is the most important part of giving your voice an emotional quality or expression. Whether you speak loudly, softly, or somewhere in between (volume), whether you speak rapidly or slowly or at a moderate speed (pace), or whether you speak in a high voice or a low voice (pitch), you are giving your audience cues about how they should feel about what you are saying. (You are also helping to keep them awake.) Often it is important to pause at important moments in your speech to allow your words to sink in. Volume, pace, and pitch all make up the tone of a speech. Another important part of expression is inflection. When you use inflection, you are changing the pitch (the highs and the lows) of your voice to grab the audience's attention. Inflection helps the audience know when it needs to be excited or laugh or get serious. We know that when a person asks us a question his voice will get a little higher at the end of his sentence. A person also sounds more uncertain or more excitable when the voice goes up. We know we're about to hear a strong statement or bad news when a person's voice goes lower. Inflection is one way to make a speech more powerful.
- **Gestures:** Beyond good posture, speakers can add extra emphasis to their words by using gestures. A raised hand or raised eyes, a fist pounding in one's hand or on a podium, arms wide open or rigidly shut—these are ways to convey new levels of meaning. It's important not to overdo gestures during a speech, because that can get a little distracting, but a well-timed gesture can really highlight an important point in a speech or recitation.

People use breathing, articulation, posture, eye contact, expression, and gestures every day when talking to one another. This is how all human beings communicate. When we deliberately use all of these tools together, when we seek to speak skillfully to an audience, we are practicing elocution.

In the past, elocution was a part of every well-educated person's schooling. The following excerpt is from a nineteenth-century manual of elocution. Though the language may be difficult for twenty-first-century students, it is included here to give you an idea of another educator's priorities in teaching elocution.

> The following rules are worthy of strict attention:
> 1. Let your articulation be distinct and deliberate.
> 2. Let your pronunciation be bold and forcible.
> 3. Acquire a compass and variety in the height of your voice.
> 4. Pronounce your words with propriety and elegance.
> 5. Pronounce every word consisting of more than one syllable with its proper accent.
> 6. In every sentence distinguish the more significant words by a natural, forcible, and varied emphasis.
> 7. Acquire a just variety of pause and cadence.
> 8. Accompany the emotions and passions which your words express, by corresponding tones, looks and gestures.[1]

1. From *The Canadian Elocutionist: Designed for the Use of Colleges, Schools, and Self Instruction* by Anna K. Howard (Toronto: Rose Publishing Company, 1885).

Glossary of Literary and Rhetorical Concepts

Abstract noun—an object that cannot be seen or touched: e.g., love, anger

Active voice—wording in which the subject of a sentence does the action of the action verb (e.g., The spider ate the fly.)

***Ad hominem* attacks**—personal attacks; generally a weak strategy for argumentation because they attack a person's appearance or character rather than his thesis and ideas

Adjective—describes a noun and helps us to "see" it more clearly: e.g., happy, silly, strange

Adverb—usually describes a verb and answers the questions how, when, and where; can also describe adjectives or other adverbs: e.g., shakily, lazily, sometimes

Allusion—a reference to a well-known idea, often found in a story, speech, or poem; can hint at the idea indirectly or borrow its words directly (e.g., I'm going to turn into a pumpkin if I don't get home before curfew.)

Amplification—a longer and more detailed version of a shorter story; *or*, enlarging a sentence with synonyms or stronger, more specific words

Analogy—a broad term for a comparison between two ideas, events, or objects that is used to describe or explain one of those things

Anecdote—a brief account of a humorous or interesting event, often used to make a larger point

Annotations—notes added to a text to help understand or explain it

Antithesis—an argument against a thesis; *or*, a rhetorical device that makes use of antonyms to consider opposing ideas; used mostly to capture interest rather than to make an argument (e.g., "The world will not long remember what we say here, but it can never forget what they did here." —Abraham Lincoln)

Antonyms—words that are opposites: e.g., alive/dead, sane/mad, joy/sorrow

Appositive—also an appositive phrase; a noun or a noun phrase that explains another noun (e.g., <u>A Spanish artist</u>, Picasso spent most of his life in France.)

Argument—a clear line of thinking aimed at proving a point

Audience—an author's intended readers or a speaker's intended listeners

Autobiography—a description of someone's life that is written by the person himself, usually in the first person

Biography—a description of someone's life that is written by someone else, usually in the third person

Body paragraphs—all the paragraphs of an essay between the introduction and the conclusion

Character—a person who has a role to play in a story; *or*, a person's moral strengths or weaknesses, as in "good character" and "bad character"

Citation—used in writing to identify a source of information

Citing—the process of identifying sources in a written piece of work

Cliché—a metaphor, simile, or other phrase that is used so often that it no longer rouses the reader's interest or emotions (e.g., I get butterflies when he smiles at me.)

Colloquialism—informal or slang expression (e.g., "Remember what you won't get if you don't mind." —Flannery O'Connor; "Mind" is a colloquialism for "obey.")

Comparison—a way of looking at two or more people, objects, ideas, or events to identify how they are alike and different

Compound sentence—two independent simple sentences combined by a linking word called a conjunction (e.g., "Keep still, you little devil, or I'll cut your throat!" —Charles Dickens)

Confirmation—the supporting argument of a thesis essay; *or*, a short essay that defends certain parts of a narrative as believable, probable, clear, or proper

Conflict—a clash between people or ideas

Conjunction—*see* coordinating conjunction; subordinating conjunction

Context—text that accompanies a quote or paraphrase to help the reader understand the quote and how the quote connects to the point being made

Coordinating conjunction—a connecting word that links together clauses or sentences of equal importance or similar construction: e.g., and, or, but

Copiousness—any large quantity or number. In rhetoric, copiousness refers to the richness and flexibility of language as expressed in many words, many ways of building sentences, and many types of rhetorical devices. Copiousness also refers to stretching exercises for students of rhetoric whereby students reach for new words to express variations of the same idea.

Dangling modifier—a modifier that isn't properly connected to what it's modifying (e.g., Hungry as a wolf, the soup was swallowed in three gulps.)

Description—a picture made of words

Dialogue—a conversation between two or more people

Direct quote—the repetition of another person's exact words enclosed in quotation marks

Dynamic character—a character who changes in the course of a narrative; also known as a round character

Elocution—the art of public speaking

Eloquence—skillful and persuasive speech and writing

Encomium—warm, glowing praise about a specific person or thing, usually in the form of a speech or an essay

Epilogue—a tidy ending to a written work

Erotema—also called a rhetorical question; a question that needs no answer; a question with an obvious answer (e.g., Does a bear have hair?)

Ethos—a type of appeal that attempts to persuade the audience that the writer or speaker is a trusted or credible authority on her subject

Evidence—facts and ideas that support the truth or validity of an argument

Exordium—Latin word for "introduction"

Fable—a short story that teaches a simple moral lesson, usually with talking animals

Fact—a truth, something known to exist or to have happened

Fairy tale—a fanciful story for children, usually with magical people or creatures

Faulty predication—a writing error in which the subject and verb of a sentence don't logically fit together (e.g., April is the month where showers will bring May flowers.)

Fiction—any imaginative story

Figurative language—wording that suggests an imaginative meaning that goes beyond what the actual words say

First person—uses the pronouns "I," "me," "my"; the narrator takes part in the story

Formal language—wording that takes a more serious, objective, or impersonal tone; appropriate for academic or professional writing

Fragment—a sentence that is incomplete

Genre—different types or shapes of stories, such as mysteries, fairy tales, and romances; a type of literature with a certain style, form, or content

History—a narrative of actual events

Hook—the attention grabber of a narrative

Hypophora—also called *anthypophora*; a figure of reasoning in which the writer or speaker asks a question and then immediately supplies the answer (e.g., Are we afraid? No, we're terrified!)

Illustration—a picture made of words

Impromptu speech—a speech given on the spot without preparation

Improper—inappropriate or immoral

Infinitive verb—the basic form of a verb; typically starts with "to": e.g., to leap, to fly, to soar

Inflection—the change in pitch or tone of the voice that is used to make spoken words more meaningful

Informal language—wording that is more casual, personal, and conversational than formal language

In-text citation—a reference within a written work that helps the reader to identify the source of certain information

Joke—typically a crisp little story told to evoke amusement or laughter

Legend—a story that begins with a real person or event that, as it is handed down by storytellers, often gets exaggerated along the way; *or*, a person who is so remarkable that he becomes extremely famous

Literal—refers to the ordinary or factual meaning of a word or saying

Literary analysis—an essay that examines a written work, whether fiction or nonfiction, and creates an argument about some aspect of the work

Logos—an appeal to reason that is often made using facts, numbers, logic, and research and helps strengthen the logic of a thesis or reveals a writer's thought process to the audience; *or*, the content of a speech

Main idea—the most important thought in a story or speech; what the story or speech is all about

Memorize—to learn something by heart

Metaphor—a comparison in which one thing is compared to a second seemingly unlike thing to show how they are similar (e.g., That test was a breeze. Love is a rose, a red and thorny flower.). It does not use the words "like" or "as."

Modifier—a word, phrase, or clause that describes another word or phrase

Moral—noun: the short lesson that explains the meaning of a fable; adjective: virtuous or good; concerning the ethical standards of right and wrong

Moral lesson—a teaching that encourages wise actions

Motives—a person's desires and the reasons for acting the way she does

Myth—an ancient story not based on actual events, with gods, goddesses, and heroes, that is used to explain life and nature

Narrative—noun: all forms of story, from fairy tale, to history, to myths, to parables, to fables; adjective: story-telling

News flash—a brief piece of urgent and up-to-the-minute news

Nonfiction—a narrative based on fact

Nonrestrictive clause—a clause that can be deleted without changing the meaning of the sentence (e.g., "The long-awaited visit, <u>for which both had prepared questions and had even anticipated answers</u>, was once more the usual everyday conversation."

—Gabriel García Márquez)

Noun—a person, place, thing, or idea: e.g., astronaut, island, sled, love

Opinion—a personal claim, not necessarily based on fact

Outline—the skeleton of a story or essay that tells what comes in the beginning, the middle, and the end

Padding—any empty word, phrase, or sentence that is used to make writing look longer, usually to fill out a page or paragraph requirement

Parable—a short story that teaches a moral lesson, always true to life

Paragraph—a group of sentences that form an idea together

Parallel structure—when a writer uses the same pattern of words in a sentence, or the same pattern of sentences (e.g., Give a man a fish and you feed him for a day. Teach a man to fish and you feed him for a lifetime.)

Paraphrasing—using one's own words and writing style to express ideas that are similar to the ideas in a source text

Participial phrase—a phrase that begins with a present participle (e.g., <u>Sniffing for clues</u>, the bloodhound stepped into the swamp.)

Passive voice—wording in which the subject of a sentence fails to do the acting and instead is acted upon (e.g., The violin was made by Antonio Stradivari.)

Pathos—an appeal to the emotions of an audience

Plagiarism—copying someone else's words without giving him credit

Plot—the plan of a story; the events that form the beginning, the middle, and the end

Point of view—a way of seeing things

Preposition—a word that shows location (on, in, under), direction (to, into, onto, from), or time (before, after, during). Some prepositions can also connect a verb to a direct object (e.g., I'm tired of this opera.) or introduce an amount of something or a length of time (e.g., She ate three teaspoons of sugar.).

Prepositional phrase—a phrase that begins with a preposition: e.g., over the moon, toward the castle, after midnight

Present participle—a verb form that ends in *-ing*: e.g., coughing, sneezing, spitting

Proofreading—looking for mistakes in written material

Proper noun—names a specific person, place, thing, or idea: e.g., Henrietta, Spain, Kleenex

Proverb—a short, pithy saying used to convey wisdom or some basic truth

Punch line—the last line of a joke that provides its humorous impact

Quarrel—any sharp or angry disagreement

Redundancy—the unnecessary repetition of ideas

Refutation—in a thesis essay, a rebuttal for an antithesis; *or*, a short essay that attacks certain parts of a narrative as unbelievable, improbable, unclear, or improper

Repetition—the repeating of words, phrases, ideas, or actions; *or*, a subset of parallelism; a rhetorical device in which a word, phrase, or idea is repeated to make a stronger point (e.g., Slavery is a blot on human history. It is evil. It involves capturing and trafficking human beings. It is evil. It destroys dreams and tears families apart. It is evil.)

Restrictive clause—a clause that can't be deleted without changing the meaning of the sentence (e.g., "The things that happened could only have happened during a fiesta." —Ernest Hemingway)

Rhetoric—the art and practice of persuasive writing and speaking

Rhetorical device—also known as a rhetorical figure; uses words in clever ways to make writing or speech more persuasive. Simile and hyperbole are two examples of rhetorical devices.

Rhetorical question—also called *erotema*; a question that needs no answer; a question with an obvious answer (e.g., Does a bear have hair?)

Rule of Three—also known as the tricolon; a writing technique that uses three repeated elements (such as words, phrases, clauses, sentences, sections, or plots) that often are parallel in structure for the purpose of delight or emphasis or to make writing flow more smoothly

Run-on sentence—a sentence that lacks proper punctuation and should really be divided into separate sentences, either with punctuation or a conjunction

Second person—uses the pronouns "you," "your"; the narrator refers to the person or persons addressed (e.g., Do you even know how lucky you are?)

Setting—the physical location and historical time of a literary work

Simile—a comparison using the words "like" or "as" (e.g., I'm as silly as a clown with a fire hose.)

Simple sentence—a complete sentence, also known as an independent clause

Slang—informal language

Speculative question—a fanciful question that relies on good guesses (conjecture) and doesn't have a definite answer; rather, it can have more than one answer, and these answers are open to opinion and debate

Static character—a character who stays the same in the course of a narrative; also known as a flat character

Subject—what the sentence is about; either a noun, a pronoun, or a noun phrase; *or*, what a story, essay, painting, or other piece of work is about

Subordinate clause—a statement with a subject and a verb that is not a complete sentence (e.g., "Never interrupt your enemy when he is making a mistake." —Napoleon Bonaparte)

Subordinating conjunction—introduces a subordinate clause; a connecting word that links together clauses or sentences, provides a transition between two ideas, and can indicate a time, place, or cause-and-effect relationship: e.g., while, although, if

Summary—a shortened or concise version of a longer text or body of information

Symbol—a person, place, sign, or other object that represents something in addition to its literal meaning

Testimony—the expert opinion or evidence of a credible witness

Textual evidence—evidence taken straight from a source

Theme—an important idea or topic that is repeated throughout a literary work

Thesis essay—a persuasive paper that defends a thesis statement

Thesis statement—the main idea or argument of an essay or oration

Third person—uses the pronouns "he," "she," "it," "one," "they"/"him," "her," "it," "one," "them"/"his," "hers," "its," "one's," "their"

Topic sentence—the sentence that tells what the paragraph is about; *or*, a sentence that tells the main idea of an essay

Transition sentence—a sentence that makes a bridge between the ideas in one paragraph and the ideas in the following paragraph

Unbelievable—hard to believe, seeming to be impossible

Unclear—hard to understand

Verb—the action word of a sentence: e.g., pass, kick, dash

Vituperation—condemnation of a specific person or thing, usually in the form of a speech or an essay

Vocabulary—a collection of words

So Long

My first experience in a natural cave was nerve-wracking. As I followed my guide into the tight, rocky hole in the ground, the only thing he had to light our way was a lousy butane lighter. Of course, you only have to crawl a little way into a cave before there is no natural light, no way to tell which direction to crawl, no way to tell if the path splits ahead or drops down a pit. I had to rely on that wavering light ahead of me, which kept going out. My guide was forced to flick the lighter wheel again and again to get us back to safety.

Nowadays when I go caving, I carry not one flashlight, not two—but four—and I bring along spare batteries as well. Never do I go alone either. I always take along two trusted friends, and each of them brings four flashlights as well. You don't want to get stuck in the dark in the middle of who knows where—and that's the point of a thesis statement. You don't want your reader to get stuck in the dark in the middle of your essay and not know where it's going. The thesis statement serves as the light, or the guide, for your entire thesis essay.

"OK, enough," you may be thinking. "I've spent an entire book on thesis writing and I *know* the purpose of a thesis statement."

True, true—but it pays to repeat the important stuff, so it sinks deep into our brains. Remember this: Your thesis statement must guide you (and your reader) safely through all the confirmations, antitheses, refutations, and supporting facts and quotes that are part of any good thesis essay. The thesis is the main point you want to make, and it organizes all the other information in your essay. You want it to be a strong, bright beam so that it's easy to follow.

Now, as you look back on your journey through the twists and turns of *Thesis Part 1*, what have you learned? As it turns out, quite a lot! You learned how to write a persuasive thesis statement in response to a speculative question. You learned how to identify different audiences and to consider your purpose in attempting to reach them. At the same time, you learned to anticipate antitheses (or objections to your thesis) and to treat these disagreements respectfully and with well-argued refutations. Next, you learned how to hook your audience in your introduction with narratives, questions, descriptions, illustrations, proverbs, sayings, quotations, provocative statements, statistics, and facts. (Just as there's a lure for every fish, there's a hook for every audience.)

As if that were not enough, you learned how to set up rings of defense around your thesis with confirmations, refutations, and solid evidence that appeals to authority. You learned that you can build your ethos—your credibility as a writer—by using quotations, paraphrases, and allusions from people who are respected experts. And with all this wondrous, newfound learning you were able to write not just one literary analysis (of a short story), but a second one (of an autobiography) as well. In your third essay you answered the very difficult, unbelievably challenging speculative question, "What is beauty?" If you gave these essays your best effort, that, my friend, is a real accomplishment.

Last, I want to come full circle and end where we began. Remember Quintilian's declaration, "I hold that no one can be a true orator unless he is also a good [person]."[1] In our next book you will study some of the great speeches of history and then apply your skill at thesis writing to creating your own speeches. But keep in mind, and never forget, that writing and speaking well avail nothing unless you are also striving for goodness.

It's time to say good-bye for now, but your next venture will be upon you soon enough. So charge up those batteries and make sure your thesis flashlights are fresh and strong—it's about to get real! See you soon!

1. Quintilian, *Institutes of Oratory*, trans. Harold Edgeworth Butler (Loeb Classical Library, 1920–1922), bk. 1, chap. 2, http://penelope.uchicago.edu/Thayer/E/Roman/Texts/Quintilian/Institutio_Oratoria/home.html.

Logic

We use logic every day, especially to distinguish *logical* arguments from those that are unreasonable. As a fundamental part of the trivium, logic is a paradigm subject by which we evaluate, assess, and learn other subjects, growing ever closer to their mastery.

Informal Logic
(Grades 7–12)

Formal Logic
(Grades 8–12)

Logic/Pre-Rhetoric
(Grades 8–12)

Speech & Debate
(Grades 8–12)

"*The Art of Argument* is a thorough study of the fallacies, written in an organized, engaging manner. It is a great mix of instruction and application. I would highly recommend it for teaching logic."
—Kathy Gelzer, *The Old Schoolhouse Magazine*

Practical Homeschooling Reader Award, Top Ranked By Homeschoolers 2017
Practical Homeschooling Reader Award, Top Ranked By Homeschoolers 2018

WELL-TRAINED MIND™ TOP RECOMMENDATION

SCHOLÉ ACADEMY
LIVE, ONLINE COURSES

Through its classical curricula and unique approach to restful learning, *Scholé Academy* has successfully achieved harmony between rigorous academics and restful contemplation (*scholé*). Scholé Academy's wide variety of classes, excellent faculty, and faithful adherence to its contemplative approach make it a top choice for home-educators.

Now Including
ST. RAPHAEL SCHOOL
Classical Education in the Orthodox Tradition

SCHOLÉ ACADEMY *is growing!*

We invite you to discover our award-winning staples:

- Live, online classes for grades 3–12
- Classical and restful Christian education
- Engaging and personal community

Join our community through a variety of new events, including:

- Open House Nights
- College Nights
- Coffee with the Principal & Teachers

Visit ScholeAcademy.com to…

- *View full course descriptions*
- *Watch sample teaching videos*
- *Learn about our tutoring center*
- *Meet our 40+ teachers*
- *Find out about our events*

Practical Homeschooling 2017 i-Learn Awards
Practical Homeschooling 2018 i-Learn Awards

SCHOLÉ ACADEMY
CLASSICAL ACADEMIC PRESS

Follow us on Facebook!

Reader Award 2017

Reader Award 2018

WELL-TRAINED MIND™ TOP RECOMMENDATION

Classical Subjects...

LATIN Alive!

...Creatively Taught

The Latin Alive! series is a relevant, rigorous, yet engaging introduction to Latin for upper-middle and high school students. This curriculum will truly make the Latin language come alive both for students who have studied Latin and for those who have not been previously introduced to Latin.

"Latin Alive! is challenging and thorough enough for the students, yet simple enough for a homeschool mom without a Latin background to implement."
—Loretta, homeschool parent

"In Latin Alive!, I believe Karen Moore and her distinguished coauthor, Gaylan DuBose, have succeeded in the lofty goal of producing a truly outstanding beginning textbook to meet the needs of this new generation of Latin teachers and students."
—Erin Davis-Valdez, MA, Hill Country Christian School of Austin

Includes Video Audio

Full Program* Includes:

- Latin Alive! Student Edition
- Latin Alive! Teacher's Edition
- Latin Alive! Streaming Video & Audio (or DVD/CD Set)
- Latin Alive! Workbook (in production!)

*Full programs available for books 1–3.

www.ClassicalAcademicPress.com

ClassicalU®
Teacher Training

We created ClassicalU with *you* in mind. We are confident this resource will inspire educators in schools, homeschools, and co-ops to dig deep into the richness of learning, no matter where you find yourself on your journey in classical education.

NOW AVAILABLE CEU credit for every course

What You Get by Subscribing

New Content Regularly
Whether it's new courses, conversations, or interviews, we are always releasing new content to help you grow.

Ambrose Curriculum Guide
View more than 250 documents, including course guides for every class in a K–12 school or homeschool.

Downloadable Resources
Download notes, articles, recommended resources, and other files associated with our courses.

ClassicalU Community
Engage other educators and administrators in conversation and share ideas and resources.

Promotional Videos
Access professionally designed videos that promote classical education to grow your school or co-op.

Over 35 Self-Paced Courses!

Course Levels

1

Level 1: Apprentice
Begin your journey toward mastery.

2

Level 2: Journeyman
Continue your journey toward mastery.

3

Level 3: Master
Train to mentor and lead other teachers.

L

Level L: Leader
Grow as a leader or administrator.

Visit www.ClassicalU.com to see free previews of every course.